Adolescent Sexuality
and Gynecology

Adolescent Sexuality and Gynecology

DONALD E. GREYDANUS, M.D.

*Chairman, Department of Pediatrics
Director, Adolescent Medicine Programs
Raymond Blank Children's Hospital
Iowa Methodist Medical Center
Des Moines, Iowa
Clinical Associate Professor
University of Iowa Hospitals and Clinics
Iowa City, Iowa*

ROBERT B. SHEARIN, M.D.

*Professor of Pediatrics
Director, Pediatric Ambulatory Services and
Division of Adolescent Medicine
Department of Pediatrics
Georgetown University
Washington, D.C.*

Consultant: David Langdon, M.D.

Lea & Febiger   *1990*   *Philadelphia · London*

Lea & Febiger
600 Washington Square
Philadelphia, PA 19106-4198
U.S.A.
(215) 922-1330

Lea & Febiger (UK) Ltd.
145a Croydon Road
Beckenham, Kent BR3 3RB
U.K.

Library of Congress Cataloging in Publication Data

Greydanus, Donald E.
    Adolescent sexuality and gynecology / Donald
E. Greydanus, Robert B. Shearin; consultant, David
Langdon.
        p. cm.
    Includes bibliographies and index.
    ISBN 0-8121-1251-2
    1. Pediatric gynecology. 2. Adolescence.
3. Teenagers—Sexual behavior. I. Shearin,
Robert B. II. Langdon, David, 1950- . III. Title.
    [DNLM: 1. Genital Diseases, Female—in
adolescence. 2. Sex Behavior—in adolescence.
WS 360 G845a]
RJ478.G74 1990
618.92'098—dc20
DNLM/DLC
for Library of Congress   89-12765
                                              CIP

PRINTED IN THE UNITED STATES OF AMERICA

Print number: 5 4 3 2 1

PREFACE

The topics of adolescent sexuality and gynecology are important for primary care physicians who have the privilege of treating adolescents. This book supplies essential information in these areas, providing physicians with the basic information needed to effectively treat youth with gynecologic problems and concerns. It is intended primarily for pediatricians, family physicians, internists, nurse practitioners, and other health care professionals offering primary care to youth. It is meant to serve as a guide to the professional who evaluates adolescents with common gynecologic symptoms. It is not intended to be a major textbook describing rare disorders. We hope this book fills a perceived need for a practical, up-to-date review of adolescent gynecology. Though this discussion focuses on the adolescent female, some aspects pertinent to the prepubertal girl and the adolescent male are summarized.

We begin with a review of basic adolescent development and adolescent sexuality. A key component to healthy development of the teenager is how she proceeds with important stages of sexuality. Adolescence is the critical period of growth from puberty to maturation and involves physiologic, psychologic, and sociologic aspects. The physician is in a better position to treat gynecologic issues in youth if he or she starts with an understanding of "normal" adolescence. Many of the problems of youth stem from variations of normalcy. During adolescence, youth must develop healthy self-esteem and also sexual comfort—learning to deal with life from an emerging "sexual" viewpoint. Sexuality is a complex phenomenon that involves complex interaction between one's biologic sex, core gender identity (sense of maleness or femaleness), gender identity (sense of masculinity or femininity) and gender role behavior (nonsexual as well as sexual). Sexuality remains a basic yet profound aspect of humanity; humans need other humans, and this human capacity to give and receive love continues from birth to death. The success or failure experienced by the teenager as her sexual system is developed has much to do with her eventual success or failure as an adult. Thus, **Chapter 1** reviews basic principles in this regard and sets the stage for understanding some of the difficulties that youth encounter, such as an increased pregnancy rate, sexually transmitted diseases, and others.

Chapter 2 presents the basics of the gynecologic history and physical examination, including the pelvic examination with supporting laboratory evaluation. The importance of a thorough history and preparation of the youth for examination is emphasized. The reader is further prepared in **Chapter 3** with a review of the endocrinology of puberty by Dr. David

v

Langdon, director of pediatric endocrinology at the Geisinger Medical Center in Danville, Pennsylvania. **Chapter 4** presents basic information on several gynecologic topics: vulvovaginitis, pelvic inflammatory disease (PID), cervical intraepithelial neoplasia (CIN), diethylstilbestrol-related disorders, toxic shock syndrome, and others. Practical issues of diagnosis and treatment are emphasized. **Chapter 5** presents an outline of normal breast development with a review of common breast pathology that the primary care physician will encounter. **Chapter 6** summarizes the complex topic of menstrual disorders, including dysmenorrhea, dysfunctional uterine bleeding, and amenorrhea, and underlying endocrinologic principles. Basic management strategies are presented to enable the physician to deal with most menstrual problems that youth encounter. **Chapter 7** reviews adolescent contraception, **Chapter 8** summarizes pregnancy and abortion, and **Chapter 9** overviews sexual assault and incest in adolescence. **Chapter 10** stresses the importance of sexuality education in the lives of our youth. We conclude that educated physicians who help educate our youth in the critical areas of sexuality will profoundly improve the many serious problems teenagers face, including nutrition and substance abuse disorders, which are described in **Chapter 11.** All primary care physicians should become knowledgeable about basic adolescent sexuality, gynecology, nutrition, and substance abuse. We hope this book will provide a worthy contribution toward this goal. D.E.G. dedicates his contribution to this book to the women in his family, Kathy, Margaret, Marissa, Elizabeth, Suzanne and Megan—you have taught me so much about humanity and I remain eternally grateful.

Des Moines, Iowa   *Donald E. Greydanus*

Washington, D.C.   *Robert B. Shearin*

CONTENTS

1

Adolescent Sexuality

Adolescence is a critical process of human development, essential to civilization because it allows a child to eventually become an adult. In this complex process, the dependent child enters a period of metamorphosis that allows him or her to emerge as a more autonomous adult, capable of functioning in a more independent manner, which is also acceptable, even helpful, to society. Various issues—physiologic, sociologic, and even psychologic—are encountered in this often turbulent tunnel of adolescence. The patterns of achievements or failures of childhood are accepted and even altered while the adolescent undergoes the necessary changes to enter adulthood.

A successful journey through adolescence requires passage through many different stages, including psychologic, cognitive, and physiologic ones. An integral aspect of these stages is the development of the adolescent as a *sexual being.* Adolescent sexuality is important to human development because it determines the type of adolescent and eventually the type of adult an individual becomes. To become a child or adolescent is to become a sexual being, requiring the love of other human beings in various complex ways. As adolescents emerge, they become aware of powerful feelings toward others of the same and opposite genders. Although society (especially parents) often deny such developments in youth out of fear of imagined negative consequences, these stages of sexuality are inevitable and important. Clearly, young people are having difficulty with their roles as sexual beings, as this book discusses. For example, there are over 1.3 million annual pregnancies among adolescents, as well as millions of cases of sexually transmitted diseases (STDs) identified annually in this population. Many of our youth must face the horror of sexual abuse, while all of our youth are profoundly affected by the quality (whether substantial or limited) of sexuality education given them. Our society is currently struggling to deal with AIDS—the most important STD of our century—further focusing attention on sexuality education.

Sexuality is a sum total of one's feelings, not only as a sexual animal but as a man or woman in a human setting. It is a process that begins at birth and continues throughout life. Sexuality is continually changing and perhaps is most confusing during adolescence and young childhood. Sexuality is a physiologic act in a psychosocial setting requiring philosophic and moral considerations. Adolescent sexuality today is confusing and difficult not only for adolescents but also for health care providers who work with this age group. Adolescent sexuality must be viewed as a physioanatomic, biologic, psychosocial, moral, and ethical phenomenon to understand all aspects of this state.

Adolescents today are striving to accomplish psychosocial tasks in the face of biologic changes and a changing social climate that sends out conflicting sexual messages. The health care provider must have basic definitions and knowledge concerning adolescent sexuality, understand the statistics, and then develop certain guidelines to approach the adolescent in his or her environment.

When examining the normal stages of adolescence, the health care provider must remember that adolescence proceeds out of childhood. The psychologic and cognitive stages of adolescence do not begin in a vacuum but start with childhood stages. Adolescence is a template for the expression of childhood experiences. Sexuality issues of adolescence begin with sexuality issues of childhood. Thus, youth who live with a childhood filled with abuse (physical or sexual), parental divorce, family chaos, and other negative experiences can be expected to develop serious problems as teenagers. Furthermore, parental attitudes toward clinically normal sexual development is vitally important to the overall development of the emerging individual.

PSYCHOLOGIC STAGES OF ADOLESCENCE

Traditionally, adolescence occurs between ages 10 and 21, and can be divided into three important periods: early (ages 10 to 14), middle (14 to 18), and late (18 to 21) (Table 1-1). Age is not the critical determinant in placing youth in these specific stages. Development in some individuals may be precocious or delayed, whereas others can be fixed at a particular level. Problems of earlier childhood along with abnormal family dynamics can have considerable influence on what psychologic stage a particular teenager may be placed. However, these stages can serve as useful

Table 1-1. Characteristics of Adolescence.

Early	Middle	Late
Preoccupation with rapidly changing events of puberty	Significant symbolic movement away from the home environment	Issues of emancipation from parents essentially resolved
Beginning of symbolic movement away from the home environment	Considerable need for independence Strong reliance on peers setting personal rules	Final pubertal changes (physiologic fine tuning) occurs
Comparison with peers and worry over perceived abnormalities	Major change in cognitive abilities and fantasy life	Finalization of secure, acceptable body image and gender role
Establishment and maintenance of same-sex friendships	Heterosexual experimentation predominates	Establishment of "adult" versus narcissistic sexual relationships; acquisition of adult lifestyle (marriage, single status)
Initial abstract thought development	Altruistic nature emerges	
	Identification with nonparental adult role models	

guidelines for health care professionals as they seek to evaluate their adolescent patients.

Early Adolescence

The psychologic aspect of early adolescence is usually dominated by the rapid physiologic changes of puberty, which are usually set in motion between age 10 and 14. As events of puberty occur, the young teenager becomes concerned with various aches and pains associated with a rapidly growing body. This young teenager can go through a normal "hypochondriacal period" until he or she develops more experience with normal physical changes. The young boy or girl begins to symbolically move away from the home environment as he or she starts the complex and inevitable process of becoming an independent individual. The need to seek friends occurs at this time and correlates with the growing need to become less dependent on parents. Friends now begin to supply a major part of one's sense of self-worth. Parents may notice a "difference" in their child and may even greet such psychologic changes with sadness. Friendships are usually with those of the same sex: boys become involved with groups of males in "gangs" of peers; girls develop several female friends, usually enclosing themselves with one or a few close girlfriends. Young people compare themselves with peers and gain much of their self-esteem from them. If adolescents feel inferior to their peers, depression may develop. However, some unhappiness with bodily contours is normal.

Homosexual experimentation is not unusual during this stage of early adolescence (see the final section of this chapter, "Homosexuality and Heterosexuality"). Appropriate education about this issue can be important to such youth. The change in abstract thought that normally occurs during early adolescence will help health care professionals who counsel their adolescent patients. Such changes in abstract thinking are discussed under cognitive stages of development.

Middle Adolescence

Middle adolescence, regardless of age, sets in motion more significant issues of adolescent development. Although precocious or delayed development is not unusual, most youth reach this important adolescent period between ages 14 and 18. The need to rely on peers and the acquisition of general independence while seeking further separation or emancipation from parents become more important to these individuals. Peers become influential in the lives of these youth, and the kind of youth with whom they associate says much about the sense of self-worth that they are developing. For example, young people who develop peer relationships almost exclusively with a drug-abusing group or a group that drops out of school often have major psychologic difficulties. Depression is particularly noted in such individuals.

Youth with healthy self-confidence and self-assurance generally seek peers of similar views. Parents should respect this need for friends and less reliance on parents. The influence of parents really rests on how they reared their children. As noted, childhood issues begin to exert major influence in adolescence and in subsequent adulthood. Certainly, parents can encourage appropriate peer friendships but, in reality, can do little to force any particular friendships on their children. When health care professionals evaluate teenagers whom parents feel are not developing properly, these normal concepts of emerging independence and reliance on peers must be kept in mind.

Some type of heterosexual experimentation is inevitable in middle adolescence as pubertal changes continue. As youth become more involved with girlfriends or boyfriends, it becomes impossible to avoid direct confrontation of heterosexual issues. The attitudes of parents and their preparation of their children for such issues now become critical. Youth who are going against authority (particularly parental authority) may choose sexual means of rebellion. Youth with low self-esteem may also choose this direction, especially if they are not fully prepared for the consequences of unprotected sexual activity. It is not inevitable that the stimulation of heterosexual interests seen in these youth will lead to coital encounters. It is not possible to state that coital activity is "normal" for youth. However, one can state that coital activity is common and that millions of youth are coitally active, resulting in 1.3 million annual pregnancies (including over 400,000 abortions to adolescents each year) and millions of cases of sexually transmitted diseases. Such factors can complicate parent-adolescent interactions considerably. Thus, dealing with adolescent development and caring for youth without incorporating adolescent sexual development is simply not providing the type of help that young people need.

As the needs for heterosexual experimentation and emancipation from parents emerge, a continuing change in the youth's cognitive abilities (see "Late Adolescence") and overall attitude toward life often occurs. Such an adolescent may develop a rich fantasy life and may express altruistic tendencies—seeking to better the world but not becoming overtly concerned with "mundane" matters such as parent-child communication, academic pursuits, and other issues. Various adults may serve as role models, for good or for ill. Though youth may seek parental advice, they often turn to other adults for counseling. Such influential adults can be teachers, health care professionals, and even other parents. The key as a counselor is to give these young people room to explore ideas, to be nonjudgmental, and not to come across in the dictatorial, authoritarian manner they perceive to be that of their parents. During this time, the youth may question moral, ethical, and religious views of parents and society at large. Moodiness, irritability, transient school dysfunction, drug experimentation, and even suicidal ideation may be noted. Parents may feel they have lost control of their children and may seek help for themselves and their children to learn how to better cope with these perceived problems. The health care professional can serve as a role model for such youth and as a valued counselor to both youth and parents in this regard.

This is not an easy task, but it can be a rewarding and important one. Helping such youth is a major way to help our future—for young people clearly represent society's future.

Certainly, not all youth go through such emotional upheavals. Some adolescents have a very difficult time, while others journey through the stage of adolescence without major difficulties—at least those that observers can spot. A quiet stage of middle adolescence may be seen in some "normal" youth. Other youth may be fixed on early adolescent issues; as such individuals get older, middle adolescent issues may emerge after the usual time. Most observers conclude that if middle adolescence is necessary, it should occur "on time" between ages 14 and 18 and not later. Perhaps midadolescent issues inspired the lament of the Greek poet Hesiod who, in the eighth century B.C., said, "I see no hope for the future of our people if they are dependent on the frivolous youth of today, for certainly all youth are reckless beyond words. . . . When I was a boy, we were taught to be discrete and respectful of elders, but the present youth are exceedingly wise and impatient of restraint."

One need not be so pessimistic when encountering youth. If extreme negative behavior does develop, the health care professional can begin counseling immediately or refer the individual (and family) to local resources for professional help. Such problems can include suicidal ideations (with or without suicidal gestures), extreme parent-youth conflicts, runaway behavior, promiscuity, academic dysfunction, substance abuse disorders, and many others. A careful interview of such youth, with the stages of normal adolescent development in mind, allows the health care professional to recommend the correct type of counseling. Appropriate adults can be helpful to youth by providing needed nonpejorative professional guidance.

Late Adolescence

As middle-adolescent issues begin to resolve, the preadult period emerges—late adolescence. Usually this period occurs between 18 and 21, but can be delayed or precociously developed much earlier. Issues of separation from parents (emancipation) should be resolved, and parents and youth should be more comfortable with the youth's emerging adulthood. The parent-youth relationship will always be unique, but it begins to take on the qualities of an adult-to-adult relationship. Some final physiologic fine tuning, such as regulation of menstruation, male muscular development, and other changes, may occur.

As the individual emerges from wrestling with early- and middle-adolescent issues, he or she should begin to establish a secure body image and gender role in late adolescence. What is emerging is a young preadult who accepts him- or herself, likes him- or herself as a male or female, and has come to grips with important concepts of human sexuality. If this is not the case, considerable anxiety or depression may ensue, requiring mental health treatment. It is difficult to become a happy, productive adult without establishing a normal sense of emancipation from parents and a normal acquisition of identity (Table 1.2) as identified in Erickson's classic *Tasks of Adolescence.* Accepting gender role and establishing a secure body image are the keys to potential success in late adolescence and adulthood.

Much of late adolescence (and even adulthood) involves the acquisition of adult lifestyles. The sexual lifestyle alternatives of today are numerous, as outlined in Table 1-3. It takes a secure individual to traverse such alternatives and avoid serious problems. Evaluation of adults reveals that they, too, struggle with their own human sexuality concepts. This struggle has resulted in a high divorce rate, rapidly changing lifestyles, sexual dysfunction, sexually transmitted diseases, and other negative consequences. Thus, the more preparation we give our children and adolescents in regard to human sexuality, the better prepared they will be for their own adulthood. A variety of sexual orientations are described (see Appendix F).

Finally, as the late adolescent deals with these various issues, considerable time must be spent in establishing appropriate vocational skills and training. The complexities of modern society frequently require extensive training, whether purely academic or vocational. One cannot successfully live today without acquiring a needed trade; the adult must become able to earn enough to establish the independence he or she was seeking throughout adolescence. Failure to achieve success in school or in vocational training often dooms the individual to a low-income job or series of such jobs, which can lead to considerable depression and limit one's potential as an adult.

Certainly these stages do not perfectly fit all youth and need considerable refinement. Many other stages can be used to improve one's understanding of normal adolescent development, e.g., Kolberg's stages of moral development, Freud's psychosexual stages, Sears' social condition stages, Havighurst's development tasks, Kinsey's scale of sexual orientation, Lidz's life stages, and others. Current researchers in female sexuality (Gilligan, Miller, and Chodorow) note that the Eriksonian views do not accurately portray the development of female adolescent sexual development. For example, they note that such views allow female adolescents (when compared with their male counterparts) to appear more dependent, immature, and depressed than is actually the case. Current parenting techniques may result in males having difficulty developing relationships, while females may have more difficulty with separation issues. However, such stages do provide the health care professional with an introduction to understanding normal adolescence. The reader is

Table 1-2. Erikson's Tasks of Adolescence.

1. Emancipation
2. Acquisition of identity (sense of uniqueness and of self-separateness)
   a. *Intellectual:* "Who am I in relation to the Universe?"
   b. *Sexual:* "Who am I as a male or female in relation to other males and females?"
   c. *Functional:* "What role do I assume in an adult lifestyle and work?"

Table 1-3. Lifestyle Spectrum in the 1990s.

1. Traditional monogamy
2. Serial monogamy (repeat marriages)
3. Single parenthood
4. Cohabitation
5. Singlehood
6. Communal living
7. Child-free relationships
8. Swinging and/or group sex
9. Group marriage (one married couple adding an additional adult)
10. Synergamous relationship (several couples with various sexual arrangements)
11. Open-ended relationship in marriage (freeing either partner to develop sexual contacts outside the marriage)
12. Celibate marriage
13. Family network systems (several families joined together with or without traditional sexual relationships)
14. Secret extramarital relationships

encouraged to add further concepts to these basic stages. Understanding the cognitive stages of Piaget is also helpful in this regard.

COGNITIVE STAGES OF DEVELOPMENT

In addition to the physiologic stages, youth also traverse important maturational stages in their thinking or cognitive skills, as classically outlined by Piaget and associates (Table 1-4). During the first 2 years of life, the individual is in the *sensorimotor stage,* during which skill develops in the complex motor-sensory systems, and some basic language skills emerge. During this time, important principles of parent-child bonding occur in which the infant and toddler learn to feel secure while acquiring the sense that they are loved in a consistent, dependable manner. Many serious problems of adolescence and adulthood stem from abnormalities of parent-child bonding that can take place during this critical period of human development. From ages 2 to 7, the *preoperational stage* occurs in which language-skill acquisition becomes important. Thinking skills increase somewhat, but the ability to use logic (especially reversed thinking) is limited. Thus, the child believes that a large nickel is worth more than the smaller dime or that the taller individual is always older than the shorter one. Such young children struggle with difficult concepts that are presented to them, whether from theology, science, or other disciplines. Youth go through various sexual stages (Table 1-5), as outlined by Freud and others. They discover masturbation and become curious about the body parts of the opposite sex. Such developments are normal and, as indicated earlier, sensitive to parental attitude and teaching.

Table 1-4. Piaget's Cognitive Stages.

1. Sensorimotor stage (birth to 2 years)
2. Preoperational stage (2-7 years)
3. Concrete operational stage (7-11 years)
4. Formal operational stage (12-16 years of age or to adulthood)

Table 1.5 Stages of Sexual Development and Their Relationship to Adolescent Periods
and Pubertal Stages.

Pubertal Stage*	Sexual Stage	Adolescent Period
Puberty Onset Females 8-14 years Males 10-14 years	Sexual Awakening	Early
Females B-2 to B-4 Males G-2 to G-3	Practicing social behavior	Early to middle
Females B-3 to B-5 Males G-3 to G-5	Developing sexual roles	Middle
Females B-4 to B-5 Males G-3 to G-5	Experiencing situational ethics	Middle to late
Females B-4 to B-5 Males G-5	Forming permanent relationships	Late

B = Breast stage
G = Genital stage
* See Tables 1-6, 1-7

Between 7 and 11 years of age, the *concrete operational thinking stage*
develops in most individuals, often lasting well into adolescence. During
this time, the child's ability to develop logical thinking patterns increases
significantly. The individual understands more and can handle more complicated tasks in school, church, synagogue, and other situations of daily
living. The youth now understands more about symmetric relationships as
well as concepts involving serializations. Children and young adolescents
can vary considerably in such abilities, and this can influence their overall
school performance and eventual self-esteem.

Concrete thinkers have real limitations, however, that parents and
health care professionals should remember. For example, questions di-
rected at youth often elicit monosyllabic responses. Although they may be
interested in physical aspects of their bodies, concrete thinkers often
cannot express themselves in detail. The use of questionnaires can save
health care professionals much time in identifying key points of a medical
history, and the liberal use of practical teaching aids (visual instruments)
will considerably extend the concrete thinker's knowledge. Also, it is
usually difficult for such youth to think in futuristic terms: their thinking is
rooted in the present. For example, trying to convince a sexually active
13-year-old teenager not be sexually active, or at least to use contraceptives because of the risk of pregnancy with a resultant baby in 9 months,
can be frustrating because of the difficulty in overcoming the youth's
concrete thinking skills. Or try to convince a 14-year-old youth not to
smoke cigarettes because of the many well-known medical complications
that can arise later. Such youth do not do well with these types of arguments based on futuristic concepts. Another problem such young people
have is with the concept of "magical thinking." Youth often feel that they
are immune from danger and thus can take risks without suffering predicted consequences because they are "special." Though magical thinking fades over time, it can persist into later adolescent stages and even

into adulthood. Just look at the large number of adults who smoke cigarettes, use other drugs to excess, take drugs while driving, and are sexually active without contraceptives, to name just a few examples.

Though many youth remain in this concrete stage (perhaps 30% or more by late adolescence), the norm is to proceed, by middle adolescence, into the *formal operational thinking stage*. At this time, the ability to use logic is much improved, equal to or even surpassing the parents' ability. Many parents become amazed at their youth, who can present an almost endless array of complicated arguments explaining why he or she should not do what the parent requests, whether in regard to dating, school work, household chores, curfews, or other matters. What makes midadolescence so fascinating is the simultaneous emergence of independence needs and formal operational thought patterns. Youth still lack experience and thus may make errors in judgment, especially if magical thinking concepts remain. Such "mistakes" can be seen in the many problems of sexuality and gynecology discussed in this book. Interaction with youth at this stage requires the parent or health care professional to prepare full explanations of the rules or recommendations they present concerning prescription of contraception, treatment of sexually transmitted disease, or other related topics.

PHYSIOLOGIC STAGES OF DEVELOPMENT

Biologic maturation in the child is the first sign of developing a concept of sexuality in adolescence. Although sexual function occurs before biologic maturation, the first signs of puberty are generally the initiation of the concept of adolescent sexuality in the individual. The phenomenon of biologic maturation creates changes in the adolescent's body as the individual grows in height and weight and develops secondary sexual characteristics. Changes in the individual generally move from the prepubertal, or childhood, stage to the adult stage in a period of 2 to 4 years, although the transition may take up to 5 years. Many factors are involved in this phenomenon. Approximately 30 years ago, Tanner started to classify adolescent biologic changes, terming the classifications "sexual maturity ratings." These are broken into stages 1 through 5, which include changes in the breast (Fig. 1-1), pubic hair, and genital growth of males and females (Tables 1-6 and 1-7 and Figs. 1-2 and 1-3).

This process, or the events of puberty, which are related to hormonal changes, occur in the hypothalamus with stimulation of the anterior pituitary. At this time, biologic changes begin to occur and puberty starts [see chapter 3]. The adolescent then moves from stage 1 to stage 5 with various hormones being responsible for particular aspects of development. Chapters 3 and 6 review some of these important events.

The tremendous biologic changes in adolescent males and females may occur at various stages, and it is best to assess the adolescent based on pubertal changes rather than on age. The first sign of puberty in the adolescent female, which starts at about 11 years of age, is the breast bud (thelarche), or Tanner stage 2. The range is wide, between 8 and 15 years.

Table 1-6. Sexual Maturity Rating or Tanner Staging in Females.

Stage	Breasts	Pubic Hair	Range
1	None	None	Birth to 15 years
2[1]	Breast bud (thelarche): areolar hyperplasia with small amount of breast tissue	Long downy pubic hair near the labia; may occur with breast budding or several weeks to months later (pubarche)	8½ to 15 years (some use 8.0 years)
3[2]	Further enlargement of breast tissue and areola	Increase in amount of hair with more pigmentation	10 to 15 years
4[3]	Double contour form: areola and nipple form secondary mound on top of breast tissue	Adult type but not distribution	10 to 17 years
5[4]	Larger breast with single contour form	Adult distribution	12½ to 18 years

[1] Peak height velocity often occurs soon after stage II
[2] 25% develop menarche in late III
[3] Most develop menarche in stage IV, 1 to 3 years after thelarche
[4] 10% develop menarche in stage V
From Greydanus DE, McAnarney ER: Overview on adolescence. In: Wasserman E, Gromisch DS, eds: Survey of Clinical Pediatrics. 7th ed. New York: McGraw Hill, 1981.

The first observable sign of puberty in the adolescent male is testicular growth, which identifies Tanner stage 2. This usually begins at 11.6 years of age, with a range of 10 to 14.8 years. As these biologic changes occur, the adolescent is developing an adult-like physique. At this time of development, the youth's sexuality is obviously being affected. At the same time, the adolescent may or may not enter into the psychologic or the psychosocial phase of his adolescent sexuality.

SOCIOLOGIC ASPECTS OF ADOLESCENT SEXUALITY

When one realizes the social influence on the sexuality of all human beings, it is apparent that social stimuli affect the sexuality of the developing adolescent. The influence of the media on adolescent sexuality has been well documented by Strasburger and others. Television (Table 1-8) is only one example of how society has affected adolescent sexuality today. The importance of this is certainly apparent when statistics on teenage pregnancy and related statistics, noted earlier, are compared with those of 20-30 years ago. Topics now discussed and publicized in movies, television, and advertising were not as pervasive 20 to 30 years ago. Therefore, social sexuality of adolescence is now a different phenomenon than it was in years past.

HOMOSEXUALITY AND HETEROSEXUALITY OF ADOLESCENCE

Any discussion of adolescent sexuality must include an acknowledgment of the concept of homosexuality and pseudohomosexuality. With increased media coverage of homosexuality, many adolescents pass through this period of life questioning their true orientation with respect to males and females. In 1973, Sorenson reported that 6% of adolescent

Table 1-7. Sexual Maturity Rating or Tanner Staging in Males

Stage	Testes	Penis	Pubic Hair	Range
1	No change, testes 2.5 cm. or less	Prepubertal	None	Birth to 15 years
2	Enlargement of testes, increased stippling and pigmentation of scrotal sac	Minimal or no enlargement	Long, downy hair often occurring several months after testicular growth; variable pattern noted with pubarche	10 to 15 years
3[1]	Further enlargements, especially in length	Significant penile enlargement, especially in length	Increase in amount, now curling	10½ to 16½ years
4[2]	Further enlargement	Further enlargement, especially in diameter	Adult type but not distribution	Variable; 12 to 17 years
5[3]	Adult size	Adult size	Adult distribution (medial aspects of thighs, linea alba)	13 to 18 years

[1] Peak height spurt usually between III and IV
[2] Axillary hair develops, as well as some facial hair
[3] Twenty percent have peak height velocity now. Body hair growth, and increase in musculature, etc., continue for several months to years
From Greydanus DE, McAnarney ER: Overview on adolescence. In: Wasserman E, Gromisch DS, eds: Survey of Clinical Pediatrics, 7th ed. New York: McGraw Hill, 1981.

females and 11% of adolescent males had homosexual experiences. A survey by Norman and Harris found that 9% of American youth report homosexual experiences. How frequently such experiences really occur is unclear, but current research does note that casual homosexual experiences do not lead to an overtly homosexual lifestyle during adulthood. It is important to show youth and their parents that such experimentation is not necessarily linked to an adult lifestyle of homosexuality. Many adolescents become concerned after such encounters and may develop negative reactions as a result.

Most gay males say that they became aware of their gay orientation during early adolescence, according to Green, and most gay women trace their commitments to late adolescence. Therefore, early adolescence is the time most male homosexuality occurs; late adolescence is the time when most lesbian activity occurs. The health care provider must be aware of this when working with adolescents and their families (see Appendix G).

The concept that homosexuality is related to a definite patient profile is not true. No definite data support the concept of a dominant mother or a weak father or vice versa with respect to the development of true homosexuality and a true gay lifestyle. Homosexual orientation for both men and women during adolescence is a reality of life. It is important for the

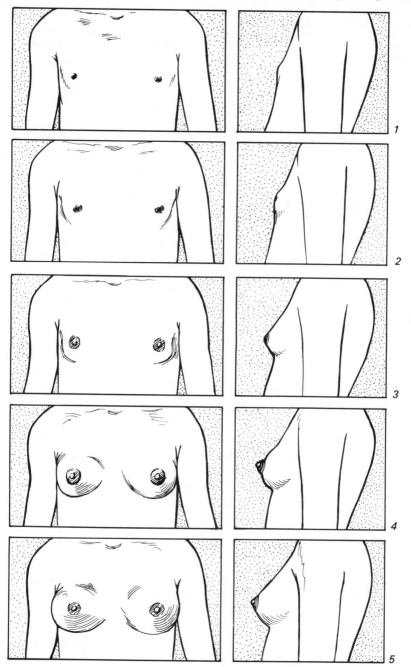

Fig. 1-1. Tanner stages for breast development.

health care provider to recognize when homosexual activity is present or when such activity is not of the adolescent's choosing, and to know when to refer. Also, conflicts concerning homosexuality may be the hidden agenda for many adolescents presenting clinical problems.

Male Tanner Staging

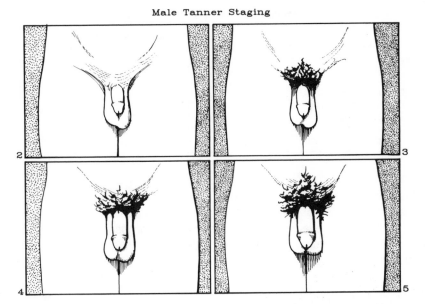

Fig. 1-2. Male Tanner staging.

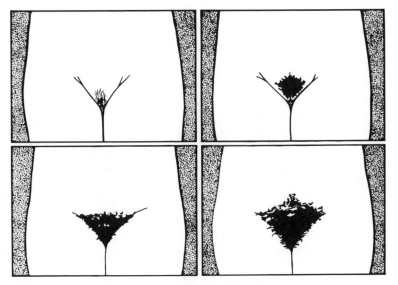

Fig. 1-3. Pubic hair ratings in female (Tanner 2, 3, 4, 5).

Table 1-8. Sexual Behaviors Portrayed on Television.

Behavior	Average Acts per Hour	
	1975	1979
Kissing	3.3	7.3
Hugging	2.6	4.9
Casual touching	68.0	62.0
Aggressive touching	5.4	6.8
Suggestiveness	2.0	13.5
Sexual intercourse	0.0	1.3
Discouraged practices	0.2	3.0

The health care provider, therefore, must take a judgment concerning the appropriateness of the sexual direction of the particular patient. The work of Meeks in evaluating heterosexual and homosexual behavior in adolescents is useful. The physician or the health care provider should keep the following points in mind:

Do the stated goals of the behavior seem realistic?

Is the sexual behavior a form of gratification or a form of punishment?

Is the sexual behavior asking for an adult role but childlike in behavior?

Does the sexual behavior represent a misdirection from hidden depression, hostility, or anxiety?

Is the sexual behavior relaxed and integrated into the individual's personality, or is it a forced activity?

Is the sexual behavior necessary to avoid anxiety-producing sexual fantasies?

Is the relationship with the sexual partner mature, sharing, and realistic, or is it immature or unrealistic?

Is the sexual behavior self-destructive?

By evaluating these eight points when observing the sexual behavior of the adolescent, the health care professional can determine whether the youth has a problem concerning sexuality. In evaluating homosexual behavior, it is important, according to Meeks that the health care professional differentiate between pseudohomosexual behavior and overtly homosexual behavior. In pseudohomosexual experience, the following points are noted:

There is uncertainty of masculinity or femininity.

There is a fear of homosexuality.

There is usually depression, anxiety, and delinquent behavior.

With overtly homosexual behavior, the following points may be made:

There is no set pattern of history with respect to family relationships or mother/father experiences.

There is aphobic avoidance of the genitalia of the opposite sex.

The total lifestyle seems to be integrated into homosexual activities and behavior.

The health care provider must understand these points and work to aid the individual while striving to help the parents to either accept the fact of homosexuality or understand the concept of pseudohomosexuality.

BIBLIOGRAPHY

Blum RW, ed: Health futures of youth: a symposium. J Adol Health Care 1988;9(suppl 6):1S-50S.

Chodorow N: The Reproduction of Mothering. Berkeley: University of California Press, 1978.

Cohen MW, Friedman SB: Nonsexual motivation of adolescent sexual behavior. Med Aspects Human Sexuality 1975;10:9-31.

Daniel WA, ed: Adolescent growth and development: update. Semin Adolesc Med 1985;1:1-96.

Deisher R: Adolescent sexuality. In: Adolescent Medicine. Hofmann AD, Greydanus DE, eds. Norwalk, CT: Appleton-Lange, 1989:337-346.

Duke P: Adolescent sexuality. Pediatr Rev 1982;4:2.

DuRant RH, Jay MS: Communication and compliance issues in adolescent medicine. Semin Adolesc Med 1987;3:79-162.

Erickson EH: Childhood and Society. New York: W.W. Norton, 1950.

Franger AL: Taking a sexual history and managing common sexual problems. J Repro Med 1988;33:639-644.

Freud S: Inhibitions, symptoms and anxiety. In: Strachey J, ed: Complete Psychological Works of Sigmund Freud. London: Hogarth Press, 1959.

Freud S: Three Essays on the Theory of Sexuality. 5th ed. London: Hogarth, 1953:125-245.

Fujii CM, Felice ME: Physical growth and development: current concepts. Prim Care 1987;14:1-12.

Gilligan C: New maps of development: new visions of maturity. Am J Orthopsychiatry 1982;52:199-213.

Gilligan C, Kohlberg L: Moral reasoning and value formation. In: Calderone MS, ed: Sexuality and Human Values. New York: Associated Press, 1974.

Green R: Homosexual behavior. In: Gillis SE, Kagan BM, eds: Current Pediatric Therapy. Philadelphia: W.B. Saunders, 1982.

Greydanus DE, ed: Adolescent sexuality. Parts I-IV. Semin Adolesc Med 1985;1(2):97-151, 1985;1(3):153-230, 1986;2(2):201-289, 1987;3(1):1-78.

Greydanus DE: Adolescent sexuality: an overview and perspective for the 1980s. Pediatr Ann 1982;11(9):714-726.

Allan Guttmacher Institute: Teenage pregnancy: the problem that hasn't gone away. New York: Planned Parenthood Federation of America, 1981.

Havighurst RJ: Objectives for youth development. In: Youth: 74th Yearbook of National Society for the Study of Education. Chicago: University of Chicago Press, 1975:87.

Hayes CD, ed: Risking the Future: Adolescent Sexuality, Pregnancy and Childbearing. Washington, D.C.: National Academy Press, 1987.

Johnson RL: Adolescent growth and development. In: Hofmann AD, Greydanus DE, eds: Adolescent Medicine. 2nd ed. New York: Appleton-Lange, 1989.

Katchadourian H: Adolescent sexuality. Pediatr Clin North Am 1980;27:17-28.

Kinsey A, Pomeroy W, Martin C, et al: Sexual Behavior in the Human Female. Philadelphia: W.B. Saunders, 1953.

Kinsey A, Pomeroy W, Martin C: Sexual Behavior in the Human Male. Philadelphia: W.B. Saunders, 1948.

Kolberg L: Moral development. In: International Encyclopedia of the Social Sciences. New York: Crowell, Collier & Macmillan, 1968.

Meeks JF: The Fragile Alliance. 3rd ed. Miami: Krueger, 1986:52.

Miller JB: Toward a New Psychology of Women. Boston: Beacon, 1976.

Norman J, Harris M: The Private Life of the American Teenager. New York: Rawson, Wade, 1981.

Orr DP, Ingersoll GM: Adolescent development: a biopsychosocial review. Curr Probl Ped 1988;18(8):447-499.

Piaget J: The intellectual development of the adolescent. In: Kaplan B, Lebovice, eds: Adolescence—Psychosocial Perspectives. New York: Basic Books, 1969.

Remafedi GJ, ed: Symposium on adolescent homosexuality. J Adol Health Care 1988;9:93.

Sahler OJZ, McAnarney ER: The Child from Three to Eighteen. St. Louis: C.V. Mosby, 1981.

Sarrell IJ, Sarrel PM: Sexual unfolding. J Adolesc Health Care 1981;2:93-99.

Sorenson R: Adolescent Sexuality in Contemporary America. New York: World, 1972.

Strasburger VC: Normal adolescent sexuality. In: Shearin R, ed: Seminars in Adolescent Medicine. New York: Thieme-Stratton, 1986;1(2):101-116.

Strasburger VC, ed: Basic Office Gynecology: An Office Primer. Baltimore: Urban and Schwarzenberg, 1990.

Strasburger VC: The Media. State of the Art Reviews: Adolescent Medicine. Philadelphia: Hanley & Belfus, 1990;1(1):90-101.

Stewart DC: Sexuality and the adolescent: issues for the clinician. Prim Care 1987;14:83-99.

Tanner JM: Growth at Adolescence. 2nd ed. Oxford: Blackwell Scientific, 1962.

2

Adolescent Examinations

The cornerstone of an accurate diagnosis in medicine is a thorough history and complete physical examination. When these elements are performed well, the problem and its ultimate solution (if any) are usually apparent. Expert diagnosticians are aware of this critical principle, and it certainly holds true in the area of adolescent gynecology.

Although the main topic of this book is the sexual health of the adolescent female, clinicians should also consider the health issues pertinent to the male. For this reason, the final section of this chapter describes genital examinations of the male.

Obtaining a useful history from an adolescent can be a difficult task, whether dealing with young adolescents who cannot provide detailed answers to important questions or with older youth who are wary of the entire medical process, especially when it includes a pelvic examination. Thus, establishing a relationship of trust between the health care professional and the adolescent patient is the first step. Table 2-1 describes the three basic types of doctor-patient relationships, whereas Table 2-2 describes the interactional factors and interviewing skills needed when dealing with adolescent patients, particularly those having gynecologic problems.

A questionnaire (Table 2-3) can be a helpful and time-saving way of obtaining useful information. Despite a fear of the examination process and a hesitancy to discuss intimate aspects of her life, the patient may find that the questionnaire helps relieve anxiety and prepares her for the kinds of questions the clinician wishes to ask. It may help the physician as well, who may be reluctant to pursue such intimate topics with a patient not well known to him or her. It is usually necessary to interview the adolescent alone, without parents, at some point in the evaluation process—especially when gynecologic-related subjects are discussed. Parents are a valuable part of the evaluation, but some private time with the teenager is necessary. There are many issues that most youth will not discuss in the presence of their parents. Parents should be made aware of this and taught not to become hurt or angry over their teenager's need for privacy. Parents who insist on knowing all about their child's behavior usually end up knowing very little about real aspects of their child's life. The child or younger teenager may wish to have a parent (usually the mother) involved during the entire process. Many clinicians start the interview process with the teenager and parent together and then see each one alone later.

When interviewing the youth alone, never pledge total confidentiality, although you can assure the individual that you will keep as much infor-

Table 2-1. Doctor-Patient Relationships.

Relationship	Description
Active–passive	An authoritarian posture, the typical doctor-patient (parent-childlike) relationship, used with infants and young children.
Guidance–cooperation	The classic doctor-patient (independent) relationship used with patients of all ages. Appropriate for most early- and middle-stage teenagers.
Mutual participation	A mutual participatory doctor-patient (independent-dependent) relationship. Appropriate for some middle- and most late-stage adolescents.

mation private as possible. Promising absolute confidentiality only sets up potential problems, such as would be encountered if a youth suggests that she may attempt suicide or run away from home but insists that the parent not be informed of such serious thoughts. When the clinician then shares this information with the parent, the trust relationship with the patient may be irreparably broken.

However, many sexuality-related issues can be held in private and much confidentiality provided. Youth who are coitally active can legally seek advice on contraceptive prescription from health care professionals without parental consent. Although it is best to include parents in such overall decision-making processes, this is not possible in all cases. Preparing the child and parent for such dilemmas while the patient is in childhood may help to alleviate such unpleasant and difficult conflicts. When the patient is a child, the physician may tell both child and parents about the impending adolescence and ascertain the ground rules expected from the emerging adolescent and the parents. Thus, the clinician can avoid such conflicts as the 14-year-old, sexually active female who seeks contraception from the physician but does not want the parents involved.

LEGAL RIGHTS OF ADOLESCENTS

Anyone involved with youth (including parents, teachers, and health care professionals) must realize that American laws now recognize that minors (youth) do have some legal rights. Understanding these rights, especially when specific issues arise, is often difficult, because the laws

Table 2-2. Interactional Factors and Interviewing Skills.

All Patients	Adolescent Patients
Relationship	Use of authority, boundaries of confidentiality, maintenance of objectivity
Communication	Purpose of the visit; sources of information other than patient; patient communication via open-ended questions, clarification of slang, and feedback (by patient and physician)
Feelings	Recognition and validation, ventilation of feelings

Table 2-3. Screening Medical Inventory for Young Adolescents.

1. Do you have frequent headaches?
2. Do you have any eye or vision difficulties?
   When was your last vision check?   Result:
3. Do you have any ear or hearing difficulties?
   When was your hearing checked?   Result:
4. Do you get frequent nosebleeds?
   Do you feel you bleed easily?   Bruise easily?
5. Do you feel you have problems with your teeth?
   Date of last dental check?
6. Do you have any lumps, bumps, or sores you are concerned about?
7. Do you tire easily?
8. Do you get short of breath easily or wheeze?
9. Do you wheeze after exercise?
10. Do you think there is anything wrong with your heart?
11. Do you have any abdominal pain you are concerned about?
12. Do you often have backaches or sore bones or sore joints?
13. Do you think you have a hernia or weak muscles?
14. Are you allergic to anything (drugs, pets, pollen, etc.)?
    If so, what?
15. Do you sleep well most of the time?
16. Do you have frequent dreams or nightmares?
17. Are you concerned about your weight?
18. Are you concerned about your height?
19. Are you concerned about your appearance?
20. Do you have any medical illnesses (epilepsy, diabetes, tuberculosis, other)?
21. Do you feel you get upset easily?
    Do others say you get upset easily?
22. Are you worried you might have a tumor or cancer?
    If so, where?
23. Are you satisfied with your progress in school?
24. Do you have skin problems?
25. Are you having problems with your parents?
26. Does it burn when you urinate?
27. Do you have any questions about menstruation?
28. Do you have questions about contraception?
29. Do you have questions about breast problems?
30. Do you have questions about sexual matters?
31. Are there any questions about pregnancy that you have?
32. Do you have any questions about discharge, genital sores, or VD?
33. Are you concerned about your sexual development or sexual feelings?
34. Do you have questions about drugs or alcohol?
35. Do you often feel moody or depressed?
36. Are there any of these or other concerns that you wish to discuss with a health professional?

Nurse: Counselor:
Physician: Other (   ):

are frequently vague. Different states disagree on certain details; thus, the caregiver must be familiar with current laws in the state in which he or she is practicing. Definition of "the law" is a compilation of various statutes, Supreme Court rulings, or decisions (state and federal), as well as interpretation of legal philosophy, that covers areas not always specifically covered by an identified law at the local, state, or federal level.

Only recently has official law identified the rights of minors (those under age 21). The first 100 years of United States history was marked by the legal philosophy that parents had essentially complete autonomy over their children. In that era, children were expected to obey parents and were punished by parents or other individuals if they disobeyed.

Toward the end of the 19th century, a shift in legal philosophy ushered in the "era of child welfare." The laws then reflected the concept that children were different from parents and needed to be *protected* from parents. If legal guardians abused their privileges, punishment was now possible. Thus, juvenile courts were established and child labor, to some extent, was forbidden.

Minors were still not allowed to make contracts of their own. Common law tradition has often held that to treat a minor without appropriate parental consent is to commit "unauthorized touching," which legally could be called "assault and battery." Much of this legal philosophy continues today, but it has become a complex issue in light of recent legal cases (Hofmann, 1989).

In 1967, the "Era of Rights of Minors" began with a well-known legal case: *In re Gault.* This involved a 15-year-old male who was sentenced by a court to several years of institutionalization after being convicted of placing obscene phone calls to a teacher. The boy's parents brought forth a successful countersuit, claiming that the original trial was not legal since it violated the minor's rights on various grounds: no official legal representative, no cross-examination, and others. Table 2-4 lists other important cases in this concept of minor's rights. The Danforth case (1976) pitted the minor's rights against the parents' rights. In this case of a late adolescent seeking an abortion from a qualified physician, the state court ruled that mature minors have the right to obtain an abortion, regardless of third-party (e.g., parental) disapproval.

Such issues are complex and far from being resolved, especially the abortion issue. However, it seems clear that youth can give consent for medical treatment in some situations and do not necessarily have to involve parents. In general, it is best to involve parents in such matters, but such is not always possible or feasible.

A nonofficial legal concept has emerged over the past generation: the *mature minor doctrine.* This implies that "emancipated" minors may seek and receive some medical treatment. However, the interpretation of "emancipation" can be vague and varies according to the different criteria used in various states (Table 2-5). Becoming familiar with one's own state's rules and philosophy is strongly recommended for those who deal with such teenagers. Tables 2-6 and 2-7 identify some of these specific concepts for the state of Iowa.

Thus, youth do have some legal rights, although the situation remains complex and in a state of constant legal flux. Problems of sterilization (especially of mentally subnormal youth), abortion, sexual assault, mental health, health record privacy, payment issues, and other areas remain critical concepts for individuals involved in the health care issues of adolescents. For many in our society, the legal complexities are crystallized in the current debate over abortion.

Table 2-4. Important Legal Cases and Laws Involving Legal Rights of Minors.

Case	Year	Significance
In re Gault	1967	Minors have right to fair trial before sentencing
Tinker v. The Des Moines Independent School District	1969	Minors cannot be removed from school unless their rights are protected
Roe v. Wade, Doe v. Bolton	1973	Women have the right to obtain a first-trimester abortion
Planned Parenthood of Central Missouri v. Danforth	1976	Mature minors have the right to obtain an abortion regardless of third-party (e.g., parental) disapproval
Bellotti v. Baird	1979	Judge can grant a minor an abortion with parental notification but without parental consent
Hyde Amendment	1979	Restricted use of federal funds to pay for legal abortions
H.L. v. Matheson	1981	It is legal to require immature and dependent minors to inform parents before abortion is obtained
Carey v. Population Services International	1977	U.S. Supreme Court rules that contraceptives must be available to minors and that states cannot prohibit it
DHHS Regulation	1983	Establishment of rules governing protection of human subjects in federally funded biomedical research
California State Law	1987	Parents must be notified before providing contraception. Minnesota has established this also. This will probably receive U.S. Supreme Court evaluation
Webster v. Reproductive Health Services	1989	Supreme Court ruling: states are given greater power to determine access to abortion. See Table 8-10.
Sexually transmitted diseases treatment	1970s	Virtually all states allow minors to consent to the diagnosis, treatment, and prevention of STD's
Substance abuse disorders	1970s	Most states allow minors to consent to medical and psychologic treatment of drug abuse
Voluntary commitment to mental hospitals	1970s	Most states allow a minor to voluntarily commit himself or herself to a mental hospital. A U.S. Supreme Court ruling notes that parents can commit their children to such facilities under special conditions, which vary from state to state
Age of emancipation	(Varies)	Mostly age 18, but with some variation: Alabama: 14, Oregon: 15, S. Carolina: 16, Nebraska: 19, and Wyoming: 19

From Greydanus DE: Abortion in adolescence. In: Premature Adolescent Pregnancy and Parenthood. McAnarney ER, ed. New York: Grune & Stratton, 1983:355.

Table 2-5. Various Criteria for Emancipation.

1. Age (often over 18, but varies from 14-19)
2. Marriage
3. Parenthood
4. Runaway status (financially independent)
5. Individuals away from the home with parent's permission
6. Individuals at home who are "essentially independent"
7. Education (such as high school graduates)
8. Member of armed forces
9. Certified by physician and others

GENERAL HISTORY

As noted, getting a youth to openly discuss her concerns with you can be a difficult task. Learn to be yourself and not to project a false image—the youth will detect falseness immediately. Asking questions about her friends or "others" may allow her to relax and then to gradually begin talking about herself. For example, the health care professional can say, "I know many youth your age are smoking cigarettes. What do you think about that? How does this affect you?" As previously stated, starting with a general medical questionnaire may help to reduce anxiety and may inform the patient as to what you consider important issues.

Seek information on demographics, past medical history, general review of systems, family history, general psychosocial data, and the status of important relationships in her life with peers and with family. Talk at her cognitive level, whether concrete or operational thinking is required. Be aware of the differences that different psychologic stages can make, and that the stages are not based solely on the patient's age (see Chapter 1). Be alert to clues in the history, such as the patient with a "smoke-screen" issue—vague complaints of abdominal pain when the real issue is concern about pregnancy. Clues to various behavioral disorders are usually contained in the thorough interview (Tables 2-3 and 2-8).

Table 2-6. Emancipation Criteria in Iowa.*

1. Age: 18 (Iowa Law Code, Section 599.1)
2. Marriage (Iowa Law Code, Section 599.1)
   (You need to be 16 years of age or over, have the consent of parents and a judge's approval to marry, if under age 18).
3. Parent-Youth Contract
   (Parent(s) and youth under age 18 can make a verbal or written contract declaring emancipation. Its legality would depend on the circumstances).
4. The following, by themselves, do not establish emancipation:
   a) Parenthood
   b) Runaway status
   c) Living away from home
   d) Living at home but "essentially independent"
   e) Education
   f) Member of the armed services
   g) Physician's certification

*Prepared in consultation with the Youth Law Center, Des Moines, Iowa.

Table 2-7. Example of Parent-Youth Contract for Emancipation.

Parents and youth under 18 can make a verbal or written contract declaring emancipation. Its legality would depend on the circumstances.

In general, individuals over age 18 are allowed to initiate such contracts, and those under 18 are not. If an individual 16 or 17 years of age seeks medical treatment, understands the physician's recommendations, and explains why parents are not to be involved, then the physician can document this, declare the patient to be an emancipated minor in need of treatment, and proceed with appropriate medical treatment. Some consultants recommend having a second physician sign this document also, but one needs remember it is not an official legal statement. The individual who is between 13 and 15 years of age represents a complex legal situation, even if he or she appears to be fully "emancipated." Minors in need of emergency care, as determined by a physician, can always be treated. Youth with possible sexually transmitted disease, pregnancy, or drug abuse can also be evaluated and treated without parent's consent or knowledge if necessary. As of this date, there has been no successful lawsuit against a physician treating a minor over 15 years of age for any purpose if the minor consented to the treatment. Also, there has not been a successful lawsuit against a physician treating a minor of any age for contraceptive-related services. When treating minors without parent's approval, the youth should be reminded of his or her obligation to follow through with medical recommendations and to consider the cost of such health care.

Again, it takes time to evaluate youth; a hurried, careless approach is not appropriate. Refer to others who can provide a thorough evaluation if your schedule or training does not permit this approach. The patient with poor eye contact or the seductive patient is alerting you to the probability of having some type of behavioral difficulty. Pursue the history further. Remain professional at all times, especially with seductive youth. Remember, they are not yet adults and are sensitive to improper suggestions.

GYNECOLOGIC HISTORY

The pertinent aspects of a gynecologic history are outlined in Table 2-9. Remember that the history, as well as the physical examination, should

Table 2-8. Behavioral Problems of Adolescents.

1. Concerns of normalcy (e.g., height, weight, appearance, pubertal status, etc.)
2. Drug abuse (marijuana, alcohol, tobacco, stimulants, depressants, hallucinogens, etc.)
3. School failure
4. Parent-youth conflicts
5. Adolescent sexuality concerns
6. Physical abuse
7. Depression
8. Suicide gesture (suicide act)
9. Anorexia nervosa
10. Juvenile delinquency
11. Personality trait disorder
12. Psychosomatic illness
13. Hyperventilation
14. Running away
15. Other psychiatric illness
16. Functional symptoms (headache, abdominal pain, etc.)
17. Other problems

Table 2-9. Outline of Basic Gynecologic History.

1. General demographic data
2. General medical history
3. General family history
4. General psychosocial data
5. Review of pubertal milestones
   a. Thelarche
   b. Pubarche
   c. Growth spurt
   d. Menarche
   e. Establishment of regular menstruation
6. Menstrual history (including the mother's history)
7. In-utero diethylstilbestrol (DES) exposure
8. Sexarche (onset of coital patterns)
9. Dating history and non-coital sexual history
10. History of sexually transmitted diseases
11. History of pregnancy and abortion
12. History of sexual (physical) abuse
13. History of previous pelvic examination
14. Other

be a valuable educational experience for the patient. The use of visual aids (charts, pictures, anatomy models, handouts, films, and others) can be helpful in explaining important concepts. For the initial interview, the patient is sitting down and fully clothed. Do not meet the patient for the first time while she is lying down, waiting for the pelvic examination. Be aware of the embarrassment that this process can be for the patient and occasionally for you. Try to be warm, professional, gentle, empathetic, and nonjudgmental. Try not to write while you ask her intimate questions; record the details later. Also, try to help the patient avoid a traumatic experience, one that can be with her for the rest of her life and negatively affect her adolescent as well as adult sexuality development.

The actual gynecologic history should detail the important events of puberty—thelarche, pubarche, height spurt, menarche, and the timing of regular menstruation. Evaluation can determine the normalcy or abnormality of sexual maturity. Many useful clinical correlations (Table 2-10) can be observed with the use of such ratings or Tanner stages (Tables 1-6 and 1-7). A careful review of the patient's menstrual history over several cycles is often helpful, as is information on the mother's menstrual pattern. Having the patient keep a menstrual-cycle diary may be helpful. Determine if the youth was prepared for thelarche or menarche and how she reacted to these important events. Discovering the role of the female in the family can provide valuable clues as to how she is functioning currently in the home, in school, with boyfriends, and with others. Seek information about possible in-utero diethylstilbestrol (DES) exposure; sometimes only the mother is aware of such exposure. Although you may be interviewing the patient alone, don't overlook the details that the mother (or other family members) may have to offer. If the answers from patient and mother are different, one can gain valuable insight into the

For clinical purposes, a nomogram such as Fig. 6-2 suggests the necessary weight for menarche for a girl of given height; regardless of height and weight, a girl whose fat content is less than 17% has a 90% probability of continued menarcheal delay. Conversely, obesity advances pubertal maturation and menarche, except in extreme obesity in which hypothalamic amenorrhea may persist.

Activity Level and Exercise

Intensive and repeated exercise such as athletic or dance training may delay menarche, just as exercise may induce secondary amenorrhea in older adolescents. Estrogen-dependent processes (breast development and menarche) are more affected by activity than androgen-dependent processes (pubic hair growth). Although the lower body fat content of girls in physical training contributes to this phenomenon, studies of young adolescent ballet dancers found delay of menarche disproportionate to their leanness (i.e., primary amenorrhea continued until the dancers achieved a body-fat content higher than that of the less active controls at their menarche). One study reported that each year of premenarcheal training delayed menarche by 5 months. When intensive training has inhibited pubertal maturation, an interruption of training such as an off-season may result in dramatically rapid physical development. There is no conclusive evidence that exercise-related delay is harmful. Again, the teleologic interpretation is that pregnancy is undesirable during major ongoing energy drain.[9]

Conversely, girls who are less active undergo earlier pubertal maturation. Studies have established that puberty occurs earlier in bedridden girls; a reasonable prediction is that this relationship holds true, to a lesser degree, for those who are simply sedentary.

General Physical and Mental Health

General health influences hypothalamic maturation and timing of puberty. As with athletic amenorrhea, obvious mechanisms involve body weight and nutritional state, but pubertal delay is observed in a variety of systemic illnesses (such as poorly controlled diabetes), even when growth and body weight appear adequate for menarche.[10] Chronic illness tends to delay menarche more than thelarche, and thelarche more than adrenarche.

Although rarer and more difficult to demonstrate, stress, environmental deprivation, depression, and major mental illness may delay menarche by the same hypothalamic mechanisms that cause secondary amenorrhea.[11]

EARLY PUBERTAL DEVELOPMENT

By definition, puberty is "early" only if it occurs long before the adolescent years. Because the process of idiopathic precocity in a 5-year-old girl may be indistinguishable from puberty in a 12-year-old, and because a disease such as congenital adrenal hyperplasia may cause pubic hair to appear in a 9-year-old, no age specification can completely separate the pathologic from the physiologic. The age guidelines in the following paragraphs are arbitrary and result in the screening of numerous early but normal girls, but are widely used to minimize the risk of neglecting a significant problem. Detailed discussion of the individual entries in Table 3-6 is beyond the scope of this book, and good reviews are available.[12,13]

Early Thelarche

Thelarche before age 8 years warrants evaluation. The following should be sought and excluded by history and examination: exogenous estrogen source; family history of early maturation; signs or symptoms of intracranial, abdominal, or pelvic disease; skin signs of neurocutaneous syndromes; neurologic or visual abnormalities; recent acceleration of growth or longstanding growth failure; signs or symptoms of hypothyroidism or hypothalamic disorder; widening of the hips; adult body odor; acne; and vaginal discharge. The presence of these features requires some or all of the following investigations: measurement of gonadotropins, estrone, and estradiol; other hormone measurements; bone-age x rays; imaging of head, abdomen, or pelvis; and referral to a pediatric or reproductive endocrinologist. Pathologic causes of early thelarche include tumors of the hypothalamus, ovaries, liver, or adrenals, or intracranial disorders initiating precocious puberty, severe hypothyroidism, rare states of autonomous ovarian hyperfunction (such as McCune-Albright syndrome), and a few others.

In the absence of the above items, breast development and growth may be observed for 6 months; lack of significant change or new features indicates that breast development is most likely isolated premature thelarche, a benign condition requiring no intervention. Early pubic hair or menarche in addition to thelarche requires fuller evaluation as described below.

Early Adrenarche

Adrenarche before age 8 years warrants evaluation. The following should be sought and excluded by history and examination: exogenous androgen source; previous vomiting episodes or siblings who died in infancy with vomiting; signs or symptoms of intracranial, abdominal, or pelvic disease; skin signs of neurocutaneous syndromes; neurologic abnormalities; recent acceleration of growth; other axillary, facial, or body hair; adult body odor; acne; and clitoromegaly, labial fusion, or genital ambiguity. A strong family history of early adrenarche, especially if combined with reports of excessive hirsutism, polycystic ovary disease, or infertility, suggests the need for adrenal testing. The presence of any of the above features requires some or all of the following investigations: measurement of androgens (DHAS, androstenedione, testosterone), 17-hydroxyprogesterone, other adrenal steroids, or gonadotropins; other hormone measurements; bone-age x rays; imaging of head, abdomen, or pelvis; and referral to a pediatric or reproductive endocrinologist. Pathologic causes of early adrenarche include tumors of adrenals or ovaries,

Table 3-6. Causes of Precocious Pubertal Development in Girls.

Precocity with episodic or sustained gonadotropin elevation
    Complete central precocious puberty
        Idiopathic
            Sporadic
            Familial
                Familial precocious puberty
                Familial, isolated LH hypersecretion
      Associated with neurologic dysfunction or abnormality
        Neurocutaneous syndromes
            McCune-Albright, neurofibromatosis, tuberous sclerosis
        Post-infectious
            Encephalitis, meningitis, brain abscess
        Post-traumatic
        Myelomeningocele
        Hydrocephalus
        Cerebral palsy
        Hypothalamic syndromes
        Intracranial mass lesions
            Ventricular cysts
            Hamartoma
            Pinealoma
            Optic glioma
            Craniopharyngioma (post-operative)
        Seizure disorder, especially gelastic epilepsy
        Intracranial hemorrhage, stroke
      Prolonged primary hypothyroidism
      Hypothalamic maturation accelerated by long androgen exposure
        Congenital adrenal hyperplasias
        Exogenous androgens
    Ectopic tumor production of LH or chorionic gonadotropin
      Intracranial teratoma
      Hepatoblastoma
      Thoracic polyembryoma
      Retroperitoneal carcinoma
      Chorioepithelioma
    Exogenous chorionic gonadotropin exposure
Estrogenic precocity with low (prepubertal) gonadotropin levels
    Isolated premature thelarche
    Isolated premature menarche
    Feminization by ovarian estrogens
      Primary ovarian precocity
      McCune-Albright syndrome
      Granulosa-theca cell tumor of ovary
      Ovarian follicular cyst
      Gonadoblastoma
      Lipoid ovarian tumors
      Cystadenoma
      Ovarian carcinoma
    Feminization by adrenal estrogens
      Adrenocortical carcinoma
      Adrenal adenoma
    Feminization by ectopic tumor estrogens
      Teratoma
      Teratocarcinoma
    Feminization by exogenous estrogens
      Oral contraceptives, estrogen creams
      Foods or other environmental estrogen sources (?)
Androgenic precocity with low (prepubertal) gonadotropin levels
    Isolated premature adrenarche
    Virilization by ovarian androgens
      Arrhenoblastoma
      Lipoid tumor
      Cystadenoma
      Gonadoblastoma
      Ovarian carcinoma

Table 3-6. Continued

Virilization by adrenal androgens
  Adrenal tumors
    Adrenocortical carcinoma
    Adrenal adenoma
  Congenital adrenal hyperplasias
    21-hydroxylase deficiency
    11 beta-hydroxylase deficiency
    3 beta-hydroxysteroid dehydrogenase deficiency
Virilization by exogenous androgens (given for blood disorders, growth stimulation, athletic abuse)

---

various forms of congenital adrenal hyperplasia, various neurologic disorders, rare cases in which adrenarche is the first manifestation of complete precocious puberty, and a few others.

In the absence of the above items, pubic hair development and growth may be rechecked after 6 months; lack of significant change or new features indicates that the pubic hair probably represents isolated premature adrenarche, a benign condition requiring no intervention. The presence of thelarche or menarche in addition to adrenarche requires fuller evaluation as described below.

Early Menarche

Menarche before age 10 years warrants evaluation. The following should be sought and excluded by history and examination: exogenous estrogen source; signs or symptoms of intracranial, abdominal, or pelvic disease; skin signs of neurocutaneous syndromes; neurologic or visual abnormalities; signs or symptoms of hypothyroidism or hypothalamic disorder; recent acceleration of growth or longstanding growth failure; thelarche; widening of the hips; pubic or other hair; adult body odor; acne; evidence of vaginal infection, foreign body, or trauma (especially sexual abuse); and other perineal bleeding sources. The presence of these features requires some or all of the following investigations: measurement of gonadotropins, estrone, and estradiol; other hormone measurements; bone-age x rays; imaging of head, abdomen or pelvis; and referral to a pediatric or reproductive endocrinologist. A strong family history of early development is reassuring unless the patient is very young (under age 5).

Some of the pathologic causes of vaginal bleeding are discussed in Chapter 6. True menarche without prior thelarche is rare. True menarche usually indicates central precocious puberty and is accompanied by other evidence of puberty, especially thelarche, growth spurt, and bone age advancement. If the source of vaginal bleeding is unknown and no other features of early puberty are present, observation for another episode (or additional evidence of precocious development) is permissible.

Precocious Puberty

Combinations of thelarche with adrenarche, thelarche with menarche, or of all three (or other evidence of both androgen and estrogen effects) are indicative of central (i.e., gonadotropin-induced) precocious puberty, although a few other rare conditions may mimic it. Central precocious puberty may be "idiopathic," indicating that no disease is demonstrable and that the process is indistinguishable (except by age) from normal puberty (Fig. 3-4). Idiopathic precocity is often familial. Alternatively, central precocious puberty may be a manifestation of many varieties of CNS dysfunction. Even in the absence of neurologic signs or symptoms, CNS imaging is necessary to discover or exclude structural abnormalities such as tumors.

With the exclusion of treatable CNS disorders, the major decision re-

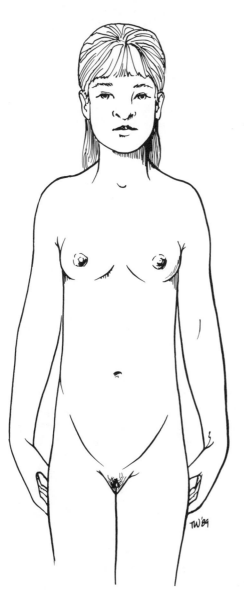

Fig. 3-4. The appearance of precocious puberty.

garding central precocious puberty is whether treatment is warranted. Primary indications for treatment include an unacceptably low predicted height (from current height, age, and bone age) or unmanageable emotional or behavioral responses (e.g., extreme social withdrawal or compulsive masturbation).

DELAYED PUBERTY AND PRIMARY AMENORRHEA

As with precocity, no precise age will cleanly separate all pathologic forms of delay from normal variations in timing. The following guidelines are arbitrary and will result in screening evaluations for many girls who are late but otherwise "normal," but are widely used to avoid undue delay in the recognition and treatment of various pathologic conditions. Absence of thelarche at age 14 years warrants evaluation. An evaluation of primary amenorrhea (absence of menarche) is warranted at age 16, or after 3 years from thelarche. Although the presence or absence of pubic hair is an important clue to the causes of delay of thelarche or menarche, concern over delay of adrenarche is an unlikely presenting complaint and, in the absence of other signs or symptoms, does not warrant evaluation.

Differential Diagnosis of Delayed Puberty

Table 3-7 lists both common and rare causes of delayed pubertal development, grouped by etiology. However, because the initial differential diagnosis depends on the physical findings, the workup will be discussed from that perspective. The small number of important conditions that constitute the majority of cases of delay are mentioned in this section and discussed in further detail below.

Delay of Thelarche, Menarche, and Adrenarche. Absence of all three aspects of puberty usually indicates general physical immaturity. A 14-year-old girl without any sign of early puberty probably has simple constitutional delay, unless there is specific evidence to suggest otherwise. As she gets older without thelarche or menarche, however, gonadotropin deficiency or other forms of hypogonadism or hypothalamic suppression become more likely.

Reversible hypothalamic delay is suggested by low weight for height, intensive athletic training, chronic system disease, or major psychologic disturbance, as discussed above. Laboratory studies demonstrate prepubertal hormone levels. Supposition of this condition may be confirmed by the onset of thelarche after weight gain, interruption of athletic training, amelioration of underlying disease, or simply the passage of time.

Evidence suggestive of more pathologic conditions, including primary or secondary hypogonadism, includes extreme short stature, poor growth velocity, past or present CNS disease, signs or symptoms of hypothyroidism, and abnormalities of the genitalia.

Initial screening evaluation may include a bone-age x ray and measurement of gonadotropins (and sometimes T4, TSH, and prolactin). A delayed bone age is consistent with a variety of diagnoses, but a bone age without delay makes constitutional delay unlikely.

Table 3-7. Causes of Delayed Puberty and Primary Amenorrhea.

Hypothalamic delay or dysfunction[2]
Constitutional delay of puberty[1]
"Homeostatic" delay of puberty[3]
Insufficient body mass[1]
Unfavorable energy balance
    Insufficient calorie intake[1]
    Excessive calorie expenditure (exercise)[1]
Psychologic delay of puberty
    Anorexia nervosa[1]
    Environmental stress or deprivation[1]
    Depression and major mental illness[1]
    Drug abuse[1]
Delay due to chronic systemic illness[1]
    Cancer
    Bowel disease with malnutrition
        E.g., Inflammatory bowel disease
            Cystic fibrosis
    Chronic renal failure
    Chronic liver disease
    Chronic heart disease
        E.g., Cyanotic congenital heart disease
    Chronic lung disease
        E.g., Asthma
    Chronic metabolic disorders or endocrinopathies
        E.g., Poorly controlled diabetes mellitus
            Adrenal insufficiency
            Cushing's syndrome
            Hyperthyroidism
    Chronic inflammatory conditions
        E.g., Juvenile rheumatoid arthritis
    Blood dyscrasias
        E.g., Sickle cell disease
            Thalassemias
    Chronic infection
        E.g., Tuberculosis
            Immunodeficiency states
    Miscellaneous genetic disorders
        E.g., Down's syndrome
Drug suppression of hypothalamic function[3]
    Major psychotropic agents, therapeutic and recreational
Endocrinopathies directly affecting hypothalamic function[3]
    Hyperprolactinemia[1]
    Hypothyroidism[1]
    Growth hormone deficiency[1]
Intrinsic hypothalamic disorders[4]
    Hypothalamic mass lesions (tumors or cysts)
    Infiltrative disease of the hypothalamus
        E.g., Histiocytosis X
            Leukemia
            Allergic or autoimmune encephalomyelitis
    Therapeutic craniospinal irradiation
    Intracranial surgery or trauma
    Ischemic or hemorrhagic lesions of hypothalamus
    Hypothalamic dysfunction syndromes[1]
        Kallmann's syndrome
        Prader-Willi syndrome
        Septo-optic dysplasia
        Laurence-Moon-Bardet-Biedl syndrome
    Idiopathic gonadotropin deficiency[1]
Intrinsic pituitary disorders[2,4]
    Empty sella syndrome
    Combined pituitary hormone deficiencies[1]
    Pituitary infarction
    Sellar tumors

Table 3-7. Continued

Traumatic or surgical stalk disruption
Abnormal, "bioinactive" gonadotropin molecules
Isolated FSH deficiency
Gonadal dysfunction[5]
   Congenital or early childhood ovarian failure
      Gonadal dysgenesis
         Turner's syndrome and partial X deletions[1]
         Pure gonadal dysgenesis[1]
         Mixed gonadal dysgenesis[1]
         Testicular dysgenesis[1,9]
      47,XXX syndrome
      Disorders of estrogen synthesis (ovaries otherwise normal)
         17 alpha-hydroxylase deficiency
         3 beta-hydroxysteroid dehydrogenase deficiency
   Later childhood or adolescent ovarian failure[6]
      Galactosemia
      Autoimmune ovarian failure
      Myotonia dystrophica
      Ataxia telangiectasia
      Idiopathic ovarian failure
      Resistant ovary syndrome (unresponsiveness to gonadotropins)
   Age-independent ovarian failure[6]
      Radiation destruction
      Surgical removal
      Cytotoxic chemotherapy
      Bilateral ovarian torsion or infarction
Abnormalities or absence of uterus[7]
   Absence of uterus in XY females with testes[8]
      Disorders of androgen synthesis[1,9]
         17 alpha-hydroxylase deficiency
         17,20-desmolase deficiency
         17-ketosteroid reductase deficiency
         3 beta-hydroxysteroid dehydrogenase deficiency
         5 alpha-reductase deficiency
      Androgen resistance syndromes
         Partial resistance syndromes[1,9]
         Complete (testicular feminization)[1]
   Absence or abnormality of uterus in XX females with ovaries
      Congenital müllerian dysgenesis syndromes[1]
         Uterine aplasia[1]
         Mayer-Rokitansky-Kuster-Hauser syndrome[1]
         MURCS association[1]
      Hysterectomy
      Radiation damage to uterus
Obstruction of outflow tract[7]
   Congenital cervical atresia[1]
   Congenital vaginal agenesis or atresia[1]
   Transverse vaginal septum[1]
   Imperforate hymen[1]
   Acquired cervical obstruction
   Agglutination of labia[1]

---

[1] Discussed further in the text because of clinical importance or frequency.
[2] All aspects of puberty are delayed, but adrenarche less so than thelarche and menarche.
[3] Puberty will usually proceed when inhibiting factors are removed.
[4] Gonadotropin deficiency is usually irreversible.
[5] There is little or no delay of adrenarche; thelarche and menarche will usually not occur
   spontaneously.
[6] If the ovaries fail after thelarche has occurred, menarche may be the only aspect of
   puberty that is delayed.
[7] All of these disorders may cause primary amenorrhea after normal thelarche and adrenarche.
[8] Adrenarche is variable and may be absent or late.
[9] Genitalia are usually ambiguous.

Extreme shortness with marginal growth velocity is suggestive of gonadal dysgenesis or longstanding hypopituitarism or hypothyroidism. Poor growth velocity without extreme shortness suggests more recent onset of hypothyroidism or hypopituitarism. Low T4 and high TSH confirm primary hypothyroidism. Growth hormone deficiency is suggested by a delayed bone age and low somatomedin C and gonadotropins in a girl with poor growth and pubertal delay. Significantly elevated gonadotropins indicate some type of primary ovarian failure, usually gonadal dysgenesis (although absence of pubic hair at age 14 or 15 years is distinctly uncharacteristic of primary ovarian failure). Referral to a pediatric endocrinologist is recommended for this category of problems.

Delay of Thelarche and Menarche, with Pubic Hair Present. If the pubic hair is less than stage 3 (suggesting presence for less than a year), the girl may still have some type of delay and the workup is as discussed in the preceding paragraphs (bone age, gonadotropins, review of growth, systemic symptoms, and causes of reversible delay).

However, absence of thelarche and menarche in a girl who has long-established pubic hair is strongly suggestive of irreversible hypogonadism, either primary or central. Full laboratory evaluation is warranted, including bone age, gonadotropins, androgens, prolactin, and general health screening (blood count, sedimentation rate, chemistries, urinalysis). Suspicion of hypogonadism is increased by a bone age greater than 13 years. Gonadal dysgenesis becomes one of the most likely possibilities, especially with elevated gonadotropins.

Delay of Menarche for More than 3 Years Past Thelarche. Thelarche indicates a functional hypothalamic-pituitary-gonadal axis and rising estrogen levels. Delay of menarche beyond 3 years suggests that the hypothalamic-gonadal axis has not matured normally, or that there is a defect of the uterus or outflow tract. Acquired failure of the hypothalamic-pituitary-ovarian system may be reversible or permanent, and is always treatable. Pubic hair may or may not be present. The pelvic examination is especially important. Initial screening tests include estradiol, gonadotropins, T4 and TSH, prolactin, and testosterone. A pregnancy test may be indicated. Primary amenorrhea due to congenital defects of the reproductive system is less often reversible but usually treatable.

The reversible disorders of hypothalamic-ovarian function are the familiar conditions: loss of weight (or extreme weight gain), intensive physical exercise, and significant systemic or mental illness. Onset of hypothyroidism or hyperprolactinemia after thelarche may disrupt hypothalamic function and prevent menarche. Androgen excess is far more likely to cause anovulatory oligomenorrhea than primary amenorrhea, but hirsutism, excessive acne, or advanced bone age may indicate long-standing androgen excess, such as congenital adrenal hyperplasia (see Chapter 6); androgen and adrenal screening should be pursued. Irreversible causes of hypothalamic or pituitary primary amenorrhea include acquired intracranial disorders, especially tumors. In some cases, atrophy of breasts or vaginal mucosa will reflect the loss of estradiol. Gonadotropins and estradiol will be at low-normal or low levels. Intracranial imaging or general health screening tests may be indicated.

Ovarian failure that develops shortly after thelarche is rare and unlikely to be reversible. This condition is suggested by signs of estrogen deficiency and marked elevation of gonadotropins.

Absence or hypoplasia of the uterus, cervix, or vagina will commonly appear as primary amenorrhea following normal thelarche and adrenarche. These are usually congenital malformations, and hormone levels are characteristic of middle puberty. One type of absence of müllerian derivatives (uterus, cervix, fallopian tubes, vagina) accompanies complete androgen resistance and is known as "testicular feminization." The diagnosis of these conditions is usually first suspected during the pelvic examination, when the vaginal opening or cervix is absent. In rare cases, the uterus and cervix are present but the escape of vaginal blood has been obstructed, resulting in distention of the uterus or upper vagina. An ultrasound will quickly define the internal anatomy, and a karyotype may be indicated.

Specific Conditions Associated with Pubertal Delay

Constitutional Delay of Puberty. Simple constitutional delay is less common in girls than in boys; it is also less likely to be considered a problem by girls or their parents.[4,14] A girl with constitutional delay is usually of normal or mildly short stature (at least third percentile), with a normal prepubertal rate of growth (at least 2 in. per year), a normal weight for height, and a negative history and physical examination. These children appear healthy but physically younger than their age. A family history of normal but delayed puberty is common but not always present. When puberty begins, it generally progresses at a normal rate to normal adult reproductive status and function.

No test absolutely confirms the diagnosis of constitutional delay. Confirmation of the delay of bone age by x ray is necessary for the diagnosis of constitutional delay (although it is not pathognomonic, as delayed bone age is common in a number of pathologic causes of delay). The delay is usually 1 to 4 years; it should be consistent with physical stages. Laboratory tests simply reflect hypothalamic and hormonal immaturity and are normal for a younger age.

A similar delay of maturation can also result from prolonged but temporary malnutrition, hormone deficiency, or major illness earlier in childhood. Growth records usually show interference with linear growth during the years of the problem. By definition, this delay is not "constitutional," although the findings and prognosis may be identical.

The most difficult aspect of differential diagnosis is distinguishing constitutional delay from ongoing hypothalamic suppression due to weight, diet, activity, and systemic or mental illness, and from gonadotropin deficiency or pure gonadal dysgenesis. Confirmation of an adequate growth velocity by reliable sequential measurements is crucial to the diagnosis of constitutional delay. Hypothalamic suppression should be suspected from the clinical circumstances. However, the history, physical examination, and laboratory findings of isolated gonadotropin deficiency are usually identical to those of constitutional delay; in some girls, only the passage of time or onset of puberty provides conclusive distinction. Gonadal dysgenesis or primary ovarian disease will be suggested by the elevated gonadotropins.

No treatment except reassurance is necessary for mild to moderate constitutional delay. Although one might consider the use of low-dose estrogen for several months in a manner analogous to the widespread use of testosterone in delayed males, this is not commonly done and may entail more disadvantages. However, when the delay is severe, or a significant chance of gonadotropin deficiency exists, as described below, a course of estrogen treatment is justified. A brief course of low-dose estrogens will not further delay normal puberty. In some cases, such a course may hasten the onset of spontaneous puberty.

Isolated Gonadotropin Deficiency. Isolated gonadotropin deficiency resembles constitutional delay, and between the ages of 11 and 15 years is likely to display at least mild delay of bone age. As mentioned above, there are no reliable distinguishing tests in early adolescence. The presence or absence of certain clinical findings may increase the suspicion of permanent gonadotropin deficiency. Marked bone age delay (more than 2 years), short stature, and delay of adrenarche are somewhat less common in gonadotropin deficiency than in delay. A history of intracranial infection, injury, surgery, or congenital abnormality increases the likelihood of deficiency. Intracranial imaging is indicated for positive neurologic history or findings, or as the diagnosis of gonadotropin deficiency becomes confirmed.[4,15,16]

In many of these cases, the gonadotropins are detectable but remain in the prepubertal range. Only when the gonadotropin levels are undetectably low and completely fail to respond to gonadotropin-releasing hormone (GnRH) can the diagnosis of gonadotropin deficiency be based on laboratory tests.

Furthermore, the only clinical evidence that allows a confident diagnosis of isolated gonadotropin deficiency is features of certain syndromes known to include hypothalamic gonadotropin deficiency, or increasing age. Although cases of many obscure syndromes have included hypothalamic gonadotropin deficiency, the two most common identifiable syndromes are Kallmann's and Prader-Willi syndromes, both of which nearly always include hypothalamic gonadotropin deficiency.

The most characteristic feature of Kallman's syndrome is hyposmia (a diminished sense of smell), which is often associated with gonadotropin deficiency. This syndrome illustrates the normal close connection between the olfactory nerves and the reproductive areas of the hypothalamus. Kallmann's syndrome occurs in both males and females; it is usually sporadic but has been reported to recur in some families. There are usually no other clinical abnormalities, although an increased incidence of color blindness in family members has been found. Partial impairment of smell (hyposmia) is more difficult to assess by history, and quantitative tests of olfaction have been devised.[17]

Prader-Willi syndrome also involves hypothalamic gonadotropin deficiency in nearly every instance. It is often diagnosed before adolescence because of its other distinctive features. Children affected with Prader-Willi syndrome display transient hypotonia in early infancy, followed by progressively severe generalized obesity with an unrestrainable appetite. Affected children are short, with a growth pattern similar to that of Turner's syndrome. Mild to moderate mental retardation is usual. Diminutive fingertips and undescended testes are common. By adolescence the severe obesity often leads to hypoventilation and cor pulmonale. Many have an abnormality of chromosome 15.[18]

Unless gonadotropins are undetectable, or features of an hypogonadotropic syndrome are present, firm diagnosis of gonadotropin deficiency must wait for the passage of enough years to reduce the probability of constitutional delay to a nonexistent level. For example, the overwhelming majority of 13-year-old girls with no thelarche have simple delay and a high likelihood of spontaneous thelarche within the next year or two. However, a 16-year-old with unexplained delay of thelarche is more likely to have gonadotropin deficiency than simple delay, and a healthy 18-year-old without thelarche has only a negligible chance of being delayed rather than deficient, if other conditions have been excluded.

Treatment of gonadotropin deficiency may be started any time after 11 or 12 years if the diagnosis is based on anosmia, undetectable gonadotropin levels, or both. In these situations, permanent deficiency may be predicted (although not guaranteed), and reassurance may be given that normal development and probably fertility may be achieved with appropriate hormone replacement.

Girls over 14 or 15 years old in whom gonadotropin deficiency is suspected but not yet confirmed may be given low-dose ethinyl estradiol (at 10 μg daily) to initiate breast development and perhaps accelerate the onset of hypothalamic puberty. After 6 to 12 months this treatment should be discontinued for several months of observation and testing; it should be stopped sooner if bleeding occurs. Further breast development and the onset of menses may then be achieved with a 6- to 12-month course of a low-estrogen oral contraceptive. After interrupting the oral contraceptive, failure to maintain at least early pubertal estradiol levels or to respond with menses to a progestin challenge (10 mg of oral medroxyprogesterone daily for 5 days) is highly suggestive of gonadotropin deficiency.

Maintenance treatment after establishing the diagnosis of gonadotropin deficiency may be provided with a cyclic oral contraceptive. When fertility is desired, further hormonal manipulation (such as GnRH by pump) by a reproductive endocrinologist will be necessary.

Hypopituitarism and Hypothalamic Failure. Hypopituitarism usually refers to the deficiency of growth hormone, with or without deficiency of other pituitary hormones. Growth hormone deficiency in childhood delays growth and pubertal development.[19] This condition can result from congenital or acquired defects of either the pituitary gland or the hypothalamus. Whether or not gonadotropins are also deficient, pubertal delay is common if the condition has gone untreated for several years.

The hallmark of growth hormone deficiency is a diminished rate of growth. A 10- to 14-year-old girl who has had growth hormone deficiency for several years will appear physically immature, usually with complete delay of puberty. A growth velocity of less than 2 in. per year excludes the diagnosis of simple constitutional delay. She is often at least mildly obese. In cases of acquired hypopituitarism due to an intracranial tumor (most often a craniopharyngioma), there may be headache, vomiting, visual disturbances, and neurologic signs in addition to pubertal delay.

In pubertal delay due to hypopituitarism, the bone age is usually 2 or more years delayed. Slow bone growth and diminished protein synthesis are often reflected by a low alkaline phosphatase level (within the adult normal range) and slightly elevated BUN level (12 to 18 mg/dl). Once hypothyroidism has been excluded by testing, growth hormone deficiency may be screened by measuring somatomedin C. A low somatomedin C level in an older child indicates a need for integrated or provocative testing for growth hormone itself; details of testing are beyond the scope of this book.

If growth hormone deficiency is demonstrated, deficiencies of thyroid-stimulating hormone (TSH) and adrenocorticotropic hormone (ACTH) must be excluded. Intracranial imaging for tumor or other structural abnormality is especially important if the growth failure is of recent onset. Regular growth hormone injections will induce rapid catch-up growth, and may allow resumption of normal pubertal development.

Although confirmation of growth hormone deficiency provides an explanation for pubertal delay, it also raises the possibility of gonadotropin deficiency. Roughly half of children with idiopathic or congenital hypopituitarism will have associated gonadotropin deficiency, as will many whose hypopituitarism is acquired in later childhood or adolescence. Associated gonadotropin deficiency may not be easy to confirm during the early teen years if bone age and gonadotropin levels are in the prepubertal range. If both gonadotropins and growth hormone are deficient, replacement will be needed as discussed above. The likelihood of gonadotropin deficiency and the optimal time and method of estrogen replacement is best determined by a pediatric endocrinologist.

Hypothyroidism. Like growth hormone deficiency, hypothyroidism causes growth failure and a general delay of physical maturation. Associated symptoms and signs (increased sleeping, decreased physical activity, cold intolerance, pallor or carotenemia, constipation, dry skin, general aches and pains) may be subtle enough that the child or family has not perceived them as a problem.[20]

It should be noted that untreated primary hypothyroidism with onset between 4 and 8 years of age may eventually result in thelarche and menarche at or before the usual age (sometimes with galactorrhea). This "unnatural" estrogenization apparently results from stimulation of gonadotropin receptors by longstanding and extreme elevation of TSH. It is the only type of premature pubertal development accompanied by growth failure and bone-age delay.

A low thyroxine and elevated TSH will commonly confirm the diagnosis of hypothyroidism. The etiology, laboratory testing, and treatment of hypothyroidism are discussed briefly in Chapter 6.

Hyperprolactinemia. Hyperprolactinemia is a common cause of secondary amenorrhea in young women. Rarely, it may occur early enough to delay puberty and cause primary amenorrhea. Galactorrhea is nearly pathognomonic, but does not occur in all instances of hyperprolactinemia. Measurement of prolactin is therefore indicated in any unexplained case of marked pubertal delay. Hyperprolactinemia is discussed in more detail in Chapter 6.

Gonadal Dysgenesis and Primary Ovarian Failure. Puberty may be delayed when the ovaries themselves are defective. Primary ovarian failure should be suspected when evidence of estrogen deficiency is accompanied by elevation of gonadotropins above the adult normal range. Although a number of unusual causes are listed in Table 3-7, varieties of gonadal dysgenesis account for the majority of cases of primary ovarian failure in the peripubertal age group.

Gonadal dysgenesis refers to ovaries that are hypoplastic or virtually absent ("streak gonads") as a result of defective development before birth or in early infancy.[21,22] The gonads have failed to develop normally because of defective genetic instructions (either single gene defects or gross sex chromosome abnormalities), environmental insults (e.g., viral infections or radiation destruction), or perhaps other factors. Strictly speaking, the diagnosis of gonadal dysgenesis depends on confirmation by inspection or biopsy, although it can sometimes be inferred from a combination of clinical and laboratory evidence. Pure gonadal dysgenesis, testicular dysgenesis, and mixed gonadal dysgenesis are less common than demonstrable defects of the X chromosome, such as those that cause Turner's syndrome.

It should be noted that although the ovaries in all forms of gonadal dysgenesis are usually completely nonfunctional, there have been numerous cases in which estrogen-induced breast development has occurred. Usually the estrogen effects are partial and unsustained, but menarche may occur, followed by premature, permanent secondary amenorrhea months or years later. There have even been rare instances of pregnancy in women with gonadal dysgenesis. These atypical examples of estrogenization or fertility have occurred mostly with a mosaic karyotype that has included a 46,XX cell line. Spontaneous estrogenization or fertility are least likely when the second X chromosome is completely absent in all cells (i.e., 45,X).

The most common identifiable cause of gonadal dysgenesis is abnormality of the second X chromosome. Common karyotypes include 45,X,

45,X/46,XX, and 46,X,iXq, but a wide variety of more complex mosaicisms, partial deletions, and malformations of the X chromosome have been found in girls with gonadal dysgenesis.

There is some degree of correlation of phenotypic features and karyotype (Fig. 3-5). The X chromosome carries genes necessary for ovarian development on both the long and short arms, so that deletions of parts of either arm usually result in gonadal dysgenesis. The short arm carries genetic information that furthers growth, so that karyotypes in which the short arm is missing are always accompanied by short stature; deletions restricted to Xq usually allow normal growth. Relationships of specific regions of the X chromosome to the other Turner's syndrome features are less well understood; in general, the fuller forms of Turner's syndrome occur when the entire second X chromosome is missing (45,X) in all cell lines.

In early adolescence, the typical girl with Turner's syndrome is short, with marginal growth velocity (1 to 2 in. per year) and slightly delayed bone age. At this age her legs are disproportionately shorter, to a mild

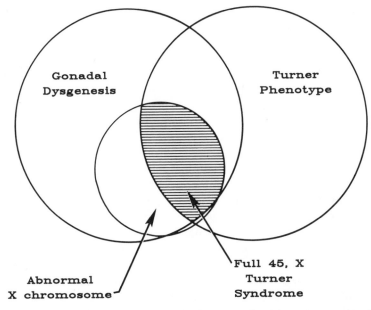

Fig. 3-5. Relationship of Turner's syndrome to gonadal dysgenesis. Various combinations of abnormal ovarian development, appearance, and karyotype occur. Gonadal dysgenesis denotes streak (or maldeveloped) ovaries, resulting in delayed or absent thelarche, primary or secondary amenorrhea, and infertility. The most common abnormal karyotype is 45,X, but mosaicism, deletions, duplications, or other abnormalities of the sex chromosomes may produce physical or gonadal abnormalities. The most invariable associated abnormality of phenotype is poor growth with characteristic body build, but other features from Table 3-8 may be present. The term "Turner's syndrome" describes patients with abnormalities of all three (gonads, karyotype, and phenotype).

degree, than her trunk. Her pubic hair has developed with minimal delay, but her breasts have not. She is likely to have some of the dysmorphic features of Turner's syndrome listed in Table 3-8. However, it should be emphasized that a minority of girls with Turner's syndrome display the severe shield chest and webbed neck illustrated in medical school lectures. In many more patients the features are subtle enough to escape the notice of most primary care physicians, so that gonadal dysgenesis cannot be excluded reliably by physical examination. The external genitalia and internal organs are normal for an immature female. The ovaries are nearly always streaks, although they should be inspected and subjected to laparoscopic biopsy if the karyotype is mosaic or unusual. Complete lack of breast development and primary amenorrhea is the rule (with rare exceptions, as noted above).

It is apparent to physicians experienced with Turner's syndrome that, although each individual is unique, certain personality and cognitive characteristics are frequently observed in this group of girls. Difficulty with tasks involving spatial orientation is common. Athletic interest or aptitude is uncommon. By adolescence, many are socially immature, and their personalities tend toward passivity. However, one must be wary of the disadvantages of such stereotyped expectations in dealing with individual patients and their families.

Management of Turner's syndrome in early adolescence requires supportive counselling of the girl and her family. At this age, the girl is generally more concerned about growth than sexual development or fertility; treatment to achieve breast development is usually deferred in favor of treatment to enhance growth. Initial management also requires testing for less obvious features of Turner's syndrome or sequelae, such as hearing loss, urinary tract malformation, and cardiac malformations (especially coarctation of the aorta). Continuing care during adolescence should include surveillance for additional late features such as hypertension, obesity (especially when full adult estrogen replacement is begun), diabetes, thyroiditis or other autoimmune diseases, and osteoporosis. If no Y chromosome is demonstrated by karyotype, the streak ovaries are not at risk for malignant transformation and need not be removed. Hormonal replacement is described below.

Mixed gonadal dysgenesis also results from abnormalities of the sex chromosomes, but the karyotype contains a Y chromosome.[22,23] Examples of karyotypes found with mixed gonadal dysgenesis include 46,XX/46,XY, 45,X/46XY, and other complex forms of mosaicism. Girls with mixed gonadal dysgenesis comprise a clinically varied group. The gonads are dysgenetic streaks, but may contain rudimentary testicular tissue. Depending on the degree of testicular hormone production in fetal life, the internal or external genitalia may show minimal or significant masculinization; the diagnosis is sometimes made in the course of evaluation of a newborn with ambiguous genitalia. If there is a 45,X cell line, there may be physical features of Turner's syndrome (Table 3-8), especially short stature. If masculinization is absent or overlooked in infancy, delay of puberty eventually leads to a workup. Abnormalities of the genitalia in a girl with delayed puberty (e.g., clitoral hypertrophy, partial labial fusion, or apparent absence of a uterus) warrant an immediate karyotype. Management requires scrutiny of internal and external anatomy; surgical correction of partially masculinized genitalia may be necessary. The nonfunctional gonads should be removed, as the Y cell line confers a risk of malignancy. Hormonal replacement is as described below.

In pure gonadal dysgenesis, the ovaries are dysgenetic despite a normal, 46,XX karyotype.[22] The growth pattern, genitalia, and body phenotype are also normal for the female, and only the ovaries themselves are defective. In a young teenager with delayed breast development and primary amenorrhea, elevated gonadotropins, indicative of primary ovarian failure, is usually the only clue to pure gonadal dysgenesis. It may recur in families, in which cases the cause is apparently a single defective gene of an autosome or sex chromosome, but sporadic cases may occur when various early environmental insults result in destruction of fetal or infant ovaries. The diagnosis is confirmed by laparoscopic inspection and biopsy. Karyotype of biopsied gonadal tissue is important because it may occasionally differ from the peripheral karyotype and may contain a Y chromosome. Removal of the gonadal streaks is unnecessary in most cases, as there is no risk of neoplastic development. However, removal may be desirable in rare instances in which remnants of ovarian stromal tissue may produce enough androgens for unwanted hirsutism or clitoromegaly. Removal is also imperative if the gonadal karyotype includes a Y chromosome. Management consists of appropriate counselling and estrogen and progesterone replacement as discussed below.

The clinical appearance of testicular dysgenesis is similar.[24] In this condition, the karyotype is XY, but an unidentified defect leads to degeneration of developing testicular tissue early in fetal life, before the fetal testes can produce significant amounts of either müllerian-inhibiting hormone or testosterone. The internal and external genitalia are therefore unambiguously female (with vagina, uterus, and fallopian tubes). Biopsy of the streak gonads may reveal elements of testicular origin. There are none of the abnormal somatic features associated with major defects of the sex chromosomes. These girls are slightly tall, and the diagnosis is not suspected until adolescence, when pubertal delay and primary amenorrhea lead to detection of elevated gonadotropins and karyotype. The XY karyotype must be explained with care and sensitivity. Because of the XY karyotype, the gonadal remnants have a high risk of malignant transformation and should be surgically removed. Otherwise, management is similar to that of pure XX gonadal dysgenesis.

Other rare causes of primary ovarian failure (Table 3-7) are suspected when evaluation of delayed thelarche and primary amenorrhea reveals elevated gonadotropin levels but normal karyotype. Differentiation from pure gonadal dysgenesis involves demonstration by imaging or laparos-

Table 3-8. Clinical Features of Turner's Syndrome.

Body size and proportions
  Short stature (<5th percentile)
  Increased upper:lower segment ratio (i.e., short legs)
Head, face, and neck
  Alopecia
  Antimongoloid slant to palpebral fissures
  Telecanthus
  Epicanthal folds
  Strabismus
  Ptosis
  Rotated ears, low-set ears
  Recurrent otitis media, hearing impairment
  High-arched palate
  Downturned corners of mouth
  Micrognathia
  Webbed neck
  Short neck, abnormal cervical vertebrae
  Low posterior hairline
Trunk
  "Thickness" of torso, stocky build
  Shield-shaped chest, widely-spaced nipples
  Hypoplastic nipples
  Scoliosis
Limbs
  Short 4th or 5th metacarpals or metatarsals
  Cubitus valgus (increased carrying angle)
  Madelung deformity of forearm
  Genu valgum
  Edema of hands and feet in neonatal period
  Nail dysplasia
  Prominent veins
  Characteristic dermatoglyphics
  Osteoporosis
  Syndactyly of second and third toes
  Abnormal carpal bones by x ray
Skin
  Multiple pigmented nevi
  Vitiligo
  Keloids
Cardiovascular system
  Coarctation of aorta
  Bicuspid aortic valve
  Mitral valve prolapse
  Hypertension
  Dissecting aortic aneurysm
Urinary tract
  Duplication of collecting system
  Horseshoe kidney
  Aberrant renal vasculature
  Rotational abnormalities of kidneys
  Unilateral renal agenesis
Gastrointestinal tract
  Inflammatory bowel disease
  Bleeding due to vascular anomalies
Endocrine system and metabolism
  Autoimmune thyroiditis, hypothyroidism
  Carbohydrate intolerance
Reproductive organs
  Ovarian dysgenesis with infertility
Psyche
  Visual-motor and spatial-coordination performance deficits

copy that the ovaries are not streaks, and confirmation of one of the other conditions by history and testing. Management again consists of counselling and hormone replacement, as described below.

Müllerian Dysgenesis and Absence of the Vagina. Some birth defects of the female reproductive tract may not be apparent until they cause primary amenorrhea, dysmenorrhea, or other perimenarcheal abnormalities in adolescence. Various degrees and forms of müllerian dysgenesis and uterine obstruction account for about 20% of cases of primary amenorrhea.[25]

Müllerian dysgenesis refers to incomplete fetal development of the müllerian derivatives: the uterus, and sometimes the vagina or fallopian tubes as well, may be absent, hypoplastic, or atretic. Ovaries are normal, as are the external genitalia (unless the vagina is totally absent). At adolescence, thelarche occurs appropriately in response to ovarian estrogen, but menarche fails to occur normally. Diagnosis is usually first suspected when an apparently healthy girl is evaluated for delay of menarche for more than 3 years past thelarche.

Complete vaginal agenesis may be immediately recognized upon perineal inspection when no vaginal introitus is found between normal vulva. Even though the lower vagina is not technically a müllerian derivative, complete absence of the vagina almost always implies complete müllerian dysgenesis (the Mayer-Rokitansky-Kuster-Hauser syndrome). One should be careful not to confuse absence of a vagina with agglutination of the labia due (presumably) to past vulvar inflammation. Although spontaneous separation will usually occur in prepubertal girls, application of an estrogen cream over several weeks and repeated gentle manual traction may be required in adolescents.[26,27]

When the vagina is short and ends blindly without a cervix, the range of diagnostic possibilities is wider. Laparoscopy or imaging may be needed to distinguish müllerian dysgenesis (uterus is hypoplastic or absent) from a condition such as transverse vaginal septum or cervical atresia (uterus is present but outflow is obstructed). When the vagina, but not the cervix, is present, one must also consider complete androgen resistance, discussed below, in the differential diagnosis. If clitoromegaly, posterior labial fusion, or other evidence of androgen excess are found, further diagnostic possibilities are complex and include many of the disorders technically listed as causing ambiguous genitalia.

Obviously, the sudden discovery of an absent or short, blind vagina must be handled with sensitivity. The best initial explanation to the patient is that the vagina "has not fully opened" and that steps will be taken quickly to ascertain why and to determine the best way to open it. Further explanation should be deferred to the appropriate consultant, optimally a gynecologic endocrinologist, to avoid unnecessary emotional trauma.

Further evaluation should include ultrasound imaging of the pelvic organs to identify and measure a uterus, and measurement of gonadotropins and testosterone to exclude androgen resistance syndromes. Karyotyping and laparoscopy are indicated in some circumstances.

If müllerian dysgenesis is confirmed, an intravenous pyelogram and spinal x rays are warranted because of the high likelihood of ectopic or aplastic kidneys or spinal anomalies. The combination of müllerian dysgenesis, renal aplasia, and cervicothoracic somite dysplasia is termed the "MURCS association."[28] Associations of other anomalies with vaginal agenesis or müllerian dysgenesis have been described.[27] In rare cases, gonadal dysgenesis may accompany müllerian dysgenesis, resulting in absence of both menarche and thelarche.

Treatment of vaginal agenesis often begins with the use of successively larger vaginal dilators, which the patient is taught to use. In some cases the vagina will gradually enlarge, and surgery may be unnecessary. The method and outcome of surgical reconstruction depend on the exact anatomic configuration.[27]

Uterine Obstruction. Congenital anomalies obstructing outflow from the uterus include imperforate hymen, transverse vaginal septum, upper vaginal atresia, and cervical atresia.[25,29,30] Delay of menarche due to uterine obstructions differs from müllerian dysgenesis because of the presence of a uterine endometrium that responds to ovarian hormones with menstrual bleeding, which is prevented from flowing through the vaginal introitus as menses. In addition to primary amenorrhea, accumulation of menstrual fluids causes distention and discomfort. If the condition has gone unnoticed in childhood, the typical adolescent presentation is recurrent pelvic pain with primary amenorrhea. External genitalia are usually normal.

When the obstruction is low, as with imperforate hymen or transverse vaginal membrane, external menstrual flow fails to occur and menarche is followed by gradual accumulation of blood and fluid visible as a bulging, bluish cystic mass in the introitus. Uterine distention (hematometrocolpos) is uncommon because of the thickness of the myometrium, but reflux of menstrual blood through the fallopian tubes (hematosalpinx) may occur. Increasing pelvic discomfort develops. A tumor or cyst must be excluded.

When the obstruction is due to absence of the cervix or atresia of the upper vagina, hematocolpos is a more common accompaniment of menarche. Hematosalpinx and endometriosis are more common in this case than with lower obstruction. To vaginal examination, upper vaginal atresia is distinguishable from cervical atresia mainly by the length of the vagina, which ends blindly in both conditions. Cervical atresia and complete uterine aplasia are tentatively distinguishable by the presence or absence of pelvic pain, and definitively by pelvic ultrasound, which usually reveals a distended uterus when only the cervix is absent.[30]

Management and prognosis depend upon the level of the obstruction. Incision and drainage may be all that is necessary for an imperforate hymen. However, a transverse vaginal membrane may be associated with stenosis of the vagina and may be more difficult to reconstruct. Vaginal atresia is usually surgically correctable with good functional outcome when the uterus and cervix are normal. When the cervix is absent, infertility is likely despite reconstructive procedures, endometriosis is common, and hysterectomy is often necessary. Compared to müllerian dysgenesis, obstructive conditions are far less likely to be associated with renal or other nonreproductive anomalies.

Androgen Insensitivity or Deficiency: XY Females. Various degrees of an inability to synthesize androgens, or insensitivity to the effects of androgens, may occur in both sexes. Diminished ability to synthesize androgens may occur when there is a reduced number of functional Leydig cells in the testes, or when an enzyme necessary for androgen synthesis is absent or reduced in activity. Insensitivity or resistance to the action of androgens results from various types and degrees of dysfunction of androgen receptors and responses.[31]

In general, diminished androgen production or response does not produce clinically significant problems in an XX female and is likely to remain undetected throughout life. However, masculinization of the external genitalia during male fetal life depends on the capacity to make and respond to androgens, especially dihydrotestosterone. Deficient synthesis or cell insensitivity to androgens during the prenatal life of an XY fetus results in diminished virilization of the genitalia, despite the presence of testes. The infant may then be raised as a girl, but various clinical problems will later appear. The nature of these problems primarily depends upon whether the deficiency or resistance is partial or complete.

When the deficiency or insensitivity is partial, genital ambiguity is obvious and the diagnosis will likely be made in infancy. If satisfactory virilization cannot be therapeutically induced, the infant will often be assigned and raised as a girl. Her testes will be removed and, if necessary, her external genitalia reconstructed to optimize her female appearance in infancy. As she approaches the age of puberty she will need estrogen replacement to induce secondary sexual characteristics, as discussed below. Furthermore, lacking ovaries and uterus, she will never menstruate or ovulate.

When androgen insensitivity or deficiency in an XY fetus is complete, no virilization occurs, the testes remain in the abdomen or inguinal canals, and an externally normal infant girl is born. Internally, müllerian-inhibiting factor from the testes prevents development of a cervix, uterus, and fallopian tubes. Complete insensitivity to androgen action is more common than complete deficiency and has been known as "testicular feminization." This term is traditional and dramatic, but misleading. The defect is not in the testes, which dutifully produce testosterone, but in the androgen receptors of the external genitalia, hair follicles, and pilosebaceous glands, and other target organs.

Because of the unambiguously female genitalia, the child is raised as a girl without suspicion of internal abnormality, except in rare cases when testes are discovered during pelvic surgery, especially inguinal hernia repair. Normal female gender identity evolves. At the age of pubertal activation of the neuroendocrine axis, the testes begin again to make testosterone and the body again fails to respond. However, enough testosterone is converted to estradiol to induce appropriate female breast development. Concern does not arise until several years pass without menarche. Thus, the most common presentation is that of primary amenorrhea in a young woman, somewhat taller than average (because of the XY karyotype), with normal breast development, minimal sexual hair or acne, and with absence of a cervix upon pelvic examination. The testosterone level is in the upper male range, estradiol is in the lower female range, gonadotropins are moderately elevated, and the karyotype is XY. The testes should be removed and estrogen replacement begun.

The clinical picture may vary, and a number of less common conditions may occur with similar features. The major disorders that may occur as a problem in an adolescent girl with an XY karyotype are listed in Tables 3-7 and 3-9.

Management of the Hypogonadal Adolescent

Hormonal Management of Hypogonadism. Young women without properly functioning ovaries need replacement of estrogens and progesterone. Major potential benefits of replacement in adolescence are the

Table 3-9. Causes of Ambiguous Genitalia in Adolescent Girls.

Female Pseudohermaphroditism (XX karyotype, ovaries)
Prenatal androgen excess (variable degrees of ambiguity)
Fetal androgen source
Congenital adrenal hyperplasias
3 beta-hydroxysteroid dehydrogenase deficiency
11 beta-hydroxylase deficiency
21 hydroxylase deficiency
Maternal androgen source
Maternal androgen-producing tumor
Maternal congenital adrenal hyperplasia
Exogenous maternal anabolic steroids
Postnatal androgen excess (clitoromegaly only)
Endogenous androgens
Polycystic ovary syndrome
Androgen-producing tumors of adrenals
Androgen-producing tumors of ovaries
Exogenous anabolic steroids
Miscellaneous genital abnormalities
Male Pseudohermaphroditism (XY karyotype, testes, raised as girls)
Androgen deficiency
17 alpha-hydroxylase deficiency
17,20-desmolase deficiency
17-ketosteroid reductase deficiency
3 beta-hydroxysteroid dehydrogenase deficiency
5 alpha-reductase deficiency
Androgen resistance
Nuclear receptor resistance to androgens
Mixed gonadal dysgenesis
True hermaphroditism

induction and maintenance of secondary sexual development (especially breasts), uterine size and endometrial differentiation, mature and lubricated vaginal mucosa, regular menses, and sexual identity and libido. Other possible advantages are attainment of normal stature and control of dysfunctional uterine bleeding. Potential long-term benefits include enhanced fertility, reduction of later risk of endometrial and other forms of cancer, and improved bone density with lower risk of osteoporosis.[32]

The method of hormonal replacement in hypogonadism depends less on the etiology of hypogonadism than on age, stature, associated internal and external abnormalities of reproductive organs, and desire for immediate fertility. As in other types of hormone deficiency, ideal treatment replicates physiologic levels of the missing hormones; however, as in other hormone deficiencies, actual treatment involves compromises for feasibility. Hormonal replacement is generally initiated at around 12 to 13 years to achieve pubertal development within a normal time frame. When the need for replacement is discovered in older girls, the only reason for delaying replacement may be treatable short stature (see below).

When one is replacing hormones in an older adolescent or young adult woman who has already achieved secondary sexual development, one of the simplest methods is an oral contraceptive that supplies both estrogen and progestin in combination. The choice of pill in this situation depends on the doses and relative ratio of estrogen and progestin necessary to maintain clinically adequate estrogen effects and regular menses without breakthrough bleeding; most patients do well with the low estrogen combination oral contraceptives (equivalent to 20 to 35 μg of ethinyl estradiol). However, because of the lack of endogenous estrogen in these cases, there is less advantage to the very low estrogen doses; the estrogen strength may be increased as needed.

A different approach for prepubertal or completely unestrogenized girls is to provide 10 to 20 μg of ethinyl estradiol daily for the first 21 days of each calendar month. If the uterus is normal, withdrawal bleeding will occur within several months. At this point (or 6 months from estrogen initiation), 2.5 to 5 mg of medroxyprogesterone acetate is added on days 12 through 21 of each month. This will produce more gradual pubertal development.[4,33]

Stature is a major consideration in the treatment of some forms of hypogonadism in early adolescence. Gonadal dysgenesis and longstanding hypopituitarism both result in severe growth impairment, and as long as a girl remains significantly shorter than all her classmates, her size will distress her far more than her lack of pubertal development. When estrogen is given to a young adolescent with significant remaining growth potential in the doses contained in traditional replacement regimens (such as those just described), it will produce a brief acceleration of growth but will also induce rapid bone maturation and closure of long bone epiphyses. Because of the possibility of improving prepubertal growth with growth hormone or anabolic steroids and the complexities of coordinating growth hormone treatment with the initation of estrogen replacement in girls with severe short stature, referral to a pediatric endocrinologist is crucial as soon as a diagnosis of hypogonadism is suspected in a short girl. This is a rapidly changing area of practice: as an example, one current experimental approach for both gonadal dysgenesis and hypopituitarism is to provide ethinyl estradiol at very low doses (4 to 8 μg daily), beginning as early as 11 to 13 years of age. At these doses, bleeding is unlikely, but growth is enhanced and pubertal development (including epiphyseal maturation) is more gradual; close monitoring of growth rates and bone age is essential.

Use of cyclic estrogen-progesterone regimens or oral contraceptives will not, of course, reverse the infertility associated with most forms of hypogonadism, and in some instances their use will further reduce the probability of pregnancy. Although the contraceptive effect is rarely unwanted in adolescence, maintenance therapy in the hypogonadal woman who desires pregnancy is more complex, and beyond the scope of this discussion. Because of the rapid changes in fertility technology (e.g., the recent implantation of a fertilized egg in the uterus of a woman with gonadal dysgenesis), the physician must be cautious in making long-term negative predictions.

Emotional Management of Hypogonadism. When hypogonadism is detected in childhood (e.g., in the case of gonadal dysgenesis), parents and physician are able to anticipate the need for hormonal replacement, and parents will be aware of future problems such as infertility or reconstructive surgery. Hormone replacement beginning before age 12 years is usually accepted well, and gradual physical development can be induced at the appropriate ages to minimize visible physical disparities. Severe emotional distress related to hypogonadism itself is uncommon in early adolescence.

Explanations of an age-appropriate nature are provided as things change and as the girl asks questions. Direct questions should always be answered directly and truthfully, but choice of words is crucial. Structural defects or anomalies of the reproductive tract should be described as "under-" or "overdeveloped" or "unopened" female organs to minimize her sense of difference; these terms are nearly universally applicable and far more understandable than some of the traditional medical terms, which may carry misleading and pejorative connotations to patients. Although parents should be fully informed, detailed discussion of fertility with a young adolescent is unnecessary; she should be allowed to assume that she "can have children when she grows up," since this is likely by adoption or as a result of rapidly changing fertility technology.

The potential for significant emotional distress is high when a major defect is not identified until middle or late adolescence, especially if it has caused, or is accompanied by, visible physical differences such as immature breast development, short stature, or dysmorphic features. These girls have often learned alternative, asexual roles centered in their homes, such as caretaker of small children, and have avoided the competition and comparisons inherent in school-centered social or athletic life. In addition, many of these girls have long been aware that "something" about themselves, related somehow to sexuality, is different or defective, and have dealt with it by denial and suppression. This type of reaction is especially likely if parents have withheld knowledge from an affected daughter because of their own discomfort. An exact diagnosis may be unwelcome as an official confirmation of a previously secret shame, even when treatment is offered. Individual or family counselling may be indicated.

Although the benefits of hormone replacement are obvious to the physician and (usually) the parents, it is common for an older adolescent with long-delayed puberty due to gonadal dysgenesis, chronic illness, or other conditions that have set her apart from her peers to be fearful at the prospect of sexual development and initially resistant to the idea. A patient, sensitive exploration for specific fears will usually suggest the best direction for reassurance and persuasion. In understanding this, the physician might consider how many "normal" adolescent girls would be reluctant if they were required to consciously choose to initiate puberty.

GENITAL AMBIGUITY IN ADOLESCENCE

Genital ambiguity is usually recognized at birth and dealt with in infancy. Rarely, ambiguity may first be recognized in an adolescent girl, either at her first pelvic examination, or during evaluation of hirsutism, virilization, pubertal delay, or amenorrhea.[34] Physical manifestations of ambiguity include posterior labial fusion (much more rarely, complete external vaginal atresia) and a phallic urethra. These findings usually indicate prenatal exposure to higher androgen levels than are typical for a female fetus. Although clitoromegaly may also result from prenatal androgens, when unaccompanied by other ambiguous features it is more suggestive of acquired androgen excess. Absence of a cervix or uterus suggests that enough testicular tissue to produce müllerian-inhibiting factor was present in fetal life (and may imply that the present gonads are in fact testes). However, since the prepubertal uterus is small, absence must be confirmed by pelvic ultrasound.

Table 3-9 lists those conditions that may cause ambiguity in an adolescent. Diagnosis is likely to be established by karyotype, various hormone measurements (especially of adrenal steroids and other androgens), and investigation of internal anatomy by ultrasound, CT scan, or exploratory laparotomy.

Although gender identity is nearly always secure at this age (and gender reassignment not an issue), an adolescent's sexual identity is vulnerable. Because of the potential for creating misconceptions not easily reversed, evaluation must be performed with rapidity, assurance, and sensitivity. Because of the rarity of these conditions and continuing changes in available therapy, referral to a pediatric or reproductive endocrinologist is recommended.

REFERENCES

1. Marshall WA, Tanner JM: Puberty. In: Falkner F, Tanner JM: Human Growth: A Comprehensive Treatise. 2nd ed. Vol 2. New York: Plenum, 1986.
2. Frisch R: Fatness and fertility. Sci Am 1988;258:88-95.
3. Wied GL, Boschann H-W, Ferin J, et al: Symposium on hormonal cytology. Acta Cytol 1968;12:87.
4. Styne DM, Grumbach MM: Puberty in the male and female: its physiology and disorders. In: Yen SSC, Jaffe RB: Reproductive Endocrinology, 2nd ed. Philadelphia: W.B. Saunders, 1986.
5. Reiter EO: Neuroendocrine control processes: pubertal onset and progression. J Adolesc Health Care 1987;8:479-491.
6. Speroff L, Glass RH, Kase NG: Clinical Gynecologic Endocrinology and Infertility. 3rd ed. Baltimore, Williams & Wilkins, 1983.
7. Yen SSC: The human menstrual cycle. In: Yen SSC, Jaffe RB: Reproductive Endocrinology. 2nd ed. Philadelphia: W.B. Saunders, 1986.
8. Rebar RW: Practical evaluation of hormonal status. In: Yen SSC, Jaffe RB: Reproductive Endocrinology. 2nd ed. Philadelphia: W.B. Saunders, 1986.
9. Henley K, Vaitukaitis JL: Exercise-induced menstrual dysfunction. Annual Rev Med 1988;39:443-451.
10. Hein K: The interface of chronic illness and the hormonal regulation of puberty. J Adolesc Health Care 1987;8:530-540.
11. Yen SSC: Chronic anovulation due to CNS-hypothalamic-pituitary dysfunction. In: Yen SSC, Jaffe RB: Reproductive Endocrinology. 2nd ed. Philadelphia: W.B. Saunders, 1986.
12. Foster CM, Kelch RP: New hope for youngsters with precocious puberty. Contemp Pediatr 1985;Apr:105-123.
13. Kulin HE: Precocious puberty. Clin Obstet Gynecol 1987;30:714-734.
14. Burstein S, Rosenfield RL: Constitutional delay in growth and development. In: Hintz RL, Rosenfield RG: Growth Abnormalities (Contemporary Issues in Endocrinology and Metabolism, vol 4). New York: Churchill Livingstone, 1987.
15. Rabinowitz D, Spitz IM, Benveniste R: Isolated gonadotropin deficiency. In: Given JR: Endocrine Causes of Menstrual Disorders. Chicago: Yearbook, 1978.
16. Kletzky OA, Nicoloff J, Davajan V, Mims R, Mishell DR Jr: Idiopathic hypogonadotrophic hypogonadal primary amenorrhea. J Clin Endocrinol Metab 1978;46:808-815.
17. Lieblich JM, Rogol AD, White BJ, Rosen SW: Syndrome of anosmia with hypogonadotropic hypogonadism (Kallmann syndrome). Am J Med 1982;73:506-519.
18. Cassidy SB: Prader-Willi syndrome. Curr Prob Pediatr 1984;14:1-55.
19. Bourguignon JP, Vanderschueren-Lodeweyckx M, Wolter R, et al: Hypopituitarism and idiopathic delayed puberty: a longitudinal study in an attempt to diagnose gonadotropin deficiency before puberty. J Clin Endocrinol Metab 1982;54:733-744.
20. Longcope C: The male and female reproductive systems. In: Ingbar SH, Braverman LE: Werner's The Thyroid. 5th ed. Philadelphia: J.B. Lippincott, 1986.
21. Lippe BM: Management of gonadal dysgenesis. J Pediatr Endocrinol 1985;1:71-84.
22. Tho PT, McDonough PG: Gonadal dysgenesis and its variants. Pediatr Clin N Am 1981;28:309-329.
23. Donahoe PK, Crawford JD, Hendren WH: Mixed gonadal dysgenesis, pathogenesis, and management. J Pediatr Surg 1979;14:287-300.
24. Simpson JL, Blagowidow N, Martin AO: XY Gonadal dysgenesis: genetic heterogeneity based upon clinical observations, H-Y antigen status, and segregation analysis. Hum Genet 1981;58:91-97.
25. Dewhurst J: Genital tract obstruction. Pediatr Clin N Am 1981;28:331-354.
26. Griffin JE, Edwards C, Madden JD, Harrod MJ, Wilson JD: Congenital absence of the vagina: the Mayer-Rokitansky-Kuster-Hauser syndrome. Ann Internal Med 1976;85:224-236.
27. Smith MR: Vaginal aplasia: therapeutic options. Am J Obstet Gynecol 1983;146:488-494.
28. Duncan PA, Shapiro LR, Stangel JJ, Klein RM, Addonizio JC: The MURCS association: Mullerian duct aplasia, renal aplasia, and cervicothoracic somite dysplasia. J Pediatr 1979;95:399-402.
29. Tran ATB, Arensman RM, Falterman KW: Diagnosis and management of hydrohematometrocolpos syndromes. Am J Dis Child 1987;141:632-634.

30. Rock JA, Azziz R: Genital anomalies in childhood. Clin Obstet Gynecol 1987;30:682-696.
31. Griffin JE, Wilson JD: The syndromes of androgen resistance. New Engl J Med 1980;302:198-209.
32. Lufkin EG, Carpenter PC, Ory SJ, Malkasian GD, Edmonson JH: Estrogen replacement therapy: current recommendations. Mayo Clin Proc 1988;63:453-460.
33. Kustin J, Rebar RW: Menstrual disorders in the adolescent age group. Primary Care 1987;14:139-166.
34. Reindollar RH, Tho SPT, McDonough PG: Abnormalities of sexual differentiation: evaluation and management. Clin Obstet Gynecol 1987;30:697-713.

4

Diseases of the Gynecologic and Genitourinary System

Diseases of the gynecologic system constitute one of the major concerns of the health care professional who is working with adolescent females. The majority of complaints seen in a clinical setting are related to the gynecologic system. This chapter details this important area and presents clinical graphs and charts that may be useful to the clinician. Specifically, the following conditions, as they relate to the adolescent female, are described: vulvovaginitis (leukorrhea and vaginitis, cervicitis, vulvitis, and miscellaneous causes); pelvic inflammatory disease (PID); and miscellaneous gynecologic topics (Fitz-Hugh-Curtis syndrome, cervical intraepithelial neoplasia (CIN), diethylstilbestrol (DES) exposure in utero, toxic shock syndrome (TSS), and acquired immunodeficiency syndrome (AIDS). A brief discussion of male genitourinary disorders is also provided.

VULVOVAGINITIS

There are many causes of vulvovaginitis in teenagers. These causes can be divided into leukorrhea or vaginitis, cervicitis, and vulvitis (Table 4-1). Before reviewing these causes, a few introductory comments are necessary.

At birth, the newborn female has an enlarged vulva and a thickened vagina, which is sterile and has a pH of 5.0 to 6.0. There may be a variable amount of a whitish discharge, which contains mucus and estrogen-effected epithelial cells caused by the maternal estrogen effect. Cultures taken after 2 days show considerable amounts of Doderlein's lactobacilli. Other bacteria are quickly added, including streptococci, staphylococci, and various *Enterobacteriaceae.*

As the maternal estrogen level falls, the infant's vulvovaginal tissue rapidly changes; in a matter of days, this tissue becomes thin and alkaline (pH 7.0 to 8.0). During childhood, a nonestrogen-effected vaginal cell structure is characteristic. Cytologic evaluation reveals no superficial or cornified cells (polygonal cells with small pyknotic nuclei), 0 to 20% intermediate cells, and 80 to 100% parabasal cells (round or oval cells with large vesicular nuclei). Vulvovaginitis occurring during childhood has many causes, including the agents discussed in this section. Frequently the cause is "nonspecific," meaning that no specific microbe is found but other factors are noted: poor hygiene, fecal contamination, improper toiletry procedure, allergy, chemical irritation, and others.

At puberty, the genital tract becomes estrogenized. This results in a growth of the vagina (longer and thicker) and an acidic pH of the vagina,

Table 4-1. Outline of Vulvovaginitis.

A. Leukorrhea and vaginitis
　　1. Physiologic leukorrhea
　　2. *Trichomonas vaginalis* vaginitis
　　3. *Gardnerella* (Haemophilus) *vaginalis* vaginitis
　　4. *Candida albicans* vaginitis
B. Cervicitis
　　1. *Neisseria gonorrhoeae* cervicitis
　　2. *Chlamydia trachomatis* cervicitis
　　3. Herpes simplex cervicitis and vulvitis
C. Vulvitis (Tables 4-10, 4-12)
D. Miscellaneous causes of vulvovaginitis
　　1. Foreign body vaginitis
　　2. Allergic vaginitis or vulvitis
　　3. Familial allergic seminal vulvovaginitis
　　4. Salivary vulvitis
　　5. Psychosomatic vulvovaginitis

often 5.0 to 5.5. This acidic pH is, in part, caused by the action of lacto-bacilli on epithelial cell glycogen, resulting in lactic acid production. This thickened, acidic environment offers some protection against infection and also accounts for the fact that most causes of vulvovaginitis in youth are "specific" in nature—that is, due to a usually identifiable microbe. Puberty also induces a change in the vaginal cell count, which becomes more adult-like: 60% superficial cells, 40% intermediate, and 0% para-basal (Fig. 4-1).

The normal vaginal flora contain numerous organisms: Doderlein's lac-tobacilli, various staphylococci, streptococci (including group B), various *Enterobacteriaceae* (especially *Escherichia coli*), *Bacteroides fragilis*, *Neisseria sicca*, *Branhemella catarrhalis*, various diphtheroids, *Candida albicans*, other yeasts, other anaerobic bacteria, and other microbes. The presence of certain potential pathogens (such as *Neisseria gonorrhoeae*, *Trichomonas vaginalis*, *Gardnerella vaginalis*, or *Candida albicans*) does

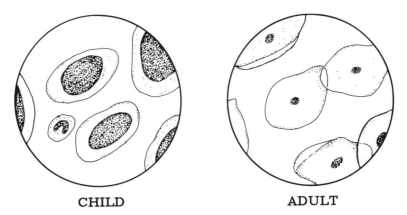

CHILD　　　　　　　ADULT

Fig. 4-1. Vaginal smear. *A.* Predominance of parabasal cells. *B.* Estrogen-induced cornified cells.

not necessarily imply an overt, symptomatic infection. A triggering mechanism, often of unknown etiology, may be necessary to convert the mere presence of an organism into an acute infection with signs of inflammation.

As noted, vulvovaginitis in the prepubertal girl may be due to "nonspecific" factors like hygiene, a foreign body, and local irritation (as from clothing, soaps, and others). Sexually transmitted diseases (STDs) can be detected in children and should be considered when a child having genital symptoms is presented. *Neisseria gonorrhoeae, Chlamydia trachomatis, Gardnerella vaginalis, Trichomonas vaginalis,* and other classic microbes of genital infections can be found in children. Other agents include *Enterobius vermicularis* (pinworms), amebiasis (*Entamoeba histolytica*), *Candida albicans,* and others. Gastroenteritis induced by *Shigella* species or typhoid can cause leukorrhea in children. Classic skin microbes (such as beta hemolytic streptococcus or *Staphylococcus aureus*) can lead to vaginal discharge, as can certain agents causing respiratory tract infections—*Haemophilus influenzae, Neisseria meningitides,* beta hemolytic streptococcus-Group A, *Streptococcus pneumoniae,* and others. Table 4-2 outlines these causes and suggests treatment plans.

Leukorrhea and Vaginitis

Physiologic Leukorrhea. Physiologic leukorrhea refers to a normal (physiologic) increase in vaginal discharge (leukorrhea) due to estrogen stimulation. This condition is often noted during the first few days or weeks of newborn life, and also in puberty, often around menarche. There are various reasons for this fluid increase, such as mucus secretion of the cervical columnar epithelium; transudation through the vaginal wall; and

Table 4-2. Causes and Treatment of Childhood Vulvovaginitis.

Cause	Treatment
1. Sexually transmitted disease agents	1. See text.

2. Nonspecific causes
    a. Hygiene
    b. Local irritation
    c. Foreign body
	2. See text.

3. *Candida albicans* vaginitis	3. Use antifungal creams, as miconazole, butoconazole, clotrimazole, others.
4. *Enterobius vermicularis*	4. Mebendazole (Vermox) 100 mg PO-one dose or Pyrantel pamoate 11 mg/kg up to 1 g, PO-one dose.
5. Gastroenteritis-induced (*Shigella* species, typhoid)	5. Treat underlying disorder—gastroenteritis.
6. Skin infection-induced	6. Treat underlying skin infection.
7. Respiratory-tract infection-induced (*Haemophilus influenzae, Neisseria meningitides, Streptococcus pneumoniae* beta hemolytic streptococcus Group A)	7. Treat underlying respiratory infection.
8. Miscellaneous vulvar disease	8. The child can develop many of the causes of vulvitis that are seen in the pubertal individual.

stimulation of sebaceous, sweat, and Bartholin's glands. Classically, this secretion begins several weeks or months before the onset of menses, and it may end at menarche or continue until regular menstruation develops.

Symptoms and Signs. A variable amount of leukorrhea occurs, which is usually clear, sticky, and nonirritating. Some individuals will note such an increase during sexual excitement and pregnancy.

Diagnostic Procedures. Microscopic study of a vaginal aspirate reveals normal vaginal cell structure but no leukocytes and no pathogenic bacteria. Cultures for bacteria and fungi (which are usually not indicated) are unrewarding.

Treatment. Since some youth think the discharge represents a sexually transmitted disease or genital injury, it is important to reassure the patient that the nature of her condition is physiologic. Frequent changes of cotton undergarments will help absorb the leukorrhea; nylon does not absorb as well. Good perineal hygiene is recommended, including frequent baths. Medication should not be given, since it is unnecessary and can cause complications such as dermatitis medicamentosa.

Trichomonas Vaginalis Vaginitis. *Trichomonas vaginalis* is a unicellular, flagellated protozoa originally described in 1836 by Donné. It has been established as an important etiologic agent in leukorrhea: the protozoa is noted in 10% of private gynecologic patients, 30% of general clinic patients, 38% of sexually transmitted disease clinic patients, and 85% of women prisoners. Many of the estimated 3 million annual cases in the United States occur in youth, frequently in association with *Neisseria gonorrhoeae* and *Condyloma acuminatum* infections.

Three *Trichomonas* species are described: in the mouth (*T. buccalis*), in the gastrointestinal tract (*T. hominis*), and in the genital tract (*T. vaginalis*). *T. vaginalis* is transmitted through sexual contact, though it may be spread through close genital contact as well. For example, the organisms can survive for a few hours in wet towels. After an incubation period of 4 to 30 days, a classic genital tract infection develops, which may involve the vagina, periurethral glands (Skene's), Bartholin's glands, urethra, bladder, and cervix.

Symptoms and Signs. The classic infection is vaginitis and cervicitis with secondary vulvitis. There is often erythema of the vagina with a profuse leukorrhea, often described as pruritic, greenish (or gray), frothy (bubbly), and malodorous. A mucopurulent or turbid vaginal discharge may also be seen, causing diagnostic confusion with gonorrhea, chlamydial infection, and herpes simplex infection. "Strawberry marks" (vaginocervical ecchymoses) and swollen vaginal papillae can also occur. The vaginal pH is 5.0 to 5.5 (or higher). Trichomoniasis can also occur with vaginal bleeding, sometimes in association with genital trauma, such as coitus or even wiping the area with a cotton swab. Dysuria is common, and severe cases may also involve lower abdominal pain as well as excoriation of the vulva or inner thighs.

Such symptoms can be intense, especially in young females. Postpartum trichomoniasis can be associated with fever, leukorrhea, and endometritis. If this condition is not adequately treated, a prolonged carrier state may develop, sometimes characterized by menses-induced, acute exacerbations. Trichomoniasis may also cause chronic pelvic congestion with resultant menorrhagia and dysmenorrhea.

Diagnostic Procedures. Trichomoniasis can be confirmed by laboratory analysis with saline drop, Pap smear, or culture. The appearance of the leukorrhea is not enough for an accurate diagnosis. For example, what seems to be an "inflamed" cervix may not be trichomoniasis but benign cervical erosion, in which endocervical columnar epithelium spreads out of the cervical canal, forming a border around the external os.

During the pelvic examination, an unlubricated speculum is used when collecting leukorrheic samples. A saline drop or wet mount is made by mixing a small amount of secretion with one or two drops of fresh saline on a glass slide. A cover slip is added, and the mixture is added microscopically. Trichomoniasis occurs with numerous, motile, pear-shaped, unicellular, flagellated organisms (protozoa), which are usually twice the size of normal leukocytes (Fig. 4-2C). They may not be seen if the patient is a chronic carrier, if she recently used a chemical douche, or if urine sediment is steady. Repeat saline preparations may be needed to confirm clinical suspicion.

Evidence of trichomoniasis may be found in an asymptomatic patient during a routine urinalysis or Pap smear. False positive and false negative results have been noted when relying solely on the smear for diagnosis. Though often not done in many laboratories, a culture of *T. vaginalis* is possible using a variety of media: Feinberg-Whitington medium, Trypticase serum of Kupferberg, cysteine-peptone-liver-maltose medium, and some transport media (such as Stuart's or Amies'). Cultures are helpful in suspicious cases in which saline microscopic preparations have proven negative.

Treatment. Metronidazole is the current treatment of choice and can be given as a single, 2-g dose (8250-mg tablets) or as a 7-day course (250 mg, 3 times daily). Young children can be treated with metronidazole at a dose of 15 mg/kg/day in three divided doses over a 7-day period; the maximum daily dose is 250 mg.

Metronidazole is not given during pregnancy (especially the first trimester) because of its teratogenic potential. Lactating women can be given the 2-g single dose if breast feeding is stopped for 1 or 2 days and then resumed. Although a carcinogenic potential has been implied by some authors, recent studies do not confirm any association between metronidazole and cancer.

Metronidazole has various well-known side effects, which are usually lessened with the 2-g dose. These include dizziness, headache, minor gastrointestinal disturbances, lethargy, depression, dermatitis, dry mucosal surfaces, transient neutropenia, and a bitter aftertaste. If the individual consumes alcohol while taking metronidazole, nausea and vomiting may result because of the disulfiram effect of this drug. Monilial vaginitis can also occur after a course of metronidazole.

Metronidazole is the currently recommended drug. If the patient is

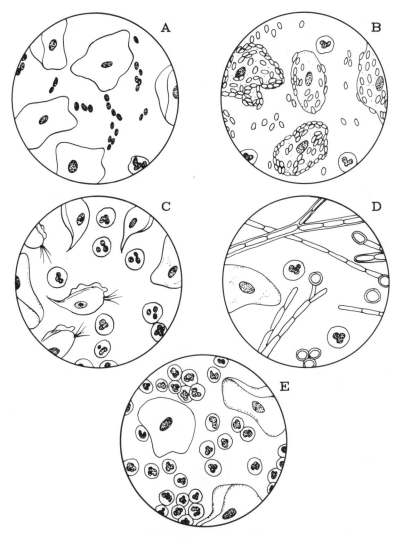

Fig. 4-2. Five different saline-preparation appearances. *A.* Normal saline drop with epithelial cells and lactobacilli. *B.* Clue cells. *C. Trichomonas vaginalis. D. Candida albicans* (hyphae and spores). *E.* Many white blood cells; consider gonorrhea or chlamydial infection.

pregnant, clotrimazole (100-mg tablet, intravaginally for 7 nights) can be used to reduce symptoms, but cure is unlikely. The patient's sex partner should be evaluated and treated with the 2-g, single-dose metronidazole regimen.

Resistance to metronidazole is reported. Often it is not resistance but simple failure to take the medication or reinfection. In actual cases of resistance, 2 g for 3 days may be effective. Continued resistance may respond to higher doses of metronidazole (such as 500 to 750 mg TID for 14 days). Oral administration of 2-g daily doses of ascorbic acid may increase metronidazole within the vagina. Some patients have been hospitalized for intravenous metronidazole treatment. If resistance continues, consult local experts.

Gardnerella Vaginitis (Bacterial vaginosis). *Gardnerella* is a gram-negative facultative anaerobe, originally identified in 1954 by Gardner and Dukes as a cause of vaginitis. Current studies note it as a common cause of leukorrhea in sexually active individuals. Originally, the name of the organism was *Corynebacterium vaginale* or *Haemophilus vaginalis;* currently, *Gardnerella vaginalis* is the term most frequently used. Although there has been some debate in the literature, most authors agree that the disease is transmitted sexually, with the male often being the asymptomatic carrier. The female develops a mild vaginitis, since the organism is a surface parasite, which rarely causes gross vulvo-vaginal changes. This organism is noted to cause 90% or more of so-called "nonspecific" vaginitis, and infrequently it is reported in prepubertal individuals.

Symptoms and Signs. G. vaginalis produces a vaginitis (currently termed "bacterial vaginosis") characterized by a gray-white malodorous leukorrhea, which is rarely pruritic but frequently "frothy." Cervicitis or cystitis does not occur. The vaginal pH is usually 5.0 to 5.5. Bacteremia has been noted, usually transiently after an abortion or delivery.

Diagnostic Procedures. A saline preparation or Gram's stain of the leukorrhea reveals classic "clue cells," epithelial cells covered (studded) with numerous gram-negative bacilli (Fig. 4-2B). A less reliable test is noticing an amine-like odor when 10% potassium hydroxide solution is mixed with a small amount of the vaginal discharge. There is a specific fluorescent antibody test for *G. vaginalis,* as well as culture media: blood agar incubated in a CO_2 environment or thioglycolate broth. Culture of the vaginal flora from individuals with this infection reveals a predominance of *G. vaginalis* and various anaerobic bacteria (such as *Bacteroides* and *Peptococcus* species).

Treatment. Recent evidence indicates that effective therapy must reduce the high level of anaerobic bacteria present. Thus, oral metronidazole (500 mg twice a day for 7 days) is the treatment of choice for *Gardnerella vaginalis* vaginitis. If the individual is pregnant, ampicillin is used (500 mg 4 times a day for 7 days), although it is not effective in all cases. Other treatment methods recommended by some include cephradine, 250 mg; cephalexin, 500 mg; and tetracycline, 500 mg—each 4 times a day for 7 full days. Treatment of the asymptomatic male partner is controversial. Though previously used, application of various vaginal creams (AVC triple sulfa, sulfisoxazole dialamine) is ineffective and not recommended.

Candida Albicans Vaginitis. *Candida albicans* (*Monilia albicans, Oidium albicans, Endomyces albicans*) is a dimorphous fungus that exists as a saprophyte or pathogen in humans. The other two genera of fungi in the human vagina—*Cryptococcus* and *Saccharomyces*—usually do not cause disease. Other species of *Candida* (*stellatoidea, parakrusel, krusei, tropicalis, pseudotropicalis,* and *guilliermondi*) are also not associated with symptoms. Occasionally, symptoms similar to monilial vaginitis are found secondary to *Torulopsis glabrata.* The relationship of yeast-like fungi to human disease was first described by Laugenbeck in 1839, whereas Wilkinson reported the presence of yeastlike organisms in vaginal secretions in 1840. An etiologic link to diabetic pruritus vulvae was noted by Hopkins in 1929 and by Hesseltine in 1933.

C. albicans is a ubiquitous organism, often found on skin (especially the foreskin and fingernails), and in the mouth, vagina, and stool. It can also be cultured from prostatic secretions and semen. Its incidence in the general population is 20%, 50% in pregnant women; it has been reported to cause up to 60% (alone or in combination) of vaginitis. Approximately 10% of cases are chronic or resistant to usual treatment, and the organism can be noted in children.

Many factors predispose women to monilial vaginitis (Table 4-3). These factors seem to work by many interrelated mechanisms, such as the following: removal of normal bacterial flora, allowing for the overgrowth of *Candida* (due to the use of metronidazole or broad-spectrum antibiotics); increase in glycogen content in vaginal epithelial cells with lowering of vaginal pH (as noted with pregnancy, diabetes, or birth control pill use); lowering of host defense factors (as with debilitating illness, iron deficiency, use of corticosteroids, aging, and others); constant reinfection exposure, as from contaminated soaps, intestinal reservoir, infected male

Table 4-3. Predisposing Factors to Monilial Vaginitis.

Common Factors	Other Factors	
Diabetes	Iron-deficiency anemia	Tight nylon undergarments
Pregnancy	Renal glycosuria	Increased sexual activity (including cunnilingus)
Broad-spectrum antibiotics	Endocrinopathies (hyperthyroidism, hypothyroidism; Addison's disease)	Drug addiction (especially heroin)
Metronidazole	Immunosuppressive drugs	Trauma to skin or vagina
Oral contraceptives	Malignancy	Infected soaps, douche bags, or other toilet articles
Obesity	Blood dyscrasias (including leukemia, agranulocytosis, aplastic anemia)	Removal of protective bacteria by antiseptic soaps
Age (over 50)	Pancreatitis	Intravenous infusions (indwelling catheters)
	Other host-factor deficiencies (such as lack of transfer factor)	Use of broad-spectrum antibiotics by male partner (as tetracycline for acne vulgaris), resulting in an antibiotic level in the ejaculate
	Malabsorption and poor hygiene	
	Large reservoir for *Candida* (skin, vagina, GI tract, mouth, semen)	? Emotional factors
	Allergic predisposition and hypersensitivity	

partners, increase in heat or moisture (tight nylon undergarments and obesity), or allergy. These factors should be considered, especially in cases of chronic monilial vaginitis. This condition is common in sexually active women.

Symptoms and Signs. Classically, moniliasis often occurs with pruritic vagino-vulvar erythema and whitish, cheese-like leukorrhea, which has a pH of 3.8 to 5.0. If antibiotics are the precipitating factors, there tends to be less discharge and more pruritus with erythema. If pregnancy is the predisposing factor, the leukorrhea is often more predominant. Various patterns can occur, such as improvement during menses and worsening both before and after menses.

Frequency, dysuria, and dyspareunia are common. Chronic infection may lead to thickened and dull-red or bronzed skin of the labia and groin. Fissuring, lichenification, and secondary bacterial infection may also occur. Intercrural, inguinocrural, and perianal involvement may be prominent. Skene's glands and the endocervical glands may be infected. Moniliids or dermatophytids may cause intensely pruritic, sterile lesions at the sides of fingers and hands.

Diagnostic Procedures. A drop of the vaginal secretion is mixed with a drop of 10 to 20% potassium hydroxide solution, which is covered with a cover slip and evaluated microscopically. *Candida* is the only yeast present in the vagina in two forms: hyphae (also called pseudomycelia or filaments) and spores (also called conidia or yeast buds) (Fig. 4-2D). Many lactobacilli are seen. A culture in Sabouraud's or Nickerson's medium may occasionally be necessary for patients who have atypical symptoms or whose potassium hydroxide preparations prove negative.

Treatment. Several effective antifungal agents are available. Currently recommended drugs include miconazole nitrate vaginal cream or suppository, clotrimazole cream or vaginal tablet, and butoconazole cream. The various forms and dosages are outlined in Table 4-4.

The agents in Table 4-4 are imidazoles. A new triazole agent, teraconazole (0.4% vaginal cream—Terazol 7, and 80-mg suppository—Terazole-3) has been introduced; it appears to be as effective as the classic imidazoles. The suppository is given once at night for 3 nights; the vaginal cream is given h.s. for 7 nights.

Nystatin vaginal tablets are effective, although the standard treatment is longer—twice daily for 14 days. Disseminated candidiasis or severe resistant vaginal candidiasis may respond to ketoconazole. For acute vulvitis, warm sitz baths with baking soda and hydrocortisone ointment may be helpful.

The adolescent with recurrent vaginal moniliasis should undergo a careful screening for underlying factors, such as diabetes, recent use of oral contraceptives or broad-spectrum antibiotics, tight nylon undergarments, infected toilet materials, and sexual activity with an infected male partner. Other treatments for *C. albicans* vaginitis include:

Treatment for an entire month through a menstrual cycle
Gentian violet solution painted in the cervix and vagina 2 to 4

Table 4-4. Forms and Dosages of Antifungal Agents.

Chemical	Trade name	Form	Prescription
Butoconazole	Femstat	2% cream	1 Application h.s. for 3 nights
Clotrimazole	Gyne-Lotrimin	100 mg tab.	1 h.s. for 7 nights
		500 mg tab.	1 tablet once
		1% cream	1 Application h.s. for 7–14 nights
	Mycelex-G	100 mg tab.	1 h.s. for 7 nights
		500 mg tab.	1 tablet once
		1% cream	1 application h.s. for 7–14 nights
Miconazole nitrate	Monistat 7	2% cream	1 application h.s. for 7 nights
		100 mg vaginal suppository	1 h.s. for 7 nights
	Monistat 3	200 mg vaginal suppository	1 h.s. for 3 nights

times every 3 days at the beginning of an infection

White vinegar douches when the pruritus begins

Treatment of the male genital monilial infection (especially the foreskin in uncircumcized males) and female introitus with candidacidal ointment

Use of a condom by the male partner

Oral nystatin, 500,000 units taken 2 or 3 times a day for 10 days by the patient and partner to eliminate the gastrointestinal tract as a reservoir

Consideration of hyposensitization with monilial antigens

Increased intake of yogurt or use of lactobacillus acidophilus douche or tampon

Cervicitis

Neisseria Gonorrhoeae Cervicitis. Infections caused by *Neisseria gonorrhoeae* remain among the most common sexually transmitted diseases in youth. This gram-negative diplococcus has a long history of infecting humans: it was known to Huang Ti in 2167 B.C., Hippocrates in 400 B.C., and Galen in 180 A.D. In 1977, a prevalence of 465.9 per 100,000 population was noted; this was reduced to 417.9 in 1982 and 387.6 in 1983. About 900,000 cases were reported in 1983, with one fourth occurring in the 16 to 19 age group and two thirds in the 15 to 24 age group. In 1980, a prevalence of 930 per 100,000 was noted for the 15 to 19 age group. The actual number of cases is felt to be about 50% higher than reported. Gonorrhea is common in 16- to 23-year-old males and in females under age 14. Asymptomatic cases are common, especially in heterosexual females and homosexual males. Carrier states of months to years are well known. Gonorrhea is nearly always transmitted sexually; when gonorrhea is found in children, sexual abuse should be suspected, as it should be in any sexually transmitted disease affecting children. The female has a nearly 100% chance of acquiring gonorrhea from an infected male partner, whereas the male has a 1 in 4 chance of acquiring it from an infected female partner.

The pathogenicity of this organism is related to the presence of pili, outer membrane proteins (such as I, II, and III), lipopolysaccharide, IgA$_1$, protease, and other components of this complex microbe. Pili and the outer membrane protein II contribute to the organism's ability to adhere to epithelial cells. The presence of sperm and *Trichomonas vaginalis* can influence the transfer of *Neisseria gonorrhoeae* into the upper female genital tract. The use of barrier contraceptive methods can block this microbe, and the use of antigonococcal spermicidal agents (such as non-oxynol-9) or oral contraceptives can reduce the presence of this organism as well. *N. gonorrhoeae* has a well-known predilection for columnar and pseudostratified epithelium. The lipopolysaccharide causes local cytotoxicity and inflammation, as well as systemic toxicity with fever. The IgA$_1$ protease inactivates human IgA$_1$ antibodies. A variety of complex factors allows some strains to be relatively resistant to neutrophil destruction.

Symptoms and Signs. *N. gonorrhoeae* causes vaginitis in prepubertal girls and cervicitis (with or without salpingitis) in both adolescent and adult females. This form of cervicitis classically appears as a yellow-green, mucopurulent or purulent endocervical discharge with variable cervical motion tenderness. The discharge may be visually indistinguishable from that caused by *Trichomonas vaginalis,* herpes simplex, or *Chlamydia trachomatis.* Symptoms of urinary tract infection and abnormal uterine bleeding are also seen with gonococcal cervicitis.

A variety of other infections in females can also occur with *Neisseria gonorrhoeae,* much the same as those noted with *Chlamydia trachomatis.* Skenitis (inflammation of Skene's glands) appears as a pea-sized tender nodule at the base of the urethral meatus along with dysuria. Bartholinitis appears as a unilateral, 2- to 7-cm tender mass within the labia majora; it represents infection of the Bartholin gland duct. A mucopurulent urethral discharge, noted with or without urethral milking, can occur with an erythematous urethral meatus. This gonococcal urethritis can develop into a chronic condition without treatment. *Neisseria gonorrhoeae* is one of the three common microbial causes of male urethritis, along with *Chlamydia trachomatis* and *Ureaplasma urealyticum.* Rectal inflammation or proctitis can develop from gonococcal cervicitis because of the close anatomic relationship between the vagina and the rectum; the infection is usually mild unless there has been direct penile inoculation. Pelvic inflammatory disease (PID) is a major complication of cervical gonorrhea and is discussed in the section on PID. A section on the Fitz-Hugh-Curtis syndrome (gonococcal or chlamydial perihepatitis) is also included. Approximately 1 to 2% of patients with gonococcal cervicitis develop septicemia with evidence of dermatitis, tenosynovitis, arthritis, meningitis, endocarditis, and others. This is called disseminated gonococcal infection (DGI) or gonococcal arthritis dermatitis syndrome (GADS).

Diagnostic Procedures. A Gram's stain of the gonococcally induced endocervical discharge reveals many pairs of gram-negative, kidney-bean-shaped diplococci locked within polymorphonuclear leukocytes (Fig. 4-2E). The normal vaginal flora contains other *Neisseria* species—*sicca, subflava, flavenscans, mucosa,* and *meningitides.* The oropharynx and rectum also contain various *Neisseria* species. Thus, a positive culture using a chocolate agar base (Thayer-Martin medium) in a 10% carbon dioxide environment is considered definitive evidence for gonococcal infection. Gram's-stain evidence for gonorrhea is usually sufficient if taken from the urethra or cervix in symptomatic females or from the urethra in symptomatic males. Gram's stains are unreliable evidence of gonorrhea if taken from the urethra of asymptomatic patients or if taken from the oropharynx or anorectal area even if the patient is symptomatic. These sites require a culture before a definitive diagnosis of gonorrhea is made. If a history of oral or rectal sex is elicited or symptoms occur in these areas, gonococcal cultures from the pharynx and rectum are necessary. When gonorrhea is present, look for other STDs, such as those caused by *Chlamydia, Trichomonas,* and *Condyloma accuminatum,* as well as others. Gonorrhea and chlamydia are often found together, and treatment schedules often cover both of these important microbes.

Treatment. Table 4-5 outlines a variety of treatment plans recommended for *Neisseria gonorrhoeae* cervicitis. Ceftriaxone (Rocephin), in a single, 125- to 250-mg intramuscular dose, has been recommended as the treatment of choice for uncomplicated gonorrhea (including penicillinase-producing strains), as well as for gonococcal pharyngitis and proctitis (CDC-recommended schedules, 1988). Alternatives to ceftriaxone for uncomplicated gonorrheal cervicitis include ampicillin, amoxicillin, aqueous procaine penicillin G, tetracycline, and others (Table 4-5). Alternatives for gonococcal cervicitis due to penicillinase strains include cefotaxime, cefoxitin, spectinomycin, and others (Table 4-5). Spectinomycin has a high rate of inducing bacterial resistance and has no effect on incubating syphilis. Spectinomycin is an alternative antibiotic for rectal gonorrhea but not for pharyngeal gonorrhea. Because of the frequent association between

Table 4-5. Treatment Plans for Uncomplicated Gonoccocal Cervicitis.*

Gonococcal cervicitis
1. Ceftriaxone, 250 mg intramuscularly (current drug of choice)
2. Aqueous procaine penicillin G (4.8 million units intramuscularly) plus probenecid (1 g orally)
3. Tetracycline (500 mg orally, 4 times daily for 7 days)
4. Ampicillin (3.5 g orally) or amoxicillin (3 g orally) plus probenecid (1 g orally)
5. Doxycycline (100 mg orally, twice daily for 7 days)
6. Erythromycin (500 mg orally, 4 times daily for 7 days)
7. Cefotaxime (1 g intramuscularly)
8. Spectinomycin (2 g intramuscularly)
9. Cefoxitin (2 g intramuscularly) plus probenecid (1 g orally)

Gonococcal cervicitis due to penicillinase-producing strains
1. Ceftriaxone (250 mg intramuscularly)
2. Trimethoprim (80 mg) plus sulfamethoxazole (400 mg), nine tablets orally in one dose for 5 days to treat pharyngeal gonorrheal infection
3. Cefotaxime (1 g intramuscularly)
4. Cefoxitin (2 g intramuscularly) plus probenecid (1 gram orally)
5. Spectinomycin (2 g intramuscularly)

---

* Most experts currently recommend treatment of chlamydia along with gonorrhea when gonorrhea has been identified, in view of the frequent association of these two microbes. Ceftriaxone is the recommended drug for uncomplicated gonorrhea, for gonorrhea of the pharynx as well as the rectum, and for penicillinase-reproducing gonorrhea.

gonorrhea and chlamydia, the following treatment schedule has been recommended by some for individuals with proven gonococcal cervicitis and possible chlamydial cervicitis: ceftriaxone (with amoxicillin as an alternative) followed by tetracycline (500 mg 4 times daily) or doxycycline (100 mg twice daily), each given orally for 7 days. This may also prevent salpingitis as a complication of early cervicitis. Pregnant patients can be given erythromycin and, if necessary, spectinomycin. Table 4-6 lists antibiotics to avoid during pregnancy, and Table 4-7 lists those presumed safe during pregnancy. Table 4-8 lists pediatric doses of some of these antibiotics. Followup culture of treated gonococcal infections is important, as is treatment of the patient's sex partner.

Chlamydia Trachomatis Cervicitis. *Chlamydia trachomatis* is an obligate, intracellular parasite that causes the most common form of sexually transmitted disease in adolescents. Two *Chlamydia* species are described: *C. psittaci* (causing psittacosis) and *C. trachomatis,* which has 15 serotypes and is implicated in causing lymphogranuloma venereum (L-1, L-2, and L-3), trachoma (A, B, Ba, and C), and a variety of infections, including urethritis, cervicitis, salpingitis, epididymitis, acute urethral syndrome, and others (Table 4-9). Like cytomegalovirus and herpesvirus, *C. trachomatis* infection can be passed from mother to fetus with resultant disease in the neonatal period, such as inclusion conjunctivitis, pneumonia, and other perinatal infections. Studies note that 15 to 37% of pregnant youth are infected with this agent; 50% of the newborns develop inclusion conjunctivitis, whereas about 20% develop pneumonia. Current studies also note that *C. trachomatis* is noted in 15 to 35% of patients in STD clinics and causes 30 to 60% of mucopurulent cervicitis, 15 to 25% of pelvic inflammatory disease, more than 50% of Fitz-Hugh-Curtis syndrome, and 25% of urethral syndrome. The cervix seems to serve as an important reservoir for this sexually transmitted agent, and a carrier state has been recognized to last for months, especially in females. This state is often asymptomatic, and surveys of sexually active, asymptomatic youth reveal a positive culture rate of over 5%. Thus, the role of *C. trachomatis* as a major STD pathogen is well recognized.

Symptoms and Signs. Infection in the cervix produces mucopurulent cervicitis, with a mucopurulent (or purulent) discharge, erythematous vaginal mucosa, hypertrophic cervical erosion, and abnormal Pap smear. *C. trachomatis* has a predilection for columnar epithelium. Youth using oral contraceptives have increased cervical columnar epithelium, and some studies have suggested that youth taking oral contraceptives have an increased incidence of *C. trachomatis* in the cervix. Thus, some have

Table 4-6. Medications for STD to Avoid in Pregnancy.

1. Tetracyclines (including doxycycline)
2. Podophyllin tincture
3. Metronidazole (at least for the first trimester)
4. Sulfonamides
5. Lindane
6. Erythromycin estolate

Table 4-7. Medications for STD Presumed Safe in Pregnancy.

1. Erythromycin (not the estolate)
2. Penicillin
3. Ampicillin
4. Amoxicillin
5. Probenecid tablets
6. Spectinomycin injection
7. Clotrimazole vaginal tablets
8. Nystatin vaginal cream
9. Trichloroacetic acid topical
10. Phenol topical
11. Crotamiton cream
12. Ceftriaxone

suggested that youth taking the pill have more chlamydial-induced cervicitis and salpingitis than those not taking the pill.

Mixed infections with *Neisseria gonorrhoeae* are common. The urethral syndrome comprises dysuria, pyuria, and a negative urine sample (i.e., less than 100,000 colonies per ml of urine, clean-catch method). Common agents implicated in the urethral syndrome include *Escherichia coli* and *Chlamydia trachomatis.* There may be an accompanying leukorrhea. *C. Trachomatis* is also one of the three main causes of male urethritis, the others being *Neisseria gonorrhoeae* and *Ureaplasma urealyticum.* (Pelvic inflammatory disease due to *Chlamydia trachomatis* is discussed in the section on PID.) This agent has a major role in the production of PID-induced infertility in youth.

Diagnostic Procedures. A positive culture taken from the cervix, using tissue culture monolayers containing McCoy cells, confirms the diagnosis of *C. trachomatis* infection. However, if the vaginal discharge alone is used, the culture is often negative. Adequate samples of epithelial cells from the cervix are necessary to ensure reliable results. Many laboratories are still not equipped for such cultures, although samples can be frozen and sent to laboratories that handle McCoy cell media.

Other tests are being marketed, and a clinician can consult local laboratories to determine which ones are available. For example, there is a fluorescent monoclonal antibody test called the Microtrak Immunofluorescent Test, which uses columnar cervical cells. Another, the Chlamydi-

Table 4-8. Pediatric Doses for Antigonococcal Antibiotics.

1. Tetracycline	40 mg/kg/day PO
2. Amoxicillin	50 mg/kg PO
3. Ampicillin	50 mg/kg PO
4. Aqueous Procaine Penicillin G	100,000 U/Kg IM
5. Erythromycin	40 mg/kg/day PO
6. Spectinomycin	40 mg/kg/day PO
7. Probenecid	1.0 gm (25 mg/kg for children under 45 kg; this is not an antibiotic but is used with some; see text)
8. Ceftriaxone	125 mg/kg/day IM

Table 4-9. Chlamydia Trachomatis Disorders.

Male urethritis	Epididymitis	Pneumonia
Cervicitis	Reiter's syndrome	Endocarditis
Salpingitis	Prostatitis	Others
Perihepatitis (Fitz-Hugh-Curtis-syndrome)	Peritonitis	
Proctitis	Arthritis	
Bartholinitis	Pharyngitis	
Acute urethral syndrome	Conjunctivitis	
Otitis media		

azyme Test, is an enzyme immunoassay. The 4-hour ELISA (Enzyme-linked Immunoabsorbent Assay) is a serologic test using a spectrophotometer. Other serologic tests are available that use complement fixation and microimmunofluorescence tests, but they have limited clinical applicability. Many clinicians favor the Microtrak test if direct cultures are not possible, since urethral and cervical secretions can be placed on glass slides, fixed, treated with the fluorescein-labeled monoclonal antibody, incubated, and read as positive or negative for *C. trachomatis*. A sensitivity of 93% and a specificity of 96% have been reported.

Treatment. Recommended therapy for uncomplicated chlamydial cervicitis (and urethritis or proctitis) includes tetracycline, 500 mg, 4 times daily; doxycycline, 100 mg, 2 times daily; and erythromycin, 500 mg, 4 times daily—each administered orally for 7 days. Erythromycin is given if tetracycline or doxycycline cannot be used, as, for example, in pregnancy when these two agents are not recommended or when the patient is allergic to them. An alternative antibiotic is sulfisoxazole, 500 mg 4 times daily, orally, for 10 days. Children over 8 years of age can receive tetracycline at a dose of 25 to 50 mg/kg/day; this is not recommended for those under 8 years of age because of the well-known effects of tetracycline on bones and teeth in children. The pediatric dose for erythromycin is 40 to 50 mg/kg/day. A 7-day course of antibiotics is usually sufficient.

If cultures or other tests are not available to confirm *C. trachomatis* infections and yet the clinical course is consistent with this diagnosis, treatment with one of the above agents is recommended. For example, this would occur in a youth with mucopurulent cervicitis with a gram-negative stain and negative culture for *Neisseria gonorrhoeae*. Also remember that gonorrhea and chlamydia are often found together. As with other STDs, treatment of the sex partner is important, and you must try to educate the sexually active youth about STDs.

Herpes Simplex Virus Cervicitis. Herpes simplex virus (Types I and II) belong to a viral group called the herpesvirus, which also includes varicella-zoster virus, cytomegalovirus, and Epstein-Barr virus. Type I herpes simplex causes herpes labialis, gingivostomatitis, keratitis, and eczema herpeticum. Type I is implicated in about 10% of herpes kenitalis cases, whereas 90% result from Type II infections. Recurrent infection, despite the presence of serum antibodies, is characteristic of this viral agent. An incubation period of days to weeks is observed for the primary infection, and most clinicians feel that the cervix serves as a reservoir for this microbe. This infection represents one of the most common sexually transmitted diseases in the adolescent population. Surveys note that 3 to 12% of sexually active youth have positive cultures for herpes simplex. Active lesions are very infectious, with 30 to 70% of exposed individuals developing the disease. A major concern with herpes in pregnancy is its potential transmission to the newborn, which occurs at a rate of 30% with Type I and 70% with Type II; neonatal herpes infection can be a serious disease. Another concern is the potential, but unproven, link between herpes cervicitis and cervical cancer.

Symptoms and Signs. Herpes genitalis infection usually appears as a form of cervicitis with ulcers on the vulva (Fig. 4-3), The initial finding is an area of hyperesthesia or itching, which leads to small groups of vesicles placed on erythematous bases. The vesicles develop into ulcers within 24 hours, last 3 to 14 days, and then heal without scarring. These tiny, superficial, painful ulcers are characteristically located on the cervix, vulva, or periurethral area, but can spread to the urethra, vagina, thighs, buttocks, or other regions. Cervical herpes produces a purulent or mucopurulent leukorrhea, which is also seen with chlamydia, gonorrhea, trichomoniasis, and other STDs. Primary herpes infection leads to worse symptoms than the recurrent disease. Primary infection can result in one (or several) deep ulcers in association with various symptoms—fever, general malaise, anorexia, headache, and others. This occurs in addition to cervicitis and tender inguinal lymphadenopathy. The differential diagnosis of the genital ulcer syndrome includes herpes, syphilis, chancroid, granuloma inguinale, lymphogranuloma venereum, Behçet's disease, trauma, and others (Table 4-10). Reported herpes genitalis complications included erythema multiforme, radiculomyelitis with acute urinary retention, ascending myelitis, hepatic failure, meningitis, and others. Complications can be especially severe in immunocompromised hosts.

Diagnostic Procedures. Microscopic examination of collected material from the vesicles or ulcers that have been treated with Giemsa or Wright's stain (Tzank Test) demonstrate characteristic balloon cells with intranuclear inclusion bodies or multinuclear giant cells; these giant cells are also seen with herpes zoster and varicella. The Pap smear reveals multinuclear giant cells and can be up to 75% accurate when compared with viral cultures. Electron microscopy can demonstrate viral herpetic particles; definitive diagnosis is by way of specific viral cultures along with typing using immunofluorescent techniques. Viral serology is possible, but is of limited usefulness.

Treatment. There is no specific cure for herpes simplex infections, and treatment remains preventive and symptomatic. Methods used to reduce pain include warm-water sitz baths, analgesics, anti-inflammatory agents, petroleum jelly, viscous xylocaine jelly or ointment, and povidone-iodine (Betadine) solution. Betadine solution is not given to pregnant individuals, since iodine can be absorbed through the vagina and may reach the fetus.

Currently, acyclovir has been advocated in the treatment of herpes genitalis. Current recommendations are to apply 5% acyclovir ointment every 3 to 4 hours for 7 days. If given within 6 days of symptom onset,

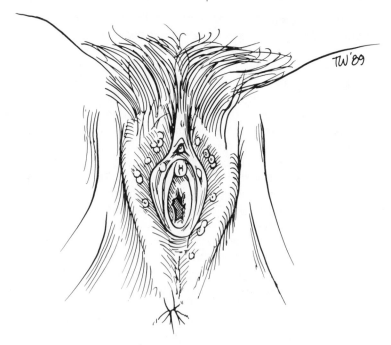

Fig. 4-3. Genital herpes simplex infection.

acyclovir can reduce viral shedding and disease duration. The use of oral and intravenous forms of this chemical is under evaluation. The oral form may serve as a prophylactic for those with severe, frequently recurrent disease, as well as for those who are immunocompromised. It is given at a dose of 200 mg 5 times per day (every 4 hours during waking hours) for 10 days with primary disease and for 5 days for recurrent herpes. A dose of 200 mg 3 times a day has been used for up to 6 months as chronic suppressive therapy for severe recurrent disease. A 7-day course of in-

Table 4-10. Vulvar Ulcerations and Erosions.

1. Syphillis
2. Chancroid
3. Lymphogranuloma venereum (LGV)
4. Granuloma inguinale
5. Herpes simplex virus genitalis
6. Behçet's disease
7. Reiter's syndrome
8. Erosions secondary to vaginal or endocervical discharge (*Neisseria gonorrhoeae; Candida albicans*)
9. Traumatic ulcers or erosions (post-coital)
10. Amebiasis
11. Regional enteritis
12. Bullous diseases (pemphigus)
13. Lichen simplex chronicus
14. Tropical ulcerations (tuberculosis, filariasis, schistosomiasis, LGV, and amebiasis)
15. Others

travenous acyclovir has been used in cases not responding to topical or oral acyclovir therapy. This medication is not recommended for pregnant or lactating females, but has been used in children with severe infection. Interferon and monoclonal antibody therapy may also serve a role in the management of this disease; both are under current study.

If secondary bacterial infection occurs, a broad-spectrum antibiotic can be helpful. If herpes infection develops during pregnancy while labor is imminent, a Caesarian section is recommended to reduce (but not elim-inate) the risk of neonatal herpes. The American Academy of Pediatrics and the American College of Obstetricians and Gynecologists have de-veloped guidelines for managing pregnant individuals and their offspring who are exposed to or infected with herpes. Those with painful lesions and certain complications (such as acute urinary retention) may require hospitalization. Catheterization with antibiotic coverage for a potential uri-nary tract infection is recommended for those with acute disease, and condoms can be useful during asymptomatic periods to reduce the risk of transmission. An annual Pap smear is recommended for youth with a history of herpes genitalis, in light of its possible link to cervical intraepi-thelial neoplasia (CIN) and cervical cancer. Recent literature suggests an even greater association between CIN and human papillomavirus (HPV) infection.

Vulvitis

Inflammation or infection of the vulva may cause many diverse disor-ders in the adolescent female, especially if she is sexually active. Accord-ing to Young, 161 of 375 patients (43%) at a vulvitis clinic (primarily for adult women) had a sexually transmitted disease. General treatment in-cludes adequate perineal hygiene (including the use of Tuck's pads); plain, warm-water sitz baths; frequent changes of white cotton undergarments (if vaginal discharge is present); and use of hydrocortisone ointment or cream for severe inflammation. Cooling compresses with Burrow's solu-tion or colloidal bath compresses may be helpful. Treatment of secondary bacterial infection is important. Over-treatment resulting in sensitization, dermatitis medicamentosa, secondary eczema, or monilial vaginitis should be avoided.

Table 4-10 lists some causes of vulvar erosions or ulcerations that may be observed in teenaged or adult women. The most frequently occurring of these disorders are briefly described in this chapter. It should always be remembered that more than one STD can occur at the same time; thus, if one is found, always look for others.

Syphilis

Evaluation of a vulvar (or vaginal) ulcer must always include the possi-bility of primary syphilis, especially if the ulcer is a single, punched-out, nontender sore with a serious discharge in association with inguinal lymphadenopathy. A darkfield examination for *Treponema pallidum* on three successive days is recommended, as well as serologic testing for syphilis at the time the ulcer is noted, 6 weeks later, and at a 3-month followup evaluation. Secondary syphilis should be considered if influenza-like symptoms are associated with generalized lymphadenopathy and a generalized skin and mucous-membrane rash. The manifestations of secondary syphilis are diverse, including vulvar swelling as the initial symptom.

Treatment. Standard treatment of primary or secondary syphilis is with 2.4 million units of benzathine penicillin G intramuscularly. The Jarisch-Herxheimer reaction is common after the penicillin treatment of secondary syphilis, and less common with primary syphilis. Alternate treatments include 15 days of tetracycline or erythromycin at a dose of 500 mg 4 times daily.

Chancroid

Chancroid is caused by *Haemophilus ducreyi,* a gram-negative coccobacillus with an incubation period of 3 to 5 days. Although *H. ducreyi* is usually dismissed as a tropical infection, recent studies note that it may occur in temperate climates also. The large number of persons who travel about the world is certainly one factor in this microbe's widespread occurrence.

Symptoms and Signs. Tender, shallow, purulent, sharply circumcised ulcers of the vulva or cervix with inflamed inguinal lymph nodes (buboes) develop. Secondary bacterial infection and autoinoculation that produce multiple lesions may be observed. The differential diagnosis includes syphilis, herpes, lymphogranuloma venereum, granuloma inguinale, traumatic ulcers, and others (Table 4-11).

Diagnostic Procedures. A Gram's or Giemsa stain of ulcer or lymph node material reveals gram-negative, pleomorphic organisms in clusters. Biopsy of the ulcer, skin testing, complement fixation titers, and culture may be helpful. Culture techniques have recently improved and are now considered by many to be the diagnostic procedure of choice for chancroid.

Treatment. Ceftriaxone (250 mg intramuscularly once) or erythromycin (500 mg, orally for 7 days) is the current treatment of choice. An alternative is trimethoprim with sulfamethoxazole (2 tablets twice daily for 7 days).

Lymphogranuloma venereum

Lymphogranuloma venereum (LGV), a tropical venereal disease, is caused by *Chlamydia trachomatis* (different serotypes than those implicated in nongonococcal urethritis) and has an incubation period of 7 to 85 days. Approximately 25,000 cases are reported annually in the United States.

Symptoms and Signs. A painless ulcer of the vulva, vagina, or cervix is present but disappears in a few days, followed in 2 to 6 weeks by suppurative inguinal buboes. Inguinal or femoral lymphadenopathy may be the only sign. If both of these lymph node areas are noted together,

Table 4-11. Chancroid: Differential Diagnosis.

Syphilis
Herpes progenitalis
Lymphogranuloma venereum
Granuloma inguinale
Behçet's disease
Reiter's syndrome
Traumatic ulcers
Others (See Table 4-10)

separated by the inguinal ligament, this is called the "groove sign" and is characteristic of LGV. Other conditions that may be noted include fever, arthralgia, erythema nodosum, headache, conjunctivitis, and proctitis. Healing may be delayed with resultant scarring and stricture of the urethra or rectum, or both. In addition, an increased incidence of carcinoma in these patients has been suggested by some authors.

Diagnostic Procedures. Although the Frei test was previously used, it is not currently available, and so serial LGV complement fixation testing is currently the diagnostic procedure of choice. A 1:64 titer is considered diagnostic. Other procedures are possible, including immunofluorescence, counter-immunoelectrophoresis, and culture (though difficult). Lymphography may be useful to monitor some of the sequelae.

Treatment. Various antibiotics, including sulfisoxazole, erythromycin, tetracycline, minocycline, and doxycycline, are given for a 2- to 4-week period.

Granuloma inguinale

Granuloma inguinale is caused by *Calymmatobacterium (Donovania) granulomatis,* a gram-negative coccobacillus that has an incubation period of approximately 8 to 10 weeks. Though granuloma inguinale should be considered in the differential diagnosis of genital ulcers, it is a relatively rare STD in most parts of the United States.

Symptoms and Signs. Painful ulcers of the vulva, vagina, or cervix develop, which appear as classic red granulation tissue. Inguinal lymph nodes enlarge when there is secondary bacterial infection. Sclerosing types are described, and vaginal lesions may cause the initial sign of vaginal bleeding.

Diagnostic Procedures. A Wright's or Giemsa stain reveals Donovan's bodies, whereas a biopsy shows granulation tissue. Culturing the organism is difficult.

Treatment. The usual treatment includes oral tetracycline, oral erythromycin, or parenteral gentamicin (40 mg twice daily for 14 days). Chloramphenicol, streptomycin, and trimethoprim-sulfamethoxazole have also been used.

Amebiasis

Vulvar ulcerations can be caused by an *Entamoeba histolytica* infection in rare situations.

Symptoms and Signs. Amebiasis starts as an ulcer with a raised, thickened edge and white membranous flora. It slowly develops into a painful, foul-smelling eschar, and is associated with a blood-stained, malodorous leukorrhea and amebic enteritis. Oral-ano-genital sex can be an important precipitating factor in amebiasis, as well as in giardiasis and shigellosis, especially among homosexuals. Other parasitic gynecologic diseases include schistosomiasis, trichomoniasis, and even pinworm infection *(Enterobius vermicularis).*

Diagnostic Procedures. The organism may be identified by wet (saline) preparation from the ulcer or vaginal secretion, a Pap smear, or a biopsy of the eschar or cervix.

Treatment. Therapy with metronidazole (750 mg orally 3 times daily for 7 to 10 days) has been suggested.

Behçet's Disease

"Behçet's disease" (mostly found in Eastern Mediterranean countries and Japan) refers to a classic triad of symptoms (recurrent genital ulcers, iritis or uveitis, and recurrent aphthous stomatitis) often in association with a variety of other conditions, such as thrombophlebitis, vasculitis, ulcerative colitis, epididymitis, arthritis (arthralgias), pyodermas, erythema multiforme, and meningoencephalitis. Psychiatric manifestations have also been described. Theories regarding the etiology of Behçet's disease (such as environmental pollutants or viruses) are unproven.

Symptoms and Signs. The hallmark of Behçet's disease is the oral, painful, single or multiple aphthous ulcer, which has the appearance of a canker sore. Genital lesions are protein in nature: red macules, papules, follicles, pustules, or 1- to 2-cm aphthous-like ulcers, which generally heal within 1 to 2 weeks. Blister formation or an inflammatory reaction may occur at the site of a venipuncture or scratch in some cases. Prognosis may be poor with chronic eye disease or central nervous system manifestations.

Diagnosis. No universally accepted definition of Behçet's diseases exists, but the combination of recurrent oral ulcers with two or more of the above-mentioned signs is consistent with this diagnosis. An increase in HLA-B5 antigen has been noted in many patients. Behçet's disease has also been classified in a group of arthritic disorders, which are seronegative for rheumatoid factor. This group includes ulcerative colitis, Crohn's disease, ankylosing spondylitis, psoriatic arthritis, and Reiter's disease. Differentiation from recurrent herpes simplex infection may require careful evaluation.

Treatment. Currently, no proven therapy exists. Oral prednisone or oral contraceptives have been tried, as have a wide variety of other drugs, including chlorambucil, cyclophosphamide, levamisol, tetracycline, azathioprine, 6-mercaptopurine, colchicine, and others.

Miscellaneous Disorders Affecting the Vulva

Table 4-12 lists various disorders that can affect the vulva in the course of their disease processes. A few of these are described.

Molluscum contagiosum. Molluscum contagiosum is caused by a large pox virus that has an incubation period of 3 to 6 weeks. This disease is spread by close contact and tends to affect the skin and mucous membranes of the trunk, abdomen, and genitals. Chronic molluscum contagiosum infection may be noted in some patients with impaired cellular immunity.

Symptoms and Signs. Discrete, flesh-colored or pearly gray papules, 1 to 6 mm in diameter with central umbilication, are classic. Plaques can develop because of several papules coalescing. These lesions commonly last 4 to 6 months, but occasionally may be present for years.

Diagnostic Procedures. Potassium hydroxide preparations of curetted specimens pressed between a slide and cover slip demonstrate diagnostic intracytoplasmic inclusions (Lipschutz cells). Wright's, Giemsa, Gram's, or Pap staining of the specimen is helpful; biopsy is confirmatory. Differentiation must be made from epidermal cysts, eruptive xanthomas, flat warts, and others.

Treatment. Open each papule and apply phenol, trichloracetic acid, liquid nitrogen, podophyllin, carbolic acid, tretinoin, or even cantharadin. Curettage or electrodesiccation is also used in some cases, as are silver nitrate applications. Griseofulvin therapy has been used for extensive lesions.

Condylomata Acuminata. Condylomata acuminata (venereal warts) are due to an infection with a papilloma virus (human papillomavirus, especially types 6 and 10) that has an incubation period of a few weeks to several months. Condyloma acuminatum is sexually transmitted and is often associated with other STDs (such as trichomonal vaginitis, monilial vaginitis, and gonococcal cervicitis). As many as 70% of an infected patient's sex partners have or have had these warts. The potential of the condylomata for possible malignant changes was recently noted by many authors. Human papillomaviruses, types 16 and 18, have been linked to cervical intraepithelial neoplasia (CIN) and carcinoma in situ of the cervix. See the section on CIN.

Symptoms and Signs. Condylomata acuminata may involve any part

---

Table 4-12. Miscellaneous Vulvitis.

1. Molluscum contagiosum
2. Condyloma acuminatum
3. Scabies
4. Pediculosis pubis
5. Tinea
6. Psoriasis
7. Furunculosis
8. Hidradenitis suppurativa
9. Intertrigo
10. Hemangiomas
11. Herpes zoster
12. Erythema multiform
13. Pruritus vulvae
14. Others

of the genitals (including the vagina, urethra, bladder, or anal canal) and can be extensive (Fig. 4-4). They seem to worsen in individuals with vaginal discharge, poor hygiene, or heavy perspiration, as well as in pregnant individuals. Lesions resistant to treatment are reported in some individuals with insulin-dependent diabetes mellitus and with immunosuppression disorders.

Diagnostic Procedures. The presence of squamous papillomas in moist mucocutaneous areas of the external genitalia and perianal regions is usually sufficient for its diagnosis. Biopsy is confirmatory and mandatory if lesions are resistant to podophyllin therapy. Voiding cystourethrography will demonstrate intraurethral spread.

Treatment. Therapy of concomitant venereal disease and use of 3 to 25% tincture of podophyllin (podophyllum resin in tincture of benzoin) on the lesions are often helpful, especially if the areas are less than 2 cm in diameter. White petrolatum jelly is then added, and this mixture is thoroughly washed off in 2 to 4 hours. There are other techniques for using podophyllin, but they all stress that normal tissue must be protected from the caustic podophyllin. Weekly applications may be necessary and seem to be most effective with moist, fleshy, sessile genital warts. The role of more frequent applications is under study. Podophyllin is not used for cervical warts or for pregnant patients. If there is no regression after four

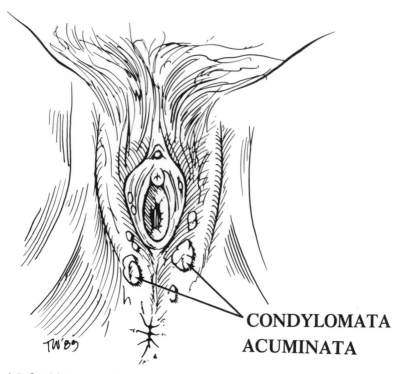

CONDYLOMATA ACUMINATA

Fig. 4-4. Condylomata acuminata.

weekly trials, other methods are used and referral to a gynecologic consultant is recommended. Topical chemotherapeutic agents (such as dinitrochlorobenzene or 5-fluorouracil) have been used as a supplement to topical podophyllin treatment. Methods recommended as alternatives to podophyllin therapy include curettage, electrodesiccation, surgical excision, and cryotherapy (with liquid nitrogen or solid carbon dioxide). Immunotherapy with an autogenous vaccine (prepared from excised warts) has been attempted, but without proven success. Laser treatment has also been used successfully. Recently, the injection of interferon (alpha 2b) into genital warts has been proven effective. Because of recent data linking vulvar, vaginal, or cervical warts with cervical and vulvar dysplasia (and cancer), patients with these warts need Pap screening and possibly colposcopy.

Scabies. *Sarcoptes scabiei var hominis* causes scabies. This pruritic dermatitis is spread by close contact and involves an incubation period of up to 2 months. The differential diagnosis includes atopic dermatitis, contact dermatitis, and neurodermatitis.

Symptoms and Signs. When burrow lesions or nodular areas are noted in the genital area, a diagnosis of scabies should be entertained. Excoriated papules may also be found in the webs of fingers, flexural surfaces of the elbows, axillary folds, and buttocks. Generalized, persistent, severe pruritus is common; secondary infection or secondary eczema is also noted in some individuals. Other STDs (such as syphilis or gonorrhea) may occur with scabies. Steroids may reduce the symptoms of scabies, masking its diagnosis.

Diagnostic Procedures. The scrapings from a suspected lesion are placed on a slide with mineral oil or 10% potassium hydroxide. Microscopic evaluation may yield mites, eggs, or fecal pellets (scybala). A biopsy may also demonstrate mites.

Treatment. Recommended therapy includes 1% lindane cream or lotion, crotamiton (Eurax) 10% cream or lotion, 25% benzyl benzoate emulsion, or 5 to 20% precipitated sulphur in petrolatum. If the patient is pregnant or under 10 years of age, use 10% crotamiton or 6% sulphur in petrolatum. The patient's family and sex partner(s) should be treated, and fomites (underwear, shorts, pillowcases, and pajamas) are to be cleaned. A hypersensitivity state is commonly noted that is characterized by pruritus for several days or weeks after the mites are dead. In addition, overuse of the medication should be avoided because of neurologic and other sequelae.

Pediculosis Pubis. Pubic lice *(Phthirus pubis)* are also common in teenagers. The lice are spread by close contact, and are often noted with other STDs (Fig. 4-5).

Symptoms and Signs. This condition should be considered when there is intense pruritus in hairy parts of the body, especially the genitals.

Diagnostic Procedures. Careful examination may demonstrate nits (ova) connected by cement-like material to hair shafts (Fig. 4-5) and maculae caeruleae (sky-blue spots), evanescent blue maculae on the trunk or thighs, which may represent blood pigment or excretion. Severe pruritus can occur because of a secondary allergic sensitization and excoriation with pyodermas due to scratching.

Treatment. Pediculosis pubis is treated with 1% lindane, 25% benzyl benzoate lotion, or DDT powder. Pyrethrins with piperonyl butoxide (such as Rid) and permethrin (Nix) are also useful. Family members should be treated if necessary, and clothes cleaned. The adolescent should be examined for other, concomitant sexually transmitted diseases.

Miscellaneous. Tables 4-10, 4-11, and 4-12 list disorders that can affect the vulva. It should be noted that Reiter's syndrome (a sexually transmitted disorder usually diagnosed in males with arthritis, urethritis, conjunctivitis, and HLA-B27 tissue-typing antigen) is infrequently observed in females. In these cases, vaginal and cervical discharge, vulvar erosions, or erythema nodosum have been reported.

When vulvar itching is a symptom, the term "pruritus vulvae" is used. As listed in Table 4-13, this condition may be due to many disorders. A related condition is pruritus ani, which may appear as or cause pruritus vulvae.

Because of the large numbers of STDs and pregnancy in teenagers, the practitioner inevitably will see both of these conditions in the same pa-

Fig. 4-5. Phthirus pubis infestation with egg (magnified view).

tient. Indeed, certain STDs (monilial vaginitis, condyloma acuminatum, and possibly gonococcal arthritis) may develop or worsen during pregnancy. Treatment must be tempered with awareness of which medications are contraindicated in pregnancy and which may be safe. Physicians must constantly review the safety of any medication given to the pregnant individual.

Finally, other lesions, including true neoplasms, of the lower genital tract in adolescent girls are rare. However, lichen sclerosis et atrophicus, leukoplakia, hidradenoma, vulvar sarcomas or carcinomas, DES-induced vaginal adenosis, or DES-induced vaginal or clear-cell adenocarcinoma, sarcoma botryoides, and other lesions are occasionally seen in teenage girls. Excellent reviews are provided by Underwood and Kreutner et al., as well as by Carlson. If the patient's mother has a history of DES use, if atrophic changes or unusual lesions of the lower genital tract are noted, or if the more common causes of vulvovaginitis presented in this discussion are refractory to standard treatment, referral to a gynecologist or dermatologist is indicated. Also, the clinician must constantly be aware of the ever-expanding range of STDs noted in sexually active individuals. Recent interest in AIDS is a clear example of this principle (see the section on AIDS).

Table 4-13. Pruritus Vulvae.

A. Systemic Causes
  1. Diabetes mellitus
  2. Seborrheic dermatitis
  3. Part of systemic drug reaction
  4. Lichen planus
  5. Leukemia
  6. Psoriasis
  7. Disorders with jaundice
  8. Rhus dermatitis
  9. Severe anemia
 10. Avitaminosis A
 11. Psychosomatic pruritus vulvae
B. Local Causes
  1. Infections
    a. Cutaneous candidiasis (Diabetic vulvitis)
    b. Pediculosis pubis
    c. *Sarcoptes scabiei*
    d. Tinea cruris (*Epidermophyton floccosum; Trichophyton mentagrophytes; Trichophyton rubrum*)
    e. *Enterobius vermicularis*
    f. Other: flea, tick, mosquito, bed bug, chigger
  2. Contact vulvovaginitis
  3. Dermatitis medicamentosa
  4. Neurodermatitis
  5. Pruritus ani
  6. Lichen sclerosis et atrophica
  7. Vulvar dystrophies
  8. Carcinoma-in-situ
  9. Fox-Fordyce disease
 10. Atrophic vulvovaginitis
 11. Others

Miscellaneous Causes of Vulvovaginitis

Foreign Body Vaginitis. Objects left in the vagina can induce vaginal discharge in infants, children, adolescents, and adults. This is not a rare cause of leukorrhea in mentally subnormal individuals. Although a forgotten tampon is probably most common, any number of objects can be seen: contraceptive sponges, paper, tissue paper, bits of clothing, marbles, etc. Eventually, an intensely malodorous leukorrhea develops, which can be described as bloody, purulent, or mucopurulent. Variable symptoms arise, including dyspareunia, pruritis vulvae, and backache. Inflammation and infection of the bladder, urethra, and Skene's glands can occur. Recurrent cystitis has been described. A Gram's stain of the discharge reveals numerous polymorphonuclear leukocytes. General vaginal culture identifies various gram-positive and -negative bacteria, indicating a mixed infection. Treatment consists of proper diagnosis, foreign-body removal, and appropriate hygienic measures.

Allergic or Contact Vaginitis. Erythema of the vulvovaginal tissues with pruritus, edema, pain, and vaginal discharge may develop after contact with a local allergen. These symptoms can be induced by various chemicals, including chemical douches, perfumes, sanitary napkins (especially with "deodorant" agents added), feminine deodorant sprays, bubble bath soaps, various cleaning agents, contraceptive foams (or similar agents), and many others. Treatment consists of proper diagnosis, removal of the inciting chemical, and sometimes application of hydrocortisone or antihistamine cream or ointment to the inflamed vulvar tissues. The patient can be advised to avoid the use of tight nylon undergarments, which can worsen the situation. Also, an allergic type of vaginitis has been linked to hayfever.

Familial Allergic Seminal Vulvovaginitis. An unusual cause of allergic or contact vaginitis has been reported in which the above symptoms develop in females after contact with sperm. The use of a condom by the male partner may be sufficient treatment, and supportive treatment measures described under the section on contact vaginitis usually help.

Salivary Vulvitis. Oral-genital sexual contact may induce vulvar inflammation with erythema and pain. A thorough sexual history from the patient will reveal this diagnosis, and it can be suspected if one sees a patient with nonspecific vulvar inflammation without overt vaginitis and sometimes with a vaginal culture suggesting infection with *Haemophilus influenzae* or beta hemolytic streptococcus. Abstaining from this form of sexual contact for a short time is usually sufficient treatment.

Psychosomatic Vulvovaginitis. This diagnosis can be suspected in individuals with a chronic history of vague, nonspecific vulvovaginal symptoms, including pruritus, burning, pain, discharge, and others. A gynecologic disorder is not identified and numerous specialists are often consulted. There is no positive response to different therapeutic suggestions. Further evaluation reveals that the patient evidences behavioral difficulties, including concerns about her female sexuality. Treatment for the behavioral concerns usually resolves the gynecologic complaints. Although reported in adult females, this condition is not well described in adolescents.

PELVIC INFLAMMATORY DISEASE

A very significant sexually transmitted disease confronting the American adolescent of the 1990s is pelvic inflammatory disease (PID). Current estimates identify 300,000 to 400,000 annual cases of adolescent PID in the United States. Because PID is not a reportable disorder, all statistics are estimates—probably conservative ones at that. Most of the reported cases involve patients under age 25; PID is also noted in nulliparous women. Because infertility is a common sequela to inadequately treated PID, numbers such as those cited above reveal the enormous negative impact this disorder can have on the adolescent population. PID literally translates into millions of patient visits and billions of health care dollars each year when the general population is considered.

The literature of the 1970s presented evidence that millions of American teenagers were sexually active, usually with minimal knowledge of contraception and venereal disease. Thus, it is not surprising to see so many cases of PID, especially when realizing that few teenagers have ever heard of PID. It is a disorder that clinicians who deal with teenagers will see if a strong index of suspicion is developed. Early, aggressive treatment of the youth with PID will certainly prevent enormous potential morbidity. As clinicians, we must teach our youthful patients about this potentially devastating disorder, and we must also teach ourselves as to its proper diagnosis and treatment.

PID can be associated with various factors, including surgery, malignancy, instrumentation, pregnancy, and sexually transmitted diseases. A review of the literature on PID can sometimes become confusing when all these factors are mixed together. This section focuses on a discussion of this disorder as it concerns sexually transmitted diseases in the adolescent female; awareness of this orientation is important to the reader as further thoughts on this important disease are presented.

Pathophysiology. PID refers to an infection of the lower genital tract, specifically the fallopian tubes and uterus. Numerous microorganisms can be found at various stages of this infection. Table 4-14 lists some of the bacteria implicated during different times in this complex disease. Classic theory states that most cases are initiated by *Chlamydia trachomatis* or *Neisseria gonorrhoeae*. A much smaller number are started by *Mycoplasma hominis,* while there are unusual case reports identifying *Neisseria meningitidis* and even Group A beta hemolytic streptococcus. Studies vary, reporting from 30 to 80% of cases initiated by *N. gonorrhoeae*. In most reviews, *Chlamydia trachomatis* is the other major precipitant of PID development. This primary invasion (with *Neisseria gonorrhoeae* or *Chlamydia trachomatis*) causes fallopian tube injury and often results in eventual mixed bacterial infection—especially the coliform bacteria and anaerobic microbes (specifically *Bacteroides fragilis*). It is this "super infection" that can cause difficulty in effective treatment and lead to a high rate of complications.

It is proper to speak of three main types of adolescent PID: gonococcal, chlamydial, and polymicrobial. The longer the interval from initial monomicrobial infection, the more likely that it is polymicrobial. Because teenagers often delay treatment (out of fear of the physician or parents, or because of ignorance of the disease), they may, unfortunately, present with this type of PID. *Actinomyces israelii* may be seen, especially if an intrauterine device is present when the PID develops. The role of viruses (such as herpes simplex or cytomegalovirus) remains unproven. Recent literature suggests that autoimmune phenomena may be present, but more studies are necessary to clarify the possibility that PID may be in part an immunologic disorder in some individuals.

Trying to decide which agents are responsible for PID symptoms can be difficult. When you compare your experiences with those of others, more difficulties arise. Many factors influence the specific culture results. For example, different culture sites can be used—rectum, cervix, fallopian tubes, or peritoneum—sometimes with different results. The timing of each culture can be important in identifying a monomicrobial or polymicrobial infection. The gonococcal toxin may cause injury even without evidence of a major genital gonococcal invasion. The mere presence of an agent in the cervix does not mean that PID is inevitable. For example, classic studies suggest 10 to 20% of cervical gonorrhea eventually becomes PID. Parallel figures for chlamydia are unknown. The presence of the menstrual period may be important, since over two thirds of gonococcal PID occurs within 7 days of menstruation. Even coitus can be a factor, since recent evidence suggests that sperm can carry bacteria to the fallopian tube. Other factors that play a role in the production of PID include the exact type of bacteria (such as auxotype or colony phenotype in *Neisseria gonorrhoeae*), antimicrobial susceptibility of the involved microbe(s), local (genital) antibody activity, serum bactericidal activity, and others.

Various studies have identified more general risk factors for PID. The teenager is at special risk for PID, since some youth change sex partners frequently, often without knowledge of their partner's current or past sex practices. A young age combined with multiple sex partners can lead to high risks for PID. A history of previous PID is also important; for example,

Table 4-14. Bacterial Agents of Pelvic Inflammatory Disease.

Chlamydia trachomatis
Neisseria gonorrhoeae
Mycoplasma hominis
Group A beta-hemolytic *Streptococcus*
Neisseria meningitidis
Coliform bacteria: *Enterobacteriaceae*
Bacteroides fragilis
Streptococcus faecalis
Other anaerobic microbes
Other aerobic microbes

20% of those with gonococcal PID have had at least one additional episode. Youth with an intrauterine device run additional risks for severe PID episodes since the IUD dramatically changes endometrial defense mechanisms. A nidus infection may develop with pain and bleeding. Submucosal microabscesses may occur with subsequent endometritis, as well as eventual severe fallopian tube infection and injury. Adolescents using an IUD have a three- to nine-fold increase in risk of PID. Youth using oral contraceptives may have a greater risk for the development of chlamydial-induced PID and a reduced risk for gonococcal-induced PID. The pill can prevent the normal recession of cervical ectopy, thicken cervical mucus, and shorten menses. This seems to increase the risk of cervical infection with *Chlamydia trachomatis* and resultant PID.

Interestingly, PID is unusual during pregnancy, probably because of the anatomic protection pregnancy affords. Also, recent studies note that individuals using oral contraceptives have a significantly lower incidence of gonococcal-induced PID and clinically less severe PID episodes than those not taking oral contraceptives. The reasons for this important observation are unclear; however, this observation should be remembered when counseling sexually active youth who are at risk for pregnancy as well as PID.

Diagnosis. Diagnosing PID is usually not an easy task and presents a considerable challenge to the clinician. One must approach the evaluation of abdominal pain in the sexually active adolescent female with much caution and respect. In our view, *any* sexually active adolescent with lower abdominal pain has PID until a careful clinical assessment clearly reveals another explanation. Cervical and uterine tenderness with motion and adnexal tenderness are noted with PID. Only 20% of patients present with "classic" PID findings: fever, leukorrhea, adnexal tenderness, leukocytosis, and elevated erythrocyte sedimentation rate.

Most individuals have abdominal (adnexal) tenderness, but only half present with abnormal vaginal discharge. Adnexal enlargement is noted in only 25%, whereas the classic tubo-ovarian abscess is described in only 10% of cases. Episodes of "painless" PID are well described when *C. trachomatis* is the responsible bacterial agent. Perhaps 10% of *C. trachomatis*-induced PID cases may have minimal abdominal and adnexal tenderness. Laparoscopy is thus advocated by many as a way of identifying PID—especially atypical types.

The differential diagnosis of PID is considerable (Table 4-15). Various medical, as well as surgical, causes of abdominal pain must be carefully considered. One must not conclude that serious causes of abdominal pain are only revealed to the emergency department. Astute clinicians can find PID in office practice, especially early cases in which treatment is easier and more effective. A careful history and a physical examination (with pelvic evaluation) are vital to making the correct diagnosis. Lower abdominal pain (especially adnexal tenderness) is highly suggestive. But remember that variable symptoms are classic for PID.

A negative serum pregnancy test is an important tool, often screening out an ectopic pregnancy. Cultures can be negative, and routine blood tests (such as white blood counts or erythrocyte sedimentation rate) can be normal or elevated. Recent studies allege "increased" white blood counts in vaginal wet smears or peritoneal fluid, increased inflammatory plasma proteins (such as C-reactive protein or antichymotrypsin), or even various ratios of genital isoamylases in peritoneal fluid versus the serum. Unfortunately, these tests do not have current general clinical usefulness for the diagnosis of PID. Ultrasonography or culdocentesis may be helpful in some cases.

Current literature emphasizes the importance of laparoscopy, since the wrong diagnosis can be made if one decides that PID is present after only a history is taken and a physical examination is performed. One need only review the classic work of Jacobson and Westrom to appreciate this fact. Their well-known studies note that even experts who base their diagnosis of PID on general clinical grounds (such as history and physical examination) will correctly identify salpingitis in only 65% of the cases when laparoscopy is used to confirm the correct diagnosis. These studies note that other diagnoses are present in 12%, and a normal pelvis is present in 23%. These studies on mainly adult women remind us to diagnose PID with great care in adolescent patients. Laparoscopy is an excellent tool, especially in cases that are initially confusing or in which rapid response to appropriate treatment plans does not occur. We do not recommend that laparoscopy be used in every case of suspected PID. The well-trained individual can also use the laparoscope as an excellent means to obtain cultures directly from the fallopian tube. However, laparoscopy will not always correctly diagnose PID, especially with very early cases. Current studies indicate that laparoscopy can be used to correctly diagnose PID in about 95% of cases.

It should be remembered that early diagnosis with aggressive treatment is the key to reducing the many potential sequelae of PID. These complications include infertility, ectopic pregnancy, Fitz-Hugh-Curtis syndrome, tubo-ovarian abscess, chronic abdominal pain complex, dysmenorrhea, dysfunctional uterine bleeding, and others. The studies of Westrom contend that one severe episode of gonococcal PID can cause bilateral tubal occlusion in 13% of cases. If there are two such episodes in one individual, she has a 35% chance of becoming sterile; if there are

Table 4-15. Differential Diagnosis of Pelvic Inflammatory Disease.

Appendicitis
Endometriosis
Ectopic pregnancy
Ovarian cyst (with or without torsion or rupture)
Pyelonephritis
Mesenteric lymphadenitis
Inflammatory bowel disease
Diabetic ketoacidosis
Henoch-Schönlein syndrome
Hemolytic-uremic syndrome
Gastroenteritis (due to *Yersinia enterocolitica* or Campylobacter fetus)
Acute intermittent porphyria
Other

three or more episodes, this figure rises to an astonishing 75%. If PID is due to chlamydia or polymicrobial etiology, these figures are thought to be even higher. During the 1970s, an estimated 100,000 cases of PID-induced infertility occurred each year—one million cases during the entire decade. Thus, the clinician must strongly suspect PID when presented with a sexually active teenager who complains of lower abdominal pain.

Treatment. A wide variety of antibiotics and therapy regimens are recommended to treat PID. Because it is difficult to know which microorganisms are responsible at a given time in a specific patient, clinical judgment is often required. Close observation is recommended, and the ability to switch to a new treatment regimen is often important. Because some teenagers do not take oral medications well, and because of the serious nature of PID sequelae, we recommend early hospitalization of most youth with PID for vigorous parenteral treatment, even though most adults with PID need not be hospitalized. Hospitalization is clearly warranted if an oral medication plan has already failed, the patient has been ill for several days, peritoneal signs are noted, the diagnosis is unclear, enlarged adnexa develop, or pregnancy occurs with PID.

If uncomplicated gonococcal or chlamydial cervicitis is diagnosed, various treatment plans have been suggested (Table 4-16). If broader antibiotic coverage is needed, metronidazole (500 to 750 mg, 3 times daily) can be combined with doxycycline (100 mg, twice daily) or tetracycline (500 mg, 4 times daily), all administered orally. These three medications should not be given to pregnant teenagers. Metronidazole is especially useful for its antianaerobic coverage (especially against *Bacteroides fragilis*). Metronidazole has proven to be a safe drug for youth, but patients should know that they need to abstain from alcohol while taking it because of its well-known disulfiram effect.

A wide variety of intravenous antibiotic therapy plans are available (Table 4-17). The point is that PID, which continues for several days, may be due to multiple bacteria—aerobic and anaerobic. Thus, appropriate broad-spectrum antibiotic therapy is necessary to limit the PID sequelae. We recommend early, aggressive treatment for teenagers. Intravenous treatment plans are used until there is clinical improvement; then oral medications can be given, for a total of 10 to 14 days of antibiotics. If there is a question regarding the diagnosis or if the treatment plans are not successful, a laparoscopy should be performed to more accurately identify the exact pathology. This topic is an important one and should not be lightly dismissed by the clinician who deals with teenagers. PID is one of the most significant sexually transmitted diseases of the past generation for adolescent females.

MISCELLANEOUS GYNECOLOGIC TOPICS
Fitz-Hugh—Curtis Syndrome

The Fitz-Hugh-Curtis syndrome (perihepatitis) is due to inflammation of the liver capsule after genital infection with *Neisseria gonorrhoeae* or *Chlamydia trachomatis*. There may or may not be symptomatic genital infection at the time the perihepatitis appears.

Table 4-16. Treatment of Uncomplicated Gonococcal and Chlamydial Cervicitis.

1. Tetracycline 500 mg QID for 7 days
2. Doxycycline 100 mg BID for 7 days
3. Erythromycin 500 mg BID for 7 days

Symptoms and Signs. Acute, severe, knife-like, right upper quadrant pain develops with or without right shoulder pain, right costal margin friction rub, and abdominal rebound or rigidity. Fever, nausea, emesis, hiccups, pleurisy, and pleuritic chest pain may also occur. The erythrocyte sedimentation rate is elevated; a brief elevation of the liver enzymes and amylase often occurs. A laparoscopy will usually demonstrate the perihepatic inflammation and presence of adhesions between the anterior abdominal wall and the liver. Most acute cases will have a positive cervical culture for gonorrhea or chlamydia.

Diagnostic Procedures. The differential diagnosis includes other sources of right upper quadrant pathology, including cholecystitis, pancreatitis, peptic ulcer disease, hepatitis, pyelonephritis, pleurisy (with or without pneumonia), pulmonary embolism, pleurodynia, herpes zoster, and others. A rapid response to antibiotics is usually noted. Some individuals develop chronic pain due to the adhesions. Correct diagnosis is based on a high index of suspicion in a sexually active female with right upper quadrant pain and chlamydial or gonococcal infection.

Treatment. The pain is diminished with antibiotics (Tables 4-16, 4-17). Adhesions require lysing for relief of pain via laparoscopy.

Cervical Intraepithelial Neoplasia

Recent studies note that sexually active youth are at risk of developing premalignant cervical dysplasia, termed cervical intraepithelial neoplasia, or CIN. Such lesions are often asymptomatic and are initially detected with a Pap smear. Cytologic evaluation allows use of a grading system, which consists of grade I, mild dysplasia; grade II, moderate dysplasia; grade III, severe dysplasia; and grade IV, carcinoma in situ. The malignant potential of CIN is unknown, but all grades can progress into higher levels of dysplasia at unpredictable times. Grades I and II can also spontaneously resolve. Youth with CIN are at risk for invasive cervical cancer later in adulthood. Sadeghi, in an analysis of a mass screening program involving

Table 4-17. Intravenous Anti-PID Antibiotic Therapy Plans.

1. Cefoxitin (2 g, four times daily) with doxycycline (100 mg, twice daily) until improvement is seen; for at least 4 days; then doxycycline (100 mg twice daily) orally to complete a 10- to 14-day course.
2. Doxycycline (100 mg, twice daily) with metronidazole (1 g, twice daily) until improvement is seen; for at least 4 days; then oral doses of these same antibiotics to complete a 10- to 14-day course.
3. Clindamycin (600 mg, four times daily) with gentamicin (2 mg/kg once, followed by a dose of 1.5 mg/kg three times daily) until improvement is seen; followed by clindamycin (450 mg, four times daily) orally to complete a 10- to 14-day course.
4. Others (such as mezlocillin, or penicillin-G and tobramycin)

796,337 women in 1981 (which included 194,069 youth), noted that the prevalence of dysplasia was 1.7% in the 15- to 19-year-old age group and 2.8% in the 20- to 29-year-old age group. The prevalence of carcinoma in situ (CIS) in 15- to 19-year-olds was 0.26%; no cases of invasive carcinoma were noted in this age cohort. The prevalence of grade III (CIN) and grade IV (CIS) was 0.33% in the 20- to 29-year-old age group, whereas invasive cervical carcinoma was observed in nine of the 20- to 22-year-old females.

Symptoms and Signs. Sexually active youth appear to be at considerable risk for CIN. Various factors increase this risk, including early coital activity (sexarche), multiple sex partners, poor hygiene, exposure to STDs, impaired immunity, and others. Human papillomavirus (types 16 and 18) and herpes simplex virus have specifically been linked to CIN. The increased risk for CIN noted in youth may be due to the active physiological changes occurring during normal adolescence. At puberty, the junction of squamous and columnar epithelial cells is on the exocervix and is exposed to the vagina. At the squamocolumnar epithelial zone, the columnar cells are transformed to squamous epithelial cells. The cells in this zone (T zone) are immature and possibly more susceptible to carcinogens than the other cells. Changes in this zone occur most dramatically in utero, at menarche, and during the first pregnancy. This T zone, or transition zone, moves into the endocervix and up the cervical canal as the female matures, and thus becomes less exposed to the vagina. Therefore, teenagers who start sexual activity at an early age and are exposed to STDs do so at an age when the T zone is undergoing active metaplasia and is more openly exposed to the vagina, and thus may have an increased susceptibility to dysplasia, which can lead to CIS and eventually invasive cervical carcinoma.

Exposure to mycoplasma, syphilis, *Trichomonas,* and cytomegalovirus may also prove to be risk factors for the development of CIN and CIS. Further study is needed in this regard. Whether or not there are "male" factors, such as sperm, that increase the risk is unclear. Early detection of CIN is made with frequent Pap smears. The prevalence of abnormal Pap smears and CIN in sexually active 15- to 19-year olds is about 2%. According to DiSaia and Creasman, transition time of normal cervical cytology of mild or moderate dysplasia can average 1.62 years; from normal to moderate or severe dysplasia, 2.2 years; and from normal to CIS, 4.5 years.

Diagnostic Procedures. Current recommendations are to perform yearly Pap smears on sexually active youth. If an abnormal Pap smear is found, careful evaluation is necessary. The use of a cervigram, in addition to the Pap smear, may improve chances of early identification of CIN. Referral to appropriate gynecologic consultants is then recommended. If mild cervical atypia is reported by the cytologic laboratory, check for the presence of STDs and treat if found. After treatment, repeat the Pap smear in 3 months. If atypia again is noted, colposcopy is performed. If the cytologic evaluation reveals CIN at any time, colposcopy is immediately recommended to give the examiner a magnified view of the epithelial and vascular pattern of the cervical, as well as vaginal, area. Biopsy and endocervical curettage can then be performed. If the entire abnormal area can be seen and invasive carcinoma ruled out, cryosurgery or laser surgery of the abnormal area is recommended; a 90% success rate has been reported. If these lesions extend into the cervical canal and invasive disease cannot be ruled out, cervical conization is performed. This latter procedure should not be done in youth unless clearly necessary, since it can lead to later pregnancy complications.

Treatment. Vaginal intraepithelial lesions are treated with cryosurgery or laser surgery in most cases. Multiple vaginal diseases may respond to topical application of 5-fluorouracil. Invasive disease is treated according to stage and usually requires a hysterectomy as well as extensive surgical resection. Thus, primary care physicians should perform yearly Pap smears on sexually active youth and carefully treat any observed STD. Referral to appropriate gynecologic consultants is recommended for abnormal Pap smears, particularly if CIN is reported. Careful followup of such patients is important. Particular attention is necessary for individuals with herpes simplex virus and human papillomavirus (types 16 and 18) infection. Recent literature strongly implicates HPV and CIN/cervical cancer, and more evidence of this link is expected in the future. Educating youth to such risks is important.

Diethylstilbestrol Exposure in Utero

Diethylstilbestrol (DES) is a nonsteroidal estrogen that was synthesized in 1938 and suggested in 1946 as a way to both prevent and treat abortion and various pregnancy complications. In 1970, Herbst and Scully observed an unusually high number of vaginal adenocarcinoma cases in young women between ages 15 and 22; in 1971, an association of these cases with in-utero DES exposure was reported. Currently, it is estimated that between the latter part of the 1940s and 1971 (when the Food and Drug Administration banned the prescription of DES during pregnancy), 2 to 3 million pregnant women were given DES, resulting in as many as 1.5 million female offspring with in-utero exposure to this drug. In 1971, a registry was established, which through 1985 had studied 497 cases of clear-cell adenocarcinoma of the vagina and cervix; 63% of the 466 with accessible maternal histories had in-utero DES exposure. It is currently estimated that the risk of clear-cell adenocarcinoma in such individuals under age 24 is 0.14 to 1.4 per 1000. This condition has been diagnosed in females between ages 7 and 33, with 95% of cases in those 14 years of age or over and with a mean age of 19 at diagnosis. Table 4-18 lists various abnormalities noted in such DES-exposed individuals. The 5-year survival rate with stage I adenocacinoma is 90%; with clear-cell adenocarcinoma, 80%.

Individuals with a history of in-utero DES exposure should be thoroughly examined once menarche occurs or by age 14, whichever is sooner. An examination should be done immediately if vaginal bleeding or unusual discharge starts before this. Examination includes a full pelvic examination, including application of Lugol's solution and colposcopy. Biopsy of areas that do not stain with the iodine solution or appear suspicious on colposcopy will help define the pathologic nature as well as what type of treatment and followup are necessary. Evaluation of prepubertal individuals does not include application of Lugol's solution, since their immature tissue does not stain the abnormal areas. Patients with definitive or possible in-utero DES exposure should be referred to gynecologic consultants well versed in the evaluation required. Fortunately, the number of DES cases appears to be declining. The peak years of DES exposure were between 1946 and 1953. These exposed individuals are now between 36 and 43 years of age. An annual examination of individuals at risk who have had previously normal examinations is still recommended.

Toxic Shock Syndrome

Toxic Shock Syndrome (TSS) has been well described since Todd's classic article in 1978, which reported on seven children with a scarlet-fever-like illness in probable association with *Staphylococcus aureus* infection. Since then, numerous cases of TSS have been reported, with a peak incidence in 1980. Approximately 80 to 90% of cases are noted in menstruating women; the incidence is 5 to 10 cases per 100,000 menstruating women. Table 4-19 outlines a case definition for toxic shock syndrome. High-risk factors for the development of TSS include infection with a TSS toxin producing *S. aureus* strain, absence of antibody to this toxin, age under 35, and continuous use of superabsorbent tampons during menstruation. Another high-risk factor is nasal surgery that includes nasal packing. Moderate-risk factors include the regular use of normal-absorbing tampons during menses, alternating the use of tampons with pads, and the use of the contraceptive vaginal sponges. Isolated reports of TSS have been reported with the diaphragm, IUD, early postpartum period, and various surgical wound infections. TSS in males and females has been reported following a wide variety of surgical procedures, pre-

---

Table 4-18. Abnormalities Noted in DES-Exposed Individuals.

1. Cervical ectropion
2. Vaginal adenosis
3. Cervical/vaginal adenocarcinoma
4. Vaginal structural abnormalities: incomplete vaginal septum, absence of fornix, and vaginal ridges
5. Cervical structural abnormalities: collars (complete and incomplete), hoods, protuberance (cocks's combs), pseudopolyps, hypoplasia, and endocervical os stenosis
6. Extended transformation zone (T-zone)—studies have revealed a variable CIN incidence in these patients (0 to 18%)
7. Uterine structural abnormalities: T-shaped uterine, hypoplasia, constriction bands, and others
8. Various fallopian tube defects
9. Oligomenorrhea studies reveal conflicting results
10. Possible reduced fertility rate
11. Various pregnancy complications (ectopic pregnancy, premature birth, stillborn)
12. Others

sumably related to *S. aureus* wound infections. A few studies have suggested that the birth control pill may offer protection.

Symptoms and Signs. Most patients with TSS develop an abrupt onset of fever, vomiting, myalgia, lightheadedness, and rash. The TSS rash is a sunburn-like macular erythema, which often develops on the trunk and thighs but can be variable and transient. Hyperemia can also be seen in the conjunctiva, mouth, pharynx, and vagina. In 7 to 10 days, desquamation of the involved skin occurs. A wide variety of symptoms can then be seen, including headache, diarrhea, cough, edema, confusion, syncope, stiff neck, abdominal pain, arthralgia, and others. In a small number of patients, shortness of breath and arthritis can develop. The arthritis, if present, usually involves the small joints of hands and feet, but can also involve the knee, ankle, wrist, and others. Physical examination of these patients usually demonstrates macular rash, hypotension, fever, muscle aches, and eventually desquamation of the involved skin. Some patients present in extreme prostration with severe hypotension and even shock. Many TSS patients have evidence of conjunctivitis, pharyngitis, strawberry tongue, nonpitting edema, and vaginitis.

A pelvic examination may reveal the vaginal erythema with tenderness, along with a variable, purulent, malodorous cervical discharge sometimes in association with adnexal tenderness. Multiple punctate pustules or ulcers on the genital tissues may also occur. A Gram's stain of the leukorrhea reveals clusters of gram-positive cocci in association with polymorphonuclear leukocytes, and a culture reveals *S. aureus*.

In many cases, a youth will present to the clinician with onset of vomiting, irritability, muscle aches, and rash. There may be a distinctive gy-

---

Table 4-19. Case Definition for TSS.

Fever: temperature $\geq$ 38.9°C (102°F)
Rash: diffuse macular erythroderma
Desquamation: 1-2 wk after onset of illness, particularly of palms and soles
Hypotension: systolic BP $\leq$ 90 mm Hg for adults or below fifth percentile by age for
   children below 16 yr of age, or orthostatic drop in diastolic BP $\geq$ 15 mm Hg from
   lying to sitting, or orthostatic syncope, or orthostatic dizziness
Multisystem involvement—three or more of the following:
   GI: vomiting or diarrhea at onset of illness
   Muscular: severe myalgia or CPK level at least twice the upper limit of normal for
     laboratory
   Mucous membrane: vaginal, oropharyngeal, or conjunctival hyperemia
   Renal: BUN or creatinine at least twice the upper limit of normal for laboratory or
     urinary sediment with pyuria ($\geq$ 5 leukocytes per HPF) in the absence of urinary
     tract infection
   Hepatic: total bilirubin. SGOT or SGPT at least twice the upper limit of normal for
     laboratory
   Hematologic: platelets $\leq$ 100,000/cu mm
   CNS: disorientation or alterations in consciousness without focal neurologic signs
     when fever and hypotension are absent
Negative results on the following tests, if obtained:
   Blood, throat, or cerebrospinal fluid cultures (blood culture may be positive for *S.
     aureus*)
   Rise in titer to Rocky Mountain spotted fever, leptospirosis, or rubeola

necologic history, and a pelvic exam, as described, often reveals vaginal erythema with leukorrhea and a variety of other gynecologic symptoms. The laboratory results are also variable and indicate the multisystem involvement so characteristic of TSS. Most TSS patients have an elevated white blood count (with an increase in polymorphonuclear leukocytes), elevated liver function tests (SGOT, SGPT, alkaline phosphatase, and bilirubin), hyponatremia, hypocalcemia, hypophosphatemia, hypoalbuminemia, and others. Many will have an elevated blood urea nitrogen, elevated creatinine, increased phosphokinase, pyuria, proteinuria, hypokalema, hypomagnesemia, thrombocytopenia, and anemia, as well as an increased amylase and positive stool guaiacs, and others. Coagulation studies are usually normal to slightly prolonged; occasionally, however, disseminated intravasular coagulation may be in evidence. If the patient has not been given antibiotics, *S. aureus* can be cultured from the vagina (cervix) in patients with the menstrual-type TSS or cultured from the wounds of patients with postsurgical infections.

Diagnostic Procedures. The differential diagnosis list of TSS is long and reflective of its variable course and multisystem involvement. Such a list includes Kawasaki's disease, Stevens-Johnson syndrome, scarlet fever, numerous viral syndromes, gram-negative shock, and many others. The diagnosis should not be difficult in the common case of the tampon-using menstrual female with an abrupt onset of classic symptoms along with gynecologic symptoms (such as vaginal erythema and vaginal discharge) and a vaginal Gram's stain suggestive of staphylococcal overgrowth. The culture should confirm the diagnosis while identifying the strain and toxin.

Treatment. Treatment essentially remains supportive and involves early diagnosis, hydration, and (if still present) removal of the tampon, surgical packing, or other occlusive factors. Many clinicians use antistaphylococcal antibiotics (such as nafcillin or oxacillin), although their benefit in acute cases remains unproven. Some studies note that such antibiotic use reduces the incidence of recurrent TSS in menstruating women. The severity of the illness dictates whether oral or intravenous antibiotics are given. Most begin with intravenous antibiotics along with intravenous hydration. Although a wound infection is often irrigated, vaginal irrigation is not recommended because of concern over resultant toxin absorption or bacteremia. The use of immunoglobulin in an attempt to replace absent antibodies to the toxin (called TSS toxin) is unproven, as is the use of corticosteroids. Other treatment methods depend on the nature of the complications, whether disseminated intravascular coagulation, acute renal failure, adult respiratory distress syndrome, peripheral gangrene, bowel infarction, or others. Mortality rates of 2 to 4% are currently reported, in contrast with mortality rates of up to 10% in earlier studies.

Prevention of menstrual TSS can be accomplished, to some extent, by avoiding the use of superabsorbent tampons and by not alternating the use of regular tampons and pad (napkins) during menstruation. If the youth develops a "flu-like" illness during menstruation, immediate evaluation by the clinician is recommended. Attention to the other high-risk factors, as mentioned previously, may be helpful. Some evidence suggests that the use of antistaphylococcal antibiotics during acute TSS may reduce the chances of recurrent TSS, perhaps to as low as 5%. Identification of those at risk and those with absent antibody to the TSS toxin would also be helpful.

MALE GENITO-URINARY DISORDERS

A brief discussion of male genitourinary disorders is now provided. The most common manifestation of sexually transmitted disease in the male is urethritis, which is usually seen with a urethral discharge and dysuria. Urethritis is detected by the presence of bacteria (such as gram-negative diplococci) or five or more white blood cells in a urethral discharge. The most common bacterial causes are *Neisseria gonorrhoeae, Chlamydia trachomatis,* and *Ureaplasma urealyticum.* Current treatment recommendations for gonococcal urethritis include ceftriaxone (Rocephin), 125 to 250 mg IM once, and the acceptable alternatives, as follows: amoxicillin, 3 g orally (with oral probenecid, 1 g once) or spectinomycin, 2 g IM once (Table 4-5). Ceftriaxone is thought to be effective against incubating syphilis but not against *Chlamydia.* Rectal and pharyngeal gonorrhea can also be treated with ceftriaxone. Alternative treatment for rectal gonorrhea includes penicillin G procaine, 4.8 million units IM (with 1 g probenecid by mouth) or spectinomycin, 2 g IM. Alternatives to pharyngeal gonorrhea include penicillin G with probenecid (the same dose as for rectal gonorrhea) or trimethoprim-sulfamethoxazole, 9 tablets daily in one dose for 5 days. Treatment for gonorrhea should also include a regimen to cover *Chlamydia trachomatis* because of the frequent occurrence of both of these common sexually transmitted disease agents together (Table 4-16).

Current treatment recommendations for *C. trachomatis* urethritis include doxycycline (100 mg twice daily orally for 7 days), tetracycline (500 mg 4 times daily orally for 7 days) or erythromycin (500 mg 4 times daily orally for 7 days). Sulfamethoxazole (500 mg orally 4 times daily for 10 days) is an alternative treatment. The use of doxycycline, tetracycline, or erythromycin is also effective for proctitis due to *C. trachomatis.* Tetracycline or erythromycin is also effective against *Ureaplasma urealyticum* urethritis. Tetracycline-resistant *Neisseria gonorrhoeae* and *Ureaplasma urealyticum* strains have been reported. During pregnancy, ceftriaxone, spectinomycin, and erythromycin (not the estolate form, because of an increased risk for cholestatic hepatitis) are safe. Tetracyclines are not used in pregnancy because of potential adverse effects on fetal teeth and bones. Other less common causes of male urethritis include: *Candida albicans, Gardnerella vaginalis,* herpes simplex, *Staphylococcus saprophyticus, Escherichia coli,* and others.

Scrotal Disorders

A *hydrocele* is a cystic collection of clear or slightly yellow fluid within the tunica vaginalis or processus vaginalis. A hydrocele is usually a congenital lesion, detected during childhood. Occasionally, the lesion may be caused by scrotal trauma, epididymitis, or a testicular tumor. A hydrocele usually appears as a nontender, firm or tense intermittent scrotal swelling that transilluminates with a bright light. The testes on the affected side may not be palpated, and an inguinal hernia can also be present. The differential diagnosis includes a varicocele, a hernia, a hematocele (trauma-induced), and a testicular tumor. Aspiration is not done because of the possible complication of infection and bowel perforation. A hydrocelectomy is indicated for discomfort, for cosmetic reasons, and as an additional procedure when repairing a coexistent hernia.

The *varicocele,* found in approximately 15% of males between ages 15 and 25, consists of a tortuous dilatation of pampiniform scrotal veins. A primary varicocele (usually on the left) is caused by an imperfect venous valve system that permits retrograde blood flow. It is hypothesized that the primary varicocele is on the left because of the heightened gravitational effect of a longer left (versus right) spermatic vein. Secondary varicoceles (usually on the right) are due to overt mechanical blockage of a lower abdominal or pelvic vein; they may signify a renal or retroperitoneal tumor. Infertility is noted in some individuals with primary varicoceles, and recent studies note some semen and histologic abnormalities in the testes of those with varicoceles, even if asymptomatic. Examination of the standing youth reveals the classic varicocele appearance: dilated worm-like cords within the scrotal sac. A primary varicocele disappears when the patient is recumbent, whereas a secondary varicocele does not. Patients with an asymptomatic primary varicocele could be checked every several months; no specific treatment is usually recommended. Some experts have suggested obtaining a baseline semen analysis. Surgical ligation of a primary varicocele is recommended for oligospermia, severe physical discomfort, ipsilateral testicular volume loss, other semen abnormalities, and psychologic distress. If a secondary varicocele is suspected, a thorough search for the underlying etiology is mandatory.

Testicular torsion refers to spermatic cord twisting that leads to twisting and then blockage of the testicular-epididymal vasculature. This condition results from abnormal enclosure of the testicle by the tunica vaginalis and is a bilateral congenital defect. It is usually a sudden unilateral event, but the risk for an acute event with the other side does exist. The peak incidence is during adolescence. Testicular torsion usually appears with the sudden onset of scrotal pain with concomitant swelling and discoloration of the affected side, as well as possible nausea and vomiting. Although usually spontaneous, this condition may be precipitated by trauma or exercise. The examination demonstrates a tender testicle that lies in a high transverse scrotal location. The epididymis is also tender and lies in an antero-posterior position (as opposed to its normal posterolateral location). The Prehn sign is negative (that is, testicular elevation does not relieve the pain), the cremasteric reflex is absent, and there is no transillumination or urethral symptoms. A urinalysis is negative and a scrotal scan with Technetium-99m reveals vasculature perfusion; a scrotal ultrasound may be diagnostic.

The differential diagnosis of testicular torsion can vary significantly (Table 4-20). The usual differential diagnosis is to distinguish testicular torsion from epididymo-orchitis. Irreversible testicular cell necrosis can occur within a matter of hours; thus, surgical relief of the obstruction is necessary as soon as the diagnosis is suspected. The torsion is reduced and both the ipsilateral testicle and the contralateral testicle are fixed to prevent recurrence. Orchiopexy is also recommended for situations characterized by intermittent testicular torsion; in such cases there can be long intervals between the torsions, a horizontal or very mobile testicle, an anterior epididymis, or partial torsion-induced congestion of the spermatic cord. Torsion of the appendix testis (hydatid of Morgagni) or appendix epididymis can simulate acute testicular torsion as well, although the symptoms are usually milder. Surgical treatment is usually unnecessary.

Acute epididymitis or inflammation of the epididymis can be precipitated or induced by numerous factors (Table 4-21). Most cases in teenagers are caused by infections with sexually transmitted disease agents (*Neisseria gonorrhoeae* or *Chlamydia trachomatis*). Other "idiopathic" cases are often related to trauma or exercise-induced reflux of sterile urine through the vas deferens with resultant chemical irritation. Often, the testicle is inflamed, resulting in epididymo-orchitis. There is a sudden or gradual onset of epididymal (and sometimes testicular) pain with local swelling. The Prehn sign is positive (improvement or relief of the pain is noted with testicular-epididymal elevation), the cremasteric reflex is normal, "urologic" symptoms are present (such as dysuria, urethral discharge, fever, and toxicity), and a urinalysis reveals pyuria and bacteriuria; cultures of the urine or urethra may reveal the causative bacteria. A scrotal scan reveals increased vascularity. If the inflammation persists beyond 14 days despite treatment, consider a testicular tumor. Surgical exploration is necessary if a diagnosis of testicular torsion is not excluded from the differential diagnosis. Epididymitis due to chlamydia or gonorrheal infection should be treated with ceftriaxone (250 mg IM) followed by doxycycline (100 mg twice daily orally for 10 days). Amoxicillin (3 g orally once) with probenecid (1 g orally once), followed by doxycycline, can serve as an alternative treatment. Idiopathic epididymitis not due to infections will be improved with the use of anti-inflammatory agents and rest.

Testicular Neoplasm

Though uncommon in youth, testicular tumors are the most common solid neoplasms in the teenage population, representing approximately 1% of all cancer in this age cohort and noted in 1 out of every 10,000 young adult males. Thus, providing genital examinations and teaching the patient to perform testicular self-examinations is prudent. A firm, painless unilateral testicular mass arouses suspicion of a testicular neoplasm unless proven othewise. Two tumor types, which are both of germ-cell origin, predominate: seminoma (most common) and embryonal carcinoma. Other tumors—granulosa cell, Sertoli cell, interstitial—are infrequently encountered, sometimes in association with precocious puberty,

Table 4-20. Causes of Scrotal Pain and Swelling.

Epididymitis (epididymo-orchitis)
Testicular torsion
Varicocele
Hydrocele
Spermatocele
Testicular tumor
Torsion of appendix testis (hydatid of Morgagni)
Torsion of appendix epididymis
Orchitis
Hernia (strangulated)
Hematocele
Acute idiopathic scrotal edema
Henoch-Schönlein purpura (with spermatic cord vasculitis)
Generalized edema
Scrotal cellulitis
Fat necrosis

feminization, or persistent gynecomastia. Youth with undescended or ectopic testes are at greater risk for testicular tumors than the general population. A full "oncology" workup is required, and treatment includes radical orchiectomy, chemotherapy, and radiotherapy. Specific treatment depends upon the type and stage of the tumor.

There are other causes of genital lesions. For example, a spermatocele can appear as a small, typically nontender cyst that develops from epididymal tubules. Further evaluation shows positive transillumination and that the lesion contains a milky, sperm-filled fluid. Such a lesion may be confused with testicular torsion until surgical excision reveals its precise nature. Epididymal cysts have also been noted as a consequence to prenatal DES exposure, which can also lead to hypertrophic testes and semen abnormalities. Other genital abnormalities can be noted during examination. The reader is referred to the Hofmann-Greydanus textbook.

ACQUIRED IMMUNODEFICIENCY SYNDROME (AIDS) (HIV INFECTION)*

One of the most devastating and complex conditions to occur to date is the acquired immunodeficiency syndrome (AIDS or HIV infection). The general mortality rate has been approximately 80%. Most cases thus far have been in adolescents and young adults. The possibility of AIDS in this age group must be considered with certain malignancies (such as Kaposi's sarcoma) and any opportunistic infections (such as recurrent candidiasis or herpetic infections) and other chronic states in which recurrent sexual activity is noted. Homosexuals, drug abusers, hemophiliacs, and other individuals have been noted to have this condition.

A human retrovirus, variously called the human T-lymphotrophic retrovirus type III (HTLV-III), human immunodeficiency virus (HIV), lymphade-

---

* The literature on this most important STD of the twentieth century has exploded and is constantly changing. Only a brief comment is made in this book, though a number of references that provide much more information are provided.

Table 4-21. Precipitants or Causes of Epididymitis.

1. Urethritis	6. Respiratory tract infections
2. Urinary tract infection	7. Genitourinary tuberculosis
3. Prostatitis	8. Mumps
4. Testicular tumor	9. Other viral infections
5. Urologic surgery	10. Other bacterial infections (with a hematogenous spread)

nopathy-associated virus (LAV), and AIDS-associated retrovirus (ARV), has been isolated from peripheral blood lymphocytes, serum, semen, saliva, tears, breast milk, and cerebrospinal fluid of patients with AIDS, patients with less severe forms of the infection (called AIDS-related conditions, or ARC), and asymptomatic patients.

Retroviruses are RNA viruses that contain an enzyme (reverse transcriptase) that transcribes DNA from RNA, a process used in the replication of viruses. HTLV-III/LAV, like HTLV types I and II, primarily infects the thymic-derived lymphocytes that are responsible for cell-mediated immunity. HTLV-III/LAV preferentially infects the subset of T lymphocytes known as T-helper lymphocytes (T4), which augment the immune response.

The distribution of adolescent cases reported is as follows: New York 19 cases; California, 8 cases; Florida, 6 cases; Puerto Rico, 5 cases; and Pennsylvania, 4 cases. More than half of adolescent cases have occurred in blacks (41%) and Hispanics (16%). The number of cases increases with age.

The incubation period for AIDS averages about 2 years in adults and about 1 year in young children, but has been as long as 5 to 7 years. Mathematical models have estimated that the incubation period may average 5 years and last as long as 15 years.

Symptoms and Signs. Clinically, the spectrum of illness in persons infected ranges from no symptoms to clinical fever, night sweats, malaise, diarrhea, weight loss, generalized lymphadenopathy, and oral candidiasis. Symptomatic infections are generally chronic.

AIDS Testing. Several tests have been developed to detect antibodies to the human immunodeficiency virus (HIV). The screening tests licensed in the United States are based on the enzyme-linked immunosorbent assay (EIA). The test is used primarily to screen blood donors and individuals at risk for AIDS. The incidence of false-positive tests remains high, particularly for people with a low risk of infection. Consequently, an initially reactive EIA test is repeated in duplicate. If one of the duplicates is also reactive, the sera or plasma should be retested for HIV antibody with a supplemental assay, such as the Western blot. The sensitivity and specificity of currently available EIA tests are good; however, it should be remembered that these tests detect antibody to HIV, not antigen. Therefore, EIA may not detect HIV-infected individuals prior to seroconversion, which usually occurs within 2 to 5 months, or longer. The incidence of false-positive reactions is significant, particularly for individuals with a low risk of HIV infection. Consequently, repeatedly reactive results are validated by more specific tests, such as the Western blot test. A positive supplemental test is *not* diagnostic of AIDS or ARC, but is indicative of past exposure to HIV. Such an individual is presumed to be infected and capable of transmitting the disease.

The Western blot test identifies HIV antibodies to specific viral proteins. Only one Western blot test kit (DuPont) has been approved by the FDA, but many laboratories use unlicensed kits. The problem with the Western blot is that it is technically difficult, relatively expensive, and subjectively interpreted.

Less frequently used tests to confirm a positive EIA are the indirect immunofluorescence assay (IFA) and the radioimmunoprecipitation assay (RIPA). The IFA is comparable to the Western blot in sensitivity and specificity and can be performed in less than 2 hours, compared with 24 hours for the Western blot. Furthermore, IFA is not as technically sophisticated. Unfortunately, reagents, procedures, and performance vary according to laboratory, and the FDA has not licensed any IFAs.

RIPA is considered by some to be more sensitive and specific than Western blot or IFA. However, it is cumbersome and expensive. It also requires maintenance of infected cell lines and use of isotopes.

Treatment. Vaccines for HIV are not available; therefore, prevention of HIV infection is the key. Local and national education programs for patients and the health care industry are a must. Screening of all adolescents for HIV is not recommended, since the prevalence of the virus is rare overall. Counseling and education are important, and testing should be made available to those who want or need it from a medical standpoint.

The Public Health Service recommends that the following groups of individuals be counseled and tested for HIV antibody:

>   Persons who have sexually transmitted diseases
>   Intravenous drug abusers
>   Individuals who consider themselves at risk
>   Women of childbearing age identified as being at risk for AIDS
>   Couples considering marriage, depending on the prevalence of
>   HIV infections in the geographic area and other relevant con-
>   siderations
>   Persons undergoing medical evaluation or treatment
>   Persons admitted to hospitals
>   Persons in correctional systems
>   Prostitutes (male and female)
>   Hemophiliacs who have received factor concentrates since 1977
>   Males who have routine intercourse with other males

BIBLIOGRAPHY
AIDS

Amman AJ: The acquired immunodeficiency syndrome in infants and children. Ann Intern Med 1985;103:734-737.

Barbour SD: Acquired immunodeficiency syndrome of childhood. Ped Clin North Am 1987;34:247-268.

Barrett DJ: The clinician's guide to pediatric AIDS. Contemp Ped 1988;5(1):24-55.

Cunha BA: AIDS: a symposium. Postgrad Med 1988;83:135-194.

Curran JW, Morgan WM, Hardy AM, et al: The epidemiology of AIDS: current status and future prospects. Science 1985;229:1352-1357.

Eickhoff TC, Lewis CE, Calia FM, et al: The acquired immunodeficiency syndrome (AIDS) and infection of the human immunodeficiency virus (HIV). Health and Public Policy Committee, American College of Physicians and Infectious Diseases Society of America. Ann Intern Med 1988;108(3):460-469.

Fischl MA, Dickinson GM, Scott GB, et al: Evaluation of heterosexual partners, children, and household contacts of adults with AIDS. JAMA 1987;257:640-644.

Francis DP, Chin J: The prevention of acquired immunodeficiency syndrome in the United States: An objective strategy for medicine, public health, business, and the community. JAMA 1987;257:1357-1366.

Francis DP, Jaffee HW, Fultz PN, et al: The natural history of infection with the lymphadenopathy-associated virus human T-lymphotrophic virus type III. Ann Intern Med 1985; 103:719-722.

Garrison J, ed: Symposium on AIDS and adolescents: exploring the challenge. J Adol Health Care 1989;10(3 Suppl):1S-67S.

Helgerson SD, Petersen LR: The AIDS Education Study Group. Aids and secondary school students. Pediatrics 1988;81(3):350-355.

Ho DD, Pomerantz RJ, Kaplan JC: Pathogenesis of infection with human immunodeficiency virus. N Engl J Med 1987;317:278-286.

Jenness D: Scientists' roles in AIDS control. Science 1986;233:835.

Kaminski MA, Hartmann PM: HIV testing. Amer Fam Phys 1988;38:117-122.

Landesman SH, Minkoff H, Willoughby A: HIV disease in reproductive age women. JAMA 1989;261:1326-1327.

Macher AM: Acquired immunodeficiency syndrome. Am Fam Phys 1984;30:131-144.

Martin JL: The impact of AIDS on gay male sexual behavior patterns in New York City. Am J Publ Health 1987;77:578-581.

Marx J: The slow, insidious nature of the HTLVs. Science 1986;231:450-451.

Miles SA: Diagnosis and staging of HIV infections. Amer Fam Phys 1988;38:248-260.

Mok JQ, DeRossi A, Ades AE, et al. Infants born to mothers seropositive for human immunodeficiency virus. Lancet 1987;1:1164-1167.

Morgan WM, Curran JW: Acquired immunodeficiency syndrome: current and future trends. Public Health Rep 1986;101:459-465.

Nicholas SW, Sondheimer DL, Willoughby AD, et al: Human immunodeficiency virus infection in childhood, adolescence and pregnancy. Pediatrics 83:293-308, 1989.

Oleske JM: AIDS in children in 1988. Pediatr Ann 1988;17:319-365.

Osborn JE: AIDS: politics and science. N Engl J Med 1988;318(7):444-446.

Ostrow DG, Gayle TC: Policy guidelines for resolving psychosocial problems. Diagnosis 1987;6:82-90.

Padian N, Marquis L, Francis DP, et al: Male-to-female transmission of human immunodeficiency virus. JAMA 1987;258:788-790.

Pomerantz RJ, de la Monte SM, Donegan SP, et al: Human immunodeficiency virus (HIV) infection of the uterine cervix. Ann Intern Med 1988;108(3):321-327.

Quinn TC, Zacarias FR, St. John RK: AIDS in the Americas: an emerging public health crisis. N Engl J Med 1989;320:1005-1007.

Recommendations for prevention of HIV transmission in health-care settings. Morb Mort Week Rep 1987;36(2S):3S-18S.

Rogers MR, Lifson AR: Acquired immunodeficiency syndrome and HTLV-III/LAV infection. Semin Adolesc Med 1986;2:163-173.

Rogers MF: AIDS in children: a review of the clinical, epidemiologic and public health aspects. Pediatr Infect Dis 1985;4:230-236.

Sivak SL, Wormser GP: How common is HTLV-III infection in the United States? N Engl J Med 1985;313:1352.

Wofsy CB: Human immunodeficiency virus infection in women. JAMA 1987;257:2074-2076.

Behçet's Disease

Ammann AJ, Johnson A, Fyfe GA, et al: Behçet syndrome. J Pediatr 1985;107:41.

Jayakar VV: Behçet's syndrome. J Postgrad Med 1980;26:201-302.

O'Duffy JD: Summary of an international symposium on Behçet's Disease. J Rheumatol 1978;5:229-233.

Cervical Intraepithelial Neoplasia

Appenheimer AT: Screening and diagnosis of cancer in office practice. Prim Care 1987; 14:255-269.

Cates W, Rauh JL: Adolescents and sexually transmitted diseases: an expanding problem. J Adolesc Health Care 1985;6:257.

DiSaia PJ, Creasman WT: Clinical Gynecologic Oncology. St. Louis: C.V. Mosby, 1984:1-13.

DiSaia PJ: Conservative management of the patient with early gynecologic cancer. CA 1989;39:135-154.

Furguson JH: Positive cancer smears in teenage girls. JAMA 1961;178:365.

Lake P: Herpes simplex virus infections: Present scope and future prospects. Semin Adolesc Med 1986;2:113-120.

LaVecchia C, Franceschi S, Decarli A, et al: Sexual factors, venereal diseases and the risk of intraepithelial and invasive cervical neoplasia. Cancer 1984;58:935-641.

Nelson JH: Cervical intraepithelial neoplasia and early cervical carcinoma. CA 1989;39:157-178.

O'Reilly KR, Aral SO: Adolescence and sexual behavior. J Adolesc Health Care 1985;6:262.

Piver MS, Baker TR: Cervical cancer in the adolescent patient. Pediatr Ann 1986;15:536-541.

Planner RS & Hobbs JB: Intraepithelial and invasive neoplasia in association with HPV. J Repro Med 33:503-509, 1988.

Sadeghi SB, Hsieh EW, Gunn SW: Prevalence of cervical intraepithelial neoplasia in sexually active teenagers and young adults. Am J Obstet Gynecol 1984;148:726-729.

Sanz LE, Gurdian J: Human papillomavirus and cervical intraepithelial neoplasia. Semin Adolesc Med 1986;2:121-124.

Condylomata Acuminata

Eron LJ, Judson F, Tucker, et al: Interferon therapy for condylomata acuminata. N Engl J Med 1986;315:1059-1064.

Howley PM: On human papillomaviruses. N Engl J Med 1986;315:1089.

Kinghorn GR: Genital warts: incidence of associated genital infections. Br J Dermatol 1978;99:405-409.

Moore GE, Norton LW, Meiselbaught DM: Condyloma. A new epidemic. Arch Surg 1978;113:630-631.

Oriel JD: Genital warts. Sex Trans Dis 1981;8:326-329.

Powell CL: Condyloma acuminatum: Recent advances in development, carcinogenesis and treatment. Clin Obstet Gynecol 1978;21:1061-1079.

Sanz LE, Gurdian J: Human papillomavirus and cervical intraepithelial neoplasia as sexually transmitted diseases. Semin Adol Med 1986;2:121-124.

Diethylstilbestrol

Bibbo M, Gill WB, Azizi F, et al: Follow-up study of male and female offspring of DES-exposed mothers. Obstet Gynecol 1977;49:1-8.

Barones AB, Colton T, Gundersen J, et al: Fertility and outcome of pregnancy in women exposed in utero to diethylstilbestrol. N Engl J Med 1980;302:609-613.

Herbst AL, Scully RE: Adenocarcinoma of the vagina in adolescence: a report of 7 cases including 6 clear cell carcinomas (so called mesonephromas). Cancer 1970;25:745-757.

Herbst AL, Ulfelder H, Poskanzer DC: Adenocarcinoma of the vagina: Association of maternal stilbestrol therapy with tumor appearance in young women. N Engl J Med 1971;284:878-881.

Herbst AL, Hubby MM, Azizi F, et al: Reproductive and gynecologic surgical experience in diethylstilbestrol-exposed daughters. Am J Obstet Gynecol 1981;141:1019-1028.

Kaufman RH, Binder GL, Gray PM, et al: Upper genital tract changes associated with exposure in utero to diethylstilbestrol. Am J Obstet Gynecol 1977;128:51-59.

Kaufman RH, Adam H, Binder GL, et al: Upper genital tract changes and pregnancy outcome in offspring exposed in utero to diethylstilbestrol. Am J Obstet Gynecol 1980;137:299-308.

Report of the Recommendation of the 1985 DES Task Force of the US Dept of Health and Human Services. JAMA 1986;255:1859.

Robboy SJ, Szyfelbein WM, Goellner JR, et al: Dysplasia and cytologic findings in 4589

young women enrolled in diethylstilbestrol adenosis (DESAD) project. Am J Obstet Gynecol 1981;140:587-589.
Senekjian EK, Herbst AL: Diethylstilbestrol exposure in utero, in Lavery JP, Sanfilippo JS (eds): Pediatric and Adolescent Obstetrics and Gynecology. New York, Springer-Verlag, 1985, pp 149-161.

Male Genito-Urinary Disorders

Berger OG: Varicocele in adolescents. Clin Pediatr 1980;19:810.
Boyd AS: Variococeles and male infertility. Amer Fam Phys 1988;37:252.
Goven DE, Kessler R: Urologic problems in the adolescent male. Pediatr Clin No Amer 1980;27:109.
Greydanus DE, Hofmann AD: The genitourinary disorders. In: Hofmann AD, Greydanus DE, eds: Adolescent Medicine. 2nd ed. Norwalk, CT: Appleton-Lange, 1989:163-172.
Kass EJ, Chandro RS, Bellman AB: Testicular histology in the adolescent with a varicocele. Pediatrics 1987;79:996.
Keith LG, Berger GS, eds: The clinical and laboratory diagnosis of sexually transmitted diseases; a symposium. J Repro Med 1985;30(Suppl):235.
Murphy MD: Office laboratory diagnosis of sexually transmitted diseases. Pediatr Infec Dis 1983;2:146.
O'Brien WM, Lynch JH: The acute scrotum. Amer Fam Phys 1988;37:239.
Treatment of sexually transmitted diseases. Med Lett Dr Ther 1988;30:5-10.
Witherington R: The acute syndrome. Lesions that require immediate attention. Postgrad Med 1987;82:207

Miscellaneous Vulvar Diseases

Carlson JA: Gynecologic neoplasms. In: Lavery JP, Sanfilippo JS, eds: Obstetrics and Gynecology. New York: Springer-Verlag, 1986:134-148.
Daunt S, Kotowski KE, O'Reilly AP: Ulcerative vulvitis in Reiter's syndrome. A case report. Br J Vener Dis 1982;58:405-407.
Fish SA: Special problems in managing vulvar disease. Consultant 1976;16:155-160.
Kaufman RH: The many causes of pruritus vulvae. Consultant 1975;15:182-196.
McMillan A: Reiter's disease in a female, presenting as erythema nodosum. Br J Vener Dis 1975;51:345-347.
Smith L: The long-standing problem of anal itching. Consultant 1977;17:115-118.
Underwood PB, Kreutner A: Neoplasms and tumorous conditions of the lower genital tract and uterus. In: Kreutner AK, Hollingworth DR, eds: Adolescent Obstetrics and Gynecology. Chicago: Year Book, 1978:479-502.

Pediculosis

Honig PJ: Bites and parasites. Pediatr Clin North Am 1983;30:563-582.
Orkin M, Epstein E, Maibach HI: Treatment of today's scabies and pediculosis. JAMA 1976;236:1136.

Pelvic Inflammatory Disease

Brookman RA: Infections of the male and female reproductive tracts. In: Hofmann AD, Greydanus DE, eds: Adolescent Medicine, 2nd ed. Norwalk, CT: Appleton-Lange, 1989:359-361.
Centers for Disease Control. 1985 STD Treatment Guidelines. Atlanta: CDC, 1985.
Eschenbach D: Fitz-Hugh Curtis syndrome. In: Holmes KK, Mardh PA, Sparling PE, et al, eds: Sexually Transmitted Diseases. New York: McGraw Hill, 1984:633-638.
Freij BJ: Acute pelvic inflammatory disease. Semin Adolesc Med 1986;2:143-154.
Hager WD, Eschenbach DA, Spence MR, et al: Criteria for diagnosis and grading of salpingitis. Obstet Gynecol 1983;61:113-114.
Hofmann AD, Greydanus DE, eds: Adolescent Medicine, 2nd ed. Norwalk, CT: Appleton-Lange, 1989:359-361.
Hemsell DL, Nobles BJ, Heard MC, et al: Upper and lower reproductive tract bacteria in 126 women with acute pelvic inflammatory disease. J Repro Med 1988;33:799-805
Hemsell DL: Acute pelvic inflammatory disease. Etiologic and therapeutic considerations. J Repro Med 1988;33(Suppl 1):124-127.

Holmes KK, Eschenbach DA, Knapp JS: Salpingitis: overview of etiology and epidemiology. Am J Obstet Gynecol 1980;138:893-900.

King LA: Pelvic inflammatory disease: its pathogenesis, diagnosis and treatment. Postgrad Med 1987;81:105-112.

McAnarney ER, Greydanus DE: Disorders of the adolescent. In: Kempe CH, Silver HK, O'Brien D, eds: Current Pediatric Diagnosis and Treatment. 9th ed. Los Altos, CA: Lange, 1987:237-242.

Mercer LJ: Treatment and prophylactic considerations in ob/gyn infections. A Symposium. J Repro Med 1988;33:85-168.

Method MW: Laparoscopy in the diagnosis of pelvic inflammatory disease. J Repro Med 1983;33:901-906.

Reilly KR, Aral SO: Adolescence and sexual behavior: trends and implications for STDs. J Adolesc Health Care 1985;6:262-270.

Sanfilippo JS, Schikler KN: Mezlocillin versus penicillin and tobramycin in adolescent pelvic inflammatory disease: a prospective study. International Pediatrics 1989;4:53-56.

Semchyshyn S: Fitz-Hugh and Curtis syndrome. J Repro Med 1979;22:45-48.

Sexually transmitted diseases treatment guidelines—1982. Morb Mort Week Rep 1982; 31:33S-60S.

Shafer MB, Irwin CE, Sweet RL: Acute salpingitis in the adolescent. J Pediatr 1982;100:339-350.

St John RK, Brown ST, eds: International symposium on pelvic inflammatory disease. Am J Obstet Gynecol 1980;138(7):845-1112.

Treatment of sexually transmitted diseases. Med Lett Dr Ther 1988;30:5-10.

Venezio FR, O'Keefe JP: Microbiologic considerations in the treatment of serious pelvic infections in women. J Repro Med 1899;33(Suppl 1):124-127.

Wang SP, Eschenbach DA, Holmes KK, et al: Chlamydia trachomatis in Fitz-Hugh-Curtis syndrome. Am J Obstet Gynecol 1980;138:1034-1038.

Toxic Shock Syndrome

Chesney PJ, Davis JP, Purdy WK, et al: Clinical manifestations of toxic shock syndrome. JAMA 1981;248:741.

Chesney PJ, Crass BA, Polak MB, et al: Toxic shock syndrome: management and long-term sequelae. Ann Intern Med 1982;96(pt 2):847.

Crowder WE, Shannon FL: Colposcopic diagnosis of vaginal ulcerations in toxic shock syndrome. Obstet Gynecol 1983;61:505.

D'Angelo LJ: Young teens and tampons: a crisis in waiting. J Adol Health Care 1986; 7(6):423-424.

Follow-up on toxic-shock syndrome. MMWR 1980;29:441.

Friedrich EG Jr, Siegesmund KA: Tampon-associated vaginal ulcerations. Obstet Gynecol 1980;55:149.

Kasper DL: CPC-Toxic shock syndrome N Engl J Med 1986;314:302-309.

MacDonald KL, Osterholm MT, Hedbery CW, et al: Toxic shock syndrome. A newly recognized complication of influenza and influenza-like illness. JAMA 1987;257:1053-1058.

Markowitz LE, Hightower AW, Broome CV, et al: Toxic shock syndrome. Evaluation of national surveillance data using a hospital discharge survey. JAMA 1987;258:75-78.

Petitti DB, Reingold A, Chin J: The incidence of toxic shock syndrome in Northern California. JAMA 1986;255:368-372.

Reed KL, Christian CD: Toxic shock syndrome: the keys to successful management. Hosp Pract 1987;21:111-119.

Shands KN, Schmid GP, Dan BB, et al: Toxic shock syndrome in menstruating women: Association with tampon use and Staphylococcal aureus and clinical features in 52 cases. N Engl J Med 1980;303:1436-1442.

Smith CB, Jacobson JA: Toxic shock syndrome. DM 1985;32:79-118.

Todd J, Fishaut M, Kapral F, et al: Toxic-shock syndrome associated with phage group-1 staphylococci. Lancet 1978;2:116-118.

Wagner GP: Toxic shock syndrome. Am J Obstet Gynecol 1983;146:93-102.

Vulvovaginitis

Altchek A: Recognizing and controlling vulvovaginitis in children. Contemp Pediatr 1986;3:59-70.

Amsel R, Totten PA, Spiegel CA, et al: Non-specific vaginitis. Am J Med 1983;74:14-22.

Asgeirsson G, Wientzen RL: Epidemiology and pathophysiology of Neisseria gonorrhoeae infection. Semin Adolesc Med 1986;2:99-105.

Binder MA, Gates GW, Emson HE, et al: The changing concepts of condyloma. Am J Obstet Gynecol 1985;151:213-219.

Brookman RR: Infections of the Male and Female Reproductive Tract. In: Hofmann AD, Greydanus DE, eds: Adolescent Medicine, 2nd ed. Norwalk, CT: Appleton-Lange, 1989:355-370.

Brown ER, Nair V: Laboratory identification of sexually transmitted diseases. J Repro Med 1985;30:237-243.

Buntin DM: Cutaneous features of sexually transmitted diseases. Postgrad Med 1985; 78:121-128.

Carlson JA: Gynecologic neoplasms. In Lavery JP, Sanfilippo JS, eds: Pediatric and Adolescent Obstetrics and Gynecology. New York: Springer-Verlag, 1985:124-148.

Chacko MR, Louchik J: Chlamydia trachomatis in sexually active adolescents: prevalence and risk factors. Pediatrics 1984;73:836-840.

Corey L: Diagnosis of genital herpes simplex virus infections. J Repro Med 1985;30:262-268.

Donowitz GR, Mandell GL: Beta-lactas antibiotics. N Engl J Med 1988;318:419-426.

Dunlop EMC: Sexually transmitted diseases. Clin Obstet Gynecol 1977;4:451.

Emans SJ, Woods ER, Woods NT, et al: Genital findings in sexually abused symptomatic and asymptomatic girls. Pediatrics 1987;79:778-785.

Emans SJ: Vulvovaginitis in the child and adolescent. Ped in Rev 1986;8:12-19.

Faro S: Chlamydia trachomatis infection in women. J Repro Med 1985;30:273-278.

Felman YM, Nikitas JA: Granuloma inguinale. Cutis 1981;27:364-277.

Fiumara NJ, Calhour J: Multiple sexually transmitted diseases. Sex Trans Dis 1982;9:98-99.

Friedman-Kien AE, Eron LJ, Conant M, et al: Natural interferon alfa for treatment of Condylomata acuminata. JAMA 1988;259(4):533-545.

Fusger CD, Neinstein LS: Vaginal chlamydia trachomatis prevalence in sexually abused prepubertal girls. Pediatrics 1987;79:235-238.

Gibbs RS: Sexually transmitted diseases in the female. Med Clin North Am 1983;67:221-234.

Gilchrist MJ, Rauh JL: Office microscopy: low-cost screening for STDs. Contemp Ped 1987;4:50-58.

Gilly PA: Vaginal discharge: its causes and cures. Postgrad Med 1986;80:231-237.

Greydanus DE, Sladkin K, Rosenstock R: Vulvovaginitis in children and adolescents. In: Strasburger VC; ed: Basic Office Gynecology: An Office Primer. Baltimore: Urban & Schwarzenberg, 1990.

Grimes DA: Deaths due to sexually transmitted diseases. JAMA 1987;255:1727-1729.

Guinan ME: Treatment of primary and secondary syphilis: defining failure at three and six-month follow-up. JAMA 1987;257:359-360.

Hammerschlag MR: Chlamydial infections. J Pediatr 1989;114:727-734.

Handsfield HH: Sexually transmitted diseases. Hosp Pract 1982;17:99-116.

Henry-Suchet J: Chlamydial infections and infertility in females. J Repro Med 1988;33:912-914.

Hernandez TJ: Adolescents and sexually transmitted diseases. Am Fam Phys 1987;34:127-132.

Hook EW, Holmes K: Gonococcal infections. Ann Intern Med 1985;102:229-243.

Horsburg CR, Douglas JM, LaForce FM: Preventive strategies in sexually transmitted diseases for the primary care physician. JAMA 1987;258:814-821.

Johnson J: Sexually transmitted diseases in adolescents. Prim Care 1987;14:101-120.

Kirby P: Interferon and genital warts: Much potential, modest progress. JAMA 1988;259(4):570-573.

Kitchener HC: Genital virus infection and cervical neoplasia. Br J Obstet Gynecol 1988;95:182-191.

Krieger JN, Tam MR, Stevens E, et al: Diagnosis of trichomoniasis. JAMA 1988;259(8):1223-1227.

Lake P: Herpes simplex virus infections: present scope and future prospects. Semin Adolesc Med 1986;2:113-120.

Lefrock JL, Molavi A: Metronidazole. Am Fam Phys 1981;24:185.

Lindner LE, Nettum JA, Altman KH: Clinical characteristics of females with chlamydia cervicitis. J Repro Med 1988;33:684-690.

Lossick JG: The diagnosis of vaginal trichomoniasis. JAMA 1988;259(18):1230.

Lossick JG: Sexually transmitted vaginitis. Semin Adolesc Med 1986;2:131-142.

Lynch PJ: Therapy of sexually transmitted diseases. Med Clin North Am 1982;66:915-926.

Martien KM, Emans SJ: Treatment of common genital infections in adolescents. J Adolesc Health Care 1987;8:129-136.

McCormack WM, Evard JR, Laughlin CR, et al: Sexually transmitted conditions among women college students. Am J Obstet Gynecol 1981;139:130-133.

McGregor JA: Trichomoniasis: a common challenge in STD treatment. STD Bulletin 1989;8(6):3-11.

Moscicki B: HPV infections: an old STD revisited. Contemp Pediatr 1989;6:12-48.

O'Reilly KR, Aral SO: Adolescence and sexual behavior: trends and implications of STD for sexually active teenagers. J Adolesc Health Care 1988;2(2):43-51.

Owen WF: Medical problems of the homosexual adolescent. J Adolesc Health Care 1985;6:278-285.

Paavonen J, Stevens CE, Wolner-Hanssen P, et al: Colposcopic manifestations of cervical and vaginal infections. Obstet Gynecol Survey 1988;43:373-381.

Panconesis E, Zuccati G, Cantini A: Treatment of syphilis: a short critical review. Sex Trans Dis 1981;4:321-325.

Paradise JE, Campos JM, Friedman HM, et al: Vulvovaginitis in premenarcheal girls: clinical features and diagnostic evaluation. Pediatrics 1982;70:193-198.

Pheifer TA, Forsyth PS, Durfee MA, et al: Nonspecific vaginitis. Role of Haemohilus vaginitis and treatment with metronidazole. N Engl J Med 1978;298:1429.

Pitegoff JG, Cathro DM: Chlamydial infections and other sexually transmitted diseases in adolescent pregnancy. Semin Adolesc Med 1985;2:215-230.

Robinson GE, Forster GE, Munday PE: The changing pattern of sexually transmitted disease in adolescent girls. Gentourin Med 1985;61:130-132.

Rose FB, Camp EJ: Genital herpes. Postgrad Med 1988;84:81-88.

Sanfilippo JS: Adolescent girls with vaginal discharge. Pediatr Ann 1986;15:509-519.

Schneider GT: Vaginal infections. Postgrad Med 1983;72:255-262.

Schmied GP: The treatment of chancroid. JAMA 1986;255:1757-1762.

Sexually transmitted diseases treatment guidelines, 1982. Morb Mort Week Rep 1982; 31:33S-59S.

Siegal D, Washington AE: Updated approach to an old disease. Postgrad Med 1987;81:83-90.

Silber TJ: Genital ulcer syndrome. Semin Adolsc Med 1986;2:155-162.

Singleton AF: Vaginal discharge in children and adolescents. Clin Pediatr 1980;19:799-804.

Speigel CA, Amstel R, Eschenbach D, et al: Anaerobic bacteria in non-specific vaginitis. N Engl J Med 1980;303:601-606.

Teraconazole for Candida vaginitis. Med Lett Dr Ther 1988;30:118-119.

Treatment of sexually transmitted diseases. Med Lett Dr Ther 1988;30(Jan 15):5-10.

Warner-Hanssen P, Krieger NJ, Stevens CE, et al: Clinical manifestations of vaginal trichomoniasis. JAMA 1989;261:571-576.

Washington AE, Browner WS, Korenbrot CC: Cost-effectiveness of combined treatment for endocervical gonorrhea. Considering co-infection with Chlamydia trachomatis. JAMA 1987;257:2056-2060.

Weinstein AJ: Sexually transmitted diseases and other genital infections during adolescence. J Repro Med 1984;29:411-415.

Whittington WL, Rice RJ, Biddle JW, et al: Incorrect identification of Neisseria gonorrhoeae from infants and children. Pediatr Infect Dis 1988;7:3-10.

Wilfert CM, Gutman LT: Chlamydia trachomatis infections of infants and children. Adv Pediatr 1986;33:49-70.

Witkin SS, Jeremias J, Ledger WJ: Recurrent vaginitis as a result of sexual transmission of IgE antibodies. Amer J Obstet Gynecol 1988;159:32-36.

Wysoki RS, Willic D: Granuloma inguinale (Donovanosis) in the female. J Repro Med 1988;33:709-714.

Young AW, Tovell HMM, Sadri K: Erosions and ulcers of the vulva. Diagnosis, incidence and management. Obstet Gynecol 1977;50:35-39.

5

Breast Disorders

Society has long emphasized the breast and body image. Five years ago a book entitled *The Breast: A Gentleman's Guide to Proper Examination* was on the best-seller list. Today, one need only look at the various lay publications to see the great emphasis placed on breast size, shape, and contour. Obviously, adolescent females are aware of this social message; it is therefore important that the health care professional always include an examination of the breast and a discussion of possible anomalies. It is important that the physician's approach be professional and nonthreatening. Therefore, a regular history, especially a family history, is important before an examination. The health care provider should know if there is a family history of breast cancer.

Breast cancer is the most common form of cancer in women in the United States. Each year, approximately 114,000 women get breast cancer. Two thirds of them will be more than 50 years of age, but breast cancer does occur in younger women and in about 900 men per year. Although rare in youth, breast cancer should be considered when examining the breasts of adolescents (Greydanus, 1989).

Most breast lesions in children and adolescents are benign. In a series of 207 children who were managed for breast lesions during a 10-year period at St. Louis Children's Hospital, 161 girls (78%) were evaluated. Surgery was performed on 64%, with the most common lesions being fibroadenoma (84), gynecomastia (23), and inflammatory processes (4). An evaluation not requiring surgery was carried out in 73 (36%) of these individuals. In this particular study, the most common diagnoses in this group were premature thelarche (35), gynecomastia (16), precocious puberty (13), and exogenous drug stimulation (3). This study reinforces the benign nature of breast masses in adolescents and young adults.

The roles of the health care provider when working with the adolescent female generally are identifying anomalies or other nonneoplastic conditions and teaching detection of possible breast anomalies. The breast examination is an important detector of early cancer in women of all ages. Therefore, the first step is to teach the adolescent proper breast examination. Many instructional pamphlets are available, such as the National Cancer Institute's "Breast Exams: What You Should Know" and the American Cancer Society's "How to Examine Your Breasts."

Between the ages of 9 and 14, the majority of girls begin breast development. Because breast development is often regarded as the principal sign of feminine sexuality, mothers and adolescents often worry inordinately about minor asymmetry or "inadequate" development. It is often difficult for the teenager to accept small breasts as "normal." On the other hand, reassurance is in order only if the rest of the examination and history excludes an endocrine disorder. Recent national publicity on breast cancer has made adolescents exceptionally anxious about cystic changes and fibroadenomas. Perhaps this fear can be used constructively to encourage patients to begin monthly self-examination.

BREAST EXAMINATIONS

All patients should have a careful breast examination regardless of whether specific complaints are mentioned. Table 5-1 outlines the steps in a routine breast examination. The patient is first asked to sit facing the examiner, and the breasts are inspected for asymmetry, retraction of the nipples, and dimpling of the skin. In the young patient with no history or asymmetry of breast masses, the sitting part of the examination may be omitted. The patient is then asked to lie supine with her arms extended over her head. Breast development should be recorded using Tanner stages B1 through B5. If asymmetry or development disorders are a concern, exact measurement of the areola and breast should be included at each exam. For example, one might record the following:

	Areola	*Breast*
Right	2.5 cm	8 × 9 cm
Left	2.5 cm	9 × 10 cm

The first number in the breast figure is the upper-to-lower measurement; the second number is the right-to-left measurement.

The breast tissue should be carefully palpated in a straight line from the margin of the breast inward, clockwise around the breast. The flat portion of the fingers should be moved in a slightly rotatory fashion to feel abnormal masses. Normal glandular tissue has an irregular granular surface like tapioca pudding; a fibroadenoma feels firm and smooth. The areola should be gently compressed to assess any abnormal discharge.

Table 5-1. Outline of the Breast Examination.

---

1. Inspect the patient while she is sitting
   a. With her arms at her side
   b. With her arms pressed against her hips
   c. With her arms raised
   d. While she bends forward
2. Inspect the patient while she is supine
   Place a small pillow under the side of the breast being evaluated
   Examine the inner aspect of the breast with her arms raised
   Examine the outer aspect with her arms at her sides
   Examine the nipple and areola with the arms raised
3. Observe for:
   Pubertal status of each breast
   Asymmetry
   Palpable lesions (check each quadrant)
   Nipple discharge
   Supraclavicular and axillary masses

BREAST SELF-EXAMINATION

Instructing the adolescent in self-examination during the physician's examination often puts the modest young adolescent at ease (Fig. 5-1). It is particularly helpful for the patient to begin self-examination after a normal examination at the office visit so that she can be assured that the lumps that she is feeling are normal glandular tissue. Also, breast pamphlets (previously noted) should be given to the patient at the time of the

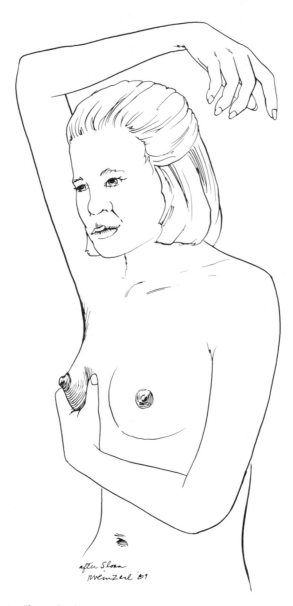

Fig. 5-1. Breast self-examination.

initial gynecologic visit. Breast self-examination (BSE) can be accomplished in the following manner:

1. Stand before a mirror. Inspect both breasts for anything unusual, such as discharge from the nipples, puckering, dimpling, or scaling of the skin.

   The next two steps are designed to emphasize any change in the shape or the contour of your breasts. As you do these steps, you should be able to feel your chest muscles tighten.

2. Watching closely in the mirror, clasp hands behind your head and press hands forward.

3. Next, press your hands firmly on the hips and bow them slightly toward your mirror as you pull your shoulders and elbows forward.

   Some women do the next part of the exam in the shower. Fingers slide over soapy skin, making it easy to concentrate on the texture underneath.

4. Raise your left arm. Use three or four fingers of your right hand to explore your left breast firmly, carefully, and thoroughly. Beginning at the outer edge, press the flat part of your fingers in small circles, moving the circles slowly around the breast. Gradually work toward the nipple. Be sure to cover the entire breast. Pay special attention to the area between the breast and the armpit, including the armpit itself. Feel for any unusual lump or mass under the skin.

5. Gently squeeze the nipple and look for a discharge. Repeat the exam on your right breast.

6. Steps 4 and 5 should be repeated lying down. Lie flat on your back, left arm over your head and a pillow or folder towel under your left shoulder. This position flattens the breast and makes it easier to examine. Use the same circular motion described earlier. Repeat on your right breast.

ANATOMIC AND PHYSIOLOGIC CONSIDERATIONS

The general development of the male and female breasts are described in Chapter 3 and the sexual maturity changes are in Chapter 1. The actual changes in the breast and various conditions through sexual maturity ratings may be normal or abnormal. Abnormalities must be related to these ratings. The major conditions that the health care provider considers are the following:

Asymmetry of the breast
Congenital anomalies

Hypoplasia, hypertrophy, and atrophy of the breast
Premature breast development
Galactorrhea and hyperprolactinemia
Gynecomastia
Breast masses
Fibrocystic disease versus fibroadenoma of the breast
Inflammation and trauma of the breast
Neoplastic processes of the breast

The health care professional should look for these conditions after instructing the patient as to the proper approach to breast self-examination. Breast anomalies in the adolescent usually are asymptomatic and are detected on routine examination or through a concerned individual who has a family history of cancer.

BREAST PATHOLOGY

Asymmetry

Asymmetry of the breasts is a common complaint, especially from those in the early stages of development. Since the breast bud may initially appear on one side as a tender, granular lump, mothers are often concerned about the possibility of a tumor. Breast asymmetry may be minimal or marked, and may be physiologically normal or a result of hypoplasia, hyperplasia, or anomalies of one of the breasts (Fig. 5-2). In evaluating breast asymmetry, it is important to recognize conditions such as scoliosis or rib-cage asymmetry, which may give the illusion of unequal breasts (Greydanus, 1989).

Asymmetry of normal breasts is common and usually minor. It may be more apparent early in puberty, arising from differences in the timing of development between the two breasts. A young adolescent whose breasts are Tanner stage 2 or 3 can be reassured that the condition will improve. By the late teens and stage 5, asymmetry is unlikely to change.

Asymmetry due to hypoplasia or aplasia of one breast (hypomastia or amastia) is less common (see below). The affected breast is more clearly abnormal, and it may be absent or minimally developed. The breast may have a normal nipple but lack underlying breast tissue, or the structure may be an unusual shape. In rare cases, even the nipple is absent. The condition is unlikely to be due to systemic problems such as chromosomal or hormonal abnormalities, but may be a sporadic birth defect due to local embryonic factors, usually unidentifiable. In some cases, there may be associated abnormalities of the chest wall (e.g., pectus excavatum) or the ipsilateral pectoralis muscle or upper limb (e.g., Poland's syndrome). A breast may also develop abnormally if injured prepubertally by infection, trauma, or surgery (including biopsy of an early breast bud).

Enlargement of one breast may signify diffuse hypertrophy or an intrinsic mass. Virginal breast hypertrophy may be unilateral, but is usually bilateral (see below). Intrinsic masses large enough to produce asymme-

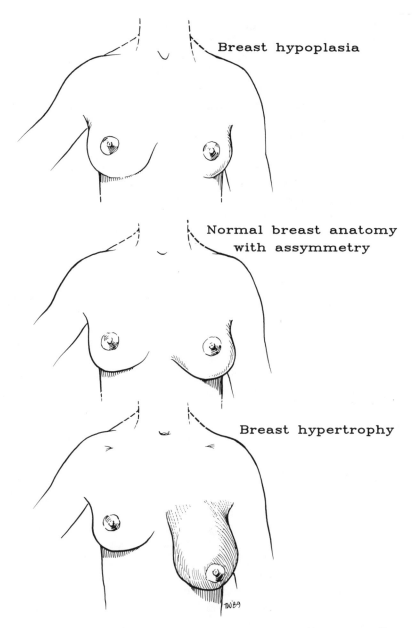

Fig. 5-2. *Top:* breast hypoplasia. *Center:* normal breast anatomy with asymmetry. *Bottom:* breast hypertrophy.

try are uncommon and generally benign, but require surgical excision. Juvenile giant fibroadenomas and cystosarcoma phylloides are rapidly growing tumors that occur more commonly in black girls in middle to late adolescence. Fibroadenomas are usually solitary and may blend into the normal breast tissue. The overlying skin is typically taut, and there is dilatation of the superficial veins. A hemangioma, lipoma, or neurofibroma may also be large enough to distort the breast.

The physician can play an important role in counseling the patient about asymmetric breast development. The young adolescent needs to hear that many other adolescent girls and adult women have asymmetric breasts and that she may be unaware of it because she only sees them clothed. It is helpful to let the 13- or 14-year-old girl know that most teenagers at the age of 18 or 19 are coping well with the degree of asymmetry they have, and that most decide not to correct the difference with surgery. Many younger adolescents are anxious to have their breasts equalized and their body image made "normal" as quickly as possible without regard to possible risks or long-term complications of augmentation mammoplasty. The young teenager can be told that the physician understands how asymmetry may cause worries, and that an annual examination is important to determine the degree of asymmetry and to help her decide, when she completes her growth, whether intervention beyond simple bra pads is warranted. Since bathing suit fittings can be difficult for girls with asymmetric breasts, girls should be encouraged to try on a large number of styles with breast supports. Slightly padded bras also make asymmetry less pronounced.

A major difference in breast size can be treated with foam inserts (available in department stores for mastectomy patients). If asymmetry is marked at the end of full growth (between 16 and 18 years of age), patients will often wish to explore the option of mammoplasty. Patients should be referred to a plastic surgeon who can discuss the risks and benefits of various options without pushing the patient in the direction of surgery. However, in cases of major disparities, surgical success can be dramatic.

Congenital Anomalies

Congenital anomalies may involve one or both breasts and are usually limited to the granular tissue. Ectopic supernumerary or accessory nipples (polythelia) are fairly common, occurring anywhere between the knees and the neck, but are of solely cosmetic significance. They occasionally have underlying breast tissue (polymastia). If the nipples are of exceptional size, they may require surgical removal. Extra nipples occur along the embryonic "milk line" (Fig. 5-3). An association between polythelia and urologic-cardiovascular anomalies has been reported.

An inverted nipple (Fig. 5-4) can be noted from birth and consists of a nipple that does not extend beyond the breast surface. Infection can develop unless excellent hygiene is practiced. The patient may be concerned about the nipple's cosmetic appearance, lack of lactation potential, or both. Surgical correction involves division of breast ducts and elevation of the nipple. Surgery prevents breast-feeding potential.

Hypoplasia

Symmetrically small breasts may be normal but distressing. If the breasts are at Tanner stage 2 or 3 and the patient is premenarcheal, the

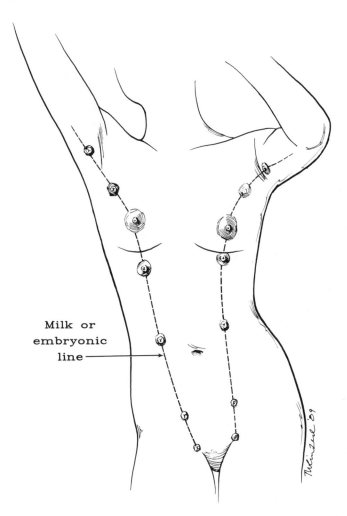

Milk or
embryonic
line

Fig. 5-3. Breast disorders: milk or embryonic line. Breast tissue begins development during the sixth fetal week, when epidermal cells migrate into the underlying mesenchyme to produce milk lines, or primitive mammary ridges. Thickening of the ectoderm occurs, extending from the axilla to the groin. During the tenth fetal week there is a normal atrophy of the upper and lower parts of these ridges, leaving the middle, or pectoral, ridges to later develop into breast tissue. Persistence of the upper and lower ridges can lead to polythelia, polymastia, or both along the milk or embryonic line, as illustrated.

physician may assure her of further growth. Menstruation demonstrates adequate estrogen levels. After menarche, if breasts have reached stage 5, the physician may offer reassurance of normality and the option of augmentation mammoplasty. Girls with a tall, thin habitus and less subcutaneous fat tend to have smaller breasts, and an association with connective tissue disorders and mitral valve prolapse has also been reported.

Bilateral hypoplasia of the breasts (hypomastia) may be difficult to distinguish from small but normal breasts. Often the nipples of hypoplastic

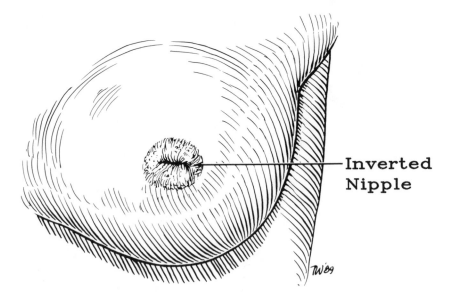

Fig. 5-4. Inverted nipple.

breasts are smaller, less pigmented or estrogenized, and lack protuberant papillae. Breast hypoplasia may occur as a result of androgen excess in fetal life or early infancy. The most common cause is congenital adrenal hyperplasia. Any condition that prevents ovarian maturation and estrogen secretion will cause deficient breast development at puberty. Appearance of pubic hair without thelarche and delay of menarche are common features. Gonadal dysgenesis, preadolescent hypothyroidism, and gonadotropin deficiency are important causes of delayed puberty (see Chapter 3).

Hyperplasia

Neonatal breast hypertrophy is a well-known phenomenon in the newborn and occurs as a result of breast stimulation from maternal estrogen (Fig. 5-5). This condition usually resolves spontaneously in a few weeks. Infection can occur, perhaps due to excessive breast manipulation. Aggressive antibiotic treatment, and perhaps surgical drainage, may be necessary.

In the adolescent, large, as well as small, breasts are usually normal. Extreme bilateral hyperplasia of the breasts (macromastia) is rare and is usually associated with some degree of asymmetry. The causes of extreme breast hypertrophy are not well understood. Virginal breast hypertrophy, characterized by rapid growth of the breasts to massive (and socially disabling) size, generally begins in early adolescence. The cause is unknown, and the only effective treatment is reduction mammoplasty.

Atrophy

Bilateral atrophy of previously developed breasts most commonly occurs during severe weight loss, especially in cases of anorexia nervosa.

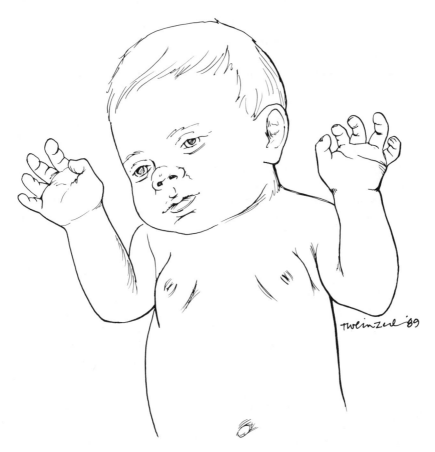

Fig. 5-5. Normal breast enlargement in a newborn.

The breasts may become wrinkled, flattened, and senile in appearance. Hormone therapy with a combination oral contraceptive as weight is optimized may help to restore shape. Atrophy may also occur if estrogen production ceases because of premature ovarian failure (see Chapter 6). Secondary amenorrhea usually precedes atrophy.

Premature Breast Development

Early breast development or premature thelarche can occur at any age before 8, but is more common between ages 2 and 4 years. Despite the early development of breasts to a Tanner stage of 2 or 3, there is no other evidence of puberty. The breast development does not represent an organic disorder and is not a form of precocious puberty. The development may recede or remain, with further progression when puberty normally occurs later. No treatment is necessary, and reassurance is given to often upset parents that premature breast development is a benign process.

Galactorrhea and Hyperprolactinemia

Galactorrhea is the secretion of fluid from a nonpuerperal breast. The fluid may be clear or milky, scanty or copious, and Sudan staining should reveal fat globules. Although the breasts of many normal adult women may yield drops of fluid when squeezed, galactorrhea of any degree is sufficiently uncommon in nulligravid adolescents to warrant evaluation. Secretions can be caused by conditions ranging from normal variations to serious diseases (Table 5-2).

Important aspects of evaluation include (1) ascertainment of repeated stimulation, trauma, or abnormality of breasts or chest, (2) thorough drug history, (3) review of pubertal growth and sexual development, especially interruption or regression, (4) menstrual history and current sexual function and practices, especially oligomenorrhea or loss of libido, (5) assessment of hirsutism, (6) recognition of neurologic or visual abnormalities, including visual fields, (7) mental status examination and assessment of current psychosocial functioning and stress, and (8) evidence of abdominal problems, significant weight changes, or hypothyroidism or hyperthyroidism.

A common cause of galactorrhea in adolescent girls is oral contraceptives. The estrogen stimulates prolactin, and the galactorrhea occurs most commonly after discontinuation (estrogen withdrawal) and may be accompanied by amenorrhea. Elevated estrogen levels may also contribute to the occasional occurrence of galactorrhea in girls with polycystic ovary syndrome. Hypothyroidism and, rarely, hyperthyroidism have been associated with galactorrhea in both adolescent and preadolescent girls.

Measurement of prolactin is important, since hyperprolactinemia is the most commonly identifiable cause of galactorrhea in adolescents and adults of either sex. In women with galactorrhea and hyperprolactinemia, secondary amenorrhea is usually present, but any two of the three may occur, and the third may appear with time. Dysfunctional uterine bleeding or hirsutism are occasionally present with hyperprolactinemia, and younger adolescent girls may have primary amenorrhea.

Prolactin is secreted episodically. Since stress, meals, and sleep will elevate prolactin, blood for basal prolactin measurement is best obtained when the patient is relaxed, preferably at least 2 hours after a meal or after awakening. Prepubertal girls generally have basal prolactin levels of less than 12 ng/ml, which rise in early adolescence to the adult range of up to 30 ng/ml, with minimal change through the menstrual cycle. Levels of 30 to 50 ng/ml are difficult to interpret and should be repeated. Many women on oral contraceptives will have such levels, which are only rarely associated with adenomas. Most pituitary prolactinomas produce levels of 80 to 200 ng/ml, or even higher.

The spectrum of pituitary hyperprolactinemia ranges from overproduction by overstimulated or uninhibited lactotroph cells (a microadenoma) to a tumor large enough to erode the sella and impinge on the optic nerves. The condition may progress through all three stages or even regress spontaneously. It apparently results from impairment of the normal hypothalamic inhibition of the pituitary lactotroph cells by dopamine. The tumors are not malignant and often respond to dopaminergic drugs such as bromocriptine.

Table 5-2. Causes of Galactorrhea.

Recent pregnancy terminated by spontaneous or induced abortion
Neurogenic, psychogenic, and miscellaneous
  Chest wall disorders
    Bronchiectasis and chronic bronchitis
    Herpes zoster
    Chronic crutch use
    Thoracotomy or thoracoplasty
    Burns to chest wall
    Breast manipulation or stimulation
    Chronic inflammatory disease or abscess of breast
  Psychogenic, including pseudocyesis and pseudonursing
  Miscellaneous
    Hysterectomy or uterine tumors
    Laparotomy
    Spinal cord disorders and surgery
    Idiopathic normoprolactinemic, with or without amenorrhea
Central nervous system abnormalities
  Diffuse brain disease
    Coma
    Pseudotumor cerebri
    Encephalitis and sequelae
    Uremia
  Tumors, infiltrations, structural abnormalities
    Neurocutaneous syndromes
    Craniopharyngioma
    Pineal tumors
    Other intracranial tumors, cysts and masses
    Histiocytosis X
    Sarcoidosis
  Pituitary
    Stalk section
    Empty sella syndrome
    Pituitary infarction and Sheehan syndrome
    Hyperprolactinemia with or without prolactinoma
    Other functional pituitary tumors
Systemic endocrine or metabolic disorders
  Hypo- and hyperthyroidism
  Hypogonadism
  Adrenal tumors and hypernephromas
  Nelson syndrome
  Testicular and ovarian tumors
  Contraceptive pills or other estrogen or progesterone
  Polycystic ovary syndrome
  Acute intermittent porphyria
  Starvation or refeeding, including anorexia nervosa
Drugs
  Phenothiazines, thioxanthines, other major tranquilizers
  Tricyclic antidepressants
  Opiates, including codeine and heroin
  Monoamine oxidase inhibitors
  Amphetamines
  Chlordiazepoxide
  Meprobamate
  Metoclopramide
  Bromocriptine withdrawal
  Cimetidine and ranitidine
  Tamoxifen
  Verapamil
  Isoniazid

Before embarking on an extensive evaluation of the adolescent girl with hyperprolactinemia, the physician should keep in mind that use of oral contraceptives may not be admitted to by a patient in front of her parents, and a recent abortion is even more likely to be concealed. Since elevated prolactin and pituitary hyperplasia often occur in primary hypothyroidism, TSH and T_4 should be measured in every case of hyperprolactinemia. In addition, since hyperprolactinemia is occasionally associated with over-production of another pituitary hormone, whose effects may or may not be clinically apparent, evaluation should include measurements of growth hormone, somatomedin C, and gonadotropins, as well as a dexametha-sone supression test.

Hyperprolactinemia requires sellar imaging. If no tumor is demon-strated and the symptoms are not distressing, treatment is unnecessary, although yearly prolactin measurement and sellar imaging are recom-mended until the hyperprolactinemia is resolved. If the galactorrhea or amenorrhea are considered troublesome, if fertility is desired, or if an adenoma is discovered, bromocriptine is the initial treatment of choice. However, some adenomas require surgery or radiation.

Prolactin levels should be checked regularly if galactorrhea persists, but some cases of galactorrhea are not associated with hyperprolactinemia or any other apparent disease and remain idiopathic. No treatment is nec-essary, although regular followup and a more intensive search for unusual causes are recommended.

Gynecomastia

A visible or palpable mammary gland development in males is called gynecomastia (Fig. 5-6). It can be divided into Type I (benign adolescent hypertrophy) and Type II (physiologic, either with or without evidence of underlying organic disease, including effects of medication). Enlargement of the mammary gland is not visible until it reaches a diameter of 1.5 to 2 cm or greater. This condition can be noted in one half to two thirds of teenage males, usually between Tanner stages 2 and 4. It usually lasts for several months and then resolves spontaneously. It usually starts as a unilateral process and can progress to bilateral involvement. It typically appears as a small, tender, firm subareolar mass. Gynecomastia, which approximates Tanner stage 3 or greater (female), often does not recede spontaneously and requires surgical correction.

The cause of benign adolescent hyperplasia or Type I gynecomastia is unclear and often theoretically linked to increased sensitivity to pubertal hormones, alterations in testosterone-estrogen ratios, and others. Various organic causes may be noted in Type II gynecomastia. If a male presents with breast development and small testes, consider Klinefelter's syn-drome. There are many organic causes of Type II gynecomastia, as listed in Table 5-3. Treatment is dependent on the underlying cause. Consider the possibility of organic causes, especially when the breast development is noted at a time other than early puberty between Tanner stages 2 and 4.

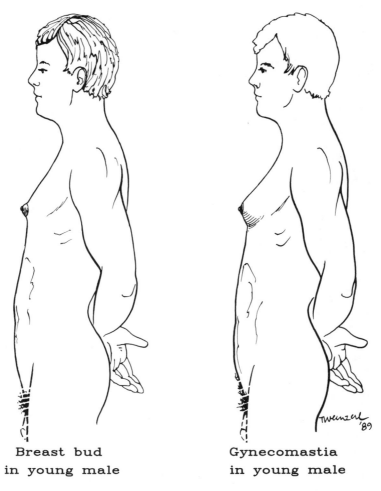

**Breast bud
in young male**

**Gynecomastia
in young male**

Fig. 5-6. *Left:* Gynecomastia (breast bud) in a young male. *Right:* Gynecomastia in young male.

Most young teenage males with Type I gynecomastia can be reassured that this condition is benign. Type I gynecomastia can be distressing to young males seeking to develop a normal body image. The facts are not commonly known by teenagers, who may fear that they are becoming female or are not fully male. Youth can become anxious about possible homosexuality when, in the midst of their sexual development, breasts appear! Thus, the clinician should not underestimate the importance of counseling in this situation. Most males can be reassured that the condition will disappear over the next several months (or 1 to 2 years). Pseudo-gynecomastia should be excluded—pectoral muscle development or obesity may give the appearance of breasts. Large male breasts usually do not recede satisfactorily; subcutaneous mastectomy will correct the situation.

Table 5-3. Organic Causes of Gynecomastia.

---

1. Familial gynecomastia
2. Klinefelter's syndrome
3. Testicular feminization syndrome
4. Miscellaneous tumors (teratoma, seminoma, Leydig-cell tumor, hepatoma, bronchogenic carcinoma, others)
5. Cirrhosis of the liver
6. Thyroid dysfunction (Hypo/hyper-thyroidism)
7. Male pseudohermaphroditism
8. Leukemia
9. Hemophilia
10. Traumatic paraplegia
11. Starvation (on refeeding)
12. Chronic glomerulonephritis
13. Miscellaneous drugs
    Amphetamines
    Anabolic steroids
    Birth control pills
    Busulfan (and other chemotherapeutic agents)
    Cimetidine
    Corticosteroids
    Digitalis
    Estrogens
    Human chorionic gonadotropin
    Insulin
    Isoniazid (and other anti-tuberculosis drugs)
    Marijuana
    Methodone
    Reserpine
    Spironolactone
    Testosterone
    Tricyclic antidepressants
    Others

Breast Masses

Breast masses usually are asymptomatic in adolescent females and are detected during routine examination or through a patient who expresses concern. Most masses are unilateral and are caused by a post-traumatic state or fibrocystic disease. Fibrocystic disease is the most common cause of breast mass in the adolescent female, excluding the post-traumatic state. Most breast masses are asymptomatic and enlarge with the menstrual cycle. Physical changes are noted at various times of the month. The physician has simply to identify the mass and repeat an examination of the area at a later date.

Fibrocystic Disease

Fibrocystic disease is probably responsible for most breast masses found in the adolescent. In the typical patient, the breasts have diffuse, cordlike thickenings and lumps that may become tender and enlarged prior to each menses. Physical findings tend to change each month, so the suspected cyst should be followed carefully. It is important to encourage the teenager to become aware of her cysts through monthly self-examination.

Fibroadenoma accounts for 75 to 95% of pathologic breast masses in adolescents. These masses occur in the outer quadrant of the breast and generally are present at all times of the menstrual cycle. They are clearly defined and freely movable, and may enlarge with manipulation. These masses can be followed for two menstrual cycles; if necessary, they can be excised. Needle biopsy of the area has been recommended by some. Generally, this can be done by a gynecologist.

A fibroadenoma is usually firm, rubbery, and mobile, and usually has a clearly defined edge. The breast mass may remain unchanged or increase in size with subsequent menstrual periods. Recurrent or multiple fibroadenomas are not uncommon.

If an abnormal mass is palpated, the adolescent should be instructed to return after her next period. If the lesion has disappeared, it was probably a cyst. If the lesion remains unchanged or has increased in size, it should be aspirated with a 23-gauge needle on a 3-ml syringe. No anesthesia is required for aspiration. The majority of adolescents are cooperative during this procedure. Any material obtained (even if only on the tip of the needle) should be smeared on a ground glass slide and sent in Papanicolaou fixative for cytologic examination. If the breast mass collapses after aspiration, it is assumed to be a cyst; the mass is then reevaluated in 3 months.

When aspiration of a persistent, discrete mass is not feasible or is nonproductive, or when masses are enlarging, tender, or a source of considerable anxiety, the patient should be referred for an excisional biopsy. Unless there are underlying medical conditions, such as cardiac or pulmonary disease, an excisional biopsy can be done in an ambulatory setting under general or local anesthesia, depending on technical considerations and on the patient's preference and ability to cooperate. Since breast scars can be cosmetically deforming, the optimal incision for a lesion near the center of the breast is circumareolar. Curvilinear or semilunar incisions are superior to radial incisions in terms of wound healing and cosmetic results.

In a review of 51 patients, aged 8 to 20 years, who underwent excision of breast masses (a total of 63 procedures) at the Children's Hospital in Boston, 81.4% of the masses were fibroadenomas. The pathology report on the remainder of the biopsy specimens showed fibrocystic disease, simple cysts, capillary hemangiomas, fat necrosis, adenomatous hyperplasia, and normal breast tissue (in one patient). This is similar to the spectrum of breast disease reported by Daniel and Matthews, who found that fibroadenomas accounted for 94% of the breast tumors from adolescents between 12 and 21 years of age. Followup is particularly important in these cases because new cysts and fibroadenomas can occur.

The issue of benign breast disease remains poorly studied and controversial (Greydanus et al., 1989). Youth can also present with painful breasts termed "mastalgia" or "mastodynia." This appears to be a hormonally induced process that can be cyclic or noncyclic and can be related to various swellings and nodularities of the breast. Some experts attribute it to a relative hyperestronism, perhaps due to deficient corpus luteum activity. Standard treatment includes the use of a firm brassiere support and mild analgesics, including the nonsteroidal antiinflammatory agents. Popular but unproven treatment methods of mastalgia (and for various forms of benign breast disease) include vitamin E (600 IU/day of alpha tocopherol), restriction of various foods (such as methylxanthines— coffee, tea, cola; dairy products; chocolate; and others), and oral contraceptives. Some experts have used such various medications as bromocriptine, danazol, or tamoxifen for adult women with severe mastalgia. These are expensive drugs with significant side effects. Fortunately, mastalgia is a mild process in most cases when noted in adolescents.

Inflammation and Trauma of the Breast. By far the most common breast conditions that bring adolescents to the doctor are post-traumatic or inflammatory situations. Infectious processes are uncommon in the adolescent age group but can be seen following lacerations, bites, or tears of the breast tissue. Another cause can be acne with secondary infection of lesions through manipulation or squeezing. The etiologic agent generally is a staphylococcal aureus infection that has developed into cellulitis. Usually, patients will present with redness of the skin, which may spread. Treatment generally includes antibiotics, systemic antibiotics, and incision and drainage of the lesion. Trauma of the breast usually occurs in the young adolescent following athletic exercise, sexual activity, or accidental trauma in a school situation. The individual will present with a poorly defined, tender area, which may have been present for several weeks. There may be palpable scar tissue and also an area of fat necrosis if the condition has lasted for several months. The individual will usually present because of concern over cancer, forgetting that the trauma occurred.

Tumors of the Breast. The term "tumor of the breast" generally denotes a neoplastic process of some kind. In the adolescent female, the carcinoma is the most common neoplastic process seen. Carcinoma of the breast is rare in children and adolescents, although it has been reported in seven children between the ages of 3 and 15. Primary carcinoma of the breast accounts for less than 1% of all primary carcinoma in adolescent females. Cystosarcoma phylloides, though rare, is the most common form of malignant breast tumor in youth. It appears as a slow-growing, painless breast tumor that is often 8 to 10 cm at discovery. It may appear with bloody nipple discharge. Approximately 80 to 90% are benign. The differential diagnosis of a rapidly enlarging breast mass includes a fibroadenoma, juvenile or giant fibroadenoma, virginal hyperplasia, cystosarcoma phylloides, and others. (See Greydanus et al., 1989.)

Metastatic sarcomas can also occur but, again, are rare, affecting less than 1% of youth. Usually, metastatic sarcomas are nontender, and they may occur in the intraductal space. Intraductal neoplastic processes can also occur in adolescents but are rare and require immediate attention by a gynecologist. Most breast masses that are of a nontraumatic nature will be fibrocystic disease or fibroadenoma; an approach must be developed that is acceptable to both physician and patient.

Mammography remains a controversial diagnostic tool for youth. The American Cancer Society, National Cancer Institute, and American College of Radiology recommend a baseline mammogram in women between ages 35 and 40, an annual or biennial mammogram in women between 40 and 49, and an annual examination in those over 50 years. A mammogram and physical examination are combined to maximize the results in early cancer detection. The clinical evidence in supporting mammograms is based on a number of studies, including the Health Insurance Plan of Greater New York Screening Project (1963 to 1970) and an ongoing 11-year-old Swedish study of women aged 30 to 70. Whether using zeromammography or the film-screen imaging technique, the risk of radiation is low, the risk of pain is minimal, and the overall cost is worthwhile for adult women when considering the benefits of mammography. What about adolescents?

There is no reason for mass mammography screening in teenagers. The dense breast tissue characteristic of adolescent breasts usually makes the use of mammography impractical, and the rarity of breast cancer in this age group negates any real benefit from mass screening. Individual families with unusually high risk for breast cancer at an early age may warrant the use of mammography. A consultant in this area should be involved when dealing with such high-risk families. Prophylactic mastectomy has been recommended by some for high-risk patients such as the youth whose family has a history of breast cancer in each generation.

In summary, the role of the health care provider, with respect to breast disorders in the adolescent, is, first, to educate the patient about proper self-examination of the breast and, second, to recognize conditions of significant pathology that require either reassurance or further treatment.

BIBLIOGRAPHY

Ashikari W, Jun MY, Farrow JH, et al: Breast carcinoma in children and adolescents. Clin Bull 1977;7:55-62.

Bauer BS, Jones KM, Talbot CW: Mammary masses in the adolescent female. Surg Gynecol Obstet 1987;165:63-65.

Beach RK: Routine breast exams. Contemp Pediatr 1987;4(10):70-100.

Carlson HE: Gynecomastia. N Engl J Med 1980;303:795-799.

Cavanaugh RM: Breast self-examination in adolescents. Am Fam Phys 1983;27:189-190.

Chang RJ: Hyperprolactinemia and menstrual dysfunction. Clin Obstet Gynecol 1983;26:736-738.

Daniel WA, Mathews MD: Tumors of the breast in adolescent females. Pediatrics 1968;41:743-749.

Dewhurst J: Breast disorders in children and adolescents. Ped Clin North Am 1981;28:287-308.

Diehl T, Kaplan DW. Breast masses in adolescent females. J Adol Health Care 1985;6:353-357.

Dudgeon DL: Pediatric breast lesions: take the conservative approach. Contemp Pediatr 1985;5:61-66.

Ettinger DE, Wilcox PM: Benign breast disorders: a symptomatic approach. Primary Care 1987;22(9A);75-82.

Greydanus DE, McAnarney ER: Breast disorders in adolescents. In: Kempe CH, Silver KH, O'Brien D, eds: Current Pediatric Diagnosis and Treatment. Los Altos, CA: Lange, 1987:227-230.

Greydanus DE, Parks D, Farrell E: Breast disorders in children and adolescents. Ped Clin North Am 1989;36:601-638.

Hagerty RC: The adolescent female breast. In: Hofmann AD, Greydanus DE, eds: Adolescent Medicine. 2nd ed. New York: Appleton-Lange, 1988.

Jimerson GK: The adolescent breast: disorders and evaluation. Med Aspects Hum Sex 1985;19:66-78.

Kaplan AS, Wollerton MA, Rachlin JA: Selecting a screening mammography facility. Amer Fam Phys 1977;38:143-147.

Knorr K, Bidlingmaier F: Gynaecomastia in male adolescents. Clin Endocrinol Metabol 1975;4:157-171.

McDivitt RW, Steward FW: Breast carcinoma in children. JAMA 1966;1955:388.

Mitchell GW: The gynecologist and breast disease. Clin Obstet Gynecol 1977;20:865-880.

National Cancer Institute: Breast Exams: What You Should Know. NIH publication no. 83-2000, 1983.

Pietsch J: Breast disorders. In: Lavery JP, Sanfilippo, eds: Pediatric and Adolescent Obstetrics and Gynecology. New York: Springer-Verlag, 1985:96-104.

Rohn RD: Nipple (papilla) development in puberty: longitudinal observations in girls. Pediatrics 1987;79:745-747.

Rohn RD: Galactorrhea in the adolescent. J Adol Health Care 1984;5:37-49.

Rosenberg CA, Derman GH, Grabb WC, et al: Hypomastia and mitral-valve prolapse. New Engl J Med 1983;309:1222-1230.

Shapiro S, Venet W, Stra P, et al: Selection, follow-up, and analysis in the health insurance plan study. Natl Cancer Inst Monogr 1985;67:65-74.

Schydlower M: Breast masses in adolescents. Am Fam Phys 1982;25:141-148.

Schydlower M: Adolescent breast disorders. Semin Adolesc Med 1988;4:123-144.

Seashore JH: Breast enlargements in infants and children. Pediatr Ann 1975;4:8-47.

Shearin RB: Handbook of Adolescent Medicine. Washington, D.C.: Georgetown University Medical Center, 1983.

Tabar L, Fagerberg CJ, Gad A, et al: Reduction in mortality from breast cancer after mass screening with mammography. Randomized trial from the Breast Cancer Screening Working Group of the Swedish National Board of Health and Welfare. Lancet 1985;1(8433):829-832.

Teasdale C, Baum M: Breast cancer in a school girl. Lancet 1976;2:627.

Turbey WJ, Buntain WL, Dudgeon DL: The surgical management of pediatric breast masses. Pediatrics 1975;56:736-739.

Wilcox PM, Ettinger DS: Benign breast disease: diagnosis and treatment. Prim Care 1977;4:739-754.

Wile AG, Kollin M: Office management of the breast mass. Postgrad Med 1987;81:137-143.

6

Disorders of the Menstrual Cycle

THE NORMAL MENSTRUAL CYCLE

The menstrual cycle consists of three phases: follicular, ovulatory, and luteal (Fig. 6-1).[1,2,3]

The follicular phase begins with the first day of menstrual bleeding and lasts about 14 days, although this phase may vary in length. The onset of menses signals the end of the prior luteal phase and is accompanied by rising FSH levels. During the early follicular phase, the FSH "recruits" a number of follicles, which begin to develop. Within 5 to 7 days, a single follicle becomes dominant and the others begin to degenerate, becoming atretic. Between the seventh and fourteenth days the dominant follicle produces a rising level of estradiol, gradually suppressing FSH. The proliferative phase of the uterine endometrial cycle begins at the conclusion of menstrual flow and continues until ovulation; the endometrium gradually increases in thickness from about 0.5 mm to as much as 5 mm.

The ovulatory phase begins on approximately day 14 and lasts for about 36 hours. It appears to be initiated as the hypothalamus responds to the rapidly rising estradiol with an abrupt surge of LH. The LH surge builds to a peak in about 14 hours and falls back to basal levels over the next 36 hours. FSH levels rise and fall in a parallel pattern, though less steeply. Ovulation, the release of a fertilizable oocyte from the dominant follicle, occurs approximately 34 hours after the LH surge begins and about 20 hours after the peak. An area of the follicle wall dissolves and the oocyte is extruded from the cortex of the ovary. The estradiol levels drop as the LH surge begins. However, progesterone, produced by the ovulating follicle, rises steeply.

The luteal phase begins immediately after ovulation, lasts another 14 days, and terminates the day prior to the onset of menstrual bleeding. The released oocyte is moved through the fallopian tube toward the uterus during the next 2 days and must be fertilized during this time. Also during the first few days, the granulosa cells of the follicle become the new corpus luteum, secreting rising levels of progesterone and estradiol. During the week after ovulation, the endometrium becomes "secretory" in response to the estrogen and progesterone, producing changes in the structure of glands and blood vessels. Progesterone levels remain high through the middle of the luteal phase, as, to a lesser degree, do estradiol levels. Between the eighth and thirteenth postovulatory days the endometrium differentiates further in preparation for implantation (the implantation phase). If fertilization has not occurred by 2 or 3 days from the beginning of the next menses, the corpus luteum degenerates (luteolysis),

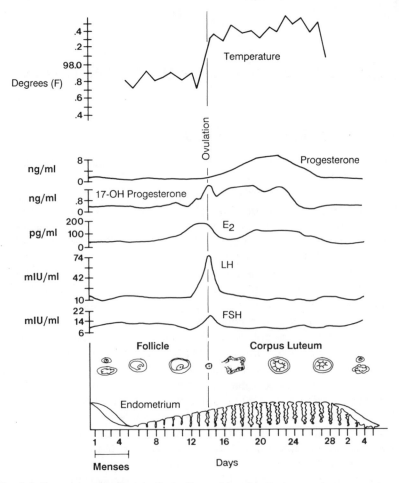

Fig. 6-1. Normal menstrual cycle fluctuations of basal body temperature, progesterone, 17-hydroxyprogesterone, estradiol, luteinizing hormone (LH), follicle-stimulating hormone (FSH), ovarian follicle, and endometrium throughout a typical menstrual cycle.

perhaps as a result of the high estradiol levels. Progesterone and estradiol levels fall quickly after luteolysis; their abrupt withdrawal produces vasomotor constriction of the endometrial vessels, leading to generalized ischemia and sloughing of most of the endometrial lining.

Menstrual flow consists of a sloughed endometrial tissue and bleeding from exposed and ruptured arterioles and capillaries. Most of the blood loss occurs in the first 3 days of menses. Flow stops several days into the follicular phase as renewed estrogen levels induce clotting and healing.

ABNORMALITIES OF THE MENSTRUAL CYCLE: INTRODUCTION

Irregularities of menstrual bleeding in adolescents commonly reflect immaturity, normal variation, pregnancy, or temporary and reversible influences of weight, diet, stress and activity, rather than disease intrinsic to the reproductive system. Cyclic pelvic and systemic disorders of adolescents likewise rarely indicate structural disease of the reproductive organs.

Abnormalities of Menstrual Bleeding

Maturation after Menarche. For most girls, the menstrual cycles in the year after menarche are anovulatory and prolonged, with the first ten cycles occurring over 15 months.[4] Prolongation of the interval between menses is primarily due to slower follicular development with a longer follicular phase. The interval between menses may vary considerably in over half of girls in the first postmenarchal year. Fertility during this time is uncommon.

Irregularities decrease over the next few years.[2] Two thirds of girls establish regular, ovulatory cycles (and fertility) within 2 years after menarche. Nearly all achieve a stable adult pattern by 7 years after menarche, and those who are still irregular or anovulatory are unlikely to correct spontaneously.

Normal Variation of Menstrual Cycles. Normal ranges of cycle length and duration of menses, as defined in Table 6-1, are statistical rather than absolute. Many normal young women experience spotting or even brief outright bleeding with ovulation in midcycle. A small percentage of women with apparently normal fertility will consistently have cycle lengths shorter or longer than the defined "normal range".[2] Regular menses 6 to 8 weeks apart are likely to represent normal variation if the woman has symptoms of ovulation and basal body temperature change 2 weeks prior to menses, or if she has dysmenorrhea or premenstrual symptoms.

Hypothalamic Suppression and Chronic Anovulation. It has long been known that female reproductive function is reversibly influenced by a variety of exogenous and endogenous factors. Diet and weight, activity level, stress, and illness, especially in various combinations, are common causes of adolescent menstrual irregularity and are discussed in more detail below. In general, these factors influence menstrual function by altering the amplitude or frequency of gonadotropin-releasing hormone secretion by the hypothalamus, causing anovulation. Menstruation and ovulation will generally return promptly when the interfering factor is removed. It is difficult to resist the teleologic interpretation that anovulation in these circumstances is a normal homeostatic response to a condition uncongenial to healthy pregnancy.

However, chronic anovulation has a significance beyond infertility. Ovulation is the key event in the middle of the normal mature menstrual cycle and results in the formation of a hormonally active corpus luteum, which participates in normal neuroendocrine feedback and function. The alterations that follow chronic anovulation affect the entire neuroendocrine-gonadal axis and contribute to the major abnormalities of the female reproductive system: amenorrhea and oligomenorrhea, dysfunctional uterine bleeding, hirsutism, and infertility. In addition, prolonged estrogen

Table 6-1. Definitions.

Menarche The first menstrual bleeding in a girl's life.
Thelarche The onset of visible breast development.
Pubarche The appearance of the first pubic hairs.
Adrenarche Strictly, the onset of adrenal maturation that leads to the appearance of pubic hair, but commonly used to refer to appearance of pubic hair (equivalent to pubarche).
Ovulatory cycle A mature menstrual cycle with positive feedback and release of an ovum (ovulation), followed by corpus luteum formation.
Anovulatory cycle A menstrual cycle without ovulation or production of a corpus luteum, so that the endometrium remains in the proliferative phase.
Amenorrhea Absence of menses in a female old enough to menstruate. Primary amenorrhea refers to the delay or absence of menarche beyond the age of 15 years. Secondary amenorrhea refers to cessation of previously established menses, for at least 6 months, at any time between menarche and menopause.
Oligomenorrhea Reduction in the regularity or frequency of menstruation with prolongation of the time between menses to more than 40 days; periods may seem to be "skipped."
Dysfunctional uterine bleeding (DUB) Any abnormal postmenarcheal uterine bleeding, including abnormally heavy or long or frequent menses, as well as nonmenstrual bleeding, i.e., bleeding occurring before or after menses or caused by a process distinct from the mechanism of cyclic menstruation. Polymenorrhea, hypermenorrhea, menorrhagia, metrorrhagia, and menometrorrhagia are all forms of DUB. Although some authorities subsume all abnormal patterns of menstrual bleeding, including oligomenorrhea, hypomenorrhea, and amenorrhea, under DUB, this broader application is not used here.
Polymenorrhea Increased frequency of menses due to shortening of menstrual cycle to less than 21 days.
Hypomenorrhea Decreased amount of blood flow with a normal menstrual cycle ("light periods").
Hypermenorrhea Increased amount of blood flow with a normal menstrual cycle ("heavy periods"), exceeding 8 saturated napkins, or 10 tampons, or 100 ml per 24 hours.
Menorrhagia Excessive menstrual blood flow due to prolonged duration of menses (more than 8 days).
Metrorrhagia Episodes of uterine bleeding between menses; intermenstrual "spotting."
Menometrorrhagia Irregular or frequent uterine bleeding, with excessively prolonged bleeding during menses.
Dysmenorrhea Painful menstruation, either "primary" or secondary to various pelvic diseases.
Mittelschmerz Pain occurring regularly between menses, usually at the expected time of ovulation.
Premenstrual syndrome One or more symptoms regularly occurring in the days prior to the onset of each menstrual period (late luteal phase).

---

unopposed by progesterone may induce endometrial hyperplasia and has been implicated in later development of fibromyomas, endometriosis, various breast disorders, and possibly uterine and breast cancers. Many women with chronic anovulation have decreased bone density, which may raise their risk of eventual osteoporosis. These secondary consequences can be more troubling than the original cause of anovulation.[1,5]

Ovulatory and anovulatory cycles differ. Ovulatory cycles are more consistent in length, and the menses are more consistent in duration and amount of flow. Mittelschmerz, increased midcycle quantity and stretchability of cervical mucus, dysmenorrhea, and premenstrual symptoms such as breast tenderness are common with ovulatory cycles but rare during anovulatory cycles. Ovulation is reliably signaled by the midcyle rise in basal body temperature. Progesterone levels in the last 10 days of the cycle are lower in anovulatory cycles. The lower progesterone levels are associated with continued endometrial proliferation; as the endometrium outgrows its vascular supply, desquamation and bleeding occur. Compared to ovulatory menses, anovulatory bleeding may be delayed and is often heavier and more prolonged because of the thicker endometrium and less synchronous desquamation. Anovulatory endometrium has a characteristic proliferative appearance; it may evolve into atypical endometrial hyperplasia.

Distinctions between secondary amenorrhea, oligomenorrhea, and dysfunctional uterine bleeding are empiric rather than etiologic, as anovulation may cause all three conditions. Anovulatory DUB often progresses to oligomenorrhea and then to secondary amenorrhea. Causes of chronic anovulation are listed in Tables 6-2 and 6-3.

Whether to treat anovulation in adolescence remains controversial.[3,5,6] Anovulation in the first 5 postmenarchal years has such a high rate of spontaneous resolution that treatment is unnecessary unless there are sufficiently troublesome symptoms, such as chronic hypoestrogenism, severe dysfunctional uterine bleeding, or marked hirsutism. Reversal of anovulation is also necessary when pregnancy is desired. However, there is insufficient evidence that cyclic progesterone or various other treatments for anovulation in older adolescents significantly reduce later risks of cancer, osteoporosis, reproductive problems, or other disorders.

Oligomenorrhea and Secondary Amenorrhea. The causes of oligomenorrhea and secondary amenorrhea are nearly identical and in most cases can be readily ascertained, despite the number of possibilities (Table 6-3).

Pregnancy should be considered, regardless of the duration of amenorrhea. An overweight teenager may carry a pregnancy to term without arousing suspicions in family and friends. Pregnancy may occasionally result from the first ovulation after a period of amenorrhea without an intervening menses to warn of fertility. It is also possible for gestational tumors such as choriocarcinoma to appear as secondary amenorrhea.

Persistent secondary amenorrhea in adolescents is most often due to the common causes of reversible suppression of hypothalamic function: abnormalities of weight, activity, stress, and systemic illness. In these conditions, both steroid and neuroendocrine hormone patterns revert to an early pubertal or even prepubertal state characterized by low gonadotropin levels and decreased levels of both androgens and estrogens.[7] These factors are fairly common, even in adolescents with normal menses; experienced clinical judgment may be required to decide whether such a factor is a sufficient explanation for amenorrhea in an individual case.

Body Fat, Starvation, and Anorexia Nervosa. Effects of reduced or excessive weight reflect increased or decreased percentages of body fat, which plays an important role in storage and metabolism of steroid hor-

Table 6-2. Causes of Oligomenorrhea and Secondary Amenorrhea.

Pregnancy
  Trophoblastic gestational tumors
Hypothalamic, reversible, with chronic anovulation
  Immaturity (early postmenarcheal period)
  Obesity
  Dietary restriction, deficient body fat, malnutrition
    Anorexia nervosa
    Involuntary starvation
  High activity level, physical training
  Emotional stress
    Depression, psychosis
    Change of environment (e.g., college)
    Withdrawal from drug addiction
    Pseudocyesis
Systemic illness
  Cancer
  Inflammatory bowel disease
  Cystic fibrosis
  Diabetes mellitus in poor control
  Head trauma
  Spinal cord injury
  Others
Drugs and toxins
  Exogenous hormones
    Withdrawal of oral contraceptives
    Exogenous androgens
    GnRH analogs
  Psychotropic agents
    Narcotics, especially heroin
    Phenothiazines and other antipsychotics
    Tricyclic antidepressants
    Marijuana and tetrahydrocannabinol
  Antihypertensives
    Reserpine
    Alpha-methyldopa
  Cancer chemotherapy
  Etretinate
  Vitamin A toxicity
  Chronic alcoholism
  Others
Hormonal abnormalities
  Hyperprolactinemia
  Hypothyroidism
  Hyperthyroidism
  Adrenal insufficiency
  Cushing's syndrome
  Hyperandrogenism
    Polycystic ovary syndrome
    Congenital adrenal hyperplasia
    Androgen-secreting tumor (adrenal or ovarian)
  Hyperestrogenism
    Estrogen-secreting tumor
      Granulosa or theca cell tumor of ovary
      Adrenocortical carcinoma
  Acromegaly
  Gonadotropin-secreting tumor
    Pituitary adenoma
    Hepatic tumor
    Germ cell tumor of ovary
Disorders of hypothalamic steroid sensitivity or feedback response
Hypothalamic infiltration or destruction, irreversible

Table 6-2. *Continued.*

Hypothalamic space-occupying tumor or cyst
Infiltrative destruction
   Leukemia
   Metastatic malignancy
   Histiocytosis X
   Sarcoidosis
   Tuberculosis
   Other infection, including viral
Radiation
Surgery or trauma
Allergic or autoimmune encephalomyelitis
Ischemic or hemorrhagic stroke
Pituitary dysfunction, usually irreversible
Pituitary infarction (Sheehan's syndrome), apoplexy
Empty sella syndrome
Tumor
Radiation
Viral or autoimmune hypophysitis
Trauma or surgery, pituitary stalk disruption
Obstruction of aqueduct of Sylvius
Gonadotropin deficiency
   Isolated
   Abnormal, "bioinactive" LH molecule
   Combined pituitary hormone deficiencies
Ovarian failure, irreversible
Autoimmune
Galactosemia
Atypical gonadal dysgenesis
47,XXX syndrome
Premature menopause
   Idiopathic
   Familial
   Small Xq deletion
Radiation
Surgical oophorectomy
Bilateral ovarian torsion or infarction
Toxins and drugs
   Cytotoxic chemotherapy
Resistant ovary syndrome
Uterine abnormalities
Loss of endometrium
   Excessive curettage (Asherman's syndrome)
   Endometritis, especially gonococcal or septic abortion
   Infection with tuberculosis or schistosomiasis
Hysterectomy
Acquired cervical obstruction
Radiation damage
Vaginal obstruction

mones. The association of delayed menarche with low body fat was discussed in Chapter 3. After menarche, weight loss may either disrupt menstrual cycling or restore it, depending on initial body weight. The Frisch fatness nomogram (Fig. 6-2) is useful in estimating body fat from height and weight in young women.

It has long been recognized that starvation, whether voluntary (e.g., dieting) or involuntary (e.g., famine), is commonly accompanied by revers-

Table 6-3. Causes of Abnormal Vaginal Bleeding.

Exclude rectal, urethral, and other perineal bleeding
Vaginal or uterine abnormalities
  Trauma (coitus, rape, abuse)
  Foreign body (IUD, tampon, etc.)
  Infection
    Vaginitis (trichomonas, gonorrhea)
    Cervicitis
    Endometritis (tuberculosis)
    Pelvic inflammatory disease
    Venereal condylomata of cervix or vagina
  Tumor
    Clear-cell carcinoma of cervix or vagina (DES)
    Sarcoma botryoides
    Polyps
    Ovarian cyst or tumor
    Leiomyomatosis
  Endometriosis
  Congenital malformations of uterus
Complications of pregnancy
  Threatened or spontaneous abortion
  Ectopic pregnancy
  Molar pregnancy
  Induced abortion
Coagulopathy
  Generalized
  Uterine production of menstrual anticoagulants
Dysfunctional uterine bleeding
  Normal variation
    Midcycle ovulatory bleeding
    Early postmenarcheal anovulation
    Early postmenarcheal estrogen irregularities
  Chronic anovulation
    Exogenous steroids
      Oral contraception
        Midcycle breakthrough bleeding
        Relative luteal progesterone deficiency
      Progestagens
      Continual estrogens
    Systemic diseases
      Hypothyroidism
      Adrenal insufficiency
      Cushing's syndrome
      Diabetes mellitus
      Chronic liver disease
    Hyperprolactinemia
    Androgen excess (see Table G)
      Polycystic ovary syndrome
      Congenital adrenal hyperplasia
      Exogenous androgens
      Androgen-producing ovarian or adrenal tumor
    Estrogen excess
      Granulosa-theca cell tumor of the ovary
      Other tumors
    Hypothalamic
      Emotional stress
      Physical stress, especially exercise
  Ovulatory
    Short luteal phase
    Prolonged luteal phase (Halban disease)
    Luteal progesterone insufficiency

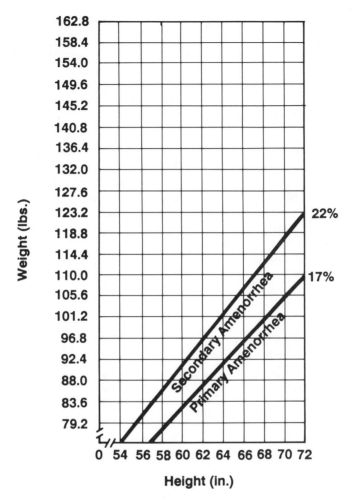

Fig. 6-2. Fatness nomogram. This simplified Frisch nomogram can be used to determine whether a young woman has a body-fat content sufficient for menarche or continued menses. The diagonal lines indicate the weights corresponding to fat contents (expressed as percentages of total body weight) of 17 and 22%. It has been found empirically that menarche will rarely occur when the body-fat content is less than 17%, and that secondary amenorrhea will usually occur if the body-fat content falls below 22%. Adapted from Frisch RE: Fatness and fertility. Sci Am 1988;258:90.

ible amenorrhea or oligomenorrhea. It has been observed that after age 16 years, a reduction of body fat to below 22% of total body weight is likely to disrupt menses; a nonobese person may achieve this during a 10-15% reduction in body weight.[8] Hormone levels and neuroendocrine secretion patterns revert to pre- or early pubertal states.[7] Ultrasound imaging of the ovaries commonly shows multiple follicular cysts with decreased ovarian tissue mass and may help to confirm that amenorrhea is due to weight loss or an eating disorder.[9] Menses will generally resume within 3 months of regaining critical body fat.

Anorexia nervosa is a special example of amenorrhea due to starvation and decreased body fat.[7,10,11,12] DSM III criteria for diagnosis of anorexia nervosa include refusal to maintain normal body weight with loss of 25% of initial body weight, disturbance of body image, intense fear of becoming fat, and no underlying medical or psychiatric disorder contributing to weight loss or abnormal behavior.

Anorexia nervosa is currently considered a primary psychologic disturbance, although the possibility of predisposing neurochemical abnormalities has not been excluded (Table 6-4). Emotional stress and hyperactivity contribute to amenorrhea; cessation of menses occasionally precedes severe weight loss. Excessive and compulsive exercise is primarily part of the effort to reduce weight. Most, but not all, of the laboratory abnormalities are a result of starvation. Table 6-5 is a fuller list of clinical and laboratory features that have been reported; some are controversial.

When all of the major features of anorexia nervosa are present, malnu-

Table 6-4. Psychosocial Features of Anorexia Nervosa.

Psychosocial aspects
  Predisposing cultural characteristics
    Overvaluation of thinness
    Learned dependence of self-esteem on attractiveness
  Predisposing family characteristics
    Upper middle class
    Poor family communications and conflict resolution
    Avoidance and denial of conflicts in family
    Enmeshment
    Overprotection
    Rigidity of family structure and interactions
    Alcoholism in family members
    Depression in family members
    Expectations of compliance, accommodation, and self-sacrifice
  Predisposing personal characteristics
    High previous academic performance
    Perfectionism
    Impaired psychologic development
      Decreased oppositional and independent behavior in infancy
      Poor awareness of body sensations
    Tendency to asceticism and self-denial
    Denial or fear of sexuality
    Taking on added work or family burdens
  Abnormal attitudes and behavior toward food and nutrition
    Hoarding or hiding food
    Obsession with food
    Taking pleasure in food refusal
    Postprandial vomiting
  Disturbed body image
    Intense fear of fat
    Perception of underweight body as fat
    Denial of signs and symptoms or malnutrition
    Resistance to recommendations of weight gain
  Depression
  Periodic overactivity

Table 6-5. Clinical Features of Anorexia Nervosa.

Altered body composition and function due to malnutrition
  General
    Dehydration
    Decreased muscle mass
    Emaciation and decreased adipose tissue
    Fluid retention and ankle edema
    Weakness and fatigability
    Decreased body temperature and basal metabolic rate
    Heat or cold intolerance with decreased shivering
  CNS
    Cerebral atrophy
    Sleep disturbances
    Sensory hypersensitivity
    Hyperactive or hypoactive reflexes
  Reproductive
    Amenorrhea, primary or secondary
    Chronic anovulation
    Small uterus
    Hypoestrogenized vaginal mucosa
    Decreased breast mass with sagging or skin wrinkling
  Circulatory
    Bradycardia (below 60 beats per minute)
    Hypotension (systolic blood pressure below 70 mm Hg)
    Mitral valve prolapse
  Skin and hair
    Cold, dry, mottled, skin
    Skin yellowed or "dirty" in appearance
    Easily plucked hair
    Lanugo hair
    Irritation or abrasions over bony prominences and sacrum
  Gastrointestinal and abdominal
    Gastric dilatation and tenderness
    Hypoactive bowel sounds and decreased motility
    Palpable stool in abdomen, constipation
  Decreased bone density
  Bone marrow suppression
  Anergy to skin testing
  Decreased urinary concentrating ability, partial diabetes insipidus
Laboratory changes
  Blood tests
    Hypoproteinemia with decreased albumin, transferrin
    Megaloblastic or normocytic anemia
    Thrombocytopenia
    Leukopenia
    Low sedimentation rate
    Hypokalemia
    Hypophosphatemia
    Hypomagnesemia
    Increased carotene
    Increased cholesterol
    Metabolic alkalosis
    Increased BUN
  Neuroendocrine abnormalities
    Low T3 and high reverse T3
    Low LH and FSH levels
    Decreased circadian differences in LH and FSH
    Decreased estradiol levels
    Diminished LH and FSH response to GnRH
    Increased cortisol levels
    Nonsuppressibility of cortisol by dexamethasone

Table 6-5. *Continued.*

Elevated basal growth hormone
Increased endogenous opioid activity
Increased cerebrospinal fluid vasopressin
Abnormal cerebrospinal fluid monoamine levels
Electrocardiogram
    Decreased voltage
    Atrioventricular block
    Sinus bradycardia
    Inverted T waves
Echocardiogram
    Decreased contractility
CT scan of head
    Cerebral atrophy
X rays
    Gastric distention
    Osteoporosis
    Narrow cardiac silhouette

trition may be life-threatening and require intravenous or tube feedings with attention to fluid and electrolyte deficiencies and cardiac function. Because girls with full-blown anorexia nervosa strenuously resist intervention, treatment can be frustrating and difficult. The currently favored approach for these cases is prolonged, intensive nutritional and behavioral treatment in an inpatient setting by a team with both medical and psychotherapeutic expertise.

Less severe, or "incomplete," forms of anorexia nervosa that lack one or more major features are common. Explanation of "healthy" body weight and the relationship between weight and amenorrhea may be enough to induce the patient to relax her dieting. Calorie counts should be kept, and weight should be checked frequently, with the understanding that hospitalization will be necessary if the weight falls.

Anorexic "variants" or "equivalents" include laxative, enema, diuretic, or thyroxine abuse, bulemia, and intentional undertreatment of diabetes mellitus or hyperthyroidism; although the psychodynamics may be similar, the malnutrition tends to be less severe, amenorrhea is less common, and the conditions are less refractory to intervention.

Obesity. Significant obesity is also associated with menstrual disruption (especially oligomenorrhea or secondary amenorrhea) due to chronic anovulation.[13] Aromatization of androgens by excess adipose tissue provides higher levels of estrogens. A probable second mechanism is the complex interaction of hyperandrogenism and hyperinsulinism characteristic of the polycystic ovary syndrome (discussed below); an obese adolescent may manifest any combination of features. In some women, anovulation and obesity may be secondary to an underlying hypothalamic dysfunction, such as hypothyroidism (discussed below) or Prader-Willi syndrome (discussed in Chapter 3). In some cases, depression and emotional stress associated with obesity may contribute to chronic anovulation. In the absence of an underlying systemic disorder, weight loss usually results in resumption of menses.

Exercise and Athletic Training. Menses may cease during intensive athletic training.[3,12,14] This appears to be a homeostatic response of the hypothalamus to some or all of the following: (1) the unfavorable reproductive state created by a major energy drain; (2) a reduction of body fat below a critical percentage; (3) the emotional stress of training and competition and its adrenal response; (4) elevated endogenous opioids which may suppress gonadotropin release; (5) dietary changes such as reduced protein intake; and (6) differences in reproductive history in those inclined to exercise.

Athletic amenorrhea occurs most commonly when frequent, prolonged exercise is combined with strenous efforts to minimize body fat, such as long distance running and ballet. In one study, amenorrhea was reported by nearly half of women running 80 miles per week, but by only 5% of women running less than 10 miles per week. The diagnosis of athletic amenorrhea should be doubted if the girl is not extremely lean, or if the exercise is not intense and nearly daily. Evidence of other causes of amenorrhea should be assessed and pursued appropriately. Conclusive proof, of course, is prompt resumption of menses upon interruption of training, as with injury or the end of the athletic season.

Whether this "homeostatic" amenorrhea is harmful has not been conclusively established. One consequence appears to be decreased bone density, which may predispose the athlete to osteoporosis as she ages. For this reason, some investigators advocate treatment with sequential estrogen-progestin combinations, especially if there is evidence of hypoestrogenism (vaginal dryness, breast atrophy, low estradiol levels, or lack of withdrawal bleeding after progestin challenge), although this recommendation is often rejected by the athletes.[3] Surveys have not found prolonged athletic amenorrhea in adolescence to increase the likelihood of later reproductive dysfunction, although exceptions may be found.[12]

Emotional Stress and Psychologic Amenorrhea. The susceptibility of reproductive rhythms to psychologic and emotional stress is well known.[3,11,15] In adolescents experiencing a marked change of environment (e.g., college, boarding school, or prison), transient amenorrhea is common and requires no intervention. Depression and anxiety may also disrupt menses, particularly if sedative, hypnotic, or antidepressant drugs are used. Amenorrhea is common during withdrawal from drug addiction, even months after last drug use. The mechanisms are complex and involve endorphins, catecholamines, cortisol, and the limbic system, resulting in decreased amplitude and frequency of GnRH release.[7]

Pseudocyesis, or "false pregnancy", is an extreme demonstration of psychologically altered neuroendocrine function. LH and prolactin secretion are increased to levels sufficient to maintain persistent luteal function and galactorrhea; these levels promptly fall when the diagnosis is revealed to the patient.[6] The fantasy of pregnancy may be a defense against depression.

Systemic Illness. In general, the regression of hypothalamic reproductive function in chronic systemic illness is similar to that seen in starvation, with contributions by psychologic stress and malnutrition, and sometimes by altered steroid metabolism. Typical conditions in which secondary amenorrhea is common include poorly controlled diabetes mellitus, tuberculosis, chronic renal failure, cancer, cystic fibrosis, chronic active hepatitis, systemic lupus erythematosis, and other rheumatoid diseases. Amelioration of the disease often allows resumption of menses; regularity of menses may be an index of disease activity.

It is uncommon for oligomenorrhea or secondary amenorrhea in adolescents to be due to undiagnosed illness. One exception deserving mention is inflammatory bowel disease, which may inhibit growth and menstrual function without prominent bowel symptoms.[11]

Drugs and Toxins. Of the many drugs and toxins that can interfere with regular menses (Table 6-2 is a partial list), few are important in adolescence. Termination of oral contraceptive pills is followed by amenorrhea of at least 6 months' duration in a sizable minority of young women; menses resumes spontaneously in most, but a workup is warranted after a year or if there is evidence of another disorder.[12]

Oral etretinate is occasionally used for acne in adolescence. The effects of psychotropic agents on menstrual periods are varied and generally dose-related. Amenorrhea of narcotic addiction and other drug abuse may arise from weight loss, malnutrition, and psychologic stress, as well as endorphin-related neuroendocrine effects.

Endocrine Disorders. Nearly all significant deficiencies or excesses of major hormones may disrupt menstrual cycles, either by directly interfering with neuroendocrine feedback and control systems at a variety of levels, or by adversely affecting general health as other systemic illnesses do.[3,16] Either way, the result is interference primarily at the hypothalamic level, resulting in anovulation, dysfunctional uterine bleeding, or amenorrhea. In a younger girl these conditions may delay or interrupt puberty.

Hyperprolactinemia, a common cause of secondary amenorrhea in young women, is discussed in detail in Chapter 5. Although the combination of galactorrhea and secondary amenorrhea nearly always indicates hyperprolactinemia, galactorrhea is absent in many cases of hyperprolactinemic amenorrhea. Hyperprolactinemia may also be a secondary feature of hypothyroidism.

Acquired hypothyroidism may cause dysfunctional uterine bleeding or secondary amenorrhea. Hypothyroidism develops insidiously enough that it is commonly missed for long periods of time, partly because the patient is unaware of a clear transition from "well" to "ill." Clinical findings in adolescent girls vary. Typical features are listed in Table 6-6; less obvious or uncommon findings are omitted. Goiter is not always present, and mild enlargement of the thyroid gland is easily missed. The diagnosis is confirmed by decreased T4 and increased TSH. Levels of free T4, T3, and T3 resin uptake are also low or low normal. In early or mild hypothyroidism, the TSH is barely elevated and T4 may be in the lower half of the normal range. Less universally accepted are claims that menstrual irregularities without other signs and symptoms may be caused by "subclinical

Table 6-6. Features of Hypothyroidism in Adolescence.

Decreased spontaneous energy and activity
Increased sleeping or tiredness
Weight gain, often with decreased appetite
Depression, social withdrawal, apathy
Cold intolerance
Loss of color in face
Loss of sharpness of features, facial puffiness
Loss of hair, loss of hair luster
Dryness and coolness of skin
Aches and pains, especially in large joints
Slowing of speech and thinking
Decreased resting pulse and pulse pressure
Swelling of ankles with minimal pitting (myxedema)
Diminished reflexes and spontaneous motion
Hypercholesterolemia
Anemia, normocytic or macrocytic
Elevated prolactin
Multicystic ovaries by ultrasound

hypothyroidism" with TSH as well as T4 within the lower normal range; in such cases, an exaggerated TSH response to TRH may justify a trial of thyroxine replacement.

Nearly all hypothyroidism acquired in adolescence is due to autoimmune thyroiditis, which can be confirmed by demonstrating antimicrosomal and antithyroglobulin antibodies. Adolescents with diabetes or a family history of thyroid disease are at higher risk. Other thyroid tests, such as imaging or uptake tests, are rarely necessary if antibodies are positive. Hypothyroidism secondary to hypothalamic or pituitary insufficiency (indicated by low T4 and TSH) is rare, and is commonly accompanied by other pituitary hormone abnormalities. Adolescents with hypothyroidism are best treated with 0.125 to 0.2 mg of L-thyroxine daily.

Hyperthyroidism in adolescent girls commonly appears with emotional lability, nervousness, poor sleep, heat intolerance, and increased appetite. Disruption of menses is less common, unless there has been significant weight loss. A goiter is nearly always present but may be minimal by palpation. Eye signs are present in most, but not all patients. The T4, free T4, T3, and T3 resin uptake levels are elevated, and TSH is suppressed. Thyrotoxicosis in adolescence is nearly always autoimmune; if the gland is symmetric and antibodies (antimicrosomal, antithyroglobulin, or thyroid-stimulating immunoglobulins) are present, imaging and isotope testing are unnecessary.

Acquired adrenal insufficiency (Addison's disease) is more common than Cushing's syndrome in adolescents. Oligomenorrhea and amenorrhea are common, especially with marked weight loss. Addison's disease should be suspected in teenagers with fatigability, depression, and weight loss; this condition can resemble anorexia nervosa, drug abuse, or primary depression. In the United States, variations of skin color due to tanning and race are common enough that hyperpigmentation is usually unnoticed until after Addison's disease is suspected. Mucocutaneous candidiasis, diabetes mellitus, hypoparathydroidism, or a family history of autoimmune endocrinopathy indicates increased risk. Diagnosis is supported by a low 0800 cortisol, poor response to cosyntropin stimulation, and positive antiadrenal antibodies.

Cushing's syndrome as a cause of menstrual irregularity occurs in most large series. It may be iatrogenic or due to pituitary overstimulation of the adrenals, an adrenal adenoma, or carcinoma. Malar flush, fat cheeks, mild obesity, and hypertension are early features. Marked obesity, buffalo hump, striae, bruising, diabetes, myopathy, and hirsutism occur with advanced disease. It may resemble the polycystic ovary syndrome. The overnight dexamethasone suppression test and a 24-hour urine collection for cortisol are the initial screening tests.

Androgen excess, discussed below, is frequently associated with anovulation and menstrual irregularities. The most common condition is polycystic ovary syndrome and its variants and partial forms.

Chronically elevated, acyclic estrogen levels cause anovulation by suppressing the hypothalamus. Conditions of estrogen overproduction are less common than syndromes of androgen excess. Granulosa-theca cell tumors of the ovary often produce estrogens. Such tumors may also secrete androgens in a manner similar to that of polycystic ovary syndrome; differentiation should be possible through pelvic ultrasound. The rare adrenal tumors that produce estrogen are likely to secrete excess androgens as well.

With the exception of hyperprolactinemia, pituitary adenomas are extremely rare causes of adolescent amenorrhea. Growth hormone excess beginning in childhood causes acromegalic tall stature; later onset only thickens the features and enlarges the jaw and digits. Somatomedin C is the initial screening test. Acromegaly is often associated with hyperprolactinemia. Gonadotropin excess from a pituitary adenoma may also cause menstrual irregularity, but nearly all reported cases have been in older adults. Rare liver or ovarian tumors producing human chorionic gonadotropin may produce a similar picture.

Hypothalamic or Pituitary Disorders. In some women with adequate estrogenization and normal levels of LH and FSH, anovulation and amenorrhea without other symptoms result from altered sensitivities or dysfunctional feedback responses of the hypothalamus to circulating steroids.

Hypogonadotropic anovulatory amenorrhea can also result from irreversible destruction of parts of the hypothalamus and pituitary gland by trauma, tumor, infiltration, or infarction (Table 6-2). Amenorrhea may be the patient's initial complaint, but neurologic symptoms or evidence of other pituitary hormone deficiencies may also be present. Gonadotropin levels are low, as are estrogen and androgen levels. Signs of estrogen deficiency tend to be less marked than in primary ovarian failure. Most of these diagnoses are confirmed by computerized axial tomography or magnetic resonance imaging, which may be more sensitive for small deep lesions.

Leukemia and histiocytosis X are the most common infiltrative hypothalamic disorders in adolescents. With the exception of craniopharyngioma (discussed in Chapter 3), intracranial tumors cause headaches and neurologic complaints more often than they do amenorrhea. Poorly understood viral, autoimmune, or allergic processes, represented by a few adult case reports and animal models, account for an unknown proportion of idiopathic hypothalamic amenorrhea cases. Craniospinal irradiation for cancer treatment may result in hypothalamic or pituitary dysfunction. The empty sella syndrome has been reported in a number of adolescents; an apparent absence of pituitary tissue by CAT scan may or may not be accompanied by anterior pituitary hormone deficiencies, especially of gonadotropins or growth hormone.

Ovarian Failure. Primary, irreversible ovarian failure is an occasional cause of oligomenorrhea progressing to amenorrhea in young women. The principal clue to ovarian failure is elevation of LH and FSH above the adult normal range. Signs of estrogen deficiency and typical menopausal vasomotor symptoms may be present.

Autoimmune destruction of the ovaries (confirmed by demonstrating anti-ovarian antibodies) may occur in women with other autoimmune endocrinopathies such as Addison's disease, thyroiditis, diabetes, or myasthenia gravis, or may be an isolated problem. "Premature menopause," or idiopathic ovarian failure indistinguishable from menopause, is rare in adolescence. Galactosemic patients will have been long identified prior to a complaint of amenorrhea, but may suffer either primary or secondary amenorrhea due to ovarian atrophy. The resistant ovary syndrome is characterized by apparent ovarian failure with elevated gonadotropins, although the ovaries appear normal histologically.

Although gonadal dysgenesis (discussed in more detail in Chapter 3) usually results in primary amenorrhea, menarche is sometimes followed by sporadic menses, and eventually amenorrhea, presumably due to the presence at puberty of a few remaining follicles.[17] Affected patients, although often short, usually do not have marked Turner's stigmata, and may have evidence of limited estrogen effect. The karyotype is usually abnormal, revealing mosaicism or partial X chromosome deletions more often than the 45,X of Turner's syndrome. Very small band deletions of the long arm of the X chromosome have recently been found to cause premature ovarian failure without any features of Turner's syndrome. Women with 47,XXX karyotype also have a high rate of secondary amenorrhea without complete hormonal deficiency.

Both radiation and a variety of cytotoxic chemotherapeutic agents may damage the ovaries reversibly or irreversibly in a dose-related manner.[18] Prepubertal ovaries may be less susceptible than postpubertal ovaries to damage by radiation or chemotherapy. Fewer but higher doses of radiation are more damaging than the same cumulative dose delivered in smaller amounts over a longer time. Of the chemotherapeutic agents, the alkylating cytotoxic agents used to treat nephrotic syndrome and various cancers (e.g., cyclophosphamide and vincristine) have been most often associated with ovarian toxicity. Combining chemotherapy with radiation synergistically enhances toxicity. Predictions as to future function or fertility made at the time of radiation or chemotherapy should be cautious.

Acquired Abnormalities of the Uterus and Vagina. Structural abnormalities of the uterus and cervical or vaginal outflow tracts are uncommon in adolescent women, although endometrial sclerosis may follow gonorrhea or complicated abortion. Asherman's syndrome refers to endometrial destruction by excessive curettage or other trauma. Pelvic radiation therapy may also damage the uterus.

Evaluation. Oligomenorrhea in an apparently healthy teenager rarely requires an extensive workup. For 2 years after menarche, oligomenorrhea is so common that laboratory evaluation is not indicated unless there is additional evidence of a medical problem. Evaluation may be justified by the following conditions: persistence of oligomenorrhea for longer than 2 years; onset and persistence of oligomenorrhea for 6 months in a girl with previously regular menses; excessive, recurrent pregnancy anxiety; or signs or symptoms suggestive of a significant disorder. Likewise, in the absence of other apparent problems, laboratory evaluation of secondary amenorrhea may be justifiably postponed until it has persisted for 4 to 6 months.

A thorough history of pubertal development, past and present menstrual patterns, menstrual and premenstrual symptoms, recent sexual activity, and oral contraceptive use should be obtained. Secondly, a complete review of systems and physical examination including a pelvic exam may suggest the possibility of one of the disorders discussed above. Particular attention should be paid to significant changes in life circumstances and emotional health, major weight changes, level of physical activity, hirsutism, and the possibility of pregnancy.

The laboratory tests useful enough to be frequently obtained include those for chorionic gonadotropin (hCG), LH, FSH, and prolactin. In many circumstances, estradiol or androgen levels are informative. Other tests may be indicated by specific symptoms or findings. Normal values for various hormones are provided in Chapter 3.

Testing for pregnancy is usually justified; the hCG test is highly accurate after the first missed period. An elevated hCG also occurs with choriocarcinoma.

The highest yield of clinical information is obtained from measurement of the gonadotropins. Levels of both LH and FSH above the adult normal range indicate ovarian failure with a reliability proportional to the magnitude of the elevation. It is often difficult to distinguish low from normal levels of gonadotropins, particularly in early adolescence, although undetectable gonadotropins usually indicate irreversible hypothalamic or pituitary deficiency. Levels that are mildly depressed or in the low-normal range usually indicate a state of reversible hypothalamic suppression and chronic anovulation. Further questioning and tests or referral to a specialist may be required at this point. An LH persistently and disproportionately higher than the FSH is often found in the polycystic ovary syndrome or hyperestrogen states.

Clearly elevated prolactin levels suggest that hyperprolactinemia is the cause of amenorrhea; there may be no other clinical clues. However, prolactin levels are commonly high in primary hypothyroidism, and may be mildly elevated in polycystic ovary syndrome.

A normal mature estradiol level helps to indicate functional ovaries, but interpretation must take into account the menstrual phase in which it was drawn. Significantly low levels suggest ovarian failure if accompanied by high gonadotropins, or pituitary deficiency if gonadotropins are low. Estradiol levels near the lower edge of normal, with low gonadotropins, are common with hypothalamic suppression. Estradiol levels may be normal or mildly elevated in polycystic ovary syndrome and some other hyperandrogen states. The vaginal maturation index is a less reliable index of estrogenization.

Hirsutism or virilization requires androgen screening, as discussed below. Cases of amenorrhea related to excess androgens without hirsutism are rare but have been reported.[19]

A 5-day progesterone challenge, as described in Chapter 3, should be followed by withdrawal bleeding if the endometrium has been adequately estrogenized. Bleeding also implies a hypothalamus and pituitary capable of some response, the presence of an endometrium, and a patent outflow tract. It usually indicates that amenorrhea was caused by hypothalamic suppression or reversible chronic anovulation. Scant bleeding implies mild hypoestrogenism. A non-response occurs with ovarian failure, loss of the endometrium, outflow-tract obstruction, or prolonged hypoestrogenism of any cause. A non-response with normal or low FSH occurs with severe impairment of the hypothalamic-pituitary axis.

Bleeding after a full cycle of estrogen-progestin oral contraceptive pills indicates a structurally intact endometrium and outflow tract, although this test is rarely necessary in adolescent secondary amenorrhea.

If pelvic symptoms or a possible mass are present, an ultrasound examination is the easiest and safest imaging screen for cysts, tumors, uterine obstruction, or other pelvic abnormalities.

High resolution intracranial imaging should be arranged to exclude a tumor or intracranial abnormality if neurologic symptoms or signs are present, or if no cause is apparent for hypothalamic amenorrhea.

Management. Management depends upon diagnosis. Systemic illnesses, hormone excesses and deficiencies, and tumors should be appropriately treated. Hyperprolactinemia and polycystic ovary disease are discussed elsewhere.

Primary failure of the ovaries requires replacement of estrogen and progesterone, normally with a sequential, low-dose estrogen-progestin oral contraceptive (discussed more fully in Chapter 3).[3] One should be cautious in predicting future infertility, as rare pregnancies have been reported in hypergonadotropic hypogonadism with estrogen replacement.[1]

When hypothalamic suppression and anovulation are expected to be temporary (because of such factors as immaturity, stress, weight loss, exercise, and discontinuation of birth control pills), patience and reassurance of reproductive normality should suffice. A progesterone withdrawal test may help demonstrate this. Oral contraceptives should not be given just to induce periods, especially within the first 5 postmenarcheal years.[1,3,20]

The decision to treat persistent anovulation in young women more than 5 years from menarche is not as straightforward, and some differences of opinion exist.[3,5,6,12] Some of the circumstances in which treatment of adolescent anovulation may be indicated include the following:

> Prolonged amenorrhea with hypoestrogenism
> Heavy dysfunctional uterine bleeding
> Apparent permanent hypothalamic or pituitary failure
> Polycystic ovary syndrome
> Desire for pregnancy

If pregnancy is not desired and estrogen levels are adequate, 10 mg of oral medroxyprogesterone acetate (Provera) can be taken daily for the first 10 days of each month. Alternatively, or if signs of estrogen deficiency are present or if greater contraceptive assurance is desired, a sequential combination oral contraceptive can be used.

Abnormal Vaginal Bleeding. Abnormal vaginal bleeding is a common problem in adolescence.[3,11,12,21-25] Occasionally, rectal, urethral, or other perineal bleeding may be mistakenly thought to be vaginal. Trauma to the introitus, hymen, urethra, or rectum due to coitus, rape, or abuse may be denied initially, especially if parents are present; such possibilities should be re-explored privately if examination warrants it. Foreign bodies such as an intrauterine contaceptive device or a forgotten tampon may cause bleeding.

Vaginal or Uterine Abnormalities. Infections such as vaginitis, cervicitis, or pelvic inflammatory disease may occur with bleeding.[21-23] However, there is usually a discharge, local tenderness, or visible inflammation; cultures will help to confirm the diagnosis. Tuberculous endometritis is rare, but skin testing is recommended in endemic areas or with exposed patients.

Neoplasia of the uterus or vagina is also rare.[21-23] Clear-cell carcinoma of the vagina or cervix may occur in girls exposed in utero to DES, although few are still in adolescence. Polyps, sarcoma botryoides of the cervix, uterine leiomyomatosis, venereal condylomata of the vagina or cervix, and ovarian tumors or cysts may cause vaginal bleeding. Tumors should be identifiable during pelvic examination by appearance, tender adnexal mass, or pap smear. Bleeding from tumors usually has no relation to menses, and is unlikely to rapidly respond to estrogen treatment.

Endometriosis (discussed below) is more common in late adolescence and may cause premenstrual spotting. Rarely, congenital malformations of the genital tract may cause nonmenstrual bleeding. For example, duplication of the müllerian system with unilateral partial obstruction and communication can result in slow, dark intermenstrual bleeding, as well as dysmenorrhea.[21]

Complications of Pregnancy. Complications of pregnancy are also common causes of adolescent bleeding.[22] Unexpected pregnancies are frequent in teenagers, and bleeding may occur in 20% of these pregnancies because of threatened or completed spontaneous abortion, induced abortion, ectopic pregnancy, or molar pregnancy. A negative history should not necessarily be taken at face value. A sensitive hCG test will detect any pregnancy advanced enough to cause bleeding. The possibility of an unwanted or complicated pregnancy is the only common indication for endometrial curettage in young adolescents.

Coagulopathies. Coagulopathies accounted for a fifth of one series of adolescent patients with abnormal bleeding.[23] Menorrhagia at menarche is highly suggestive of a congenital coagulopathy such as von Willebrand's disease or Glanzmann's thrombasthenia. There may be a history of bleeding of the gums or nose, but often there are no such problems. Platelet disorders (especially idiopathic thrombocytopenic purpura or leukemia) are the most common acquired coagulopathies capable of causing menorrhagia after several years of normal menses; bruises or petechiae are usually present. Rarely, anticoagulant drugs, including aspirin, may produce menorrhagia. Therefore, any unusually heavy vaginal bleeding at menarche that lowers the hemoglobin to 10 g/dl or requires transfusion, or any history of other bleeding problems, warrants measurement of platelet count, bleeding time, prothrombin time, and partial thromboplastin time. Although hypochromic anemia is an obvious result of excessive bleeding, some authorities also list it as a potential cause of abnormal bleeding.[12,25] It has also been suggested that some adolescents without general coagulopathy or abnormal hormonal patterns develop dysfunctional uterine bleeding due to locally produced anticoagulant substances in their menstrual flow.[25]

Dysfunctional Uterine Bleeding. The above causes of bleeding must be identified or excluded, but account for only a minority of abnormal vaginal bleeding cases. The majority of cases involve painless, irregular endometrial bleeding referred to as dysfunctional uterine bleeding (DUB). DUB may occur in a number of patterns, with distortion of menstrual bleeding (hypermenorrhea, polymenorrhea, menorrhagia) being more common than intermenstrual (metrorrhagia or menometrorrhagia).

DUB in the adolescent may result from immaturity, variation of normal function, or abnormality of hypothalamic, pituitary, ovarian, and/or other hormones (Table 6-3). Chronic anovulation (discussed above) is the factor common to most pathologic adolescent DUB because it is usually accompanied by prolonged, uninterrupted estrogen stimulation of the endometrium, which becomes hyperplastic but fragile and friable and will bleed spontaneously.[3] This "estrogen breakthrough bleeding" can be prolonged and excessive as various areas break down, desquamate, and heal in a random, asynchronous manner.[1] Another mechanism of prolonged bleeding may be insufficient exposure of the basal glands and cornual residual tissue to allow complete endometrial surface restoration.[1] Therefore, any disorder that causes anovulation may result in DUB, often in combination with oligomenorrhea, and sometimes preceding or following secondary amenorrhea.

Anovulation is common in the first years after menarche and is often reflected in prolonged, irregular menstrual cycles. The menses during this time may be heavy, but intermenstrual DUB is uncommon.[3] In fact, DUB is uncommon enough when compared to anovulation in the first years after menarche that some authorities attribute early adolescent irregularities of bleeding to fluctuations of estrogen levels rather than anovulation.[25]

Bleeding with birth control pills is common (see Chapter 7). Midcycle breakthrough bleeding in the initial cycles of low-estrogen pills usually stops spontaneously by the second or third cycle. If not, it can often be controlled by a pill with more estrogen. Hypermenorrhea, or the onset of breakthrough bleeding after longer use of a particular pill, may indicate relative progesterone deficiency and usually responds to a pill with a higher progestagen content. DUB can also be an occasional result of medroxyprogesterone prescribed to control previous irregularities.

Certain specific causes of anovulatory DUB must be recognized and treated appropriately. Menometrorrhagia occurs frequently in hypothyroidism, generally in association with other signs and symptoms; T4 and TSH will confirm or exclude this diagnosis. Polycystic ovary syndrome and other excess androgen states (discussed above), hyperprolactinemia (discussed in Chapter 5), adrenal insufficiency, Cushing's syndrome, and diabetes mellitus are all more likely to cause reduced rather than excessive bleeding, but DUB has been reported. DUB may develop in the rare adolescent with chronic liver disease because of reduced estrogen clearance or hypoprothrombinemia.

For some young women, scanty midcycle spotting during ovulatory cycles may be a normal variation that requires no treatment. Other patterns of DUB in adolescents with ovulatory cycles may indicate that the luteal phase after ovulation is too short, too long, or produces insufficient progesterone for any of several reasons. In these conditions, the DUB is easily corrected with oral contraceptives, but specific recognition and management may eventually be required for fertility.

Evaluation and Management. Heavy blood flow during regular menses (menorrhagia) rarely needs evaluation or treatment other than supplemental iron. However, nonsteroidal anti-inflammatory agents (e.g., mefenamic acid, 500 mg t.i.d. for 3 days, or naproxen, 500 mg initially followed by 750 mg daily for 5 days) may reduce unacceptably heavy blood loss.[24]

Diagnostic evaluation of abnormal vaginal bleeding primarily involves the exclusion, by history and by examination, of the entities described above. Pelvic examination should confirm that the uterus is the origin of the bleeding (or identify another source). Laboratory tests are generally done only when indicated by specific evidence, although some (e.g., pregnancy test, Pap smear, cultures, thyroid functions, prolactin, and clotting studies) require minimal justification.

Measurement of LH, FSH, estradiol, progesterone, or androgens may be worthwhile in some circumstances. Significant abnormalities are mentioned with the various conditions. Repeated determinations of gonadotropins may be necessary because of fluctuations. Interpretation of gonadotropin, estradiol, and progesterone levels requires correlation with phase of the menstrual cycle or with pubertal stage or both. Androgens fluctuate less through the cycle, but change with pubertal maturation. A pelvic ultrasound will help define possible masses, although small ovarian cysts are common normal findings. Dilatation and curettage, endometrial biopsy, or hysteroscopy are rarely necessary for diagnosis of adolescent DUB.

Management depends upon the cause and the severity of the bleeding. Reassurance and observation suffice for heavy or irregular periods occurring in the first postmenarcheal year in the absence of anemia or other pathologic features. If bleeding is persistently abnormal and distressing or causes significant blood depletion, regular and moderate menses can usually be achieved with an oral contraceptive. A pill equivalent to 35 to 50 μg of ethinyl estradiol with 1 mg of norethindrone is generally effective.[12]

To stop an ongoing episode of heavy bleeding, a similar oral contraceptive can be used at an increased dose.[11,22] One method is to have the patient take 4 pills per day until the bleeding stops, which will usually occur within 48 hours. Then reduce the dosage to 1 or 2 pills a day for 3 weeks, and stop for 5 days to allow menses. After this cycle, the pill can be resumed in a normal manner. The pill may be discontinued after 6 months to see if normal menses will ensue. Risks associated with use of oral contraceptives for DUB include the possibility of emotional dependence or a sense of reproductive inadequacy, persistent suppression of the neuroendocrine axis causing postpill anovulation, masking of unrecognized medical conditions, and the small risks of thrombosis and lipid alterations.[20] Iron should be replaced.

A gynecologist should be consulted when bleeding is severe enough to require hospitalization. Intravenous conjugated estrogens (Premarin) are used during the first 24 hours as the oral estrogen-progestagen combination is begun.[3] Curettage is a last resort.

ANDROGEN DISORDERS

Hirsutism, Virilism, and Androgen Excess

Excessive body hair (hirsutism) is distressing to an adolescent girl. Although hirsutism usually does not represent a diagnosable hormone disorder, it is important to distinguish benign hirsutism from those conditions that signify androgen excess and are dangerous or treatable (Table 6-7), and from those conditions merely suggestive of androgen excess (Table 6-8).

Table 6-7. Causes of Hirsutism and Virilization in Females.

Increased androgen-dependent hair and virilism
  Genetic and familial increased androgen sensitivity
  Androgen excess
    "Psychogenic" hirsutism
      Stress
      Schizophrenia
    Exogenous androgens
      Medical
        Hypoplastic anemias
        Growth stimulation
        Adrenal replacement
        Danazol
        Synthetic progestins in oral contraceptives
        ACTH therapy
      Nonmedical
        Bodybuilding and athletic anabolic steroids
        Female to male transexualism
      Environmental (?)
        Skin contact with male using topical testosterone
        Anabolic steroids given to livestock
        Plant or microorganism androgens
    Adrenal androgens
      Congenital adrenal hyperplasias
        21-hydroxylase deficiency
          Classic
          Late-onset
        3-beta hydroxysteroid dehydrogenase deficiency
          Classic
          Late-onset
        11-hydroxylase deficiency
          Classic
          Late-onset
      Adrenal tumors
        Adrenocortical carcinoma
        Testosterone-secreting adenoma
        Adrenal rest adenoma and carcinoma
      Cushing's disease
    Ovarian androgens
      Polycystic ovary syndrome
        Stein-Leventhal PCOS
        Conditions associated with PCOS
          PCOS with ovarian tumor
        Pineal gland hyperplasia and diabetes
          Congenital lipoatrophic diabetes
          Hyperprolactinemia
          Hyperthyroidism
          Hypothyroidism
      Androgen-secreting cysts and hyperplasias
        Stromal hyperplasia and hyperthecosis
        Solitary follicle cyst
        Hyper-reaction luteinalis of pregnancy
      Androgen-secreting ovarian tumors
        Arrhenoblastoma (androblastoma)
        Thecoma-fibroma group tumors
        Granulosa cell tumors
        Lipid cell tumors
        Gynandroblastoma
        Epithelial tumor
        Luteoma of pregnancy
  Testicular androgens in XY females
    5-alpha reductase deficiency
    Mixed gonadal dysgenesis
    True hermaphroditism
    17-beta hydroxysteroid dehydrogenase deficiency
    Other rare intersex conditions

Table 6-8. Disorders to be distinguished from hyperandrogenism.

Hirsutism
  Generalized hypertrichosis
    Idiopathic
    Familial
    Drugs and toxins
      Diphenylhydantoin
      Minoxidil
      Diazoxide
      Phenothiazines
      Cyclosporine
      Hexachlorobenzene poisoning
      Streptomycin
      Penicillamine
      Cobalt
      Acrodynia
    Rare genetic syndromes
      Hypertrichosis lanuginosa or universalis
      Hepatic and erythropoietic porphyrias
      Laurence-Moon-Biedl syndrome
      Morgagni-Stewart-Morel syndrome
      Seckel bird-headed dwarfism
      Cornelia de Lange's syndrome
      Trisomy E
      Hurler's syndrome
    Chronic systemic illness
      Chronic renal failure
      Dermatomyositis
      Cancer
    Chronic central nervous system dysfunction
      Cerebral palsy
      Spina bifida
      Multiple sclerosis
      Postencephalitic states
      Others
    Endocrine disorders
      Hypothyroidism
      Growth-hormone-secreting pituitary adenoma
      Hyperprolactinemia
    Chronic malnutrition
      Anorexia nervosa
  Localized hirsutism or hypertrichosis
    Hairy nevus (several types)
    Broken extremity bone
    Extremity lymphedema
    Repeated local trauma
Clitoromegaly without ambiguity
  Clitoral priapism
  Fibroma of clitoris
  Chronic vulvovaginitis
Acne
  Cushing's syndrome
  Exogenous exacerbating agents
    Androgenic steroids
    Synthetic progestins
    Glucocorticoids
    Lithium
    Diphenylhydantoin
    Barbiturates
    Isoniazid
    Rifampin

Table 6-8. *Continued.*

Iodides
Kelp and other seaweed
Bromides
Persistent unpleasant body odor without apparent disease
Foreign body (especially in the nose or vagina)
Genetic disorders of organic acid metabolism
Trimethylaminuria
Dietary spices
Poor hygiene

Androgen-responsive (or "sexual") hair includes pubic hair with extensions to the thighs and up the linea alba, axillary hair, mustache and beard hair, and chest and shoulder hair. The sites are listed in roughly ascending order of the magnitude of androgen effect necessary to stimulate and maintain the hair; i.e., higher levels of androgens are required to initiate beard hair than pubic hair. Sexual hair is usually coarser, darker, longer, and curlier than other body hair. Conditions of androgen excess (or increased hair follicle responsiveness) in females of all ages may result in the appearance of sexual hair.

In addition to sexual hair, androgens also enhance body odor, oiliness of skin, and acne in normal girls. When androgen effects are more marked, the exaggeration of these features and the appearance of other androgen-dependent body changes is referred to as virilization. Anovulation, menstrual irregularity or amenorrhea, vocal deepening, clitoral enlargement, increased musculature (especially chest and shoulder), decreased subcutaneous fat, breast atrophy, and frontal balding roughly indicate progressively more severe degrees of virilism. Androgens may also have psychologic effects in women, including increased libido and aggressiveness. The development of the polycystic ovary syndrome as an important consequence (as well as a cause) of various conditions of androgen excess is discussed separately below.

Other androgen effects are age-limited. Exposure of a female fetus to excessive androgens may masculinize the genitalia, whereas after birth, androgen-induced virilization of the genitalia is limited to clitoral enlargement. Androgens in the first and, to a lesser degree, second trimesters of pregnancy enlarge the phallus and move the urethra toward the end of the phallus. High levels of androgens will fuse the labioscrotal folds and obliterate the vaginal opening; lower or later androgen exposure causes partial labial fusion. Mild posterior labial fusion may be the only indicator of prenatal androgen excess at birth. When there is evidence of virilism in a girl of any age, the presence of labial fusion dates the onset of androgen excess to the prenatal period. Of less clinical use is evidence that fetal androgens may negatively influence the potential for future breast development.

Prolonged exposure of a prepubertal or early pubertal girl to excess androgens will induce a growth spurt but cause disproportionate acceleration of bone maturation with the possibility of premature closure of the epiphyses and reduction of ultimate height. A history of early adrenarche from a teenager with hirsutism, acne, or anovulation suggests an adrenal androgen source, possibly one of the congenital adrenal hyperplasias.

Various causes of androgen excess are listed in Table 6-7 and discussed in the following paragraphs. Also discussed below and listed in Table 6-8 are a variety of conditions that may initially raise the possibility of androgen excess.

Genetic Hirsutism. Genetic factors clearly influence hair, and the clearest example of this is the variation of body hair in various ethnic or racial groups. Women of southern European or Middle Eastern ancestry tend to have more facial hair than do women of northern European, African, or Oriental ancestry, but may be troubled by it if they compare themselves to current American standards of cosmetic "normalcy."[26] Even without identifiable ethnic variation, females in some families may tend to have more (or darker) facial hair, and a physician may be reassured if a girl's mother has a similar amount of hair. However, in this context one should be reminded that some of the identified defects of androgen metabolism may be familial, and that some of them (e.g., variants of 21-hydroxylase deficiency) occur more commonly in populations of southern and eastern European ancestry.[27]

Simple or Idiopathic Hirsutism. Most young women with mild to moderate hirsutism do not have one of the major, long-recognized causes of hyperandrogenism, and their complaint has been described as simple, idiopathic, or constitutional hirsutism. This is now understood to be a heterogeneous group that includes those individuals distressed by normal facial hair, those with partial forms of polycystic ovary syndrome, those with subtle defects of androgen regulation, those whose skin and hair are more responsive to androgens, and those for whom no abnormality of androgen metabolism can yet be demonstrated.[16,27-30] Among the defects of androgen regulation and metabolism reported in young women with "idiopathic hirsutism" are mild degrees of ovarian overproduction of testosterone and androstenedione, adrenal overproduction of DHAS or other androgens, late-onset or partial forms of congenital adrenal hyperplasia, increased peripheral generation of dihydrotestosterone and 3-alpha-androstanediol, decreased levels of sex-hormone-binding globulin, and variations in clearance rates. Some of these alterations are interdependent. These subgroups are not easily separated from each other by the simple androgen levels used for screening. The initial clue to those with metabolic defects may be a borderline or modest elevation of DHAS, testosterone, or 17-hydroxyprogesterone. Idiopathic hirsutism will often respond to suppression with either oral contraceptives or glucocorticoids.[29] An approach to differentiation and management is provided below.

Polycystic Ovary Syndrome. The classic polycystic ovary syndrome (PCOS), also referred to as the Stein-Leventhal syndrome, includes obesity, amenorrhea, and hirsutism (Fig. 6-3).[13,16,48] The obesity is often accompanied by elevated insulin levels with relative insulin resistance, impaired glucose tolerance, and acanthosis nigricans. The secondary amenorrhea reflects chronic anovulation, which may also be manifested by

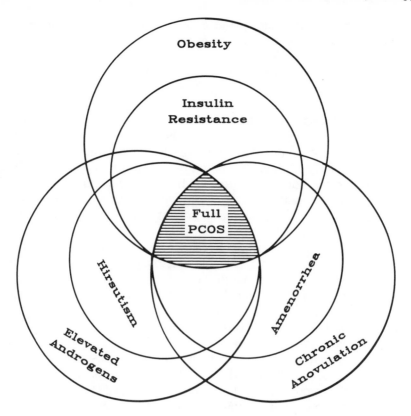

Fig. 6-3. Components of the polycystic ovary syndrome (PCOS). The complete PCOS includes all of the labeled features, but the features may occur in various combinations; patients who display some of these features are more common than those
who display all of them. The features of a single patient may change over time.

oligomenorrhea or, less commonly, dysfunctional uterine bleeding or primary amenorrhea. The hirsutism is a result of excessive androgen production by both adrenals and ovaries, and may be accompanied by other
androgen manifestations, including virilism. Many young women will display one or two of the three major features of PCOS and may progress to
fuller expression of the syndrome.

PCOS is a state of abnormal hypothalamic stimulation of the pituitary,
abnormal pituitary stimulation of the ovaries, and abnormal steroid feedback to the hypothalamus.[3,13,48] Presumed increases in gonadotropin-
releasing hormone (GnRH) stimulation of the pituitary result in higher
amplitude LH secretion with a higher baseline. Tonic elevation of LH with
inhibition of FSH results in overstimulation of ovarian secretion of both
estradiol and androgens but defective follicular maturation and anovulation. Increased adrenal secretion of androgens and increased peripheral
generation of estrogens from androgens also contribute to the high circulating steroid levels. The elevated androgens and estrogens help per-
petuate increased but acyclic hypothalamic GnRH production in a vicious
cycle of anovulation and hyperandrogenism.

In most patients, an original abnormality that triggered the cycle cannot be determined. Evidence that many girls who develop PCOS display obesity and early or excessive sexual hair before menarche suggests that an "exaggerated adrenarche" may help establish PCOS.[16] However, in some patients, PCOS develops secondarily to an underlying condition of increased adrenal androgen secretion (e.g., congenital adrenal hyperplasia or Cushing's syndrome), increased ovarian or peripheral estrogen production (e.g., granulosa-theca cell tumor), or disrupted hypothalamic GnRH release (Table 6-7).

The ovaries are enlarged, with a thickened capsule and numerous follicular cysts with hyperplasia of the theca interna. This can be confirmed by ultrasound. LH levels are nearly always mildly elevated, and FSH levels tend to be near the lower limits of normal; the usual LH:FSH ratio is thus reversed. Estradiol and estrogen levels are moderately elevated. Androgen levels, including free and total testosterone, dehydroepiandrosterone sulfate, androstenedione, and urinary 17-ketosteroids, are mildly to moderately elevated. Prolactin and 17-hydroxyprogesterone are also usually slightly increased.

Treatment must be individualized. Ovarian and hypothalamic suppression with oral contraceptives (discussed below) is the usual initial step in management. Precipitating or underlying endocrinopathies must be reversed if present. Clomiphene, wedge resection of the ovaries, or various other treatments are reserved for refractory cases or for when fertility is desired.[48]

Stress and Psychogenic Hyperandrogenism. Women respond to stress with increased androgen production, and there has been anecdotal or circumstantial evidence that emotional stress may cause or exacerbate androgen-dependent hirsutism.[26] Possible mechanisms include stimulation of adrenal androgens by stress-induced ACTH, increased ovarian androgen release as a result of stress-induced hypothalamic anovulation,[1] or poorly understood neurotropic influences on hair growth. Hirsutism has also been reported with schizophrenia. Significant virilism cannot be blamed on the psyche.

Exogenous Androgenic Agents. The medical benefits of androgens in conditions such as aplastic anemia must be balanced against the virilizing effects, which usually appear in weeks or months. Lower doses of synthetic anabolic steroids such as oxandrolone have been used to stimulate growth in Turner's syndrome and other conditions of impaired growth. Although the steroids are tailored to maximize the ratio of anabolic to virilizing effects, mild androgen effects occur in many of the girls.

Synthetic progestins in oral contraceptives (e.g., levonorgestrel) will occasionally cause mild but undesirable hirsutism. Danazol is a synthetic androgen-like steroid used for a variety of unusual conditions such as hereditary angioneurotic edema; side effects may include hirsutism. ACTH therapy is more likely to induce hirsutism than are various glucocorticoids because it stimulates adrenal androgens.

The use of anabolic steroids by female athletes and bodybuilders has increased dramatically; such use may not be admitted readily. National competitors in track and field events are said to have the highest rate of use. Synthetic steroids will not be detected by the androgen screening tests discussed below, so the physician will need to persuasively question young women in the high-use groups.[31] Asymptomatic hyperlipidemia and liver damage may occur with high-dose anabolic steroid use.

Research interest in environmental androgens is increasing, although there have been few confirmed cases of clinical significance. Several plants and microorganisms produce androgens. Synthetic androgens have also been administered widely to livestock to promote growth; laws require discontinuation of androgen use well ahead of slaughter. Many steroids may be absorbed by skin; women have been virilized by sexual contact with males using topical testosterone.

Congenital Adrenal Hyperplasias. A number of inborn enzyme defects in the pathway of cortisol synthesis result in overstimulation of the adrenal gland by ACTH to compensate for impaired cortisol production. In several types of congenital adrenal hyperplasia (CAH), the hyperplastic adrenal glands overproduce various androgens, with variable degrees of virilization in females (Table 6-7).

In the complete (or classic) forms, androgen overproduction and virilization begin prenatally, and the genitalia are mildly to severely masculinized.[30,32] If unrecognized in infancy, excess androgen production continues through childhood. This results in accelerated growth, early appearance of pubic hair in childhood, and ultimate short stature due to early closure of epiphyses. Untreated adolescent girls have severe hirsutism, virilism (including masculinization of the genitalia), poor breast development, and oligomenorrhea with polycystic changes in the ovaries. Carefully adjusted glucocorticoid replacement from infancy will minimize these effects. It is now unusual for the diagnosis of the complete forms to be missed in childhood.

In addition to the androgen effects, the classic forms of CAH in XX females may be distinguished by the following features:

> 21-hydroxylase deficiency
>> Hypotensive salt wasting crises in infancy in about 50%
>> Marked elevation of 17-hydroxyprogesterone (17-OHP)
>> Moderate elevation of testosterone
> 11-beta hydroxylase deficiency
>> Hypertension
>> Elevation of deoxycorticosterone and 11-deoxycortisol
> 3-beta-hydroxysteroid dehydrogenase deficiency
>> Only mild genital virilization (clitoromegaly)
>> Salt wasting in infancy in a minority
>> Extremely elevated dehydroepiandrosterone (DHA)

Within the last decade, it has been discovered that a significant number of women with "idiopathic" hirsutism or acne of adolescent or late childhood onset have partial deficiencies of any of the above enzymes.[28,32-36] These variants, also termed late-onset, nonclassic, or cryptic CAH, may be more common than the full classic forms of CAH. The clinical manifestations are indistinguishable from each other and from other idiopathic hirsutism and acne, without noticeable changes of the genitalia and without effects of glucocorticoid or mineralocorticoid deficiency. A history of precocious adrenarche is common but not invariable. Baseline serum levels of 17-OHP, deoxycortisol, testosterone, and DHA are in the upper normal range or marginally elevated.[34-36] The diagnosis of the late-onset forms of CAH is made by recognizing the distortions of the steroid pattern following ACTH stimulation. These late-onset forms usually respond well to glucocorticoid therapy.

The treatment of all forms of CAH involves suppression of the ACTH stimulation of adrenal androgens with glucocorticoid. Dosage is usually at replacement amounts (20 to 25 mg of cortisol equivalent orally), although this may need to be adjusted for a variety of reasons. The late-onset forms may respond to even lower doses.

Cushing's Syndrome and Adrenal Tumors. Cushing's syndrome in an adolescent commonly causes anovulation and disruption of menstrual cycles.[16] Hirsutism or acne occurs in the majority of cases of endogenous Cushing's syndrome. Nearly all will have at least mild obesity and a malar flush. Other common but not universal features include hypertension, glucose intolerance, striae, weakness or muscle wasting, osteoporosis, easy bruisability, depression, and peripheral edema. The signs and symptoms may resemble PCOS or common obesity. The best, most reliable screening tests are a 24-hour urine-free cortisol and a 1-mg overnight dexamethasone-suppression test; further testing will be necessary to distinguish among the types of endogenous Cushing's syndrome. The most dangerous type is due to adrenocortical carcinoma.

Ovarian Tumors and Disorders. A variety of ovarian tumors (Table 6-7) may secrete androgens with effects ranging from hirsutism of recent origin to severe virilism. There may or may not be local pelvic symptoms or a mass. Most of the tumors are malignant, but benign androgenic cysts have also been described. Girls with mixed gonadal dysgenesis (in which at least some cells have a Y chromosome) are at risk of androgen-producing gonadoblastomas.

Ovarian hyperthecosis is a non-neoplastic condition similar to PCOS.[37] The ovaries have islands of thecal cells in the ovarian stroma that produce high levels of testosterone, androstenedione, and dihydrotestosterone. LH levels are variable. The consequent virilization may be severe. Treatment is surgical.

Testicular Androgens in Intersexual Conditions. In a number of rare conditions (Table 6-7), the genitalia of an XY fetus are inadequately masculinized, and the baby is raised as a girl. In some of these cases, the testes at puberty will make enough testosterone to result in substantial virilization of the unfortunate young lady. In nearly all of these conditions there is some degree, even if not previously recognized, of genital ambiguity, especially posterior labial fusion. Because of the presence of internal testicular tissue, the uterus is usually undeveloped and the girl has primary amenorrhea. Breast development is variable. Suspicion of this type of problem should lead to prompt and sensitive referral to an endocrinologist for hormonal definition and explanation. In most cases, testes are removed and appropriate estrogen replacement begun.

Disorders to be Distinguished from Hyperandrogenism. The following conditions are sometimes referred because of concern about androgens.

Generalized hypertrichosis, increased hair over much of the body, does not indicate a condition of androgen excess. It is often idiopathic or familial, but may also result from drugs. A generalized increase in fine, lanugo-type hair occurs with starvation and weight loss (especially anorexia nervosa). This increase also occurs in malignancy, chronic illness, a few endocrine disorders, several genetic syndromes, and in a variety of nonprogressive neurologic disorders, though never as the only initial sign. In some endocrine and genetic conditions, hirsutism may also involve accentuation of sexual hair and be harder to distinguish from disorders of androgen excess. Hypertrichosis is rarely a cosmetic problem and requires no treatment. Localized hypertrichosis results from local factors unrelated to androgens.

Clitoromegaly may indicate prenatal or postnatal hyperandrogenism, but is unlikely to do so in the absence of labial fusion, hirsutism, or other androgen effects. Isolated, acquired clitoromegaly may be the patient's initial complaint for several rare conditions unrelated to androgens (Table 6-8). Occasionally, a clitoris of normal size may appear enlarged because of underdevelopment or loss of surrounding subcutaneous tissue, as with the emaciation of anorexia nervosa.

Acne vulgaris is an androgen-dependent disease of the hair follicles and their sebaceous glands. However, the severity of acne is also affected by the presence of particular bacteria, by the severity of the inflammatory response, and by individual differences in keratinization.[38] Excessive endogenous or exogenous glucocorticoids may also exacerbate acne, as will certain drugs. The role of hormones in the etiology and treatment of acne is discussed below.

Body odor results from complex combinations of organic acids in sweat; sweat composition is partially androgen-dependent. Although prepubertal children do not usually develop noticeable body odor until several days without a bath have elapsed, parents commonly notice that adrenarche is accompanied by the development of an adult-type body odor and the need for more frequent bathing. Excessive or abnormal body odor of childhood or adolescent onset is an unusual and unpleasant problem. It is often idiopathic and has not been found to be a result of abnormal or excessive androgens unless other evidence of hyperandrogenism is present. The differential diagnosis is beyond the scope of this chapter and is available elsewhere.[39]

As a general rule, androgens need not be measured in isolated hypertrichosis of nonsexual hair, mild acne without hirsutism, isolated clitoromegaly without labial fusion and hirsutism, and body odor without hirsutism.

Evaluation of Hirsutism and Virilism. The first step in determining whether hirsutism in an adolescent requires laboratory evaluation is distinguishing androgen-influenced hair from generalized hypertrichosis, which requires no androgen measurements.

The second step is to assess the degree of androgen effect by recognizing other androgen-dependent features. Moderate facial hair gradually developing from puberty in an otherwise healthy young lady with black hair is usually genetic (familial or ethnic), while recent appearance of hair in an adolescent of fair complexion provides a greater justification for testing. Because of the low yield, it is difficult to provide precise indications for androgen measurement in isolated mild hirsutism or acne. However, virilism, as opposed to hirsutism, nearly always indicates a diagnosable condition of androgen excess.

The third step, regardless of presence of absence of virilism, is to identify signs or symptoms (e.g., features of Cushing's syndrome or pelvic or abdominal pain) suggesting one of the significant causes of hirsutism in Table 6-7; these signs or symptoms also warrant appropriate further evaluation.

Whether prompted by the severity of hirsutism or acne, the presence of virilism, or concurrent signs and symptoms, the goal of "further evaluation" is to confirm excessive levels of androgens and identify their source. Testosterone (T) and dehydroepiandrosterone sulfate (DHAS) have now replaced 24-hour urine 17-ketosteroids as the initial screen for androgen-producing tumors and should always be obtained promptly if recent virilism is present.[1,30] Testosterone is the primary androgen produced by virilizing ovarian tumors; substantial elevation (total T above 150 ng/ml) in females of any age suggests ovarian tumor, which can be confirmed by pelvic and abdominal imaging in preparation for surgery. DHAS is quantitatively the most important adrenal androgen and is significantly elevated with virilizing adrenocortical carcinoma or other adrenal tumors. DHAS levels above 700 μg/dl warrant adrenal imaging by CT scan or other high-resolution methods. If the T and DHAS levels are normal or marginally high and there are no palpable masses or symptoms, imaging procedures of ovaries or adrenals are not necessary to exclude tumors.

Additional tests are indicated by specific circumstances, one of which may simply be the level of the patient's concern. Marginal elevations of T or DHAS may indicate one of the congenital adrenal hyperplasias, especially if the androgen effects had an early age of onset. Suspicion of this may be pursued with measurement of 17-hydroxyprogesterone and androstenedione, but referral to an endocrinologist for ACTH stimulation testing of other adrenal steroids is usually warranted. Cushing's syndrome can be excluded by a 24-hour urine collection for free cortisol, and by an overnight dexamethasone suppression test (1 mg dexamethasone orally at bedtime followed by measurement of cortisol at 0800 the next morning). Measurement of LH and FSH can help confirm the PCOS.

Management of Hirsutism. Management of hirsutism involves camouflage or eradication of the unwanted hair and removal or suppression of the androgen source. Kirschner provides a fuller description of these methods.[29] Various pharmacologic approaches to hirsutism are used if hair removal techniques alone are unsatisfactory.[40]

Facial hair may be bleached as often as daily by swabbing with 6% hydrogen peroxide. Hair may be removed temporarily by tweezer plucking, hot wax epilation, chemical depilatories (e.g., Nair or Neet), or shaving. Plucking, wax, and chemicals carry some risk of skin irritation or folliculitis. Shaving, despite popular belief, does not speed hair regrowth, but the stubble may be unacceptable. Hair may be removed permanently and relatively painlessly by electrolysis, which destroys the hair root; an experienced electrolysist should be sought.[29]

Hyperandrogenism secondary to a tumor or other treatable disease may often be eliminated by specific treatment for that condition. For adolescents with idiopathic hirsutism, PCOS, and the milder defects of androgen metabolism, the two traditional methods for suppression of androgen production are oral contraceptives and glucocorticoids.[29,40]

Combination oral contraceptives reduce androgen effects by reducing LH stimulation of ovarian androgen production and by increasing sex-hormone-binding globulin levels (thereby decreasing free testosterone), and may act as androgen antagonists in the target tissues (e.g., hair follicles and pilosebaceous glands).[29,30] These pills are more effective when the ovaries are contributing substantially to the androgen levels, as in the PCOS. In anovulatory women, combination oral contraceptives provide menstrual regularity and the benefits of regular progestin exposure to the endometrium. In general, a moderate estrogen dose (30 to 50 μg of ethinyl estradiol) and a non-androgenic progestin such as norethindrone or ethynodiol are recommended.[30] As the response is slow, 6 months should be allowed to assess effectiveness.

Glucocorticoids will suppress ACTH secretion and reduce adrenal androgen output, but are less likely to be of use in adolescent women.[30] A trial of glucocorticoid suppression is warranted by elevation of DHAS, exaggerated androgen response to ACTH, or other evidence of substantial adrenal contribution to the androgens. Significant suppression of mildly elevated androgens after 2 days of dexamethasone may also predict response to glucocorticoid suppression.[41] The dosage should be equivalent to, or somewhat lower than, maintenance hydrocortisone (20 to 30 mg daily for young women): i.e., 0.25 to 0.5 mg dexamethasone or 2 to 5 mg prednisone daily. This dosage may be assumed to produce some degree of adrenal suppression with use for more than a few days, and instructions for stress supplementation should be given upon discontinuation. It may take several months to assess effectiveness.[49]

Spironolactone and cyproterone acetate are anti-androgens that are still considered experimental drugs for adolescents.[29,30,40] Spironolactone is available but expensive, and long-term safety is not established. Cyproterone acetate is widely used in Europe but is not available in the United States.

If a young woman is obese, especially with features of PCOS, some reduction of androgens and their effects will be achieved with weight loss.[29] One should not overstate this, as it may be discouraging to simply add hirsutism to the list of problems blamed on the obesity, for which the patient may privately blame herself and which she may consider "unfixable."

Management of Virilization. The management of virilization depends upon the source of the excess androgens. Tumors should be removed. The benefits of exogenous androgens should be weighed against their virilizing effects. Congenital adrenal hyperplasia cannot be cured, but glucocorticoid in replacement doses will suppress the androgens. Virilization of the genitalia of prenatal onset may require surgical correction. In general, an adolescent girl virilized by androgens for up to a few years may expect that removal of the androgens will result in regression of nearly all of the features except the change in voice.

Hormonal Aspects of Acne Management. Hair follicles and sebaceous glands have androgen receptors; androgens strongly influence sebum production. The first comedones tend to appear with adrenarche. Acne rarely occurs in the absence of androgens. Women with androgen excess are likely to have acne, and there is a moderate correlation between androgen levels and severity of acne.[38,42] This relationship of androgens and acne has two implications.

First, moderate to severe acne in an adolescent may, but does not necessarily, imply hyperandrogenism. Androgen measurement has been considered of minimal value in young adolescent girls with mild acne and no hirsutism, but every young woman with acne should be examined for other signs of androgen excess. Also, a recent study described several young women with isolated moderate acne, or with mild acne and hirsutism, who had elevations of free testosterone or DHAS and exaggerated or abnormal androgen responses to ACTH stimulation suggestive of mild forms of congenital adrenal hyperplasias or "exaggerated adrenarche."[28] It is not yet possible to estimate the percentage of girls with isolated acne who might have such a condition. Characteristics that may justify androgen screening include acne of at least moderate severity despite conventional therapies, cystic acne, late onset of acne or persistence of it into the twenties, concurrent hirsutism or other androgen signs, an anovulatory menstrual pattern, a history of early development of pubic hair (before age 11 years), and a family history of hirsutism, amenorrhea, or similar problems.[29,42]

Second, a variety of hormonal manipulations similar to those used for hirsutism have been used therapeutically, with or without establishing the presence of hormone abnormalities.[38] Oral glucocorticoids at maintenance dosage (20 to 30 mg/day of hydrocortisone equivalent) or lower may improve acne, especially in patients with demonstrated elevations of

DHAS. Cyclic sequential combination oral contraceptives with moderate ethinyl estradiol content (30 to 50 μg) are especially useful when acne is accompanied by features of the polycystic ovary syndrome. A number of reports from Europe have found a combination of cyproterone acetate (an androgen antagonist) and estrogen to be effective. Hormone therapy should be preceded by an endocrine evaluation.

OTHER DISORDERS ASSOCIATED WITH MENSTRUAL CYCLES

Mittelschmerz

Midcycle pain with ovulation is much more common in older teenagers than in younger ones. The pain is crampy, lateralized, and rarely severe. It is generally fairly transient, lasting only a few hours (rarely, 2 to 3 days). The diagnosis of mittelschmerz is confirmed by documenting the recurrent midcycle pattern. Occasionally, mittelschmerz must be differentiated from appendicitis, ovarian cyst or torsion, or ectopic pregnancy. Reassurance and mild analgesics suffice. Mittelschmerz does not seem to occur in anovulatory cycles.

Premenstrual Discomforts

"Premenstrual syndrome" refers to a wide range of discomforts experienced each cycle in the days prior to menses by many adolescent women.[12,43,44] Onset of menstrual bleeding typically brings rapid relief. Common complaints include tension, irritability, moodiness, withdrawal, difficulty concentrating, food cravings or anorexia, breast swelling or tenderness, lack of libido, pelvic discomfort, headaches, and fatigability. Especially prominent are subjective complaints of bloating, fluid retention, and facial puffiness, sometimes with objective weight gain, tightness of clothes, and edema. Less common somatic symptoms include exacerbations of acne or furunculosis, stomatitis, constipation, or diarrhea. Also infrequent but more troublesome are psychologic symptoms such as hostility, paranoia, panic attacks, crying spells, psychotic episodes, or violence (including rare but widely publicized recurrent criminal acts). Some studies have shown a higher suicide rate in young women during the premenstrual week.

The etiology of premenstrual discomforts continues to be debated.[43,44] Since a majority of women report some premenstrual changes correlated with luteal phase hormone changes, the more severe forms of the syndrome may represent the extremes of a normal distribution, an increased sensitivity to physiologic effects, or an amplification of normal processes by a number of potential contributing factors. There is still no conclusive evidence of any distinct pathologic processes. Suggested hormonal factors include relative luteal phase progesterone deficiency, lower progesterone-estrogen ratio, and alterations of endorphins, vasopressin, aldosterone, adrenal androgens, hypothalamic neurotransmitters, prolactin, or thyroid hormones, but research studies suffer from lack of objective definitions or measures of the syndrome, unavoidable placebo effects, and the impossibility of differentiating causal hormone abnormalities from secondary changes. Underlying personality and emotional predispositions and cultural expectations also influence the expression of symptoms.[44]

No single treatment is consistently effective, as is evidenced by the endless list of proposed remedies, which has included exercise, baths, food avoidance and assorted diets, vitamins, minerals, herbs, nutritional supplements, various forms of psychotherapy, hormone desensitization, and even oophorectomy. Among hundreds of drugs recommended for premenstrual symptoms, some in recent use are progesterone, danazol, oral contraceptives, prostaglandin inhibitors, bromocriptine, lithium, GnRH analogs, clonidine, pyridoxine, tranquilizers, antidepressants, thyroxine, naltrexone, and diuretics.

The symptoms of premenstrual syndrome are so nonspecific that the diagnosis is best confirmed simply by demonstrating, by diary or daily checklist, that the symptoms occur almost exclusively in the 5 to 10 days prior to menses. Although there are no other diseases with similar pattern, it is important to identify any coexisting condition, especially psychiatric, that may be amplifying the symptoms. The most useful approach in explaining the symptoms to the patient is to emphasize the commonness and "normality" of her feelings, that they are neither imaginary nor in themselves indicative of psychiatric disease, that they affect every individual differently, and that it may take some experimentation to find effective countermeasures. It may be possible to limit the adverse effects of the monthly symptoms on school or work performance, or on family relationships, by providing some insight and specific behavioral guidelines to the patient and her family. Further management should address particular complaints. If depressive or violent symptoms are prominent, an assessment of suicidal or other risk and appropriate referral are indicated. Prostaglandin inhibitors may help pelvic or breast pain. Mild salt restriction and diuretics (e.g., chlorothiazide 500 mg qd) are widely used for feelings of fluid retention. It should be noted that diuretics are among the most widely used drugs by young women, who often obtain them without prescription or deny their use; when used excessively, diuretics can exacerbate edema. For more severe symptoms, a trial of oral contraception or progesterone supplementation (medroxyprogesterone 10 mg qd during the week prior to menses) may be warranted.

Dysmenorrhea

Primary Dysmenorrhea. Crampy lower abdominal pain during menses is a common complaint in adolescent girls.[12,45,46] The spectrum of primary dysmenorrhea ranges from minor cramps experienced by the majority of postmenarcheal women to symptoms debilitating enough to interfere with school or work. This condition may be accompanied by other discomforts such as nausea, vomiting, diarrhea, muscle cramps, fatigability, backache, dizziness, or headaches. Symptoms may begin with the onset of menstrual flow or hours before, and may last from a few hours to several days. This condition occurs more frequently with ovulatory than with anovulatory cycles. It is unusual for primary dysmenorrhea to begin during the 6 to 12 anovulatory months following menarche, but common for it to begin within the first 2 to 3 years after menarche. In a small minority of adolescents, dysmenorrhea is secondary to more significant pelvic disease.

The subjective symptoms of primary dysmenorrhea and their objective expression have cultural, psychologic, and "organic" components. Various studies have demonstrated associations with family symptoms and experiences, life stresses, psychologic and personality-related variables, race, and socioeconomic status. Long-recognized organic influences include an increased association with obesity, longer or heavier menstrual flow, and intrauterine devices, and a decreased association with regular exercise, parity, and oral contraceptive use. Some authors differentiate psychogenic menstrual pain from primary dysmenorrhea.[45]

However, recent research into the nature and treatment of primary dysmenorrhea has focused heavily on defective regulation of uterine prostaglandin production with consequent derangement of uterine contraction patterns.[46] Prostaglandins are a group of closely related hormones synthesized throughout the body that act locally or systemically; production is influenced by several hormones, including catecholamines, progesterone, and other steroids. Prostaglandins modulate blood flow, pain receptor sensitivity, smooth muscle tone, and contractile responses of the uterus. Women with dysmenorrhea have higher levels of prostaglandins in their menstrual fluid, as well as high uterine muscle tone and abnormal contraction patterns. Administered prostaglandins can produce dysmenorrheic symptoms, and prostaglandin inhibitors will usually relieve them.

Prostaglandin inhibition with nonsteroidal anti-inflammatory drugs is now the treatment of choice for dysmenorrhea, and has been shown to provide significant benefit in most cases.[45,46] Sample regimens for three of the drugs demonstrated to be efficacious are as follows:

Ibuprofen (Advil, Nuprin, Motrin) 400 mg q.i.d.
Mefanamic acid (Ponstel) 500 mg, then 250 mg every 6 hours
Naproxen (Naprosyn) 500 mg, then 250 mg every 4 to 6 hours

In many cases, the first dose may be taken at the first evidence of menstrual flow, or with the first symptoms, and continued for 2 to 3 days. Oral contraceptives have been used for years to reduce the severity of symptoms of dysmenorrhea, and may also be effective by reducing prostaglandin production; they represent a therapeutic alternative for the adolescent who is sexually active.

Secondary Dysmenorrhea. The diagnosis of dysmenorrhea secondary to pelvic disease depends on recognition of an atypical history or abnormal pelvic examination, such as lateralization of symptoms or signs. Other features warranting further evaluation include persistence of tenderness for hours after pelvic examination, onset of the symptoms at menarche or more than 3 years afterwards, promiscuity, dysfunctional uterine bleeding or change in menstrual pattern, history of pelvic surgery, and pain that is not crampy or colicky. Although lack of response to prostaglandin-inhibitor treatment suggests the possibility of pelvic disease, improvement with treatment does not exclude this possibility, as secondary dysmenorrhea may also be mediated by prostaglandins. When suspicion of pelvic disease arises, referral to a gynecologist for laparoscopy is appropriate.

Secondary dysmenorrhea is less common in adolescent women than it is in adult women, with a different distribution of causes, which follow:[12]

Recurrent PID
Ovarian cysts
Congenital obstructive malformations of the uterus
Uterine leiomyomata, polyps, or other tumors
Uterine adhesions or acquired cervical obstruction
Intrauterine contraceptive device
Endometriosis

Dysmenorrhea secondary to PID is often worse in the premenstrual period, with improvement as menses starts. Cervical and adnexal tenderness are usually present and there is often adnexal fullness. Ovarian cysts may or may not be palpable, but there is usually lateralized adnexal tenderness; however, a cyst may be coincidence rather than cause, as most are asymptomatic. Congenital malformations that may cause cyclic dysmenorrhea usually involve obstruction to menstrual flow (e.g., transverse vaginal septum), sometimes with duplication of part of the tract because of incomplete fusion of müllerian derivatives. In many of these cases there will be normal breast development but primary amenorrhea with cyclic dysmenorrhea and hematocolpos. Uterine tumors are rare in adolescents.

Endometriosis is an occasional cause of secondary dysmenorrhea or chronic pelvic pain in an adolescent.[12] Endometriosis is the establishment of functional endometrial tissue outside the uterus. This condition is rare in younger teenagers, in whom it usually indicates some type of obstruction to flow from the uterus, with reflux (retrograde menstruation) through the fallopian tubes of menstrual debris; this debris contains viable endometrial cells that become implanted in the pelvis or abdomen and begin to cause cyclic discomfort in response to cyclic hormone changes.[47] In some of these girls, the obstruction may be complete enough to cause primary amenorrhea, although secondary sexual development is normal. Surgical correction of the obstruction is often curative. In older adolescents, endometriosis is more common, but clearcut obstruction is less so. Diagnosis is usually made at laparoscopy or laparotomy for chronic pelvic pain, as the pain of endometriosis often occurs throughout the menstrual cycle, though accentuated during menses. Dysfunctional uterine bleeding occurs in some cases. The symptoms and signs of endometriosis may be modified by complications such as internal bleeding, adhesions, mass effects, or alteration of bowel or bladder function.

Other Systemic Problems Synchronized with Menses

A multitude of rare clinical problems are only expressed during particular phases of the cycle. Examples of the latter include acute intermittent porphyria, periodic paralysis, recurrent anaphylaxis, erythema multiforme, periodic fever, periodic hypersomnia, and many others. A variety of mechanisms may be involved, some of which are poorly understood, including estrogen withdrawal and rising levels of progesterone or prostaglandins. Nosebleeds with menses may be due to ectopic endometrial tissue in the nose.

Apart from these unusual disorders, more common chronic conditions (e.g., rheumatoid arthritis, migraine headaches) may simply be exacerbated during various phases of the menstrual cycle.

Careful correlation of phase with symptoms may suggest a rational treatment. Worsening throughout the luteal phase suggests progesterone dependence and may respond to suppression of ovulation; occurrence during the premenstrual week may be more indicative of a prostaglandin effect or inadequate luteal phase; midcycle symptoms may be related to ovulation. Total suppression of menses, if desirable, may be achieved reversibly with a GnRH analog.

REFERENCES

1. Speroff L, Glass RH, Kase NG: Clinical Gynecologic Endocrinology and Infertility. Baltimore: Williams and Wilkins, 1983.
2. Yen SSC. The human menstrual cycle. In: Yen SSC, Jaffe RB, eds. Reproductive Endocrinology. 2nd ed. Philadelphia: W.B. Saunders, 1986.
3. Kustin J, Rebar RW: Menstrual disorders in the adolescent age group. Primary Care 1987;14:139-166.
4. Altchek A: Dysfunctional uterine bleeding in adolescence. Clin Obstet Gynecol 1977;20:633-650.
5. Lauritzen C: Early diagnosis and long term treatment of anovulation during puberty. In: Bruni V, Gasparri F, Dewhurst J, Rey-Stocker I, eds. Pediatric and Adolescent Gynecology. London: Academic, 1982.
6. Dewhurst J: The early diagnosis and long term treatment of anovulation. In: Bruni V, Gasparri F, Dewhurst J, Rey-Stocker I, eds. Pediatric and Adolescent Gynecology. London: Academic, 1982.
7. Yen SSC: Chronic anovulation due to CNS-hypothalamic-pituitary dysfunction. In: Yen SSC, Jaffe RB, eds. Reproductive Endocrinology. 2nd ed. Philadelphia: W.B. Saunders, 1986.
8. Marut EL, Dawood MY: Amenorrhea (excluding hyperprolactinemia). Clin Obstet Gynecol 1983;26:749-761.
9. Adams J, Franks S, Polson DW, et al: Multifollicular ovaries: clinical and endocrine features and response to pulsatile gonadotropin releasing hormone. Lancet 1985;2:1375-1379.
10. Comerci GD, Williams RL: Eating disorders in the young: anorexia and bulemia. Current Prob Pediatr 1985;15:8:1-57, 15:9:1-59.
11. Litt IF: Menstrual problems during adolescence. Pediatr in Rev 1983;4:203-212.
12. Greydanus DE, McAnarney ER: Menstruation and its disorders in adolescence. Curr Prob Pediatr 1982;12:1-60.
13. Friedman CI, Kim MH: Obesity and its effect on reproductive function. Clin Obstet Gynecol 1985;28:645-663.
14. Loucks A, Horvath SM: Athletic amenorrhea: a review. Med Sci Sports Exercise 1985;17:56-72.
15. Youngs DD, Reame N: Psychosomatic aspects of menstrual dysfunction. Clin Obstet Gynecol 1983;26:777-784.
16. Yen SSC: Chronic anovulation caused by peripheral endocrine disorders. In: Yen SSC, Jaffe RB, eds. Reproductive Endocrinology. 2nd ed. Philadelphia: W.B. Saunders, 1986.

17. Dewhurst J: Secondary amenorrhea. Pediatr Ann 1981;10:496-500.
18. Shalet SM: The effects of cancer treatment on growth and sexual development. Clin Oncol 1985;4:223-238.
19. McKenna TJ, Moore A, Magee F, Cunningham S: Amenorrhea with cryptic hyperandrogenemia. J Clin Endocrinol Metab 1983;56:893-898.
20. Spence JEH: Menstrual abnormalities in the adolescent: abuse of the birth control pill. Pediatr Adolesc Gynecol 1983;1:125-148.
21. Reindollar RH, McDonough PG: Adolescent menstrual disorders. Clin Obstet Gynecol 1983;26:690-701.
22. Anderson MM, Irwin CE Jr, Snyder DL: Abnormal vaginal bleeding in adolescents. Pediatr Ann 1986;15:697-707.
23. Claessens EA, Cowell CA: Dysfunctional uterine bleeding in the adolescent. Pediatr Clin N Am 1981;28:369-378.
24. Smith CB: Dysfunctional uterine bleeding. Am Family Phys 1987;36:161-167.
25. Huffman JW, Dewhurst CJ, Capraro VJ: The Gynecology of Childhood and Adolescence. 2nd ed. Philadelphia: W.B. Saunders, 1981.
26. Leng JJ, Greenblatt RB: Hirsutism in adolescent girls. Pediatr Clin N Am 1972;19:681-703.
27. Lorenzo EM: Familial study of hirsutism. J Clin Endocrinol Metab 1970;31:556-564.
28. Lucky AW, Rosenfield RL, McGuire J, Rudy S, Helke J: Adrenal androgen hyperresponsiveness to adrenocorticotropin in women with acne and/or hirsutism: adrenal enzyme defects and exaggerated adrenarche. J Clin Endocrinol Metab 1986;62:840-848.
29. Kirschner MA: Hirsutism and virilism in women. Special Top Endocrinol Metab 1984;6:55-93.
30. Kustin J, Rebar RW: Hirsutism in young adolescent girls. Pediatr Ann 1986;15:522-528.
31. Strauss RH, Liggett MT, Lanese RR: Anabolic steroid use and perceived effects in ten weight-trained women athletes. J Am Med Assoc 1985;253:2871-2873.
32. New MI, Levine LS: Congenital Adrenal Hyperplasia. Berlin: Springer-Verlag, 1984.
33. Lobo RA, Goebelsmann U: Evidence for reduced 3 beta-ol-hydroxysteroid dehydrogenase activity in some hirsute women thought to have polycystic ovary syndrome. J Clin Endocrinol Metab 1981;53:394-400.
34. Emans SJ, Grace E, Fleischnick E, Mansfield MJ, Crigler JF Jr: Detection of late-onset 21-hydroxylase deficiency congenital Adrenal Hyperplasia in adolescents. Pediatr 1983;72:690-695.
35. Speiser PW, New M: Genotype and hormonal phenotype in nonclassical 21-hydroxylase deficiency. J Clin Endocrinol Metab 1987;64:86-94.
36. Dewailly D, Vantyghem-Haudiquet M-C, Sainsard C, et al: Clinical and biological phenotypes in late-onset 21-hydroxylase deficiency. 1986;63:418-423.
37. Wentz AC, Gutai JP, Jones GS, Migeon C: Ovarian hyperthecosis in the adolescent patient. J Pediatr 1976;88:488-493.
38. Lucky AW: Update on acne vulgaris. Pediatr Annals 1987;16:29-38.
39. Wilson MH: Odor (unusual urine and body). In: Hoekelman RA, Blatman S, Friedman SB, Nelson NM, Seidel HM, eds. Primary Pediatric Care. St. Louis: C.V. Mosby, 1987.
40. Biffignandi P, Massucchetti C, Molinatti GM: Female hirsutism: pathophysiological considerations and therapeutic implications. Endocr Rev 1984;5:498-513.
41. Steinberger E, Smith KD, Rodriguez-Rigau LJ: Testosterone, dehydroepiandrosterone, and dehydroepiandrosterone sulfate in hyperandrogenic women. J Clin Endocrinol Metab 1984;59:471-476.
42. Marynick SP, Chakmakjian MD, McCaffree DL, Herndon JH Jr: Androgen excess in cystic acne. New Engl J Med 1983;308:981-986.
43. Keye Jr, WR: The Premenstrual Syndrome. Philadelphia: WB Saunders, 1988.
44. Abplanalp JM, Haskett RF, Rose RM: The premenstrual syndrome. Psychiatr Clin North Am 1980;3:327-347.
45. Beach RK: Relieving the pain of menstrual cramps. Contemp Pediatr 1986;(Mar):115-134.
46. Smith RP: Primary dysmenorrhea and the adolescent patient. Adolesc Pediatr Gynecol 1988;1:23-30.
47. Huffman JW: Endometriosis in young teen-age girls. Pediatr Ann 1981;10:501-506.
48. McKenna TJ: Pathogenesis and treatment of polycystic ovary syndrome. New Engl J Med 1988; 318:558-562.
49. Emans SJ, Grace E, Woods ER, Mansfield J, Crigler Jr, JF: Treatment with dexamethasone of androgen excess in adolescent patients. J Pediatr 1988;112:821–826.

7

Contraception

The increased sexual activity and lack of birth control among adolescents and young adults are well documented. The health care provider working with adolescents must be able to advise them of the methods of contraception available today. The provider may elect not to prescribe contraceptive devices but must be ready to give birth control advice in the day-to-day clinical setting. There are two groups of contraceptives that the health care professional must consider: prescribed and nonprescribed methods. Each has certain advantages and disadvantages. This chapter approaches this complex topic in a didactic manner to provide a realistic approach to the sexually active adolescent.

BASIC CONTRACEPTIVE TECHNOLOGY

Despite the availability of effective methods of contraception, adolescents generally do not seek contraceptive advice or devices before engaging in sexual intercourse. Most adolescents have 6 to 12 months of coital experience before entering the health care system. The reasons for not using contraceptives have been summarized in the literature as follows:

Lack of knowledge about contraception
Nonavailability of contraceptive devices or materials
Ignorance of fertility periods
Belief that they are protected
Infrequent or unanticipated intercourse
Guilt about being protected (situational ethics concept)
Notion that contraception is harmful or interferes with sexual pleasure
Reluctance to request information from private doctors because of possible moral lectures or refusals
Physicians being unaware of the rights of minors as defined by various Supreme Court decisions (*In re Gault,* 1967; *Roe v. Wade, Doe v. Bolton,* 1973; *Planned Parenthood of Central Missouri v. Danforth,* 1976; *Bellotti v. Baird,* 1979; others).

When choosing a contraceptive, adolescents are interested in effectiveness more than any other factor. Physicians must consider this both from a theoretic standpoint and with regard to actual usefulness (Table 7-1). It is difficult to determine precise effectiveness. The questions that

Table 7-1. Contraceptive Methods for Adolescents

Method	Theoretical Effective-ness (%)	Actual (Use) Effective-ness (%)	Advantages	Disadvantages
Condom	98	64-97	Nonprescription; male responsible; anti-infective; easy to use	Coital-related; motivation needed; coital interference?
Foam and condom	99	95	Nonprescription; available anti-infective; no side effects	High motivation needed; high cost if intercourse frequent
Vaginal Spermicides	97	61-97	Nonprescription; no side effects; anti-infective	Motivation needed; messy; care interference with coitus, orogenital sex
Depo-Provera	100	99-100	Very effective; little motivation needed; no estrogen risks	Not FDA approved; delayed resumption of menses, ovulation
Abstinence	100	?		
Minipill	98	90	No estrogen risks	Irregular menses; ovulation frequent; discontinuation high
IUD	97-99	94	Noncoital method; relief	Daily motivation needed; estrogen side effects; possible estrogen risk
Diaphragm	97	82	No side effects; little infection; little interference with intercourse	Needs medical visit; motivation needed; messy; cumbersome

need to be asked of the adolescent population may be summarized as follows:

1. Am I afraid of using this method of birth control?
2. Would I really rather not use this method?
3. Will I have trouble remembering to use this method?
4. Have I ever become pregnant while using this method?
5. Are there reasons why I will be unable to use this method as prescribed?
6. Do I still have unanswered questions about this method?
7. Has my mother, father, sibling, or close friend discouraged me from using this method?
8. Will this method make my periods longer or more painful?

9. Will prolonged use of this method cost me more than I can afford?
10. Is this method known to have serious complications?
11. Am I opposed to this method because of religious beliefs?
12. Have I already experienced complications from this method?
13. Has a nurse or doctor already told me not to use this method?
14. Is my partner opposed to my using this method?
15. Am I using this method without my partner's knowledge?
16. Will use of this method embarrass me?
17. Will my partner or I enjoy sexual activity less because of this method?
18. Will this method interfere with our love-making?

Additional concerns of adolescents during the selection of a contraceptive must also be noted, such as the following:

1. Can I get pregnant if I have sex during my menstrual cycle?
2. Can I get pregnant if I have never had a period?
3. Are girls unclean when they are having their period?
4. Do you have to have menstrual periods before a doctor will let you have birth control pills?

FACTORS TO CONSIDER IN PRESCRIBING CONTRACEPTIVES

The health care provider generally will consider nonprescribed as well as prescribed methods of contraception when approaching the adolescent. The provider must know the patient's (1) probability of compliance, (2) frequency of intercourse, (3) risk of pregnancy, and (4) risk of morbidity and mortality.

Compliance is a difficult consideration in the adolescent and certainly is based on the patient's motivation to use various methods of contraception. If compliance is good, then all methods can be effective. Frequency of intercourse is important; if it is greater than six times a month, then an oral contraceptive agent, an intrauterine device, or a diaphragm is the best method of contraception. If compliance is poor and frequency of intercourse is great, then the prescribed method of contraception might be an intrauterine device.

The patient must be told the pregnancy rates with the various prescribed methods of contraception, which are based on compliance and frequency. Oral contraceptive agents, if used properly, have the best chance of reducing pregnancy (and are most frequently chosen by adolescents). However, the intrauterine device and the diaphragm also have very low pregnancy rates if used properly.

If sexual intercourse is infreqent, say less than two times a month, the condom and vaginal cream together are very effective. The diaphragm, which is associated with little risk except that of pregnancy (and occasional minimal irritation), may be superior to other methods from a morbidity and mortality standpoint, with abstinence obviously being associated with less morbidity and mortality. The intrauterine device is less desirable than other methods of contraception.

Additional factors to consider before prescribing any method of contraception are as follows:

Risk factors
Patient's maturity
Family history
Medical history
Physical and mental status of the patient
Parental consent
Frequent consultation
Followup visits

The issue of consent is important because of medicolegal implications. If individuals are under 18 years of age, consent from parents is unnecessary because the individual is protected by the Supreme Court decisions already cited. It is still important that the physician strive to obtain some consent from the patient, if possible.

Frequent consultations become an important aspect of contraceptive considerations in the adolescent. Certainly, frequent followup visits are important because of physiologic and psychologic changes that can occur with the various methods of contraception, especially oral contraceptive agents. Furthermore, regular followup visits enable the physician to assess the psychologic, endocrinologic, and psychosocial ramifications, as well as the role of sexuality and contraception, in the life of the patient.

NONPRESCRIBED CONTRACEPTIVES

Nonprescribed methods of contraception can be effective if sexual intercourse is infrequent and the individual understands the normal menstrual cycle. They offer many advantages in that they can be obtained without a prescription and are associated with little morbidity and mortality. The advantages and disadvantages of each of the nonprescribed methods should be part of the regular educational process for the adolescent as well as the health care professional.

Condoms. Condoms may be an excellent method of contraception for the adolescent if used properly. They can obviously protect against venereal disease as well as provide a barrier to the transmission of semen into the vagina. The condom's failure rate has been reported as three pregnancies per woman-year. The effectiveness rate approaches that of oral contraceptives when foam is used in conjunction with the condom. The high actual failure rate is often due to such bothersome problems as decreased sensation and interrupted lovemaking, which lead to irregular use. One contraindication is that some men cannot achieve an erection if a condom is used. Rarely do men or women have allergic reactions to the material from which condoms are made. Major advantages of the condom as a contraceptive in adolescents are (1) no side effects, (2) effective protection against pregnancy, (3) no prescription needed, (4) protects against sexually transmitted diseases, (5) may contribute to reduced instances of cervical cancer, and (6) can assist in relieving dyspareunia.

The health care professional should provide the following instructions to the patient in the use of the condom:

1. Use the condom for every episode of sexual intercourse.
2. Put the condom on the penis before the penis is in the vagina.
3. After intercourse, hold onto the condom while removing the penis from the vaginal area.
4. Buy a good brand.
5. Do not use condoms that are more than 2 years old.
6. Do not use petroleum jelly on the condom, as it will cause the condom to deteriorate. K/Y jelly, contraceptive foams, and saliva are excellent lubricants.
7. To increase the effectiveness of the condom, always use contraceptive foam.
8. If the condom tears or comes off in the vagina, insert contraceptive foam or jelly immediately.
9. Never reuse condoms, especially if they are used as protection against sexually transmitted diseases.
10. Some couples consider natural skin condoms to be more sensitive and natural.

Vaginal Spermicides. Vaginal spermicides can be effective if used properly, especially in conjunction with a condom and when intercourse is infrequent. Each product has different time requirements and suggestions with respect to intercourse and postcoital activity; therefore, it is crucial for the physician to advise the adolescent to read the package instructions carefully. The advantages of a vaginal contraceptive are that it (1) is relatively inexpensive, (2) has few side effects, (3) serves as a vaginal lubricant to reduce dyspareunia, (4) may protect against sexually transmitted diseases, and (5) is useful for young women who engage in sporadic intercourse. The vaginal contraceptive sponge has not proven to be useful for adolescents and is not recommended. It can be obtained in one size which, when inserted in the vagina, swells to occlude the vagina. Problems with vaginal malodor and toxic shock syndrome have been reported. The sponge is not more effective than the diaphragm.

Abstinence. The physician should encourage and support adolescents who choose to abstain from sexual intercourse until they feel psychologically and physically ready. In the United States, approximately 40 to 50% of adolescents experience sexual intercourse by their nineteenth year. Therefore, the concept of noncoital sex—that is, sexual activity that stops short of intercourse as an expression of sexual feelings—can and should be encouraged.

Rhythm Method. The rhythm method of contraception involves an understanding of the menstrual cycle and ideal times for sexual intercourse. This concept has been replaced by the method of "fertility awareness." If this method is chosen, it is important for the health care professional to advise the patient of its risks. The use of vaginal creams or condoms or both might be encouraged, but these suggestions may be rejected on moral grounds.

It is important for both partners to learn about the woman's menstrual cycle if they choose to use the fertility awareness method. Teaching teenagers this method may help them achieve a desired pregnancy later in life, as well as avoid pregnancy when it is not desired. The Natural Family Planning Kit recently developed by Telesis Corporation may be used to teach fertility awareness to adolescents.

The advantages of the fertility awareness method are as follows:

It is safe
It is free or inexpensive
It is acceptable to religious groups that oppose other methods
It is helpful for family planning

The disadvantages of this method are as follows:

Records must be kept for several cycles before it can be used
It may restrict sexual spontaneity
Charting must be done diligently to be accurate
Some women are unable to see clear cut cervical mucus and basal body temperature (BBT) patterns, even with diligent charting
Adolescents with irregular or sensitive cycles have difficulty with calendar and BBT techniques
Should pregnancy occur, risk is somewhat greater that an old egg will have been fertilized. (Researchers suspect that fetal abnormalities are somewhat higher when pregnancy results from the fertilization of an old egg.)

A group of adolescent and young adult patients is being followed at Children's Hospital, National Medical Center, in Washington, D.C. They are using the fertility awareness method as a means of contraception, but data are not yet reportable.

Douching. Douching offers little contraceptive protection and is not a method that should be promoted.

Lactation. Breast feeding does offer some protection against pregnancy, but nearly all lactating women ovulate within 1 year after delivery. The average onset of ovulation is approximately 7 months after delivery.

Coitus Interruptus. Coitus interruptus, or strategic withdrawal, has been used as a method of birth control for centuries. A couple using this method may have intercourse in an accepted way until the point of ejaculation, which must occur completely away from the vagina and external genitalia of the female, thus preventing any possible conception. The withdrawal method has distinct advantages over most other methods: it requires no devices and no chemicals and is always possible to perform. One strong disadvantage is the failure rate: 9 to 15 pregnancies per 100 women per year. This method of contraception, especially in adolescents, is not desirable.

Injectable Devices. Medroxyprogesterone acetate (Depo-Provera) has not been approved by the FDA as a contraceptive, but is approved for treatment of endometriosis and breast cancer. Therefore, it should not be used as a method for contraception.

Postcoital Contraceptives. The use of diethylstilbestrol, the so-called morning-after pill, has been approved by the Food and Drug Administration (FDA) for emergency situations such as rape. The drug is given in a dosage of 25 mg twice a day for 5 days and should be administered no later than 72 hours after intercourse. It is important that the adolescent be advised of the nausea and abdominal discomfort that may occur following use of this medication.

PRESCRIBED METHODS OF CONTRACEPTION

It is important that basic concepts concerning the prescribed methods of contraception be addressed by the health care provider. The advantages and disadvantages and morbidity and mortality of each must be discussed with the adolescent. The prescribed methods are the intrauterine device, oral contraceptive agents, and the barrier method (e.g., diaphragm).

Oral Contraceptive Agents. Hormonal steroidal contraceptives have been available for birth control pills since the early 1930s. The theoretic effectiveness of combined pills approaches 100% and, if used properly, will provide the individual with maximum protection against pregnancy. A wide variety of oral contraceptives commonly prescribed for adolescents are available today (Table 7-2).

It is important to try to select a pill for the particular adolescent based on endocrinologic and biologic considerations (Table 7-3). Estrogen-dominant pills should be considered for patients who have hirsutism and oily skin; progesterin-dominant preparations are usually preferable in those with leukorrhea, fluid retention, or fibrocystic disease of the breast. A low-estrogen pill, at least 20 mg, should always be chosen. Understanding the side effects of each oral contraceptive agent will aid in prescribing the proper one.

The side effects of oral contraceptive agents and the corrective actions to be taken are as follows:

> *Nausea, vomiting, abdominal pain:* Take the pill with food and use a lower estrogen pill.
> *Headache, fatigue:* Evaluate for psychosocial concerns and use a lower estrogen pill.
> *Weight gain:* Limit caloric intake, increase activity, and use a lower progestin pill.

Table 7-2. Oral Contraceptives Used by Adolescents.

Contraceptive	Estrogen	Progestin
Estrogen-dominant		
Enovid-E	Mestranol, 100 mg	Norethynodrel, 2.5 mg
Ovulen	Mestranol, 100 mg	Ethynodioldiacetate, 1 mg
Norinyl/Ortho-Novum 2	Mestranol, 100 mg	Norethindrone, 2 mg
Norinyl/Ortho-Novum 1 + 80	Mestranol, 80 mg	Norethindrone, 2 mg
Balanced		
Demulen	Ethinyl estradiol 50 mg	Ethynodiol diacetate 1 mg
Norinyl/Ortho-Novum 1 + 50	Mestranol 50 mg	Norethindrone 1 mg
Norinyl/Ortho-Novum 1 + 35	Ethinyl estradiol 35 mg	Norethindrone 1 mg
Progestin-dominant		
Ovral	Ethinyl estradiol 50 mg	Norgestrel 0.5 mg
Norlestrin 2.5	Ethinyl estradiol 50 mg	Norethindrone acetate 2.5 mg
Low-Dose		
Brevicon	Ethinyl estradiol 35 mg	Norethindrone 0.5 mg
Lo-ovral	Ethinyl estradiol 30 mg	Norgestrel 0.3 mg
Sequentials		
	Progestin	Estrogen
Triphasil (Wyeth)	Levonorgestrel	E. Estradiol tablets sequential regime
Ortho Novum 7-7-7		
Tri-Norinyl (Syntex)		

Leukorrhea: Investigate for infection and use a lower estrogen pill.

Amenorrhea/oligomenorrhea: Investigate for pregnancy and use a higher estrogen pill.

Hypermenorrhea: Investigate for infection and use a lower estrogen pill.

Irregular bleeding: Investigate for infection and incorrect pill-taking.

Galactorrhea: Investigate for pregnancy, CNS-pituitary lesion, and drug use.

Early-cycle breakthrough bleeding: Use a higher estrogen pill.

Table 7-3. Oral Contraceptive Agents.

First Choice	Indications
Balanced pill	Most adolescents, including first-time users and those with previous satisfactory experience with balanced pills
Estrogen dominant	Androgenic females: moderate-marked acne, hirutism, small breasts, menses usually short and scant
Progestin dominant	Estrogenic females: large breasts, leukorrhea, premenstrual edema/weight gain, menses long and heavy
Sequential pills	Normal menstrual cycle

Late-cycle breakthrough bleeding: Use a higher progestin pill.
Breast discomfort: Use a lower estrogen pill.

Interactions with other medications being taken may reduce the effectiveness of oral contraceptive agents. Therefore, the health care professional must document all medications that the adolescent is currently taking and advise her that she should check with the prescribing physician before using other medication while taking the pill. Tables 7-4 and 7-5 list drugs that can have an effect on oral contraceptive agents and should be referred to when prescribing oral contraceptive agents.

Table 7-4. Drugs that May Reduce the Efficacy of Oral Contraceptives.

Class of Compound	Drug	Proposed Method of Action	Suggested Management
Anticonvulusant drugs	Barbiturates: Phenobarbital, carbamazepine, primidone, phenytoin, ethosuximide	Induction of liver Microsomal enzymes Rapid metabolism of estrogen and increased binding of progestin and ethinyl estradiol to sex hormone binding globulin	Use another method, another drug or higher dose OCs (50 mcg ethnyl estradiol)
Cholesterol-lowering agent	Clofibrate	Reduces elevated serum triglycerides and cholesterol: this reduces OC efficacy	Use another method
Antibiotics	Rifampin Isoniazid Penicillin Ampicillin	Rifampin increases metabolism of progestins Enterohepatic circulation disturbance, intestinal hurry	For short course, use additional method or use another drug
	Metronidazole Tetracycline	Induction of microsomal liver enzymes (See above)	For long course, use another method
	Neomycin Chloramphenicol Sulfonamide Nitrofurantoin		
Sedatives and hypnotics	Benzodiazepines Barbiturates Chloral hydrate Antimigraine preparations	Increased microsomal liver enzymes (See above)	For short course, use additional method or another drug. For long course, use another method or higher dose OCs
Antacids	All	Decreased intestinal absorption of progestins	Use additional method

Table 7-5. Modification of Other Drug Activity by Oral Contraceptives.

Class of Compound	Drug	Modification of Drug Action	Suggested Management
Anticoagulant	All	OCs increase clotting factors, decrease efficacy	Do not use OC with anticoagulant
Antidiabetic	Insulin and oral hypoglycemic agents	High dose OCs cause impaired glucose tolerance	Use low dose estrogen and progestin OC or use another method
Antihypertensive agents	Guanethidine and occasional methyldopa	Estrogen component causes naretention; progestin has no effect	Use low estrogen OC or use another method
Anticonvulsant	All	Fluid retention, increased seizures	Use another method
Tricyclic	Clomipramine (possibly others)	Increased side effects, depression	Use another method
Betamimetic agents	Isoproterenol	Estrogen causes decreased response to these drugs	Adjust dose of drug as necessary. Discontinuing OC can result in excessive drug activity
Beta blocking	Metoprolol	Increased drug effect (decreased metabolism)	Adjust dose if necessary
Phenothiazine tranquilizers	All phenothiazines, reserpine, and similar drugs	Estrogen potentiates the hyperprolactinemia effect of these drugs	Use other drugs or lower dose OCs. If galactorrhea or hyperprolactemia occurs, use another method
Sedatives and hypnotics	Chlordiazepoxide Lorazepam Oxazepam Diazepam	Increases effect, increased metabolism	Use with caution

Indications, Contraindications, and Complications. To reduce morbidity and possible mortality, indications for oral contraceptive agents in adolescents are (1) frequent sexual activity (two to five times per week or greater than six times per month), (2) fear of the interuterine device or poor compliance with other methods, and (3) desire for immediate and maximum protection.

The absolute contraindications documented by the FDA are (1) thrombophlebitis and thromboembolic disorders, (2) history of thrombophlebitis and thromboembolic disorders, (3) cerebrovascular accidents or coronary artery disease, (4) breast cancer, (5) estrogen-dependent neoplasm, (6) undiagnosed abnormal vaginal bleeding, and (7) pregnancy.

Other so-called "relative" contraindications for oral contraceptive agents are as follows:

Patient due for surgery

Family history of seizures, diabetes, embolic phenomena, or metabolic disease

Adult maturity not reached (i.e., regular periods for 18 to 24 months)

Presence of hepatic, pancreatic, cardiac, renal, neurologic, or other organ system dysfunction

History of psychiatric illness, especially depression

History of ophthalmologic pathology, especially funduscopic changes

Unexplained dysfunctional uterine bleeding

Impaired liver function

Vascular or migraine headaches

Severe hypertension

Sickle-cell disease

Unreliability, strong ambivalence about use of contraceptives, problems in remembering to take the pill every day

Prolonged bed rest, leg cast, etc.

Complications associated with oral contraceptive agents include the following:

Thromboembolic disease (rare in adolescents)

Blood pressure elevation (reversible upon stopping)

Cholestatic jaundice (uncommon)

Post-pill menstrual irregularities (uncommon if none previously present)

Hepatomas (rare, particularly in first 5 years of use)

Contact lens problems (decreased tearing, corneal edema)

Increased water retention and mild weight gain

Guidelines. Specific guidelines for prescribing oral contraceptive agents to adolescents include the following:

1. There should be evidence of a mature hypothalamic-pituitary-ovarian axis without physical or psychologic pathology.
2. The patient should have a detailed history and physical examination to rule out contraindications.
3. Pelvic examinations with Pap smears should be performed initially and at 3, 6, and 12 months, unless some sign or symptom indicates more frequent tests.
4. Complete blood counts and liver function, cholesterol, and fasting glucose tests should be performed before a patient begins taking oral contraceptives. If this is not feasible, a complete blood count, a urinalysis, a detailed history, and a physical examination are needed.

5. A lower estrogen pill, 30 to 50 mg, should be selected for this age group.
6. Careful oral and written instructions on how to take the pill should be given to the patient.
7. The patient should be followed as a minimum at 1, 3, 6, and 12 months during the first year; if problems develop, the oral contraceptive should be discontinued.
8. Memory is aided by the use of a 28-day package paralleling the days of the week.
9. A backup method, such as foam or a condom, *always* should be used with each coital episode for the first month of pill taking.

Intrauterine Devices. The intrauterine device (IUD) was an excellent contraceptive method in the 1970s because of its effectiveness in the noncompliant adolescent. Copper-Ts and Copper-7s were effective in reducing pregnancy rates. The major drawbacks with them is pelvic inflammatory disease, perforation, and expulsion, making the risk of morbidity and mortality great. Still, the health care professional may prescribe use of the IUD as a method of contraception or refer the patient to a gynecologist.

The two major types of devices marketed in the United States today are the intrauterine progesterone T and the copper T380A. Studies with both types have shown good results if the patients are followed closely.

Indications and Contraindications. Indications for the intrauterine device are as follows:

Frequent sexual activity
Repeated pregnancies or abortions
Poor compliance
Low intelligence and poor motivation
Fear of the birth control pill
Hormone-releasing devices may help control menstrual cramps and heavy bleeding.

Contraindications for the intrauterine device include the following:

Possible pregnancy
History of apparent pelvic inflammatory disease, infected abortion, or postpartum endometriosis within 6 weeks
Abnormal uterine cavity
Uterine malignancy
Unexplained abnormal uterine bleeding
Severe dysmenorrhea
History of ectopic pregnancy or sexually transmitted disease
Valvular heart disease or blood dyscrasias
Cervicitis, vaginitis, or endometriosis
More than one sex partner.

Guidelines. Specific guidelines for use of the IUD are as follows:

1. Contraindications have been ruled out.
2. The procedure has been explained carefully to the patient and the string location has been emphasized.
3. The pain, nausea, increased bleeding, and syncope that may occur have been explained.
4. Use of foam or condoms or both within the first 3 to 6 weeks should be emphasized until the device has been examined and is known to be effective.
5. The patient should be followed at 1, 3, 6, and 12 months.
6. Pelvic examinations should be performed before insertion and at 1, 6, and 12 months after insertion.

Barrier Methods. Barrier methods of contraception for adolescents can be effective if used properly. The diaphragm generally is used in the older adolescent, between the ages of 17 and 25. If inserted properly before intercourse and used properly after intercourse, the diaphragm is effective; studies have demonstrated this effectiveness when compliance is good and medical and gynecologic abnormalities are not present. The diaphragm becomes an effective method of contraception for both those individuals who have consistent sexual intercourse and those individuals who have infrequent sexual intercourse. A number of types of diaphragms are available: coil spring, flat spring, arch spring, and bow-bent.

The patient must be advised that a contraceptive cream must be applied to the diaphragm before insertion 6 hours before intercourse and that the diaphragm may not be removed until 6 hours after intercourse. Proper storage is important so that the diaphragm does not become damaged.

Contraindications. Contraindications to the use of the diaphragm are as follows:

Lack of privacy
Hesitation in handling genitals, using tampons, or inserting creams
Immediate postpartum period (problems with proper fit)
Short anterior cervical wall
Severe retroversion of the uterus
Severe anteversion of the uterus
Peritoneal tears
Vescular vaginal fistulas
Complete uterine prolapse
Allergies to rubber or spermicides
Recurrent urinary tract infections
Inability of patient or partner to learn correct insertion technique

Guidelines. The following are guidelines for the use of the diaphragm:

1. Fitting for correct diaphragm size should be done by an experienced practitioner (Figs. 7-1 and 7-2).
2. Reassessment for a new size is indicated if weight changes by 15 or more pounds and following pregnancy.
3. A new diaphragm is recommended after 2 years of use.
4. The diaphragm should always be used with a spermicidal cream or jelly liberally applied to the center and the edge. Additional spermicide should be applied vaginally before each repeated coitus.
5. Petroleum products should not be used for additional lubrication because they will cause the diaphragm material to disintegrate.
6. The diaphragm can be inserted up to 6 hours before coitus. It should remain in place for at least 6 to 8 hours after the last coitus. After use, it should be cleaned, dried, dusted with plain powder or cornstarch, and stored.

Cervical Cap. In 1988, the FDA approved the marketing of a cervical cap (Prentif Cavity-Rim Cervical Cap, Lamberts Ltd., England). Previously, use of the cervical cap in the United States had not been widespread. In controlled studies, the cap was 93.6% effective compared with 95.4% for the diaphragm (Bernstein, 1986). The cervical cap has the advantage that it may be left in place for 7 days but must be reinserted before each sexual intercourse.

Adverse effects include abnormal pap smears in about 4% of users after 3 months, pain during intercourse, and *Gardnerella vaginalis* or *Mo-*

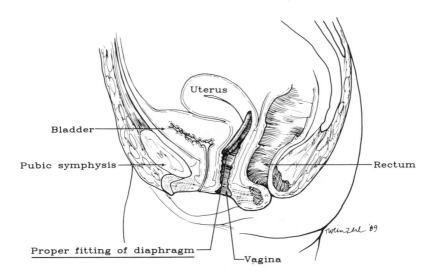

Fig. 7-1. Proper fitting of the diaphragm.

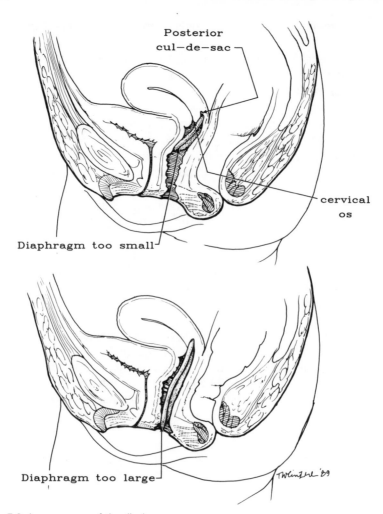

Fig. 7-2. Improper use of the diaphragm.

nilia infection. Theoretically, toxic shock syndrome and endometriosis could result from backflow of menstrual fluids.

The cap can be inserted anytime before intercourse, but must remain in place for at least 8 hours and can be left in up to 48 hours. The cap requires less spermicide than a diaphragm and is not as messy to use. Users should check regularly for holes, tears, and cracks in the cap. Users are also advised to have a Pap smear after the first 3 months, and annually thereafter. The range of sizes is limited, and the cap is more difficult to fit than a diaphragm.

POSTCOITAL CONTRACEPTION CONSIDERATIONS

Guidelines concerning postcoital contraception are as follows:

1. Used properly, postcoital methods have a low failure rate of 0.03 to 0.3%.

2. Treatment is with 25 mg diethylstilbestrol, 25 mg conjugated estrogens, or 2.5 mg ethinyl estradiol twice a day for 5 days.

3. Nausea and vomiting are common side effects and may be controlled by an antiemetic (5 to 20 mg prochlorperazine) 1 to 2 hours before each dose.

4. Use of diethylstilbestrol for postcoital contraception has become controversial because of complications from its exposure in utero. When it is used postcoitally, the practitioner should be certain that the patient is not already pregnant and that no more than 72 hours have elapsed since coitus. The patient should be informed of the possible risk to the fetus should the method fail. Some feel that postcoital diethylstilbestrol should be given only to those who agree to an abortion if the method fails; others feel it should be abandoned in favor of other estrogens.

5. If oral therapy is rejected or estrogens are contraindicated and the patient wants to initiate regular contraception, a copper-containing intrauterine device can be inserted, providing there is no evidence of infection and cultures are taken.

6. Menstrual extraction is an alternative to post-coital estrogen or intrauterine device insertion.

7. Because the risk of pregnancy from a single act of coitus is low, and because first-trimester abortion is generally safe and readily available, many advocate withholding postcoital methods and offering abortion to those few who become pregnant. The emotional effects of waiting, the difficulty of deciding to abort, or personal opposition to this procedure should be considered in each case, and the decision must be individualized.

ABSTINENCE

The health care provider should consider the following factors:

1. Abstinence always should be discussed during contraceptive counseling and supported as the safest, least expensive, most effective, and often most psychosocially appropriate method.

2. The adolescent choosing abstinence needs emotional support and assistance through rehearsal and role-playing techniques to deal with partner and peer pressures to have intercourse.

3. When abstinence is chosen, education should include alternate means of sexual gratification, the need to avoid genital closeness during ejaculation if other forms of physical intimacy are used, the risks of transmitting infection by noncoital sexual activity, and complete information about all contraceptive methods for reference in case abstinence is not sustained.

STERILIZATION

An adolescent or parent may request vasectomy, tubal ligation, or hysterectomy. Unless there are compelling medical reasons, sterilization is strongly discouraged (and of questionable legality) for anyone under 21 years of age because of the low chance of reversibility and the improbability of an adolescent's being able to make an irrevocable decision to forego childbearing for the rest of his or her life without regret. Effective contraception is a far better alternative.

Sterilization of severely retarded or mutiple-handicapped adolescents, for whom childbearing or parenthood are clearly impossible options, may be indicated in carefully selected cases. A complete diagnostic evaluation and multidisciplinary review of all circumstances are essential. The sole consideration is to enable the patient to live a heathier, fuller, and less restricted life. Continued counseling of the family and sex education of the handicapped adolescent before and after sterilization are mandatory to deal with parental guilt feelings and continued vulnerability to sexual exploitation. However, sterilization in any minor (or in any adult unable to give an informed consent), regardless of other factors—no matter how compelling—is highly controversial.

SELECTION OF THE BEST METHOD OF CONTRACEPTION FOR ADOLESCENTS

The health care professional must keep general contraceptive concepts in mind and use specific indications and contraindications to minimize patient morbidity and mortality. The key in the approach to each adolescent and young adult who seeks contraception advice and devices is *individualization,* not generalization. Keeping the basic facts and principles in mind and approaching the patient with respect to his or her sexual intercourse frequency, biologic and social maturity, and compliance are important before prescribing a method of contraception. The wishes of the patient must be considered along with his or her biologic and endocrinologic makeup.

Motivation, frequency of intercourse, side effects in each particular patient, cooperation of the sexual partner, compliance, secrecy, and psychosexual factors also must be considered when selecting the best method of contraception. By considering these factors, the health care professional can advise the adolescent about birth control and can choose to prescribe a contraceptive if deemed appropriate.

BIBLIOGRAPHY

Barnes HV, ed: Sexually active teenagers: their health care problems and needs. Soc Adolesc Med 1987;1(1):1-37.

Bernstein GS: Final Report: Use-effectiveness Study of Cervical Caps, contract N01-HD-1-2804, NICHHD, 1986.

Bracken MD: Spermicidal contraceptives and poor reproductive outcomes: the epidemiologic evidence against an association. Am J Obstet Gynecol 1985;151:552

Chvapil M, et al: Collagen sponge as vaginal contraceptive barrier: critical summary of 7 years of research. Am J Obstet Gynecol 1985;151:325.

Committee on Drugs, American Academy of Pediatrics: Medroxyprogesterone acetate (Depo-Provera). Pediatrics 1980;65:74A.

Connell EB: Oral contraceptives. The benefits and the cardiovascular risks. Postgrad Med 1987;81:46-58.

Cramer DW, Goldman MB, Schiff I, et al: The relationship of tubal infertility to barrier method and oral contraceptive use. JAMA 1987;257:2446-2450.

Goldzieher JW, Pointdexter AN: Medical aspects of contraception. Hosp Pract 1987;21:93-108.

Greydanus DE: Contraception. In: Lavery JP, Sanfilippo JL, eds: Pediatric and Adolescent Obstetrics and Gynecology. New York: Springer-Verlag, 1985:234-261.

Greydanus DE: Contraception in the adolescent. Medical Clin No Amer 1990;74:35-47.

Grimes DA: Reversible contraception for the 1980s. JAMA 1986;255:69-75.

Haspels AA, Van Santen MR: Postcoital contraception. Pediatr Adolesc Gynecol 1984;2:63.

Hormonal contraception: new long-acting methods. Pop Rep 1987;K(3):58-84.

Irwin KL, Rosero-Bixby L, Oberle MW, et al: Oral contraceptives and cervical cancer risk in Costa Rica. JAMA 1988;259(1):59-64.

Kols A: Oral contraception in the 1980s. Pop Rep 1982;A(10):189.

Kreutner AK: Adolescent contraception. Prim Care 1987;14(1):121-138.

Kreutner AK: Contraception in the adolescent female. Semin Adolesc Med 1988;5(1):45-63.

Kreutner AK: Adolescent contraception. Adolescent Med 1987;14(1):121-138.

Louik C, Mitchell AA, Werler MM, et al: Maternal exposure to spermicides in relation to certain birth defects. N Engl J Med 1987;317:474-478.

Mishell DR Jr: Current status of intrauterine devices. N Engl J Med 1985;312:984.

Neinstein LS, Katz B: Contraceptive use in the chronically ill adolescent female. Part II. J Adolesc Health Care 1986;7:350-360.

New Copper IUD. Med Lett Drug Ther 1988;30:25-26.

Nieman LK, Choate TM, Chrousos GP, et al: The progesterone antagonist RU 486. A potential new contraceptive agent. N Engl J Med 1987;316:187-191.

Ory HW, Layde PM, Rubin GL, et al: Oral contraceptive use and the risk of breast cancer. N Engl J Med 1986;315:405-411.

Rietmijer CAM, Krebs JW, Feorino PM, et al: Condoms as physical and chemical barriers against human immunodeficiency virus. JAMA 1988;259(12):1851-1853.

Rosenberg MJ, Feldblum PH, Higgins JE: Effect of the contraceptive sponge on chlamydial infection, gonorrhea, and candidiasis. JAMA 1987;257:2308-2312.

Schlesselman JJ, Stadel BV, Murray P, et al: Breast cancer in relation to early use of oral contraceptives. No evidence of a latent effect. JAMA 1988;259(12):1828-1833.

Shearin RB: Contraception in the adolescent. In: Hofmann AD, Greydanus DE, eds: Adolescent Medicine. Norwalk, CT: Appleton-Lange, 1988.

Speroff L, Diczfalusy E, eds: International symposium on contraception. Am J Obstet Gynecol 1987;157(4:Part 2):1019-1092.

Trieller K: Diaphragm and birth control pill during the first year of use among suburban adolescents. J Adolesc Health Care 1987;8:400-406.

Turetsky RA, Strasburger VC: Adolescent contraception: review and recommendations. Clin Pediatr 1983;22:337.

Tyrer LB: Oral contraceptives for the adolescent. J Repro Med 1984;29:551.

Washington AE, Gove S, Schachter J, et al: Oral contraceptives, chlamydia trachomatis infection and pelvic inflammatory disease. JAMA 1985;253:2246.

8

Pregnancy and Abortion

ADOLESCENT PREGNANCY

Currently, 12 million American teenagers are sexually active. Less than one third of them use effective contraceptive methods on a consistent basis. The result of this unfortunate situation is over 1 million pregnancies annually, including 30,000 to 40,000 pregnancies in youth under the age of 14. The pregnancy rate of teenagers from 15 to 19 years of age is 96 per 1000; this is the highest rate among developed countries. The negative effect of this phenomenon on the youth, their offspring, and society in general is enormous.

Young adolescents (ages 11 to 14) are developmentally limited in their ability to comprehend pregnancy as a definite consequence of unprotected sexual activity (see Chapter 1). Such youth are apt to deny a developing pregnancy and seek prenatal care at a much later gestation than older youth. Young adolescents are often difficult to motivate toward contraception, even though 20% become pregnant within 6 months of sexual activity initiation when no contraceptives are used. Such youth are likely to feel that they will be protected from the consequences of unprotected sexual activity. They are generally incapable of becoming nurturing mothers and often are unable to select abortion (even in the second trimester) because they do not really understand that they are carrying a human life within them. Furthermore, young adolescents are more likely to become pregnant through an incestuous relationship than are older youth.

Middle adolescents (ages 14 to 18) may actively select the option of pregnancy out of developmental pressures to prove their independence from parents. This is a time that youth find it important to become emancipated from authority figures (see Chapter 1), and pregnancy can be used as a powerful way to do this. Such youth may also use pregnancy to manipulate boyfriends or other individuals in their environment. Unfortunately, most youth find that they still have more growing up to do and learn that caring for their own infant interferes with their own continuing adolescence. The teenaged mother's need to be independent can be challenged when she is forced to spend most of her time caring for her baby. Lack of adequate support from the teenager's family or boyfriend or both complicates this picture for the teenaged mother and infant.

Late adolescents (ages 17 to 21) have a variable reaction to pregnancy. They may become pregnant to coerce a boyfriend into marriage, to solidify an existing marriage (either stable or unstable), or even to satisfy needs reflective of earlier adolescent stages. Some late adolescents may have two or more children, making their adjustment to motherhood extremely difficult. Most teenage marriages end in divorce, further compromising the adolescent mother's ability to care for her offspring. Weeks noted that youth 17 years of age and younger who marry are twice as likely to divorce as those 18 to 19 years of age and four times as likely to divorce as females 25 years of age and older. Thus, all stages of adolescence can present serious difficulties for pregnant adolescents from a developmental viewpoint.

Epidemiology

A study published in May 1985 by the Centers for Disease Control compared pregnancy and fertility patterns between 1974 and 1980. The study noted that the pregnancy rate for all 15- to 19-year-olds increased by 8.2% (88/1000), that the pregnancy rate for sexually experienced 15- to 19-year-old females decreased by 5.7% (192.8/1000), and that the pregnancy rate for those under age 15 increased by 10.3% (4.3/1000). This study also noted that the fertility rate for sexually active 15- to 19-year-olds and 12- to 14-year-olds decreased. It also noted a general national trend toward an increased pregnancy rate and a decreased fertility rate occurring simultaneously with a rapid increase in the percentage of sexually experienced 15- to 19-year-olds. In 1981, there were 3,629,238 live births; of these, 0.3% occurred to mothers under age 15; 5.2% to mothers 15 to 17 years of age; and 9.4% to mothers 18 and 19 years old. The number of births to unmarried adolescents increased between 1970 and 1981. During this period, in the 15- to 19-year-old age group, the estimated figures are as follows:

Pregnancy rate increased from 81.2 to 93.5%
Fertility rate decreased from 68.3 to 53.0%
Abortion rate rose from 12.9 to 45.1%
Rate of infants born to unmarried mothers increased from 29.4 to 49.2%
Number of births dropped from 680,500 to 562,800 (the rate of all U.S. births dropped from 18 to 15%)

If all current group pregnancy, fertility, and abortion rates remain stable, the rate of all births to adolescents should decrease to 11.8% by 1990. However, if current figures about unmarried adolescent pregnancy remain stable, more than half of all infants born to youth will be to unmarried parents. From 1960 to 1979, a 76% increase occurred in nonmarital births among teenagers. The current 1 to 1.3 million adolescent pregnancies each year represent a phenomenon that causes considerable negative impact on the youth, their offspring, and society at large. Four of every 10 women become pregnant as teenagers. In 1980, there were 1,180,450 teenage pregnancies, with nearly 50% resulting in live births, nearly 40% ending in abortion, and the rest ending in spontaneous abortion. Tables 8-1 and 8-2 summarize some of the important epidemiologic data on adolescent pregnancy. Table 8-1 includes data from 1985 as well.

Table 8-1. Number of births to Women under 20 Years of Age: 1960, 1970, 1979, and 1985

Item and Age	1960	1970	1979	1985
Total births				
Under 15	7,462	11,752	10,699	10,220
15-17	177,904	223,590	200,137	167,789
18-19	423,775	421,118	349,335	299,696
Total	609,141	656,460	560,171	477,705
Out-of-wedlock births				
Under 15	4,600	9,500	9,500	9,386
15-17	43,700	96,100	120,100	118,931
18-19	43,400	94,300	133,100	151,991
Total	91,700	199,900	262,700	280,308
Illegitimate births per 1000 unmarried women				
15-19	15.3	22.4	26.9	31.6

Data from the National Center for Health Statistics.

Adapted from Baldwin W: Trends in adolescent contraception, pregnancy and childbearing. In: McAnarney ER, ed: Premature Adolescent Pregnancy and Parenthood. New York: Grune & Stratton, 1983, and from the National Center for Health Statistics: Monthly vital statistics report. 1987;36(4 Suppl):July 17.

Pregnancy Diagnosis

Diagnosis of pregnancy in youth should be made as early as possible to enable early referral for prenatal care or, if selected, early legal pregnancy termination. Clinicians should be suspicious when dealing with young teenagers, who may delay presentation to the physician when confronted with the possibility of pregnancy. The individual who presents with vague

Table 8-2. Trends in Conception among Women 15-19 Years of Age: 1974 and 1979.

Item	1974	1979	Percentage Change
1. Women 15-19	10,186,000	10,145,000	—
2. Birth rate (per 1000)	58.7	53.4	−9.0
3. Sexual activity			
Ever married	1,272,000	894,000	−29.7
Never married women who are sexually active	2,888,000	3,922,000	+35.8
Percentage never married who are sexually active	32.4	42.4	+30.9
4. Women at risk of pregnancy (ever married and sexually active never married)	4,160,000	4,816,000	+15.8
5. Births	594,400	549,500	−7.7
6. Births per 1000 sexually active	143.1	114.1	−20.3
7. Induced abortions	278,300	449,500	+61.5
8. Estimated conceptions (births and induced abortions)	873,700	999,000	+14.3
9. Conceptions per 1000 women	85.8	98.5	+14.8
10. Conceptions per 1000 sexually active women	210.0	207.4	−1.2
11. Abortions per 1000 sexually active women	66.9	93.3	+39.5

Adapted from Baldwin W: Adolescent pregnancy and Childbearing—Growing concerns for Americans. Popul Bull 31:1-36, 1980 (updated reprint).

symptoms should be questioned about the possibility of pregnancy. The individual with early pregnancy may be under considerable stress, with development of headaches, abdominal pain, and various acting-out behaviors. One should always ask about the last normal menstrual period, especially since secondary amenorrhea is the most important early clue to the diagnosis of pregnancy. If the patient is sexually active without adequate contraception, careful observation for pregnancy is important. A missed period or even menstrual spotting may be the first indication of pregnancy. Be alert for the young pregnant teenager who may be a victim of incest. Eventually, variable pregnancy symptoms will develop, including morning sickness, fatigue, urinary frequency or dysuria, weight gain, breast swelling or tenderness, and others. Many of these symptoms improve by 14 to 16 weeks of gestation.

Clinical findings during the first 4 to 8 weeks of pregnancy include darkened areolae, enlargement of the Montgomery's glands, breast enlargement (with or without tenderness), secretion of colostrum from nipples, positive Hegar's sign (upper cervical softening), Goodell's sign (generalized cervical softening), and Chadwick's sign (bluish discoloration of the cervix). The major clinical sign of pregnancy is uterine enlargement, which can cause a general abdominal fullness and extend beyond the symphysis pubis; this sign is noted at the twelfth gestational week (Fig. 8-1). The uterus is enlarged to a point halfway between the symphysis pubis and umbilicus at 16 weeks of gestation, to the umbilicus by 20 weeks, halfway between the umbilicus and xiphoid process at 28 gestational weeks, and to the level of the xiphoid process by 40 weeks. At 12 weeks, Doppler's auscultation may reveal the fetal heart rate (120 to 180 beats per minute); first fetal movement is usually noted 16 to 20 weeks after the last menstrual period.

Early confirmation of the pregnancy is made with a pregnancy test. The serum immunoassay for the beta subunit of human chorionic gonadotropin (hCG) can be positive at 7 to 10 days after conception and has a threshold of 4 to 25 lmU/ml of serum. The urine test for pregnancy, which measures monoclonal antibodies for hCG, is positive later than the serum pregnancy test and has a sensitivity down to 174 lmU/ml of urine. The serum pregnancy test report may be quantitative, reflecting an estimate of the gestation week by the amount of hCG measured (Table 8-3). If the pregnancy test is negative, a reevaluation of the cause of the secondary amenorrhea is important. If indicated, the pregnancy test can be repeated in 7 days. The pregnancy test is specific for pregnancy (including ectopic pregnancy), with the exception of gestational trophoblastic disease (including hydatidiform mole) and certain ovarian neoplasms. Home pregnancy tests are available and currently have a 5% false positive rate and a 20% false negative rate.

Health Care of the Pregnant Adolescent

Early referral of the pregnant youth to prenatal care is important to reduce adolescent pregnancy morbidity for mother and offspring. The first

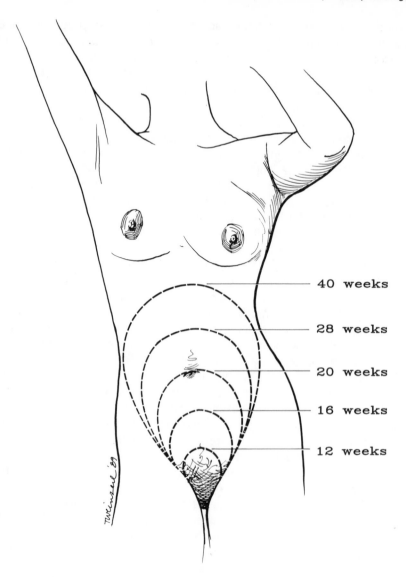

Fig. 8-1. Uterine size in pregnancy.

prenatal visit starts with a full medical history and physical examination, including pelvic evaluation. The pregnancy diagnosis is confirmed, gestational age is verified, any pelvic abnormality is identified, and clinical pelvimetry is performed to evaluate the shape and size of the pelvic bones. A general medical assessment should be made, including the recording of weight, blood pressure, and other important factors. The medical history includes inquiry about any medical illnesses, exposure to potential teratogenic drugs, any factor requiring further genetic testing, and others. General obstetric and nutritional assessment is obtained. Important initial lab-

Table 8-3. Correlation of B-hCG Level and Gestational Age.

Weeks of Conception	lmU/ml: HCG
0 weeks	Less than 5 (intermediate range: 5-23)
1 week	5-50
2 weeks	40-200
3 weeks	200-500
4 weeks	700-2000
2-3 months	12,000-200,000
4-6 months	24,000-55,000
7-9 months	6,000-42,000

oratory data include a complete blood count, syphilis serology, Rh factor and blood-type determinations, Rubella titer, Pap smear, indirect Coomb's test, toxoplasmosis titer, urinalysis, cervical culture for *Neisseria gonorrhoeae* (and *Chlamydia trachomatis*), and evaluation for other potential sexually transmitted diseases (such as trichomoniasis or HIV infection). Other laboratory data may be necessary, including screening for sickle cell disease, drug abuse, tuberculosis, and other infectious diseases.

Frequent prepartum evaluations are suggested, and various schedules are used (e.g., monthly until 28 gestation weeks, then every 2 weeks until 32 weeks, and then weekly until delivery). Visits should be educational and teach the youth as much as possible about pregnancy, including proper nutrition, normal weight gain parameters, normal activity levels (including exercise), warning signals (such as severe abdominal pain or vaginal bleeding), normal pregnancy changes, effects of drug use as well as sexually transmitted diseases on mother and child, and others. Table 8-4 presents a suggested checklist for such prenatal visits.

Considerable education can be given through prenatal classes, often offered in various hospitals. Eventually, contraceptive issues should be discussed. As the pregnancy progresses, weight gain, blood pressure, and urinalysis are carefully evaluated. Other tests include repeat hemoglobin or hematocrit, gestational diabetes screening, sexually transmitted diseases screening, repeat Rh sensitivity testing, and others as indicated by the clinical course and history. RhoGAM has been recommended in unsensitized Rh-negative women at 28 to 32 weeks of gestation.

Team Approach to Adolescent Pregnancy

Pregnant adolescents who have the best outcome are usually involved in comprehensive health care provided by an adolescent maternity project staffed by an interdisciplinary team. Pregnant adolescents, including both those who choose to keep their infants and those who place them for adoption, need comprehensive care that includes prenatal care, nutrition education, psychosocial screening, and comprehensive followup for both mother and infant. A social worker who follows the pregnant teenager throughout the pregnancy can be helpful by providing much-needed additional support. At different points in the pregnancy and postpartum pe-

Table 8-4. Checklist for Adolescent Pregnancy.

I. *Determinations: Initial visit*	
Complete blood count	
Complete urinalysis	
Blood type and group	
VDRL	
Culture for gonococcus (chlamydia and possibly other STD agents)	
Pap smear	
Sickle cell test	
Nutritional status	
Rubella titer	
II. *Discussion points with each visit*	*Suggested schedule*
1. Anatomy and physiology of pregnancy	1st visit
2. Sexual activity and venereal disease (STD)	2nd visit
3. Drug-related problems	3rd visit
4. Nutrition	Each visit
5. Family planning	4th visit
5. Childbirth phenomena	5th visit
7. Infant care	6th visit
8. Contraception	7th visit
9. Sexuality and the future	8th visit
10. Importance of followup care	9th visit
III. *Visitation*	
1. Biweekly until 34 weeks	
2. Weekly until delivery	
IV. *Educational aspects: Progress report of teacher*	
In school _____	
Homebound _____	
Other _____	
V. *Social aspects: Progress report*	
1. Parent/patient	
2. Patient/father of the child	
3. Postdelivery: progress report	
VI. *Psychologic aspects*	
VII. *Nutritional aspects: Progress report*	
VIII. *Nursing report*	
IX. *Report of neonatologist or physician who will be present*	
X. *Additional problem areas (such as risk for HIV infection or Group B streptococcus)*	

riod, the team can provide sex education, contraceptive services, and sexually transmitted disease education and screening, as well as treatment, educational counseling, vocational counseling, parenting education, financial aid, and many other services needed by the pregnant teenager.

Such programs attempt to involve the father as well. In many cases, the father is not involved with the mother and refuses to become personally or financially involved with the child. Many fathers have a history of behavioral difficulties, have not been taught responsible sexuality, and know little about pregnancy or contraception. However, some have simply been ignored and will further associate with the mother and his child when encouraged to do so. The clinician may discover a frightened young man who would welcome the chance to care for his own child.

These programs also attempt to prevent subsequent pregnancies during the mother's adolescence and help the mother continue with her education. A marked reduction in maternal and infant mortality and morbidity can be seen when patients are involved in these comprehensive programs, such as the Rochester Adolescent Maternity Project in Rochester, New York (McAnarney, 1978). In addition to comprehensive programs located in medical centers or hospitals, school-based clinics can be used to provide a wide variety of health care to youth, including prenatal care and contraceptive services. In 1968, the pediatrics department at the University of Texas established the first school-based health clinic. Many school-based clinics have subsequently been developed. In 1973, the Ramsey Medical Center of St. Paul, Minnesota established the well-known Adolescent Health Services Project in four St. Paul high schools. A 5-year followup study revealed that fertility rates were down from 59 to 21 per 1000 live births, that 80% of the pregnant teenagers finished high school (versus the national average of 50%), and that the repeat birth rate was 1.3% (versus the national average of 17%). Such programs can make a major difference in the phenomenon of teenage pregnancy. Table 8-5 reviews various programs providing educational services to adolescent mothers.

Nutrition

Most pregnant youth are ignorant of what constitutes adequate nutrition and continue poor eating patterns into their pregnancy. Various factors contribute to placing the youth at increased dietary risk, including meal skipping (especially breakfast), eating junk food, suboptimal protein intake, dietary fadism, limited income, pica, low pregnancy weight (5 to 10% or more under normal weight), insufficient pregnancy weight gains (under 24 to 28 lbs.), pre-existing medical disorders, and others. Protein deficiency is not rare in today's youth. The pregnant teenager needs extra dietary protein until she completes linear growth, which usually occurs 4 years after menarche. Some junk foods typically eaten by adolescents— hamburgers, hotdogs, pizza, peanuts, milkshakes, and others—supply considerable protein.

In general, pregnant youth require a diet that provides 2400 calories per day during the first trimester and 2700 calories during the rest of the pregnancy. Each day, pregnant youth require 76 to 78 g protein, 30 to 60 mg iron, 1.2 to 1.6 g calcium, and up to 1 mg folic acid as part of a multivitamin supplement. Iron supplementation is also recommended. If the patient is large, takes her iron supplements irregularly, has twins, or is in late pregnancy, supplementation of 60 to 70 mg of iron per day may be indicated. Teenaged vegetarians may be at risk for multiple nutritional deficiencies, including calories, protein, iron, calcium, zinc, magnesium, iodine, and various vitamins (D, B_2, B_{12}). Providing for adequate maternal nutrition will reduce maternal and fetal morbidity to a considerable extent [see Chapter 11 for further discussion of nutrition].

Maternal Risks

Conflicting articles have been published over the past 20 years regarding whether adolescents are at greater medical risk than adult women for pregnancy complications. Potential complications of pregnancy include

Table 8-5. Programs Providing Educational Services to Adolescent Mothers.[1]

| Location and Reference | Target Population | Services Provided | | Evaluation Activities* | Educational Aspirations/ Goals* | Program Outcomes | |
		Educational	Other			Educational Achievement	Other
Kalamazoo, Mich.	Emphasis on dropouts who wish to continue their schooling	Classes provided in a special school	Free day care program; outreach to help girls who dropped out or never participated in the program; help for girls' families	1963-1979	Availability of child care seemed to be very important in decision to stay in school		
Yale-New Haven Hospital, Conn.	Residents of New Haven, 18 years old or younger	Encouraged to attend classes directed by City Board of Education at McCabe Community Center		Sept. 1967-June 1969: retrospective, followed to 2 months post partum A. Examined 151 girls who delivered in clinic and attended McCabe classes B. Looked at 150 girls attending McCabe or regular classes C. Looked at 23 girls who did not attend school	A. Those who stated educational goal was college were the most likely to enroll in McCabe classes, whether or not they were in school when they registered for clinic services	A. 77% were in school or had graduated B. 86% still in school or had graduated C. 13% still in school or had graduated	A. 1. 92% of girls in school and 23% of girls not in school when registered for services, also enrolled in McCabe classes 2. Girls 15 years old, with low educational goals, and

					A. 76% of single, 23% of married girls were still in school	below their appropriate grade level, were most likely to attend class infrequently
Baylor College of Medicine, Texas	Indigent girls 18 years old or younger	Special school on hospital grounds for about 100 girls, built after program established		1968-1973 A. Questionnaires mailed at 8 months post partum to all participants; 50% response rate	A. 76% of single, 23% of married girls were still in school	
St. Paul, Minn.	Girls in the school in which clinics were located	Stayed in regular classrooms	Prenatal, post partum, and day care provided in school; delivery provided at St. Paul-Ramsey Medical Center	1968-1979 A. Retrospective: all participants B. Sample of participants (N = 36) matched to control group (N = 36)	A. 1. 85 girls delivered during 1978-1979 2. 40% decline in deliveries from 1976-1977 to 1978-1979 school year 3. No repeat pregnancies for 90.4% of girls who remained in school B. Controls began care later, had fewer prenatal visits	

Table 8-5. Continued

Location and Reference	Target Population	Services Provided			Evaluation Activities*	Program Outcomes		
		Educational	Other			Educational Aspirations/ Goals*	Educational Achievement	Other
San Francisco, Calif.: six hospital centers	City and/or county residents, over 700 school-aged girls	In-hospital classrooms, staff provided by city school district; students can return to hospital school for 1 month after delivery with day care provided	Vocational counseling, work-study program		1969-1973 A. Examined program begun in 1969 at San Francisco General Hospital; success seen as girl staying in school after leaving the program or graduating from the program		A. 1. 3.2% of those referred, 47% of those who actually entered, achieved success 2. Married girls and those closest to graduation were more likely to achieve success	
New Brunswick, N.J.	Inner-city school-aged girls	Special classes in Family Learning Center			1969-1975 A. Participants (N = 86) compared with matched controls (N = 30)		A. Participants completed significantly more schooling	
Cincinnati General Hospital, Ohio	Teenage welfare population who delivered	High school credit for those attending weekly	A control group received monthly visits; not weekly		1973-1975 A. Compared 15- to 16-year-old with 18- to 19-year-old mothers: all	B. 1. Participants in classes had higher aspirations and more		A. At recruitment, younger mothers felt they

Program/Location	Population	Setting	Program features	Study	Results
		stimulation of the infant		credit given to this group B. Examined black experimental ($N = 18$) with control ($N = 16$) mothers who participated in extended project begun Sept. 1974	controls 2. Significant difference between the two groups in the realization of school and/or employment goals ...class one night a week than did older mothers
Crittenton Hastings House, Boston, Mass.	Inner-city teenagers, about 450 served in 1973–1979	Classes under direction of Board of Education	After 1976, extended program offered counseling (through home visits) to all participants whether or not they asked for help	1973–1978 A. Examined girls who participated before 1976, until 2 years after services were received B. Examined participants ($N = 67$) who received services Mar. 1976–Sept. 1977, $\frac{1}{2}$–3 years after delivery	Academic goals generally higher after participation A. 1. 80% returned to school after delivery 2. 50% had dropped out after 2 years B. 64% dropped out by 2 years after delivery, 50% of this occurred immediately after delivery B. All but 6 of the 43 who dropped out had entered a job training program or an alternative academic program, or had obtained full-time employment
Johns Hopkins Hospital, Baltimore, Md.	Adolescents, 18 years old or younger, residing in Baltimore	Classes offered in special classrooms or regular classrooms	Included family and partner in some education and family planning activities; follow-up care (if needed) for 3 years	1974–1979 A. Examined participants at 1 year post partum B. Participants matched to control group by age, race, and delivery date; no comparison results given	A. 1. 85% of participants graduated or remained in school 2. The few mothers who married tended to drop out A. Lack of people to care for child was a major barrier to staying in school

Table 8-5. Continued

Location and Reference	Target Population	Services Provided			Evaluation Activities*	Program Outcomes		
		Educational	Other			Educational Aspirations/ Goals*	Educational Achievement	Other
Fort Worth, Texas	Students, 12-20 years old; about 425 served yearly	Continuing education unit offering credits toward a high school diploma			Jan. 1977-Dec. 1978 A. Examined sample (N = 17) of those pregnant for first time and enrolled in school	A. Strong progress was made in attaining educational goals		A. Findings (not given) showed program encouraged high school completion, job market entry, and avoidance of repeated pregnancies

* In each program summary, lettered evaluation activities correspond to goals and outcomes bearing the same letter.
[1] McCarthy J, Radish E: Education and Childbearing Among Teenagers. In McAnareny ER, ed: Premature Adolescent Pregnancy and Parenthood. New York: Grune & Stratton, 1983.

toxic conditions of pregnancy (pre-eclampsia, eclampsia, or chronic hypertension), abruptio placentae (and others causing severe bleeding), cephalopelvic disproportion, urinary tract infection, nutritional deficiency, prematurity, various psychosocial complications, and others. Reports from some earlier studies usually placed youth at greater risk than their adult counterparts. In 1976, the National Center for Health Statistics noted that adolescents accounted for 15% of all births and 25% of all premature births. The report by the Alan Guttmacher Institute, comparing data on adolescent and adult pregnancies from 1974 to 1978, noted that the maternal death rate for those under 15 years was 18 per 100,000 live births—2.5 times the 7.1 per 100,000 figure reported in individuals 20 to 24 years of age. Comparing teenagers with those 20 to 24 years old, the youth had 15% more toxemia, 92% more anemia, and 23% more prematurity. Table 8-6 presents data from four well-controlled studies comparing youth and adults.

In contrast, recent data indicate that age alone is not the sole determining factor in morbidity and mortality during adolescent pregnancy. Gynecologic age (time since menarche) alone is also not a major factor. When youth are given access to adequate prenatal care and follow through with such care, their complication rates are favorable with those of adults. Many factors complicate the obstetric risks for youth, factors such as race, parity, socioeconomic status, educational level, and marital status. There may be an increased risk factor for toxic conditions of pregnancy and cephalopelvic disproportion, but the data remain conflictual. Current data suggest pregnancy-related hypertension is actually linked to

Table 8-6. Summary of Data of Well-Controlled Studies Comparing Adolescent and Adult Outcomes of Pregnancy.

Study	Age (years)	Toxic Conditions (%)	Birth Weight under 2500 g (%)	Perinatal Mortality of Entire Group (per 1000)
Battaglia et al., 1963	Under 15 (black)	27.8*	23.4	82
	15-19 (black)	21.1*	18.3	50
	Total clinic	11.2*	16.3	—
Duenhoelter et al., 1975	Under 15	34.2†	19.2	30
	19-25	25.3†	15.9	38
Spellacy et al., 1978	Under 15 (black)	20.0*	23.5	52
	20-24 (black)	18.5*	9.6	19
	20-24 (white)	10.8*	8.1	22
Hutchins et al., 1979	Under 17	9.3‡	15.8	40
	17-19	6.7‡	15.4	40
	20-24	3.9‡	14.4	33

* Preeclampsia, eclampsia, or chronic hypertension.
† Pregnancy-induced hypertension.
‡ Preeclampsia.
From: McAnarney ER, Thiede HA: Adolescent pregnancy and childbearing: what we have learned during the 1970s and what remains to be learned. Chapter 21 in *Premature Adolescent Pregnancy and Parenthood.* (ed: ER McAnarney) NY: Grune & Stratton, 379, 1983.

nulliparity, not maternal age. As noted by Chase's 1973 study of 142,000 pregnant adolescents in New York City, psychosocial factors are as important as medical factors in determining obstetric risks. Individuals with limited health care are at increased risk for obstetric complications such as death from anesthesia and eclampsia. Certainly, complete prenatal care is essential for all pregnant women, including adolescents. This care thoroughly screens for potential complications such as eclampsia. A diastolic blood pressure over 90 mmHg with or without proteinuria should prompt a full evaluation for toxic conditions of pregnancy. The very young teenager still has a maturing pelvis and may develop cephalopelvic disproportion, prompting a difficult labor and, eventually, cesarean section. However, recent studies of teenagers versus adults show a similar cesarean section rate, with a slightly higher rate for those under 15 years. Other indications for cesarean section include inadequate labor pattern, fetal distress, breech presentation, herpes, pregnancy-induced hypertension, multiple pregnancy, placenta previa, placenta abruption, and others. In general, the medical complications of teenagers are related to a complex array of many factors, not age alone.

The psychosocial risks of adolescent pregnancy appear to be a significant problem for many teenagers. Many youth have difficulty with parenting and develop considerable financial, educational, and marital difficulties in association with pregnancy. A variety of studies have addressed the limited education many adolescent mothers have and the fact that childbearing often terminates academic education. Card and Wise have correlated the student's age at the birth of her offspring with the level of education completed. The result is lower education, limited vocational potential, and limited income. Approximately half of pregnant teenagers drop out of school before delivery, and most remain poorly educated as adults. Young teenagers under age 15, when compared with controls, complete nearly 2 years less school. Such individuals are not equipped to deal with an ever more technical society. The behavioral and cognitive outcomes of their offspring are correlated with the educational level of the parents. Such parents often stay on public assistance, and over 4.5 billion dollars are spent annually through Aid for Dependent Children (AFDC) for families with mothers who were adolescents when their children were born. The younger the adolescent mother, the more likely she is on and will stay on welfare. Furthermore, the marriages in these youth do not last; over 70% end in divorce, eventually leaving the mother to care for her children without the support of the father. In the 1970s, the number of families headed by a single parent increased by 97%. Such poorly educated, poverty stricken, often depressed individuals typically make poor parents. Though they do not physically abuse their children more than adult parents of similar socioeconomic and educational backgrounds, they may neglect their children more than adult parents. Teenage mothers are more likely than their adult counterparts to have more children, furthering the negative effect on mother, offspring, and society.

Risks to Infants of Adolescents

Further compounding the severe negative impact of adolescent pregnancy are the medical and psychosocial complications well recorded in the offspring. The increased medical risks include an increased mortality rate, prematurity, congenital defects, mental and physical handicaps (such as epilepsy, cerebral palsy, mental retardation, sensory loss, and others), increased Sudden Infant Death Syndrome (SIDS) rate, increased death from violence and accidents in childhood, and others. The neonatal mortality rate for black adolescent mothers under age 15 (the group at highest risk) is 15 per 1000 live births, versus the national average of 7.6 per 1000 live births. The increased neonatal mortality rate associated with youth is due to the increase in low-birth-weight infants born to teenagers, especially those under age 15. Teenaged mothers 15 years of age and younger have a 14% rate of infants born under 2500 g versus 5.8% described in 25- to 29-year-old women. Such small infants have a greater incidence of extensive hospitalizations, an increased mortality rate, increased neonatal complications (such as respiratory distress syndrome, seizure disorders, hypoglycemia, necrotizing enterocolitis, and others), and subsequent cognitive and behavioral difficulties. It is unclear if these infants are premature or small for gestational age; this is important, since each condition has a different etiology.

Many factors that negatively affect infant mortality and morbidity are operational in the pregnant youth. Table 8-7 reviews some of these factors. Premature births can be correlated with low prepregnancy weight, ethnic factors (increased in black teenagers), poor social conditions, being

Table 8-7. Special Risk Factors in Adolescent Pregnancy.

Under age 15 years (including low gynecologic age)
Short interpregnancy period and repeat teenage pregnancies
Low socioeconomic status
Food fadism
Drug abuse
Cigarette smoking
Alcohol abuse (over 2 oz. per day during the pregnancy or over 6 oz. per day on frequent occasions)
Heroin addiction
Others
Weight loss during pregnancy
Severe psychosocial difficulties
Presence of sexually transmitted diseases
Abuse of the pregnant youth by family or boyfriend
Third trimester coital activity
Repeat pregnancy in adolescence
Urinary tract infection
Various medical conditions
Diabetes mellitus
Asthma
Seizure disorders
Absent or limited medical care
Others

unmarried, cigarette smoking, narcotic use, anemia (hemoglobin level under 11 g/ml), primigravida status, and limited prenatal care. Intrauterine growth retardation is associated with pregnancy-induced hypertension, anemia, maternal cardiac disease, heavy smoking, collagen vascular disease, renal disease, illicit drug use, multiple gestations, chromosomal abnormalities, chronic fetal infections (TORCH), and various fetal anomalies. Preterm labor can be caused by such factors as premature rupture of membranes, multiple pregnancies, polyhydramnios, placenta previa or abruption, uterine anomalies, incompetent cervix, chorioamnionitis, pyelonephritis, appendicitis, and others.

Many youth are victims of poor prenatal care and thus do not have access to treatment that would improve or correct many of these pregnancy complications and reduce the incidence of serious maternal and fetal complications. Many youth abuse drugs, have sexually transmitted diseases, and have other risk factors (Table 8-6). Low socioeconomic status and multiple births during adolescence are especially associated with poor infant outcomes. Recent studies note that teenage mothers (at least over age 14) can have outcomes favorable to adults if they have access to adequate prenatal care and correct limiting health habits. The Merritt et al. study reviewed 70,000 teenage pregnancies and observed that the negative infant outcomes were more related to psychosocial or behavioral factors than to purely medical ones.

Drug abuse among pregnant youth is an important contributor to negative infant outcomes (Table 8-8). Teenaged mothers who smoke one pack or more of cigarettes a day give birth to infants weighing 400 g less than do nonsmoking controls. Smoking is also linked to increased spontaneous abortion, perinatal mortality, placenta previa, and placenta abruption. Excess alcohol intake can lead to the fetal alcohol syndrome with characteristic facies; intrauterine, as well as postnatal, growth retardation; mental retardation; and various skeletal abnormalities in the infant. Alcohol abuse is also linked to increased stillbirths, spontaneous abortions, and various negative effects of alcoholism. Numerous prenatal and neonatal complications are noted in pregnant heroin addicts, including fetal addiction with withdrawal syndrome, low birth weight, premature

Table 8-8. Effects of Drugs on Mother and Fetus.

Agent	Route	Teratogenic	Decreased Fetal Growth	Withdraw Maternal	Fetal
ETOH	Oral	+	+	+	+
Barbiturates	Oral	−	−	+	+
Benzodiazepines	Oral	−	−	Rare	Rare
Heroin	Intravenous subcutaneous	−	+	+	+
Methadone	Oral	−	+	+	+
Amphetamines	Oral, intravenous	−	−	+	?
Hallucinogens	Oral, intravenous	Presumed	−	−	−
Tobacco	Inhalation	−	+	+	?

rupture of membranes, pregnancy-induced hypertension, malpresentation, placenta previa, abruptio placentae, postpartum infection, and stillbirths. A possible link between amphetamines and cardiac anomalies, as well as between lysergic acid diethylamide and limb-bud anomalies, has been suggested. The link between marijuana use in the pregnant mother and infant complications is not established, though suspected. Infants born to marijuana-using mothers do appear to be smaller than those born to controls. Drug abuse in the mother suggests a troubled lifestyle, which leads to numerous negative effects on the offspring. The cumulative negative effects of various drugs used together (such as alcohol and marijuana, alcohol and cigarettes, and other combinations) is only now being appreciated. Cocaine-induced effects are now described as well (Frank, 1988).

Various *sexually transmitted diseases* can complicate pregnancy, and unfortunately these diseases are not rare in teenagers. Once the membranes have ruptured, cervical gonorrhea can ascend the genital tract, causing chorioamnionitis, postpartum endometritis, and possible neonatal septicemia. Gonococcal ophthalmia neonatorum is a complication caused by delivery through a genital tract infected with *Neisseria gonorrhoeae;* this condition is an important cause of blindness in underdeveloped countries. Cervical cultures for gonorrhea are recommended for the first prenatal visit and perhaps at 36 weeks of gestation, especially in populations at greater risk for gonococcal infections. *Chlamydia trachomatis* infection can also lead to neonatal conjunctivitis. Chlamydial infections are noted in a variable number of pregnant teens—studies reflect anywhere from 2 to 37%. Syphilis can cause a classic in-utero infection at any gestational stage, leading to stillbirth, neonatal death, and various developmental anomalies. Syphilis serology during the first and third trimester is recommended.

Genital herpes can have severe effects on the newborn if the infant is delivered in a canal having active herpes lesions. If the mother is shedding in the vagina or cervix at delivery, the risk of newborn infection is over 50% with a resultant multisystemic disease and a 70% mortality rate if untreated. Careful evaluation of pregnant patients during the third trimester is necessary if there are known herpes victims. Cesarean section is indicated if active lesions are seen 4 to 6 weeks or less prior to anticipated delivery; immediate cesarean section is done if an individual with active lesions develops ruptured membranes.

Numerous other sexually transmitted diseases can also result in neonatal complications. Hardy et al. evaluated 115 pregnant teenagers of low socioeconomic status; during the third trimester, 37% had *Chlamydia trachomatis,* 34% had *Trichomonas vaginalis,* 70% had *Mycoplasma hominis,* and 90% had *Ureaplasma urealyticum.* Infection with *Trichomonas vaginalis* may lead to reduced gestational age at delivery. Gravett and Holmes suggest that increased prematurity rate is associated with maternal infections involving *Chlamydia trachomatis, Neisseria gonorrhoeae,* group B Streptococcus, and herpes simplex virus. Infection with *Ureaplasma urealyticum* may be associated with decreased birth weight, chorioamnionitis, and stillbirths. Infection with *Mycoplasma hominis* is linked to febrile spontaneous abortions, and *Treponema pallidum* is linked to prematurity and stillbirths. Maternal postpartum infections are associated with these findings as well, except for *T. pallidum* and herpes simplex virus. The impact of AIDS is under current study, but an increasing number of children acquiring AIDS in utero is noted.

Neonatal mortality and morbidity rates are considerably increased if the pregnant teenager has more offspring during her adolescence. The perinatal death rate of 6 per 1000 live births for the first offspring can climb to 71 per 1000 for the second, and 143 per 1000 for the third. Teenage mothers have a difficult enough time coping with one child and often cannot deal with more. Such infants have increased rates of serious illnesses requiring hospitalizations as well as increased injuries requiring medical attention.

Medical illnesses can complicate the adolescent pregnancy and include urinary tract infections, diabetes mellitus, asthma, seizure disorders, and others. Gestational diabetes can be associated with prematurity, fetal distress, macrosomia, birth trauma due to the baby's large size, urinary tract infection, and others. Seizure disorders can worsen with pregnancy and can be associated with congenital anomalies possibly due to the effects of the anticonvulsant medications. The safety of various asthma medications during pregnancy must be carefully evaluated.

Various psychosocial difficulties in children of teenaged mothers have been reported in the literature, as summarized in Table 8-9. Teenaged mothers often lack important parenting skills, such as providing effective stimulation during childhood, surrounding the infant with needed love, and providing the child with a sense of security. The teenaged mother is still going through her own adolescence and may not be able to effectively deal with her offspring. Various studies show that these children and youth of teenaged mothers, when compared with controls, have lower intelligence quotients (IQs), more limited communication skills, more learning disabilities (such as reading difficulties), lower school performance, more difficulty adjusting to school, lower self-esteem, less impulse control, more attention-deficit hyperactivity disorders, and more behavioral difficulties. The cognitive and behavioral deficits start early in childhood and have a major negative impact on the lives of these children. These offspring are also more likely to grow up and become teenaged parents themselves, repeating the cycle of their parents. The individual may be more likely to have difficulties with drug abuse, sexually transmitted diseases, depression, suicide, and other serious psychosocial problems—much the same as those noted in their adolescent parents.

Adolescent Obstetrics

Labor and delivery principles are generally the same for adults and adolescents. Braxton-Hicks contractions increase in frequency during the last several weeks of pregnancy, although they do not constitute true labor. Normally, true labor contractions begin at 38 to 42 weeks of ges-

Table 8-9. Developmental Deficiencies of Children Born to an Adolescent.

Age	Deficiency	Qualifiers (e.g., Mother's Age, Race, Parity)	Children of Teenaged Mothers (COTAM)	Children of Older Mothers (COOM)	Reference
2-5 days	Less cuddly/lower Brazelton score	<18, black			Thompson
Infant	Higher risk of infant death (without intensified perinatal care)	≤16, black, primipara; white, nullipara	2% 4.19%	1.14% .54%	Hardy Teberg
	Less ability to cope with frustrating or alarming circumstances				
3½-5 years	Less adequate stimulation by mother	<18, black, white, mean IQ	23.7%	10.6%	Sugar
	Lower IQ				Lobl
	Less self esteem	Urban blacks			Furstenberg
	Lower vocabulary test scores				Vandenberg
6-8 years	More difficulty adjusting to early school				Kellam
	Lower IQ	<18, mean IQ, matched pair black, white; SES; race	86.8	89.72	Oppel NCHS
	More outgoing	<18, matched pair	36%	16%	Oppel
	More overactive, hostile, resistive, lacking impulse control	<18			Maracek
8-10 years	More reading problems: poorer vocabulary	Mean grade (reading) level, matched pairs			Oppel
	Lower weight	<18, mean weight	2.52 57.62 lbs	2.90 60.28 lbs	Oppel
	Lower height	<18, mean height	51.07 in.	51.77 in.	Oppel
	More dependent				Oppel
	More distractable				Oppel
	More likely to have infantile or acting-out type of psychiatric disturbance		33%	20%	Oppel
Adolescent	More likely to have intense psychiatric problems				Kellam
	Poorer cognitive development				Card, Presser
	Greater likelihood of teenage pregnancy				Presser, Card, Miller, Smith

From: Dennis JE: "Teenage Pregnancy: An Overview." in *Current Problems in Pediatrics*. (Eds: JF Mellinger & GB Stickler), Philadelphia: JB Lippincott chapter 11, page 148, 1983.

tation, eventually causing spontaneous rupture of the amniotic membrane. Three classic stages of labor are noted. The first begins with strong contractions that cause effacement and dilatation of the cervix, and ends at full cervical dilatation, generally lasting 12 to 20 hours. Stage two extends from full cervical dilatation to delivery of the baby, usually lasting up to 2 hours. Placental passage defines stage three. The first stage usually is more prolonged in nulliparous, as compared with multiparous, women. Failure to progress from stage one labor is defined by cervical dilatation less than 1.2 cm per hour or failure of adequate fetal progress down the birth canal. Cephalopelvic disproportion will cause poor labor progression. Young teenagers may be at risk for cephalopelvic disproportion, since the pelvic bone grows at a slower rate than the long ones that cause increase in general height. Some youth need oxytocin to initiate and maintain sufficient uterine contractions leading to a normal progression of labor. A variety of anesthetic techniques are available to relieve pain. Individuals who receive and use LaMaze training and who also have the support of their families or boyfriends may need less anesthesia. Hospital birthing rooms have become a popular option in recent times, reducing the mother's stress level and improving the mother/father-infant bonding. Fetal monitoring is often used with pregnant teenagers in labor, particularly if signs of fetal stress are observed. Pregnant teenagers are not at increased risk for breech presentation or twinning. Whether they are at increased risk for pre-eclampsia is unclear. Most studies note that pre-eclampsia is more common in nulliparous individuals.

ADOLESCENT ABORTION

Abortion in adolescence is an emotional and controversial subject. Most, if not all, individuals seem to have strong feelings when the subject of pregnancy termination in youth is presented. Many abortions occur in the United States in this age group—approximately 400,000 each year, representing nearly one third of all such procedures. For example, in 1985 428,922 reported abortions were performed in women under 20 years of age; this figure represented 27% of all abortions and 40% of all teenage pregnancies for that year. Recent studies note that abortions outnumber deliveries in those under age 15, and that adolescents account for many second-trimester abortions. Most experts agree that it is better to help youth prevent these unwanted pregnancies than to have them face a procedure as undesirable as abortion. Health care professionals need to work together with other elements of society to teach youth as much as possible about their sexuality and to allow them to come to realistic terms with their bodies long before they are confronted with unexpected, unwanted pregnancies.

Many teenagers begin coital experiences with a minimal knowledge of pregnancy and sexually transmitted diseases as possible consequences. Pregnant youth often experience a delay in diagnosis and may delay their decision about what to do—keep the child, offer the child for adoption, or abort. Health care professionals, parents, educators, religious institutions, and others often disregard the ignorance of youth about human sexuality. Physicians may not think of pregnancy as a possibility when confronted with adolescents having such difficulties. Young adolescents are especially prone to ignore such a possibility. Yet it is important for youth and health care professionals to arrive at this diagnosis as early as possible to allow sufficient time for them to make some responsible decisions. Ideally, teenagers can be taught practical, responsible sexuality and to prevent such unwanted outcomes as pregnancy and abortion. Unfortunately, such is not the case; health care professionals must deal with current reality, which involves over 1.3 million annual pregnancies and 400,000 annual abortions in the adolescent population.

Mortality Rates

A higher mortality rate is associated with pregnancy than with abortion performed by appropriately trained personnel. Tietze et al. noted a mortality rate of 11.1 per 100,000 in 15- to 19-year-old pregnant youths who deliver. This is contrasted with a mortality rate of 1.2 per 100,000 first-trimester legal abortions for this same age cohort. Published mortality rates are 0.3 deaths per 100,000 abortions at 8 weeks or less of gestation (representing 52% of all abortions), 2.5 deaths at 9 to 12 gestational weeks (38% of abortions), 11 to 12 deaths at 13 to 15 gestational weeks (5% of abortions), and over 16 deaths per 100,000 abortions at 16 or more gestational weeks (between 16 and 20 weeks, 4.1% of abortions; over 20 weeks, 0.9% of abortions). Over 100,000 second-trimester abortions are performed annually, many involving youth. Thus, current overall mortality rates for adolescents undergoing abortions could be reduced even further by having these youth undergo first-trimester rather than second-trimester procedures. Much higher mortality rates are noted when legal or illegal abortions are done by individuals with limited training; this is especially noted with illegal abortions. Tietze et al. reported a hundred-fold greater mortality rate with illegal abortions versus legally performed abortions. Complications such as infection, genital laceration, and hemorrhage are also much higher in such cases.

Counseling Issues

Pregnant youth who are contemplating an abortion should receive non-judgmental counseling to help them explore their options of keeping the infant, adoption, or abortion. The eventual decision is related to the individual's specific circumstances at the time the abortion is being considered. What an individual does at one point in her life may not be the same as what she does at another. The youth should have the support and advice of both her parents and her boyfriend during this difficult time, but often this is not the case. Youth from a religious background tend to have a very difficult time choosing a procedure that others have taught them is equivalent to murder.

Young, concrete operational youth do not really understand the meaning of pregnancy or abortion, and thus many choose abortion without understanding what it means. Young adolescents may delay the diagnosis of pregnancy until well past legal limits for abortion (usually 22 to 24 gestational weeks, depending on the specific location). Older, formal-operational-thinking adolescents generally have a greater understanding and may have a more difficult time arriving at such a decision (see Chapter 1). Some pregnancies are wanted as a means of fulfilling psychologic issues, such as the expression of anger or control toward parents, attempts at manipulation of the boyfriend, need for attention of peers, wish to improve negative life circumstances, and others. Other youth do not know whether an abortion is possible for them, where to obtain it, how to pay for it, and other important related issues.

Thus, pregnant teenagers are faced with important decisions; they should have an opportunity to receive unbiased counseling that allows open exploration of all possible legal options and helps them decide what is best for them at this time in their lives. It is easy for counselors to strongly express their views on often impressionable youth and to coerce them into making a particular decision. However, this biased type of "counseling," whether stressing abortion or arguing against it, is simply not fair to the pregnant youth. If the counselor cannot keep his or her views and prejudice out of the counseling process, the patient should be referred to someone who can. The youth, however, can be given realistic ideas of what each of the available options would mean for her life. Show her what keeping the baby means, why abortion may be a possible decision, and what abortion actually is. Whatever her decision, counseling about responsible sexuality, including future contraceptive options, should be offered at the appropriate time. If abortion is chosen, postabortion counseling and contraceptive instruction (including abstinence) should be planned.

One area of preabortion counseling that often receives minimal attention from patient and counselor is the option of *adoption*. Although one should not force the patient into any decision, the patient should look at all options and should be given a realistic look at the viable option of adoption with a responsible couple who could provide for her baby in ways that she simply cannot. There are numerous licensed groups, including those affiliated with religious organizations, who specialize in placing such babies in suitable homes. Unfortunately, only 2 to 4% of youth choose this possibility, partially because adoption is not a well known and widely accepted option. Early postpartum adoption may be an excellent choice for the well-informed pregnant youth.

Legal Issues

The subject of abortion in adolescence has stirred considerable legal debate. Table 8-10 reviews some important legal cases and laws involving minors or those under age 21. It was not until the 1967 Supreme Court decision (*in re Gault* 387 U.S. 1) that the courts addressed the important issue of minors having certain legal rights of their own (see Chapter 2). Many cases have appeared in the courts since that seek to define these

Table 8-10. Important Legal Cases and Laws Involving Legal Rights of Minors.*

Case	Year	Significance
In re Gault	1967	Minors have right to fair trial before sentencing
Tinker vs. The Des Moines Independent School District	1969	Minors cannot be removed from school unless their rights are protected
Roe vs. Wade, Doe vs. Bolton	1973	Women have the right to obtain a first-trimester abortion
Planned Parenthood of Central Missouri vs. Danforth	1976	Mature minors have the right to obtain a first-trimester abortion regardless of third-party (e.g., parental) disapproval
Bellotti vs. Baird	1979	Judge can grant a minor an abortion with parental notification but without parental consent
Hyde Amendment	1979	Restricted use of federal funds to pay for legal abortions
H.L. vs. Matheson	1981	It is legal to require immature and dependent minors to inform parents before abortion is obtained
City of Akron vs. Akron	1983	Supreme Court rejected an Akron, Ohio, city law which required parental consent before the abortion of an unmarried minor
Webster vs. Reproductive Human Services	1989	Supreme Court ruling: states are given greater power to determine access to abortion. Successful partial challenge to *Roe vs. Wade.*
Ohio vs. Akron Center for Reproductive Health	1990	Challenge to rights of teenagers to obtain abortion without parental notification. Supreme Court ruling pending.
Hodgson vs. Minnesota	1990	Challenge to rights of teenagers to obtain abortion without parental notification. Supreme Court ruling pending.
Turnock vs. Ragsdale	1990	Challenge to constitutionality of costly licensing requirements for clinics that perform abortions in the first trimester. Supreme Court ruling pending

* See page 20.
Modified with permission from Greydanus DE: "Abortion in Adolescence," in *Premature Adolescent Pregnancy and Parenthood.* Ed: ER McAnarney. NY: Grune and Stratton, chapter 20, 360, 1983.

rights. In 1973, the U.S. Supreme Court ruled that women have a legal right to seek and receive a first-trimester abortion (*Roe v. Wade* 410 U.S. 113, 1973). In addition to the debate over abortion for all women, various court decisions have addressed the issue of the legality of abortion in minors.

In 1976, the case of *Planned Parenthood of Central Missouri v. Danforth* (428 U.S. 52, 1976) noted that parents or guardians could not stop an abortion from being performed by a licensed physician on their minor when that minor has given consent for this procedure. The court ruled that

the state may not impose a blanket provision requiring the consent of a parent or person in loco parentis as a condition for abortion of an unmarried minor during the first 12 weeks of her pregnancy. . . . The state does not have the constitutional authority to give a third party an absolute, and possibly arbitrary, veto over the decision of the physician and his patient to terminate the patient's pregnancy. Minors, as well as adults, are protected by the constitution and possess constitutional rights. . . . Any independent interest the parent may have in the termination of the minor daughter's pregnancy is not more weighty than the right of the competent minor mature enough to become pregnant.

Part of this debate has involved the meaning of the "mature minor." There are individuals mature enough to seek and receive health care without parental consent. For example, youth who are married, members of the armed forces, and parents are considered mature enough to provide consent for their health care, including arranging for their own abortion. The age of consent is usually 18, but individual state variations range from 14 to 19 years of age. A recent addition to this mature minor concept involves youth who lead an "emancipated" lifestyle; this refers to individuals who are runaways from home or, for other reasons, are independent of their parents. Such emancipated youth are allowed to seek health care without parental consent in some cases. For example, youth who present to the physician with the possibility of pregnancy, sexually transmitted disease, or substance abuse disorder can be seen at any age without parental consent. Emancipated minors over age 16 often can seek medical care without parental consent if the physician declares the youth to be emancipated and feels that the youth is mature enough to accept appropriate medical advice. Individuals under age 16 are under variable state limitations, and health care professionals should be aware of the laws that address these matters in their own states (see Chapter 2 under "Legal Rights of Adolescents," pp. 18–21.)

When confronted with the difficult issue of abortion, laws become more complex. Table 8-10 reviews some pertinent legal cases that occurred after the Gault case. Current laws note that pregnant adolescents have a constitutional right to seek and receive an abortion without parental consent. However, states vary as to whether some type of parental notification is required. Health care professionals should be aware of their state's laws before performing an abortion on a youth. Current legal dynamics center on allowing a mature (versus "immature") minor to have an abortion and, in fact, whether abortion for *any* individual should be a constitutionally guaranteed right. The issue of payment for such procedures remains complex and should be discussed with youth seeking such services.

Psychologic Effects of Abortion

Concerns have often been expressed that abortion will lead to severe psychologic difficulties, and anecdotal reports testifying to this are easy to find in the literature. Such reports note the emergence of anxiety or depression in the postabortion period. Increased psychologic difficulties have been noted with various factors, including concomitant psychiatric illness, limited family support, limited counseling support, overwhelming religious views, ineffective coping skills, late gestational abortion, illegal abortion, abortion performed to avoid genetic defects, and others. Some youth are fearful of the surgery or are afraid of the anesthesia. Postabortion psychosis and suicidal ideation at the projected first birthday of the aborted fetus are rare but reported phenomena.

Studies, however, generally note that psychologic reactions are not usually seen in youth who are well prepared for the abortion and choose it after careful consideration of all appropriate options. The procedure can even mark a positive though painful development in the lives of some youth, as it forces them away from ambivalence about their sexuality and sometimes even "shocks" them into a greater sense of reality. The abortion procedure can alert the adolescent to real consequences of sexual activity and may convince her to choose abstinence or overt contraception in the future. Adjustment in the postabortion period may be better than that before the abortion, and counseling is an important step in this regard.

Repeat Abortions

Unfortunately, a small group of women use abortion as a "contraceptive" method and engage in repeat abortions. These are individuals who do not find abortion to be a strongly negative experience, who refuse contraception, and who repeatedly choose abortion when unwanted pregnancies occur. Some of these individuals have psychiatric problems, such as major affective disorders, schizophrenia, or personality trait disorders. Some remain ambivalent about their sexuality and are caught in a situation in which ethical or developmental constraints prevent them from seeking any options, such as abstinence or contraception. Others are bitter about past or current life experiences, and abortion is used as a way of expressing their negative feelings. Intensive counseling, including psychiatric care, may help some of these individuals.

Abortion Techniques

A wide variety of surgical procedures (Table 8-11) are available to the physician performing an abortion on a pregnant youth who requests this procedure. Many clinicians prefer suction curettage or menstruation extraction for first-trimester abortions. A number of methods can be used during the second trimester (Table 8-11), and controversy exists as to which is best at different times. Dilatation and evacuation is often chosen for second-trimester individuals up to 20 weeks of gestation. Intraamniotic fluid administration with hypertonic saline is the choice of some physicians at 16 to 20 weeks. The controversy heightens for gestation at 20 to 24 weeks. Clearly, abortion, if it is to be done, should be handled early during the first trimester.

Hodgson reviewed over 20,000 first-trimester abortions and concluded

Table 8-11. Methods of Abortion

General methods
Menstrual extraction
Vacuum aspiration
Dilatation and curettage or evacuation
Intra-amniotic instillation procedure (hypertonic saline, prostaglandin, or urea)
Intravaginal instillation of prostaglandin
Hysterotomy
Hysterectomy
Usual first-trimester methods
Menstrual extraction
Vacuum aspiration
Others
Usual second-trimester methods
Dilatation and curettage
Dilatation and evacuation
Intra-amniotic fluid instillation
Hysterotomy
Others

that it is a safe procedure with a relatively low complication rate when performed by well-trained individuals. Coates et al. noted a 1% or less complication rate for adolescent abortions. Problems that arise include endometritis, genital tract injury, hemorrhaging, Rh sensitization, retained fetal elements, continued gestation and, in rare cases, pulmonary embolism or death. As reviewed earlier, the mortality rate (and morbidity rate) increases in later gestation. Early diagnosis and early abortion are recommended for pregnant youth who choose abortion and for whom other options (such as delivery with keeping or adoption) are not possible. This will reduce potential psychologic and physiologic complications of abortion. Safe, legal, first-trimester abortion does not have a negative effect on subsequent fertility potential. Adolescent females do as well or better than adult women in terms of potential psychologic-physiologic complications with abortion.

Menstrual Extraction. This procedure is often done when a patient presents with a 1- to 2-week delay in menstruation and has a history strongly suggestive of pregnancy. Not all clinicians who use this method will confirm a pregnancy with a serum or urine pregnancy test. Many terms have been applied to this procedure, including miniabortion, menstrual aspiration, endometrial aspiration, menstrual regulation, and menstrual extraction. Prior to this procedure, cervical block anesthesia is used in which a short-acting anesthetic agent is injected into the cervix at several sites. After a nonrigid cannula is positioned into the cervix, the uterus is carefully aspirated or suctioned to remove the conceptus. The patient should be evaluated for the possibility of sexually transmitted diseases (such as gonorrhea or *Chlamydia*) *before* the procedure is done. A poorly performed procedure can result in continued gestation, but the risks of genital injury or other complications are very low with menstrual extraction. As is true after other abortive procedures, the patient may be placed on a broad-spectrum antibiotic for a short interval. She is given instructions to avoid coitus, tampon use, and douching for 2 to 4 weeks after this procedure.

Suction Curettage. In suction curettage (vacuum aspiration), cervical dilatation often occurs prior to the actual abortion. Laminaria (hydrophilic seaweed sticks) are placed within the cervix 24 hours prior to the procedure. These sticks swell and cause sufficient cervical dilation to allow suction curettage. Prior cervical block anesthesia is also used, although general anesthesia may be necessary in a few cases. A cannula (Hegar, Pratt, or Denniston) is placed in the cervix after the laminaria are removed. The uterus is carefully and thoroughly suctioned and then curetted to complete the procedure.

This is the procedure of choice for many who perform abortions at 12 gestational weeks. Complications, as reviewed earlier, can occur, but are not common if the procedure is performed by well-trained individuals. One should remember to evaluate the youth for sexually transmitted diseases prior to the procedure. The individual who is Rh negative should receive RhoGAM to prevent the development of Rh sensitivity. The conceptus or fetal remains are examined to confirm the gestational estimate as well as to exclude the diagnosis of molar gestation or ectopic pregnancy. The patient can usually be sent home the same day with instructions to observe for increased leukorrhea or hemorrhage, fever, abdominal cramps, dizziness, or other related symptoms. Broad-spectrum antibiotics are often given, although their role as a prophylactic agent is unproven. The patient is usually examined 3 to 4 weeks after the abortion, sooner if symptoms warrant.

Dilatation and Evacuation Curettage. With dilatation and curettage, the cervix is dilated and the conceptus is removed, mainly by curetting. With dilatation and evacuation, a variety of methods can be followed, utilizing aspiration, ring forceps, or curettage. This procedure is usually done in the 13- to 20-week gestational period, using general anesthesia. Cervical trauma is possible because of the degree of cervical dilatation necessary. The later the gestation, the greater the complication rates. Oxytocin will reduce the uterine bleeding. The patient is usually hospitalized for this procedure and carefully observed for postabortion complications such as uterine perforation, severe cervical trauma, major hemorrhaging, endometritis, and others. An incomplete abortion can lead to severe bleeding. Major cervical injury can compromise subsequent pregnancy. Prophylactic antibiotics are usually given, and the patient is asked to avoid coitus, douching, and tampon use for the next 2 to 4 weeks. A postabortion examination occurs 2 to 4 weeks after the procedure.

Intra-amniotic Instillation Techniques. A second-trimester procedure used by some clinicians is injection of hypertonic saline, prostaglandin, or urea into the amniotic sac. Hypertonic saline is the most commonly used material and is given through a transabdominally placed needle. Amniotic fluid is withdrawn and replaced with an equal volume of 20% saline. Laminaria can be used before the procedure to dilate the cervix. The result of such instillation is pituitary gland release of oxytocin, reduction of pla-

Table 8-12. Potential Complications of Intra-Amniotic Hypersaline Instillation.

Severe bleeding
Genital injury
Retained placenta
Coagulation disorders
Endometritis
Hypernatremia
Intravascular coagulopathy
Saline instilled into the mother's vascular system
Leakage of saline into the mother's peritoneal system
Delivery of a live infant

cental progesterone, and increase in the synthesis of uterine prostaglandins. Uterine contraction develops; in 1 to 3 days, fetal contents are removed. Oxytocin can be used to increase uterine contractions. Potential complications are numerous, as outlined in Table 8-12. Youth with severe cardiac or renal disorders and severe anemia are not candidates for this method. Youth should be well prepared for such a procedure, which is done in well-advanced pregnancy.

Some physicians prefer instillation of prostaglandin (PGF 2-alpha) to 20% saline since prostaglandin causes an abortion in a shorter time; however, there is more live fetus delivery and more uterine perforation because of the very strong induced uterine contractions. Other complications include severe bleeding, endometritis, retained placenta, nausea, emesis, fever, diarrhea, and bronchospasm. Prostaglandin can also be given as a 20-mg suppository to cause second-trimester abortion, induce labor after an incomplete or missed abortion, or remove a hydatidiform mole. The suppository is placed within the vagina every 3 to 4 hours until the abortion occurs in 4 to 60 hours. This procedure results in abortion in about 90% of cases. Delivery of a live fetus can occur, and 25% of patients develop a retained placenta. Other complications include nausea, emesis, fever, chills, diarrhea, and prostaglandin-induced seizures.

Hysterotomy and Hysterectomy. Hysterotomy and hysterectomy are infrequent methods of abortion for youth. Hysterotomy defines transabdominal surgical removal of a fetus; hysterectomy is a sterilization procedure that surgically removes the uterus. A complication of hysterotomy is that subsequent pregnancies may require cesarean section.

BIBLIOGRAPHY

Abortion surveillance, 1979 Provisional Statistics. MMWR 1982;31(4):47-50.

Abortion surveillance: Preliminary analysis, 1979-1980, United States. MMWR 1983;32(5):62-64.

Alan Guttmacher Institute: Teenage Pregnancy: The Problem That Hasn't Gone Away. New York: Planned Parenthood Federation of America, 1981.

Baldwin W: Trends in adolescent contraception, pregnancy, and childbearing. In: McAnarney ER, ed: Premature Adolescent Pregnancy and Parenthood. New York: Grune & Stratton, 1983.

Bellotti v. Baird 443 US 662, 1979.

Bracken MS, Klerman LV, Bracken M: Abortion, adoption or motherhood: an empirical study of decision-making during pregnancy. Am J Obstet Gynecol 1975;122:799.

Bracken MB: Psychosomatic aspects of abortion: implication for counseling. J Repro Med 1977;19:265-272.

Burkman RT, Atienza MF, King TM: Morbidity risk among young adolescents undergoing elective abortion. Contraception 1984;30:99-105.

Card J, Wise L: Teenage mothers and teenage fathers. The impact of early child-bearing on the parents' personal and professional lives. Fam Plann Perspect 1978;10:199-205.

Carrera MA, Dempsey P: The structuring of public policy priorities on teenage pregnancy. Siecus Rep 1988;16(3):6-9.

Cates W: The Hyde Amendment in action: how did the restriction of federal funds for abortion affect low income women? JAMA 1981;246:1109-1112.

Cates W: Adolescent abortions in the United States. J Adolesc Health Care 1980;1:18-21.

Cates W. Rochat RW: Illegal abortions in the US: 1972-1974. Fam Plann Perspect 1976;8:86.

Cates W Jr, Schulz KF, Grimes DA: The risks associated with teenage abortion. N Engl J Med 1983;309:621-624.

Cates W, Tietze C: Standardized mortality rates associated with legal abortion: US, 1972-1975. Fam Plann Perspect 1978;10:109.

Center for Health Promotion and Education, Centers for Disease Control: Teenage pregnancy and fertility trends—United States, 1974, 1980. MMRW 1985;34:277-279.

Chase HG: A study of risk, medical care and infant mortality. Am J Public Health (Suppl) 1973;V(63):3-16.

Chaundry SL, Hunt WB, Wortman J: Pregnancy termination in mid-trimester. Review of the major methods. Popul Rep 1976;F(5):65-83.

Committee on Adolescence: Pregnancy and abortion counseling. Pediatrics 1979;63:920-921.

Committee on Adolescence: Adolescent pregnancy. Pediatrics 1989;83:132-134.

Committee on Adolescence, American Academy of Pediatrics: Counseling the adolescent about pregnancy options. Pediatrics 1989;83:132-134.

Compton N, Duncan M, Hsuska J: How Schools Can Help Combat Student Pregnancy. Washington, DC: National Education Association, 1987.

Cook RJ, Dickens BM: A decade of international change in abortive law: 1967-1977. Am J Pub Health 1978;68:637-642.

Danforth v. Planned Parenthood of Central Missouri. Fam Plann/Popul Rep 1976;5:53-58.

DeAngelis C, Duggan A, Heald F, et al: Confronting the crisis of teenage pregnancy. Contemp Pediatr 1987;4:68-90.

Dennis JE: Teenage pregnancy: an overview. In: Mellinger JF, Stickler GB, eds: Critical Problems in Pediatrics. Philadelphia: J.B. Lippincott, 1983.

Elster AB, Lamb ME, Tavare J, et al: The medical and psychosocial impact of comprehensive care on adolescent pregnancy and parenthood. JAMA 1987;258:1187-1192.

Felice ME, Shragg P, James M, et al: Clinical observations of Mexican-American, Caucasian and Black Pregnant Teenagers. Sexually Active Teenagers. Elsevier Science Publication 1988;2:239-246.

Frank DA, Zuckerman BS, Amaro H, et al: Cocaine use during pregnancy: prevalence and correlates. Pediatrics 1988;82:888-895.

Gallagher EB, Farrall MG: Adolescent pregnancy and severe heart defects: a risky combination. J Adol Health Care 1988;9:161-163.

Gravett MG, Holmes KK: Pregnancy outcome and maternal infection: the need for comprehensive studies. JAMA 1983;250:1751-1752.

Greene KW, Resnick R: The abortion issue: past, present, and future. Curr Problem Pediatr 1977;7(10):1-44.

Greydanus DE: Abortion in Adolescence. In: McAnarney ER, ed; Premature Adolescent Pregnancy and Parenthood. New York: Grune & Stratton, 1983.

Greydanus DE, Railsback LD: Abortion in adolescence. Semin Adolesc Med 1985;1(3):213-222.

Greydanus DE, Railsback LD: Adolescent pregnancy: selected topics. Semin Adolesc Med 1986;2:175-267.

Hanson MS: Abortion in teenagers. Clin Obstet Gynecol 1978;21:1175-1190.

Hardy, JB: Preventing adolescent pregnancy: counseling teens and their parents. Med Aspec Hum Sex 1987;21(7):32-34, 36, 41, 45-46.

Hardy PH, Hardy JB, Nell EE, et al: Prevalence of six sexually transmitted disease agents among pregnant inter-city adolescents and pregnancy outcome. Lancet 1984;2:333-337.

Hayes CD, ed: Risking the Future: Adolescent Sexuality, Pregnancy and Childbearing. Washington, D.C.: National Academy, 1987.

Heisterberg L: Risk factors in first trimester abortion. Acta Obstet Gynecol Scand 1982;61:357-360.

Hern WM: Mid-trimester abortion. Obstet Gynecol Ann 1981;19:375-422.

HL v. Matheson 101S Ct 1164, 1981.

Hodgson JE: Major complications of 20,248 consecutive first trimester abortions. Problems of fragmentary care. Adv Plann Parent 1975;9:52.

Hofmann AD: A rational policy toward consent and confidentiality in adolescent health care. J Adolesc Health Care 1980;1:9-17.

Huber DH: Restricting or prohibiting abortion by constitutional amendment—some health implications. J Repro Med 1982;27:729-736.

Hyde Amendment: Appropriations year 1980—Continuance Public Law 96-123, 109, 92 Stat 926, 1979.

In re Gault, 398 US 1, 1967.

Isberner, F, Wright WR: Comprehensive prenatal care for pregnant teens. J Sch Health 1987;57(5):288-292.

Key TC, Kreutner AKK: Menstrual extraction in the adolescent. J Adolesc Health Care 1980;1:127-131.

Lovick SR: School-based clinics: meeting teens' health care needs. J Sch Health 1988;58(9):379-381.

Martin MC: Midtrimester abortion—A decade in review. Can J Surg 1982;25:641-643.

McAnarney ER, Greydanus DE: Adolescent pregnancy and abortion. In: Hofmann AD, Greydanus DE, eds: Adolescent Medicine. Norwalk, CT: Appleton-Lange, 1989:403-416.

McAnarney ER, Roghmann K, Charney E, et al: Obstetric, neonatal, and psychosocial outcome of pregnant adolescents. Pediatrics 1978;61:199-205.

McAnarney ER, Thiede HA: Adolescent pregnancy and childbearing: What we have learned during the 1970s and what remains to be learned. In: McAnarney ER, ed: Premature Adolescent Pregnancy and Parenthood. New York: Grune & Stratton, 1983.

McAnarney ER: Young maternal age and adverse neonatal outcome. Am J Dis Child 1987;141:1053-1059.

McCarthy J, Radish ES: Education and childbearing among teenagers. In: McAnarney ER, ed: Premature Adolescent Pregnancy and Parenthood. New York: Grune & Stratton, 1983.

Merino DD, King JC: Nutritional concerns during adolescence. Pediatr Clin North Am 1980;27(1):125-139.

Merritt TA, Lawrence RA, Nueye RI: The infants of adolescent mothers. Pediatr Ann 1980;9:100-109.

Meserole LP, Worthington-Roberts BS, Rees JM: Prenatal weight gain and postpartum weight loss patterns in adolescents. Sexually active Teenagers Elsevier Science Publication 1988;2:14-20.

Moore K, Waite L: Early child-bearing and educational attainment. Fam Plann Perspect 1977;9:220-225.

Morin-Gonthier M, Lortie G: The significance of pregnancy among adolescents choosing abortion as compared to those continuing pregnancy. J Reprod Med 1984;29:255-259.

National Center for Health Statistics: Annual summary of births, deaths, marriages and divorces: United States, 1982. Mon Vital Stat Rep 1983;31(13):1-28.

National Center for Health Statistics: Monthly vital statistics report: "Advance report of final natality statistics, 1985." 1987;36(4 Suppl):1-100.

Nutrient Intakes: Individuals in 48 States, Year 1977-78, Nationwide Food Consumption Survey 1977-1978. US Dept of Agriculture, Report No. 1-2, Consumer Nutrition Division, Human Nutrition Information Service, 1984.

Olson L: Social and psychological correlates of pregnancy resolution among adolescent women. A review. Am J Orthopsychiatry 1980;50:432-445.

Panzarine S: Stressors, coping and social supports of adolescent mothers. Sexually Active Teenagers 1988;2:136-144.

Paul EW, Schaap P: Legal rights and responsibilities of pregnant teenagers and their children. In: Wells CF, Stuart IR, eds: Pregnancy in Adolescence, Needs, Problems, and Management. New York: Van Nostrand Reinhold, 1983:3-24.

Planned Parenthood v. Danforth, 428 US 52, 1976.

Pritchard JA, MacDonald PC, eds: Williams Obstetrics. 16th ed. New York: Appleton-Century-Crofts, 1980.

Rhodes AM: Legal issues related to adolescent pregnancy: current concepts. Semin Adolesc Med 1986;2(3):181-196.

Report of the Committee of Infectious Diseases: The 1988 Red Book. Elk Grove Village, IL: American Academy of Pediatrics (G. Peter, Ed), 1988.

Roe v. Wade, Doe v. Bolton, 410 US 113, 179, 1973.

Sander JH, Rosen JL: Teenage fathers: working with the neglected partner in adolescent childbearing. Fam Plann Perspect 1987;19(3)107-110.

Sands L: Concepts of nutrition in adolescent pregnancy. Semin Adol Med 1986;2(3):191-196.

Sandoval JA: Impact 88: Dallas' countywide plan for reducing teenage pregnancy. SIECUS Rep 1988;16(3):1-5.

Schneider MS, Thompson DS: Repeat aborters. Am J Obstet Gynecol 1976;126:316-320.

Scholl TO, Salmon RW, Miller LK: Smoking and adolescent pregnancy outcome. Sexually Active Teenagers 1988;2(5):197-201.

Shearin RB, Burnett AM: A checklist for adolescent pregnancy. Amer Fam Phys 1976;14(1):79.

Spivak H, Weitzman M: Social barriers faced by adolescent parents and their children. JAMA 1986;258:1500-1504.

Steinhoff PG, Smith RG, Palamore JA, et al: Women who obtain repeat abortions: a study based on record linkage. Fam Plann Perspect 1979;11:30-38.

Stevens-Simon C, McAnarney ER: Adolescent maternal weight gain and birthweight: a multifactorial model. Am J Clin Nutr 1988;47:948-953.

Teenage childbearing and abortion patterns—US, 1977. MMWR 1980;29(15):157-160.

Tietze C: New estimates of mortality associated with fertility control. Fam Plann Perspect 1977;9:75.

Tietze C, Bongaarts J, Schearer B: Mortality associated with the control of fertility. Fam Plann Perspect 1976;8:14-15.

Tinker v. The Des Moines Independent School District, 393 US 503, 1969.

Tyler CW Jr: The public health implications of abortions. Ann Rev Pub Health 1983;4;223-258.

Vinovskis MA: An "Epidemic" of Adolescent Pregnancy: Some Historical and Policy Considerations. New York: Oxford, 1988.

Weeks JR: Teenage marriages: A Demographic Analysis. London: Greenwood, 1976.

Westergaard L, Philpsen T, Scheibel J: Significance of cervical Chlamydia trachomatis infection in post-abortal pelvic inflammatory disease. Obstet Gynecol 1982;60:322-355.

Wilcox AJ, Weinberg CR, O'Connor JF, et al: Incidence of early loss of pregnancy. N Engl J Med 1988;319:189-194.

Zabin LS, Hirsch MB, Smith EA: Adolescent pregnancy-prevention program: a model for research and evaluation. Sexually Active Teenagers 1988;2:125-135.

9

Adolescent Sexual Assault and Incest

Sexual abuse of adolescent males and females has become a well-described phenomenon. Unfortunately, rape is one of the fastest growing crimes of violence in the United States. The exact numbers are unknown, since most rapes (perhaps 80 to 90%) are not reported because of many underlying factors: psychologic reactions to the assault, the complex legal process following a rape report, the high acquittal rate of the rapist, fear of reprisal from the attacker, fear of embarrassment to oneself (as well as family), and other factors. Between 50,000 and 70,000 cases of rape are reported each year; the estimated number of actual cases exceeds 400,000 to 500,000 annually. In 1985, 123,000 cases of childhood sexual assault were reported. Perhaps as many as 40 million Americans have been sexually abused as children.

The rape victim risk rate varies in different communities, from 50 to 150 per 100,000 individuals. Sexual assault of children and adolescents appears to be a widespread problem, one more common than the number of reported rapes would suggest. For example, surveys of college students reveal that many have been sexually assaulted as children or youth. In a survey of 795 college students, Finkelhor reported that 19% of the females and 9% of the males had been victimized sexually. Fromuth noted this in 22% of 482 college females. This chapter reviews the common phenomena of rape and incest and discusses the important topic of examining the assaulted individual.

DEFINITIONS

Rape refers to carnal knowledge (any penile penetration) of a male or female without consent and with the use of fear, force, fraud, or all three on the part of the assailant. It is a legal term, not a medical one; and is applied by a court of law after due process. *Statutory rape* refers to coitus with a female below the age of consent, which varies from 14 to 21 years, depending on individual state laws. *Molestation* refers to noncoital sexual contact of an individual without consent, whereas *sexual assault* usually refers to sexual contact (manual, genital, or oral) with the victim's genitalia without consent of the victim and with the use of fear, force, or fraud. *Deviant sexual assault* defines contact of the individual's sex organs with the mouth or anus of another without consent. *Incest* generally defines coital contact between a blood relative and a young victim (child or young adolescent). All of these terms imply that there are many kinds of sexual

244

assault that can be perpetrated on a child or adolescent in an acute or chronic manner.

HISTORICAL PERSPECTIVE

Only recently has much attention been paid by medical and legal personnel to the topic of child and adolescent sexual assault. For centuries, the minor (any individual under age 21), especially the female, was not considered as a real person deserving fair legal treatment. The first law in Western civilization against rape was not established until 1280 A.D. in England. Incest was not defined as a crime until 1908 in England. Unfortunately, the concept of the nonpersonalization of the female has existed for a long time. Real interest in dealing with sexual assault and incest did not surface before the past 20 years. Currently, many health care professionals are involved in the research and treatment of these victims. Rape crisis centers have been established around the country, and the National Center for the Prevention and Control of Rape was established in Washington, D.C. However, many current concerns remain. For example, the movement for increased women's rights is in conflict, to some extent, with the growing number of rapes in women. Victims who actively resist a rape have a 25% chance of avoiding the rape but also increase the chance of receiving more severe physical injury. Victims who do not actively resist the assault risk condemnation by others. Also, old myths about rape continue today. Many who have been sexually assaulted feel that they brought on the assault by not being "good" enough, by not resisting enough, and other false reasons.

VICTIMS

Most raped individuals are single women between 15 and 24 years of age and are assaulted by males 15 to 30 years of age. Approximately 50% of rape victims are between 10 and 19 years of age, and half of this group are under age 16. In a study of sexually assaulted individuals by Hayman and Lanza, 66% of the female victims under age 20 were 10 to 19 years of age. The peak incidence for sexual assault appears to be at 5 and 6 and 14 and 15 years of age. According to Felice et al., over half of adolescent rape victims aged 11 to 19 had medical evidence of traumatic sexual assault. According to Hayman and Lanza, most sexually assaulted victims require physical examination because of induced trauma. Physical findings are usually noted in over 35% of female rape victims and in 50% of male victims. Risk factors for sexual assault include family discord, a child not living with his or her biologic mother, a child without active supervision (e.g., a runaway), an individual with a substance abuse disorder, an individual with a "helpless" attitude about life, the adolescent age group in general, and others.

Males may be involved as victims in 5 to 15% of reported cases and are often involved in episodes inflicted by multiple assailants with resultant severe physical damage. Males may be reluctant to report sexual assault; thus, only the more serious cases come to medical or legal attention.

Evaluation of male victims often shows more physical trauma with considerable genital injury (with urethritis), and they may be reluctant to accept help. Little is known about these male victims; hence, most of the assault literature involves the study of female victims. However, it is clear that sexual assault involves both males and females. Over two thirds of victimized children are assaulted again.

ASSAILANTS

In the hands of assailants, rape is a *pseudosexual act* and not a sexual act as such. Rape is used to express power over others, anger at others, and in a complex way, *sexuality*. Assailants generally fall into four groups of individuals. Some rape because they have an inadequate-personality disorder and are unable to control overwhelming impulses that eventually lead to rape. There are also those with a destructive personality type who have an antisocial and explosive personality. They have a deep hatred of women and use rape as an expression of their severe anger. The violence associated with such episodes worsens with each rape, and women who resist are in danger of severe physical injury. Child molesters (pedophiles), who make up the third category of assailants, are poorly understood individuals with complex psychiatric disorders driving them to seek sexual gratification from children, since they are incapable or fearful of sexual involvement with adults. Finally, incest represents the fourth group.

Unfortunately, these abusers can be anyone (parents, siblings, relatives, babysitters, casual acquaintances, and even total strangers). Incest involves 40% of reported sexual assault; thus, family members must be evaluated if a case of reported or suspected sexual assault is encountered. Unfortunately, 90% of incest cases are not reported, and the negative effects can last the lifetime of the victim. Finkelhor noted that 5 of every 1000 college females reported that they had been victims of incest by their fathers. In Weinberg's study of 103 incest cases, 78% involved father-daughter relationships; 18%, brother-sister; 1%, mother-son; and 3%, multiple incest. Societal stress may be contributing to this phenomenon. Current society witnesses considerable family discord, which leads to divorce in 40 to 50% of families. The increased phenomena of stepparents and live-in lovers of divorced parents, changing parental sex partners, and depressed parents seeking love in "all the wrong places" has lead to a dramatic rise in incest and sexual assault of children. Brother-sister incest remains a poorly reported phenomenon, which is felt to be second in frequency only to father/stepfather-daughter incest. Sibling incest appears to be more commonly reported in upper- and middle-class society.

Although the problem of father/stepfather-daughter incest appears to be more common in low- to middle-class society, it can occur in any societal stratum. Although many factors can be seen, such incest often involves a father with alcoholism or other substance abuse disorder and a limited education who turns to his daughter after serious marital issues have developed between him and his wife. In some cases, the father is diagnosed as having a psychopathic (antisocial) personality or other major personality disorder. As the marital conflict worsens, the father turns to the daughter for abnormal sexual gratification. Although any age can be noted, the daughter is often between 9 and 11 years of age. Caught in a pathologic relationship between the mother and the father, the daughter is not sure what to do. She may try to be a "good" daughter and find it difficult to disobey her father, especially when the mother silently observes the phenomenon and does not actively attempt to stop it. The father often warns the daughter not to tell anyone for fear of breaking up the home or that disclosure will lead the father to kill himself, the daughter, or immediate family members. The daughter finds herself in a terrible, seemingly hopeless situation and may allow this assault to continue for many years. As the victim grows up and leaves the home, younger females may fall into this destructive pattern unless it is interrupted and treatment initiated. Educating the child and youth to report such incidents may prevent the development of chronic sexual assault. Reporting the assault(s) to local child protective agencies for a legal evaluation is mandatory. Clinicians should be familiar with local state law in this regard.

Consequences of incest are many, including pregnancy, sexually transmitted diseases, and various behavioral disorders (Table 9-1). When evaluating youth with such problems, consider incest. Sudden runaway behavior, unusual behavioral disorders, pregnancy or sexually transmitted disease in young adolescents, and unexplained injuries (particularly genital) should raise the clinician's suspicion of incest. Silbert and Pines studied 200 juvenile and adult prostitutes and noted that 72% entered prostitution as a teenager, at an average age of 16; 96% of the juvenile prostitutes were runaways; and 60% had been sexually assaulted under age 16. In 67% of those who had been sexually assaulted, the father had

Table 9-1. Potential Behavioral Disorders of Sexually Abused Children or Youth.

Chronic drug or alcohol abuse
Sleep disturbances
Psychosomatic disturbances (chronic headaches or abdominal pain)
Persistent hyperventilation syndrome
Refractory seizure disorders
Chronic syncopal episodes
School failure
Severe parent-child conflicts
Juvenile delinquency or other aggressive behaviors
Depression
Suicide attempts
Promiscuity
Prostitution
School and work difficulties
Sexual dysfunction (anorgasmia, impotence, and dyspareunia)
Runaway behavior
Enuresis
Psychomotor retardation or agitation
Anxiety
Lowered self-esteem
Others

been involved; in 82%, the assault was forced; and 70% believed that the assault lead to their lifestyle of prostitution.

EMOTIONAL REACTIONS TO SEXUAL ASSAULT

When encountering an individual who has been involved with some type of sexual assault, clinicians should perform a thorough evaluation to determine the extent of any subsequent physical or emotional injury. Appropriate medical care (see below) should be offered, and the patient should be referred to local individuals who can handle the potentially complex aftercare such victims require.

Burgess and Holmstrom have divided their reaction of an adult to a rape incident into two phases, which collectively make up the *rape trauma syndrome* (Table 9-2). Youth can fit these categories to some extent. The first phase is the *acute phase of disorganization* in which the individual can be very upset, present in "mental shock" or dismay, and appear to be disorganized. Youth may become so upset that they do not seek medical attention for several hours to several days, or longer, after the incident. As previously noted, many never seek attention. Feelings of guilt may arise, whereby the victim feels as if she were to blame for this terrible invasion of her privacy. Young victims assaulted by family members or individuals trusted by the family may develop extreme confusion, not knowing who to turn to or how to seek help. They may turn inward and not inform anyone of the assault for years.

Middle adolescents (ages 14 to 18) who have been struggling for autonomy and emancipation may become very upset over the incident and feel that it is a punishment for their desire to be independent. Youth who feel abandoned by family and peers use such assaults as more evidence of their "worthless" nature, leading to profound depression. Many variations of the acute phases are seen. For example, if there has been previous psychologic difficulty, a *compounded reaction* can develop. A situation referred to as the silent rape reaction is created when extreme denial occurs while internal anger builds (often in association with other psychologic difficulties). Major acting-out phenomena may develop weeks to months later. Incest victims, often feeling that they contributed

Table 9-2. Rape Trauma Syndrome.

Phase	Treatment
Burgess and Holmstrom (1974)	
1. Acute phase: disorganization	1. Attention to medical needs; refer to appropriate supportive agencies (mental health clinics, rape trauma centers, others)
2. Reorganization	2. Counseling
Fox and Scheryl	
1. Acute reaction	1. Same as No. 1 above.
2. Outward adjustment	2. Offer general counseling, observe for medical needs, follow carefully.
3. Integration	3. Professional counseling.

to their assault, can develop what has been termed the *accessory-to-sex-victim reaction.* Treatment at this stage involves attention to medical needs and referral to appropriate sources that can deal with future, anticipated negative reactions. It is not possible to deal with denial at this phase. There will be time later to deal with this when the patient is ready.

The victim eventually enters the *reorganization phase* of the rape trauma syndrome in which there is an attempt to gradually develop a more normal lifestyle. The reaction at this time often depends on the way the victim's personality functioned prior to the rape. Expected reactions can include chronic depression, anxiety reactions (including phobias), and various sexual dysfunctions. This is often the best time to offer specific counseling, but only if the individual is ready. Counseling can be offered by a variety of therapists, including psychologists, psychiatrists, family therapists, primary care physicians, and others trained to deal with the complex emotional aftermath of sexual assault. Depressed individuals may benefit from the judicious use of antidepressant medications if evaluation reveals evidence for endogenous depression.

Fox and Scheryl further expanded the rape trauma syndrome into three phases (Table 9-2). Although other categorizations of the rape trauma syndrome have been developed, this one seems most useful for youth and adolescents. Phase 1, or acute reaction, is reflected by Burgess and Holmstrom's disorganization phase (Table 9-2). During this time, which can last hours to days, there may be disbelief, shock, or dismay, followed by fear (anxiety) or guilt. Much of this depends on the preassault personality and the severity of the assault. If the individual fails to report the incident for several days or longer, it may reflect the severity of the shock, guilt, or anxiety that has developed. At the time the patient presents, practical considerations are offered only in relation to immediate needs. A mental status and physical examination is performed, and immediate treatment is given for acute needs. An intense "interrogation" of the patient's psychologic reaction is not warranted at this time, and the patient can be referred to appropriate specialists. If severe psychiatric reactions are noted, such as suicidal ideations, emergency referral to such services is in order.

Phase 2 is called *outward adjustment* and defines the period when the patient is beginning practical adjustment to the severe insult she or he has sustained. A variety of defense mechanisms can be seen (Table 9-1). Extreme denial can be worrisome to the clinician who is aware of the assault. If familiar with the history, the physician can gently probe to see if the individual wishes to discuss and deal with the issue at that time. Typically, the patient will refuse to discuss the rape incident in any depth, and further probing is useless. At this point, the physician can assure him or her that counseling is available if and when the patient requests it. Assurance that the patient is not alone and that help will be offered when needed is sufficient therapy at this time. The clinician should accept the fact that the patient is not ready to deal with it and leave the established defense mechanisms alone.

Some weeks or months later, phase 3, or *integration,* may set in when the patient openly expresses a desire for help. Typically, the individual becomes severely depressed and can develop a variety of symptoms (Table 9-1). These symptoms can be viewed as cries for help, and it is during this time that active counseling may be beneficial. The depression reaction can be precipitated by various factors, including a court summons to deal with the rape charges, discovery of pregnancy or sexually transmitted diseases, and others. The court process itself can be very anxiety-provoking, with the individual having to see the accused, recount the tragic incident, hold up under cross-examination, and perhaps see the assailant go free.

Treatment at this time consists of professional counseling to allow a cathartic effect. The victim should be allowed a transient period of guilt so that this feeling can be faced openly and directly. The individual who has worried that she may have caused the incident must bring this concern out in the open, analyze it, and then let it go. Her reflections need to center on the helplessness she felt and how her inner space was cruelly invaded. She can look at her negative feelings for the assailant and any associated guilt feelings. She can be assured that depression as well as anger are natural reactions and that they will resolve over time with help. Failure to ventilate and resolve such feelings can lead to chronic, severe behavioral disorders in adolescence and adulthood. This can include continued depression or anxiety, chronic distrust of all men, continued phobias or phobic reactions to different events, sexual dysfunction, marital dysfunction, and various major lifestyle disruptions. Sexual assault in childhood or adolescence can result in various personality dysfunctions with major negative impact on the patient and, ultimately, society.

The clinician should seek to reduce the trauma of the medicolegal examination as much as possible and also attempt to deal with the negative reaction from family and friends. If the patient is prone to repeated sexual assaults by nature of his or her lifestyle, attention to this important area, if possible, is important. The empathetic and caring clinician can be helpful to the individual who has undergone an acute or chronic sexual assault.

MEDICAL EVALUATION

A thorough physical examination is recommended when evaluating a child or teenager who has been sexually assaulted. This is particularly true when encountering an individual within 2 or 3 days of the assault. The physician should always remember that his or her role is to carefully gather accurate information, not to present a demanding, pejorative demeanor to the already stressed child or adolescent patient. It is easy for the examiner to become negatively involved emotionally and to accuse patients of causing their own situation, particularly when examining a juvenile prostitute or runaway juvenile delinquent. The clinician's responsibilities are as follows:

Collect a thorough history
Perform a careful general physical examination
Perform a genital-pelvic examination
Collect appropriate materials for the forensic examination
Obtain appropriate legal consent and ensure legal release of both
information and material to proper authorities
Provide appropriate medical treatment
Refer to proper professionals

The examiner must pay attention to many details, and thus it is best to carefully use an accepted protocol, such as one of those developed by the Committee on Adolescence of the American Academy of Pediatrics or the American College of Obstetrics and Gynecology. If the patient reports a history of sexual assault, whether acute or chronic, a report may have to be filed with the local child protective authorities. The need for careful documentation despite the potential emotional reaction of the patient and the need for legal involvement can discourage physicians from becoming involved in the entire situation. However, the child or adolescent needs professional help, and clinicians should be ready to provide this in an empathetic manner.

The medical history documents how the incident occurred and what happened in the patient's own words. Table 9-3 reviews important aspects of the medical history as it seeks to document and record the details of the assault. Despite the difficulties often involved with the examination, it is important to obtain such detail, especially if a trial takes place. If the patient was using oral contraceptives, if she already has a late

Table 9-3. Medical History From Rape Protocol.

---

1. Name, age, and the usual patient demographics.
2. Date and place of the examination and of the "alleged assault."
3. Use the patient's own words and use the term "alleged assault." Write "the patient stated. . . . ."
4. How did the victim come to the examining facility?
5. How did the alleged assault occur?
6. Nature of the assault: single versus multiple rape, number of attackers, type of attack, and other pertinent descriptions.
7. Any contraceptives involved (i.e., was the victim on birth control pill or was the attacker using a condom?)
8. What is the victim's sexual and menstrual history (including last normal menstrual period, use of tampons, others).
9. Since the alleged incident, has the patient changed clothes, bathed, douched, urinated, or defecated?
10. What is the appearance of the clothes—ripped, blood- or semen-stained, others?
11. Current symptoms, including musculoskeletal, gastrointestinal, genitourinary, and others.
12. General medical history.
    a. Review of systems.
    b. Current medications.
    c. Drug or other allergies.
    d. Drug history.
    e. Others.

---

menstrual period, if she douched since the assault—these are important facts that will eventually help others reach a final opinion about the incident.

A good history can be obtained from most patients, even children. Most children are assaulted by individuals known to them, whereas adolescents are more likely to be assaulted by strangers. Communication with the child should be at his or her cognitive level. Anatomically correct dolls can be used to improve body-part vocabulary and establish what actually occurred. One can use the language of the child and ask gently probing questions. Sometimes the child is anxious and not willing to answer immediately. Patience on the part of the examiner is necessary to find the true answer. Some children will want a parent involved during the interview; however, most will not. The victim may have been threatened by the assailant; correct, as well as detailed, information often requires the establishment of trust between the examiner and the victim. One of the tragic consequences of such assault is that the victim finds it difficult to trust other individuals, particularly males.

The examiner obtaining the history should seek information on prior sexual abuse and whether this assailant was involved in similar assaults. Attackers of male children who are unknown to them are often pedophiles or gay males. Table 9-4 reviews the positive history findings of male children who were sexually abused, as documented by Spencer and Dunklee.

PHYSICAL EXAMINATION

Mental Status Examination

During the physical examination the patient's mental status should be carefully assessed. To identify major psychiatric disorders, the clinician should determine the patient's orientation toward time, place, and person and observe the patient's speech, dress, eye contact, and general degree of cooperation. The patient's affect should be carefully assessed and suicidal ideations, thought disorders, hallucinations, or delusions should

Table 9-4. Positive History in Sexually Abused Boys (Spencer and Dunklee, 1986).

Type of Abuse	Percent
Fellatio	46
Anal penetration	78
Penile	53
Digital	11
Attempted penile	9
Foreign body	5
Ejaculation	25
Fondlings	24
Masturbation	11
Fecal soiling	9
French kissing	6
Sexually transmitted disease	5
Other positives	9
Negative history	5

be carefully evaluated, as should overall intelligence, judgment, and insight into the patient's problems. If in doubt about the patient's mental status, the examiner should consult a behavioral medicine specialist.

General Physical Examination

The general physical examination, not the genital evaluation, may reveal that an assault took place. Evidence of genital injury may not be found unless the sexual assault involves a young victim with a narrow introitus or intense pubococcygeus muscles, or unless the attack was particularly vicious, perhaps involving more than one assailant. A variety of potentially severe injuries can occur, often postcoital, involving the face, neck, breasts, medial aspects of the lower extremities (thighs and lower legs), and others. Evidence of injury can include abrasions, contusions, lacerations, hematomas, ecchymoses, human bite marks, burns, fractures, and others. When collecting evidence during the examination, diagrams should be drawn or photographs taken to better document the often fleeting evidence of the assault. There may be evidence of previous abuse, such as old burns (including dugout craters from cigarettes or linear contact injuries); poor hygiene; dirty skinfolds; fecal dermal stains; nutritionally induced skin disorders (including alopecia); old fractures; strap marks; ocular damage; trauma-induced alopecia; signs of self-mutilation; and various untreated, chronic skin conditions. Chronic injury and repeated assault are common in individuals with a history of physical abuse, runaway behavior, prostitution, and others. Major trauma may lead to an acute abdomen due to ruptured viscera or even to major neurologic injury with subdural hemorrhage or hematoma, brain damage, coma, and even death. Thus, the general examination should be complete, including vital signs and evaluation of the cardiopulmonary, abdominal, musculoskeletal, neurologic, and other systems. The neurologic evaluation should include the mental status exam, along with an evaluation of cranial nerves, the sensory, motor, and cerebellar systems, and deep tendon reflexes.

Genital Examination

The pelvic examination of females may reveal diverse genital findings (Figs. 9-1 and 9-2), including hymenal lacerations, posterior fourchette erythema, first-degree vaginal lacerations, perineal tears, sexually transmitted diseases, spermatozoa, acid phosphatase, and others. Upper vaginal and cervical trauma is not common and is indicative of a vicious assault. As noted, photos and drawings are highly recommended ways of documenting the injuries. Evaluation can reveal the perineal appearance (normal, tears, hemorrhages, or ecchymoses) and the appearance of internal structures (vagina, cervix, uterus, adnexa, and rectum). One should remember that pregnancy and sexually transmitted diseases do result from sexual assault. In Hayman and Lanza's study of 451 cases of sexual assault, there were 9 pregnancies, 59 cases of gonorrhea, 3 of syphilis, and 1 of lymphogranuloma venereum. White's study of 409 sexual assault

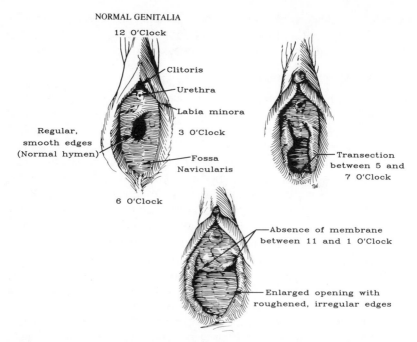

NORMAL GENITALIA

12 O'Clock

Clitoris

Urethra

Labia minora

Regular,
smooth edges
(Normal hymen)

3 O'Clock

Fossa
Navicularis

6 O'Clock

Transection
between 5 and
7 O'Clock

Absence of membrane
between 11 and 1 O'Clock

Enlarged opening with
roughened, irregular edges

Fig. 9-1. Normal female genitalia (top left) and two examples of genital injuries following sexual abuse in a prepubertal girl.

cases revealed 13% with sexually transmitted diseases, including gonorrhea, trichomoniasis, syphilis, and condylomata accuminata. Table 9-5 shows the positive findings of examinations of sexually abused male children. The current HIV infection rate must also be remembered.

The pelvic examination can be difficult to perform in rape victims, especially if the patient is young and has limited, if any, experience with this examination. Preparing the patient for the details of this evaluation may be helpful. Many male examiners may wish to have a female chaperon in the room during the evaluation of a female patient. This chaperon can be a nurse, social worker, or other, but generally not the parent. One should acknowledge that the procedure can be embarrassing to the patient and

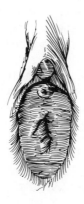

Fig. 9-2. Post-traumatic labial fusion.

Table 9-5. Physical Findings of Sexually Abused Boys (Spencer and Dunklee, 1986).

Finding	Percent
None	32
Perianal erythema/abrasions	27
Scars, skin tags, anal verge	11
Rectal lacerations and fissures	11
Perianal hyperpigmentation	10
Penile or perineal bruising	7
Sexually transmitted diseases	5
Evidence for ejaculation	5
Rectal/anal dilated veins and hematoma	4
Lax anal sphincter	3

allow him or her time to see the instruments that will be used. Drape the patient properly and have a good, reliable light source as well as the necessary equipment readily available.

Small female children can be placed in the knee-chest position on the examining table or in the usual position on the helper's lap. Female adolescents may be placed in a lithotomy or frog-leg position on the table. A careful inspection of the external genitalia can be accomplished, as discussed in Chapter 2. A gentle examination of the male genitalia can be accomplished, evaluating the penis, testicles, anus, and rectum. In the female, the examiner evaluates the mons, groin, labia (majora and minora), clitoris, hymen, and anus. Easier inspection of the hymen and lower vagina may be afforded by placing a thumb on each labial side, spreading them laterally while pushing on the perineum. It is normally difficult to absolutely state whether coital activity has occurred merely based on the hymenal ring appearance.

Instrumentation of prepubertal females can usually be accomplished with the Huffman vaginoscope or Kelly cystoscope. Colposcopy is useful in the genital examination of the female child and also in the male when sodomy has occurred. The use of such procedures may reveal microabscesses, microfissures, and petechiae.

Findings in acute sexual abuse include perineal contusions, spasm of the pubococcygeus muscle, perihymenal injury (swelling, erythema, petechiae), tense rectal sphincter, anal fissures, perianal edema, and others, such as abrasions, lacerations, avulsions, and ecchymoses. Findings of hymenal abnormalities are documented by assigning a 12 o'clock position to the urethral opening and a 6 o'clock position to the posterior fourchette. Penile penetration of a normal hymen often results in tearing of the hymenal membrane between 4 and 8 o'clock, with 6 o'clock being the most common (Fig. 9-3). Swelling may be severe, and a repeat examination may be necessary after the swelling is reduced. Digital penetration often leads to swelling and microtears in the upper half of the hymenal opening. Signs of chronic sodomy include subcutaneous lipoatrophy, coving, and microscarring in the rectum.

Other signs of chronic abuse noted by the examination include multiple hymenal transections, rounded hymenal remnants, synechiae, fourchette-

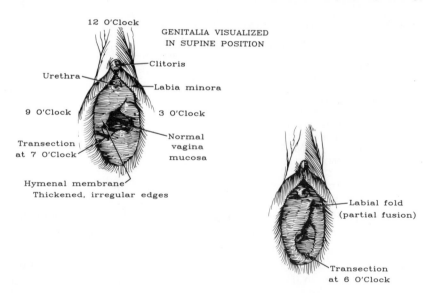

Fig. 9-3. Two examples of the results of penile penetration of the normal hymen. *Left:* transection at 7 o'clock. *Right:* transection at 6 o'clock.

hymenal lacerations, neovascularization, wide introitus (greater or equal to 4 mm at 5 years of age or more), ability to relax the pubococcygeus muscle, laxity of the vaginal-pubococcygeus muscle, reflex relaxation of the anal sphincter, and others (Table 9-6).

Boys with chronic or multiple sexual assault history may have patulous rectum, scars, fecal leaking or incontinence, perianal hyperpigmentation, decreased anal tone, and other symptoms. The Pederson speculum is suitable for most sexually active youth, whereas the thinner Huffman speculum may be preferable for virginal pubescent youth. A full speculum inspection may not be possible because of severe patient anxiety, severe injury, vaginismus, anatomic anomaly, or vaginitis (as with trichomoniasis, gonorrhea, or others). Chapter 2 discusses patient relaxation techniques and the use of medications for sedating a patient. Colposcopy and anoscopy are becoming important tools in the genital examination of pubescent females as well as children. Colposcopy can reveal evidence of trauma not appreciated without magnification of the inspected tissues.

The literature is increasing regarding the findings of acute and chronic sexual abuse in children and teenagers (Abrams, 1988; Emans, 1987; Strickland, 1989; Woodling and Hegar, 1986). Woodling and Hegar, as well as others, have made available excellent teaching videos, slides, and color photographs. Clinicians can now receive additional training in this important area and should check with local experts.

Laboratory Procedures

Diverse laboratory procedures should be performed as part of the postrape examination, according to the accepted protocol reviewed in Table

Table 9-6. Sexual Abuse Examination Terms.

Ecchymosis Small hemorrhagic spot in the skin or mucous membrane, forming a nonelevated, rounded, or irregular discolored patch

Edema Swelling; an abnormal accumulation of fluid in intercellular spaces of the body

Erythema Redness of the skin due to congestion of the capillaries

Fissure Anal fissure—a lineal ulcer, usually painful, at the margin of the anus

Funneling "Gutter-like" depression or conical appearance of the anus caused by chronic anal assault or sodomization

Gaping Orifice Abnormally large opening

Hymenal Dilatation Enlarged hymenal opening

Hypertrophy Enlargement or overgrowth of an organ or part

Leukorrhea Whitish vaginal discharge

Neovascularization Development of independent blood vessels within a scar that are clearly delineated and demarcated from the normal surrounding capillary pattern

Petechiae Minute red spot(s) due to the escape of a small amount of blood

Pigmentation Change Change from the normal coloration due to scarring

Reflex Relaxation ("+" Wink reflex) Anal sphincter reflexively relaxes when stimulated or stroked with a finger

Synechiae Adhesion; binding scar; mounted scar binding hymen to vaginal vault, post-fourchette, labia, etc.

Transection A cut through the hymen distorting normal hymenal outline, causing discontinuity of hymenal edges

Venous Pooling Abnormal collection of blood in the veins (often seen around the anus due to anal assault or sodomization)

9-7. The examiner can obtain a vaginal aspirate for *Trichomonis vaginalis* and motile sperm, as well as gonococcal and chlamydial cultures from appropriate sites (e.g., cervix, urethra, rectum, and perhaps oropharynx). Syphilis serology (at the time of the postrape examination and repeated in

Table 9-7. Laboratory Procedures in Post-Rape Evaluation.

1. Comb and pluck pubic hair.
2. Wet mount of material from vaginal fornix for motile sperm.
3. Fixed smear from vagina and/or vulva for sperm.
4. Aspirate vaginal material for acid phosphatase, ABH agglutinogen, and sperm precipitins.
5. *Neisseria gonorrhoeae* culture from cervix, rectum, urethra, and oropharynx (perform *Chlamydia trachomatis* serology or culture).
6. Collect fingernail debris.
7. Collect dried secretions from skin scrapings and stained clothes for acid phosphatase and ABH agglutinogen.
8. Various blood tests: syphilis serology, alcohol level, blood typing, and other drug tests. Consider HIV testing.

4 to 6 weeks) can be done along with other tests for potential sexually transmitted diseases. Pubescent adolescent females should be given a pregnancy test, and a serum sample should be saved that can be frozen for future testing.

The examiner can collect material suggestive of semen or ejaculate fluid, whether from pubic hair, abdomen, thighs, or other locations. Pubic hair can be combed, fingernail scrapings collected, and the patient's clothes preserved in a sealed bag—all done according to the protocol. A Wood's light examination can detect the bright fluorescence or dark coloring of semen; such material as urine, saliva, or feces is only dimly fluorescent. Suspicious material can be gently scraped off and preserved. If available, the assailant can be examined by way of blood test, saliva test, pubic hair examination, and others.

The examiner can personally observe a vaginal fluid preparation for motile sperm; vaginal washings can be obtained for acid phosphatase and ABH agglutinogen determination. Sperm can also be detected by a Pap smear. Pooled vaginal secretion can be aspirated from the vagina; a cotton-tipped applicator can also be used for this purpose. The collected material is placed on two slides, which are air dried and evaluated by appropriate forensic personnel for acid phosphatase and sperm. The aspirate can be put in a sterile tube or the swab put in 1 to 2 ml sterile saline. Vaginal washings can be obtained by irrigating the lower vagina with 10 to 20 ml sterile saline; the washings are readily collected.

Specimens collected for forensic examination are sealed and precisely labeled as to collection date and time, source of material, date of evaluation, name of patient, and name of examiner. This material is given to proper authorities after legal consent is obtained. Legal protocol should be used to avoid missing important details. Emergency departments are usually equipped with a "rape kit," which contains a legal manual outlining the protocol to be followed, important phone numbers, labels, seals, cultures, and other necessary material. This protocol can be modified according to the patient being examined, whether prepubescent or pubescent, male or female. The forensic examination is for identification of acid phosphatase or sperm, ABO sperm typing, blood typing (grouping), and others.

Legal evidence for recent coitus includes identification of motile sperm, 20+ King-Armstrong units/ml acid phosphatase from vaginal aspirates, and dried material with identified acid phosphatase. Motile sperm has been identified from the vagina up to 12 hours after rape and up to 6 hours from the rectum or mouth. Nonmotile sperm has been identified in the rectum or mouth up to 6 hours after rape, up to 4 days in the vagina, and up to 17 days in the cervix. Acid phosphatase can be seen up to 3 hours from the rectum or mouth, 48 hours from the vagina, and up to 3 hours from frozen, dried material.

TREATMENT

Treatment should include attention to injuries, wound care, and possible administration of tetanus toxoid. Attention to behavioral considerations, as discussed earlier, is important. Antibiotic prophylaxis may be indicated if the patient expresses considerable concern over the possibility of acquiring a sexually transmitted disease, if the circumstances indicate a high probability of infection, or if patient followup seems unlikely. Initial treatment should effectively cover *Neisseria gonorrhoeae, Chlamydia trachomatis,* and *Treponema pallidum.* The examiner can reculture for gonorrhea and *Chlamydia* shortly after treatment is completed. A followup syphilis serology test should be done in 4 to 6 weeks, especially if the initial test was positive or syphilis is suspected on clinical grounds.

Treatment for coverage of gonorrhea and *Chlamydia* can consist of a 7-day oral regimen of 500 mg tetracycline 4 times daily or 100 mg doxycycline twice a day (see Chapter 4). If tetracycline or doxycycline are not acceptable because of allergy, pregnancy, or other factors, 500 mg erythromycin 4 times daily for 7 days can also be prescribed. Children can be given erythromycin at a dose of 40 mg/kg/day, and children over age 8 can be given tetracycline at a dose of 50 mg/kg/day. Gonorrhea can also be treated with 3.0 g amoxicillin or 3.5 g ampicillin, each given orally with 1 g probenecid, which is also given orally in a single dose. Penicillinase-producing strains of gonorrhea are effectively treated with a number of antibiotics, including intramuscular administration of 2 g spectinomycin, 1 g cefotaxime, or 2 g cefoxitin, with 1 g probenecid orally or 125 to 250 mg ceftriaxone intramuscularly. The current drug of choice for gonorrhea is ceftriaxone. Current STD reality suggests that monitoring for AIDS may also be necessary (Chapter 4).

When evaluating an individual involved in a sexual assault, the possibility of pregnancy must always be considered. Until recently, if the individual was seen within 48 to 72 hours of the incident and the possibility of pregnancy existed, an accepted way to prevent the pregnancy was to give an oral dose of 25 mg diethylstilbestrol twice daily for 5 days. However, there is much concern about this drug's well-known effects on male and female offspring of treated mothers. Thus, current recommendations are to give 2 Ovral tablets orally and repeat in 12 hours if the patient presents within 72 hours of the assault. Ovral is an oral contraceptive that contains 0.05 mg ethinyl estradiol and 0.5 mg norgestrel. The side effects appear to be minimal (such as mild nausea), and this drug is effective at preventing pregnancy. The physician should be sure that the patient is not already pregnant, perhaps with a serum pregnancy test. A repeat pregnancy test is recommended if the patient remains amenorrheic 1 month after this treatment. The physician should obtain legal, informed consent before giving Ovral in this situation.

BIBLIOGRAPHY

Abrams ME, Shah RZ, Keenan-Allyn S: Sexual abuse in children and adolescents. A detection and management guide. The Female Patient 1988;13:17-33.
American College of Obstetricians and Gynecologists: Alleged Sexual Assault. ACOG Technical Bulletin No. 52, Nov 1978.
Backman A, ed: Child sexual abuse. SIECUS Rep 1984;13:1-30.
Blumberg ML: Sexual abuse of children: causes, diagnosis, and management. Pediatr Ann 1984;13(10):753-758.

Breen JL, Greenwald E, Gregori CA: The molested young patient: evaluation and therapy of alleged rape. Ped Clin North Am 1972;19(3):717-725.

Brookman RR: Special adolescent health issues—sexual assault. In: Hofmann AD, Greydanus DE, eds: Adolescent Medicine. 2nd ed. Norwalk, CT: Appleton & Lange, 1989:353-354.

Burgess AW, Clark ML, eds: Child Pornography and Sex Rings. Lexington, MA: Lexington Books, 1984.

Burgess AW, Holmstrom LL: Coping behavior of the rape victim. Am J Psychiatr 1976;133(4):413-418.

Burgess AW, Holmstrom LL: Rape trauma syndrome. Am J Psychiatr 1974;131(9):981-986.

Committee on Adolescence. Rape and the adolescent. Pediatrics 1983;72(5):738-740.

DeJong AR: Epidemiologic factors in sexual abuse of boys. Am J Dis Child 1982;136:990.

Deisher R, Remafedi G: Adolescent sexuality-sexual abuse and incest. In: Hofmann AD, Greydanus DE, eds: Adolescent Medicine. Norwalk, CT: Appleton-Lange, 1989:344-346.

Ellerstein NS, Canavan JW: Sexual abuse of boys. Am J Dis Child 1980;134:255.

Felice M, Grant J, Reynolds B, et al: Follow-up observations of adolescent rape victims. Clin Pediatr 1978;17(4):311-315.

Finkelhor D: Child Sexual Abuse: New Theory and Research. New York: Free Press, 1984.

Finkelhor D: Sexually Victimized Children. New York: Free Press, 1979.

Finkelhor D: What's wrong with sex between adults and children? Ethics and the problem of sexual abuse. Am J Orthopsychiatry 1979;49:692-697.

Florence R: The Best Kept Secret: Sexual Abuse of Children. Englewood Cliffs, NJ: Prentice-Hall, 1980.

Fox SS, Scheryl DJ: Crisis intervention with victims of rape. Soc Work 1972;17:37-42.

Fromuth ME: The long term psychological impact of childhood sexual abuse. Diss Abstracts Int 1984;44:2212.

Grant CA: Health assessment of the sexually victimized child. The Office Nurse 1988;1(2):21-24.

Greydanus DE: Depression in adolescence: a perspective. J Adolesc Health Care 1986;7(6):406-412.

Greydanus DE, Blum RW, eds: Sexual abuse in the adolescent. Semin Adolesc Med 1987;3:1-78.

Gross RJ, Doerr H, Caldirola D, et al: Borderline syndrome and incest in chronic pelvic pain patients. Intl J Psychiatr Med 1980;16(1):79-96.

Groth AN, Longo RE, McFadin JB: Undetected recidivism among rapists and child molesters. Crime Delinquency 1982;28:450-458.

Growth AN, Burgess AW, Holstrom LL: Rape, power, anger and sexuality. Am J Psychiatr 1977;134(11):1239-1243.

Hammerschlag MR, Cummings M, Doraiswamy B, et al: Nonspecific vaginitis following sexual abuse in children. Pediatrics 1985;75:1028-1031.

Hall ER: Abdolescents' perceptions of sexual assault. J Sex Educ Ther 1987;13(1):37-42.

Hayman CR, Lanza C: Sexual assault on women and girls. Am J Obstet Gynecol 1971;109:480-486.

Herjanic B, Wilbois RP: Sexual abuse of children. Detection and management. JAMA 1978;239(4):331-333.

Herman JL: Father-Daughter Incest. Cambridge, MA: Harvard University Press, 1981.

Hibbard RA, Orr DP: Incest and sexual abuse. Semin Adolesc Med 1985;1:153-164.

Hibbard RA, Brack CJ, Rauch S, et al: Abuse, feelings and health behaviors in a student population. AJDC 1988;142:326-330.

Hicks DJ: Rape: sexual assault. Am J Obstet Gynecol 1980;137(8):931-933.

Hofmann AD: Legal issues in adolescent medicine. In: Hofmann AD, Greydanus DE, eds: Adolescent Medicine. Norwalk, CT: Appleton-Lange, 1989:519-532.

Hunter DS, Kilstrom N, Loder F: Sexually abused children: identifying masked presentations in a medical setting. Child Abuse & Neglect 1985;9:17-25.

Jenny C: Adolescent risk-taking/sexual assault. Amer J Dis Child 1988;142(7):770-773.

Jenny C, Sutherland SE, Sandahl BB: Developmental approach to preventing sexual abuse of children. Pediatrics 1986;78:1034-1038.

Jones JG: Sexual abuse of children. Am J Dis Child 1982;136:142.

Kempe CH: Sexual abuse, another hidden pediatric problem. Pediatrics 1978;62:382.

Krebill J, Taylor J: A Teaching Guide to Preventing Adolescent Sexual Abuse. Santa Cruz, CA: Network Publications, 1988.

Krugman RD: Recognition of sexual abuse in children. Ped Review 1986;8:25.

Mann E: Self-reported stresses of adolescent rape victim. J Adolesc Health Care 1971;2:29.

Martin CA, Breen GR: Physician's management of the psychological aspects of rape. JAMA 1983;249(4):501-503.

Nadelson CC: Rapist and victim. N Engl J Med 1977;297(14):784-785.

Notman MT, Nadelson CC: The rape victim: psychodynamic considerations. Am J Psychiatr 1976;133(4):408-413.

Orr DP: Management of childhood sexual abuse. J Fam Pract 1980;11(7):1057-1064.

Orr DP, Prietto SV: Emergency management of sexually abused children. Am J Dis Child 1979;133:628-631.

Pascoe DJ, Duterte BO: The medical diagnosis of sexual abuse in the premenarchal child. Pediatr Ann 1981;10:187.

Riggs RS: Incest: the school's role. J School Health 1982;52(8):365-370.

Rimsza ME, Niggemann EH: Medical evaluation of sexually abused children: a review of 311 cases. Pediatrics 1982;69:8.

Rosenfeld AA: The clinical management of incest and sexual abuse of children. JAMA 1979;242(16):1761-1764.

Russel DEH: Child abuse. Intl J Child Abuse Neglect 1983;7(2):5.

Sarles RM: Sexual abuse in the adolescent. In: Moss AJ, ed: Pediatric Update. New York: Elsevier, 1971:73.

Sarles RM: Sexual abuse and rape. Pediatr Rev 1982;4:93.

Schaefer JL, Sullivan RA, Goldstein FL: Counseling sexual abuse victims. Am Fam Phys 1978;18:85-91.

Sgroi SM: Handbook of Clinical Intervention in Child Sexual Abuse. Lexington, MA: Lexington Books, 1982.

Shen JTY: Sexual abuse of adolescents. Postgrad Med 1982;71(6):213-218.

Silbert MH, Pines AM: Sexual child abuse as an antecedent to prostitution. Child Abuse Negl 1981;5:407-411.

Solola A, Scott C, Severs H, et al: Rape: management in a noninstitutional setting. Obstet Gynecol 1983;61(3):373-378.

Spencer MJ, Dunklee P: Sexual abuse of boys. Pediatrics 1986;78:133.

Strickland S et al: Atlas of sex abuse findings. Chicago: Yearbook, 1989.

Summit R, Kryso J: Sexual abuse of children: a clinical spectrum. Am J Orthopsychiatr 1978;48:237-251.

Tilelli JA, Turek D, Jaffe AC: Sexual abuse of children. Clinical findings, implications for management. N Engl J Med 1980;302(6):319-323.

Werthheimer AJ: Examining the rape victim. Postgrad Med 1982;71(3):173-180.

Weinberg S: Incest Behavior. New York: Citadel, 1963.

White ST, Loda FA, Ingram DL, et al: Sexually transmitted diseases in sexually abused children. Pediatrics 1983;72:16-21.

Wild NJ: Prevalence of child sex rings. Pediatrics 1989;83:553-558.

Woodling BA, Hegar A: The use of the colpolscope in the diagnosis of sexual abuse in the pediatric age group. Child Abuse Negl 1986;10:111-114.

Woodling BA, Evans JR, Bradbury MD: Sexual assault: rape and molestation. Clin Obstet Gynecol 1977;20(3):509-530.

10

Sexuality Education

Sexuality education is the knowledge that we are all sexual human beings, that our sexuality is part of our lives and can be an enhancement and enrichment of our total personality.

Mary Calderone

DEFINITION

Sexuality education, also referred to as family life education in current terminology, is a controversial topic. As noted in other parts of this book, however, sexuality is an important part of adolescent development, and lack of knowledge in this critical area can lead to serious problems, such as adolescent pregnancy and sexually transmitted diseases, to name a few. Human sexuality is a critical aspect of our lives as human beings, and when we fail to include it in the education of our children, we do so at their peril. As Reiss notes, "Human sexuality consists of those shared patterns of belief and behavior that directly or indirectly relate to erotic stimulation." Jorgenson notes that "sexuality is the total complement of an individual's attitudes, cognitives (fantasies, dreams, thoughts, beliefs, perceptions), experiences and behaviors which could result in any type of erotic stimulation" (Greydanus, 1982).

It is difficult for adults to accept the necessity for sexuality education, particularly when they have not come to terms with their own sexuality. It is also difficult because our understanding of human sexuality remains incomplete. We know that humans seek to express their sexuality from birth throughout all stages of life. The need to receive and extend love from and to others is a universal phenomenon of human beings. For each of us, the earliest erogenous zone is the skin. This complex organ is an important part of early mother-infant bonding or attachment. The importance of the genitals in the complex development of normal sexuality issues begins early. Erection occurs in utero and throughout the male's life. In female infants, vaginal lubrication has been noted at birth, and a neurophysiologic response of orgasm can be noted long before puberty.

Childhood is full of experiences that shape the eventual adult's view of human sexuality. Sexuality is more mental than physical for both children and adults. Children have no natural sense of obscenity or shame with sexual matters—such notions are taught to them by adults. Children are sensitive and quick to understand the adult's own difficulty with sexuality. Yet children are very curious: they innocently discover genital self-pleasuring and have a natural curiosity about the opposite sex. Children whose sexual expressions are generally restricted and who are taught negative aspects of human sexuality are more apt to become addicted to pornography in later adult life. Countries such as Sweden and The Netherlands, which promote open education about sexuality to children, have much lower rates of pedophilia, pornography, child sexual abuse, and teenage pregnancy than the United States.

Borneman, an Austrian researcher, has published extensively on new concepts of childhood sexuality. His current publications are based on 30 years of research interviewing over 4000 children and adolescents. Freud alerted individuals to the importance of sexuality in the development of childhood and adult psychopathology, and his psychosocial stages of childhood have given us a framework of understanding. Kinsey's reports on male and female adult sexuality stunned the American population in the late 1940s and early 1950s; however, they alerted us to the complicated sexual orientation that adults have developed.* Masters and Johnson made the first attempts at accurately measuring and studying human sexual activity. Borneman's research is also a milestone, as it expands our understanding of a poorly studied subject—childhood sexuality. His research confirms the richness and complexity of childhood sexuality as it leads to adolescent and adult sexuality. It notes that children have sexual stages corresponding to Freud's psychosexual stages, with a delay of about 2 years. Children have many hidden riddles and stories, essentially unknown to adults, that reflect the oral, anal, and phallic-oedipal phases. When confronted by adults who discourage sexuality expression, children do not reveal these sexual stories and riddles.

Borneman's research identifies two periods of "traumatic sexual repression." The first occurs in the first year of life and was termed by Freud as "infantile amnesia." It causes a block of memories regarding various sexual activities (and other memories as well) prior to the third year of life. Borneman notes that "pubertal amnesia" occurs in adolescence and reduces the memory of prepubertal sexual activities. Although Borneman's research must be studied and evaluated by other researchers, this work joins that of others in concluding that the emerging sexuality of the child and the adolescent represents an important search for identity. Failure of normal development of sexuality leads to numerous difficulties in adulthood. Thus, educating our children regarding their human sexuality is an important task, despite our current limited knowledge.

SUPPORT FOR SEXUALITY EDUCATION

Numerous studies confirm that the majority of the American population favors some type of sexuality education for their children and teenagers. According to several surveys by Davis and Smith, 56% of parents were in favor of sexuality education in 1970; 72% were in favor in 1977; and 82% were in favor in 1980. Although parents want such education for their children, they are usually reluctant to provide it. According to Roberts and Holt's study, less than 15% of mothers discussed the subject of coitus

* The Kinsey Scale of Sexual Orientation is a 7-point scale using 0 as fully heterosexual and 6 as fully homosexual (see Appendix F). The development of a homosexual identity is reviewed in Appendix G.

with their daughters and less than 8% discussed sexually transmitted diseases. Corresponding figures for fathers relating this information to their sons were less than 13% and 6%. Yet teenagers want such information. A poll in 1982 at the annual conference of the National Association of Student Councils noted that 96% (568 to 21) favored sex education, while 94% (50 to 3) of the faculty sponsors were in agreement. According to Dickman, although most surveys note that over 80% of the population favor such education, less than 10% of students currently receive comprehensive sex education.

Table 10-1 lists various groups who openly favor sex education for students. In July 1980, the American Medical Association House of Delegates adopted the following resolution:

RESOLVED, That the American Medical Association recognizes that the primary responsibility for family life education is in the home and additionally supports the concept of a complementary family life and sex education in the schools at all levels, at local option and direction; such programs should (1) be part of an overall health education program, (2) be presented in a manner commensurate with the maturation level of the students, (3) have professionally developed curricula, (4) include ample involvement of parents and other concerned members of the community, and (5) utilize classroom teachers and other professionals who have shown an aptitude for working with young people and who have received special training.

The Sex Information and Education Council of the United States (SIECUS) also supports this position. In a statement approved by the SIECUS Board of Directors on November 13, 1981, the following statement was issued:

SIECUS supports sexuality education in the public schools. Programs conducted by specially trained educators add an important dimension to the sexuality education given children by their families and religious and community groups. Such programs must be carefully formulated by each community in order to respect the diversity of values and beliefs represented in a public school classroom. SIECUS recommends that school personnel, in consultation with community representatives including parents, clergy, and health care professionals plan

Table 10-1. Organizations Officially Favoring Sex Education for Children and Teenagers.

National Council of Churches
Synagogue Council of America
American Academy of Pediatrics
American Medical Association
Society for Adolescent Medicine
American Association of School Administrators
American College of Obstetrics and Gynecology
American Federation of Teachers
American Library Association
American Public Health Association
Girls Clubs of America
National Association of State Boards of Education
National Council of Family Relations
National Education Association
National School Board Association
National Urban League
White House Council on Families

and implement public school sexuality education programs with curricula and resources appropriate to the ages of the students.

Also, the Society for Adolescent Medicine adopted this position in 1972:

The Society for Adolescent Medicine strongly endorses the position that States mandate the teaching of Health and Sex Education from kindergarten through 12th grade, as part of the overall curriculum in schools. Critical to the effectiveness of such programs is the proper training of personnel involved in teaching them.

The growing trend is to include some information on contraception and sexually transmitted diseases in school, but such information is often given when the students are well into puberty, not as part of a thorough family life education curriculum encompassing kindergarten through grade 12. Many studies note the increased adolescent sexual activity of current youth but also their limited knowledge in this area. The 1982 National Survey of Family Growth noted that 68% of 15- to 19-year-old females received formal instruction on pregnancy and birth control. However, this is not enough for today's children. They simply need more information.

All parts of America are affected by the problem of youth displaying increased sexual activity with limited knowledge of the consequences. Caplow et al. presented a detailed sociologic study of sexuality changes in a small Minnesota town with a population of 20,000 during the first part of the survey (1924-1937) and 60,000 during the second part (1976-1978). This study noted that teenagers evaluated during the second part of the survey were more sexually active at earlier ages, had greater access to birth control, and received limited sexuality education. Other studies noted that 80% of American school districts in large cities offer some sexuality education and that 67 to 85% of teenagers receive limited instruction in this area. This limited family life education must be expanded to a comprehensive sexuality education program covering kindergarten through grade 12, which would complement instruction the child receives in the home.

Sexuality education can be taught in the home and school; physicians can make their own contributions toward improving the knowledge base of their adolescent patients. As noted by Vincent:

The theoretical position that a physician cannot or should not engage in any (marriage or) sexual counseling becomes meaningless when the patients expect this role of their physician and when their illnesses have sexual (and marital) implications if not origins. The majority of physicians literally have no choice; even to do and say nothing in response to the patient's questions and/or presentation of symptoms in the sexual and marital areas is, by default, one form of counseling.

IMPACT OF SEXUALITY EDUCATION

It is difficult to measure the impact of sexuality education, since few individuals are exposed to comprehensive programs. The reviews of Dickman, Marsiglio and Mott, Dawson, Kirby, and others conclude that sexuality education, as currently taught in American school systems, has little if any effect on most teenagers when compared with the effects of parents, peers, and the media. In some situations, sexuality education can increase the student's knowledge of sexuality, increase the student's tolerance for the views of others, and lead to some decrease in teenage pregnancy as well as sexually transmitted diseases. However, these studies note that sexuality education does not lead to significant changes in the behavior or morality of the student.

Current sexuality education efforts seek to reduce the sexually transmitted disease and pregnancy rates among American teenagers. Zabin et al. showed that a school sexuality education program in Baltimore, Maryland, which was linked to specific contraceptive counseling with referral to family planning clinics near the schools, could result in youth who delay sexarche, increase their use of contraceptives, and reduce the number of adolescent pregnancies. Edwards noted that a school-based health clinic in St. Paul, Minnesota, which provides information on contraception and refers students to nearby family planning clinics, has dramatically reduced adolescent pregnancy (see Chapter 8).

The conclusions of Kirby et al., based on a government-funded research study of ten school sexuality education programs in America, were that the majority had no real impact on prevention of teenage pregnancy. The study noted that significant attitude and behavioral changes were noted in teenagers only when the community made a strong commitment in this regard. In these situations, the parents received this education along with their children, and the sexuality program in the school system was combined with a health clinic promoting contraception when abstinence was not chosen. Brown reported on a sexuality education program in St. Joseph, Missouri, that produced significant changes in student sexual behavior. The course was geared to four groups: mothers with prepubertal daughters (9 to 12 years), mothers with adolescent daughters (13 to 16 years), fathers with prepubertal sons (9 to 12 years), and fathers with pubertal sons (13 to 16 years). Unfortunately, as noted by Marsiglio and Mott, sexuality education is not given early enough in most communities to affect teenagers' decisions about coitus and the use of birth control.

Forcing sexuality education by way of state laws, without appropriate education of the general population regarding the necessity of such education, is not the answer, as noted in various states where such laws have been passed. Encouraged by a law mandating family life education in schools, the New Jersey Department of Education, in 1981, wrote: "Whether or not family life information is given or withheld from children, their experience of life itself awakens their sexuality at an early age. . . . Their world is full of interesting events that grow out of the fact that the human race is made of two sexes. . . . This reality can be ignored only at the risk of [their receiving] distorted information and ideas about sexuality, self and family living." Such a position is consistent with Mary Calderone's 1967 comments about sexuality education in schools: "Of all the institutions of society, the schools are the only ones that have the know-how and the organization and the personnel. Right now it is being romantic and totally unrealistic to say that the child should get all of their [sic] education at home." Unfortunately, passing a law requiring sexuality education without showing parents and school administrators the need for such education will doom the law to minimal compliance by the schools, resulting in considerable controversy and ineffective family life education. Muraskin has reviewed such a situation in New Jersey.

Unfortunately, resistance to family life education remains and must be dealt with by educating the general public as to the necessity of such education. Resistance is found at all levels—parents, religious leaders, teachers, and others. A major misperception continues among many individuals that teaching our children about their sexuality will have only negative effects. This misperception continues despite previously cited literature indicating that the opposite is true. Unfortunately, the vocal wishes of a minority of the population have thwarted the wishes of the majority. Some continue to believe, as noted in the June 1986 Schlafly report, that sex education and available contraception results in "incurable VD, emotional trauma, and a forfeiture of opportunities for a lifetime marriage to a faithful spouse and for career and economic advancement." Thus the debate continues, resulting in ineffective family life education for our teenagers who continue to have unacceptably high rates of pregnancy and sexually transmitted disease.

CONTENT OF SEXUALITY EDUCATION

When a community does decide to provide comprehensive family life education in its school system, it then must wrestle with the complex task of deciding what to teach. First it must teach the parents to be aware of the importance of the type of education children receive before formal education even begins. As Mary Calderone notes: "Whatever happens, it is clear that by the time the child arrives at school, it has already received, for good or ill, the most profound as well as the most unchangeable sexuality education it will ever receive in its life." As noted by Dickman, the contents of the sexuality education course can be worked out by various members of the community, such as parents, teachers, health care professionals, clergy, and others. Many books and texts are available to help with this task (see appendix). Since McCary and McCary's first college textbook on human sexuality was first published in 1967, many such texts have been written, as reviewed by Calderwood and Calderwood. A list of various sexuality education materials can be obtained by contacting SIECUS, 32 Washington Place, New York, NY 10003.

Sexuality education covers a wide variety of topics, including anatomy and physiology of sexuality, puberty, common aspects of sexuality (such as masturbation, petting, ejaculation, orgasm, and others), communication abilities between sexes, understanding as well as respecting differences in individuals' thoughts (as well as feelings and behaviors), ovulation, coitus, marriage, contraception, pregnancy, abortion, homosexuality, adoption, sexually transmitted diseases, sexual abuse, rape, incest, sexual dysfunction, and other important aspects of human sexuality. The important and potentially positive nature of human sexuality must be stressed, while emphasis can be placed on intimacy and love. Abstinence can be stressed, as can learning to avoid sexual exploitation by others. Gordon stressed teaching youth the five essential freedoms (Table 10-2). Family life education involves teaching both respect for others and sexual responsibility. Such education emphasizes the following three aspects of learning:

1. *Cognitive* (including the basic information of human sexuality)
2. *Affective* (including understanding of involved feelings, attitudes, and values)
3. *Skills* (including decision-making and communication ability)

As noted by Brick, family life education should offer an interdisciplinary model of human sexuality involving biologic, psychologic, sociologic, and ethnic dimensions. Youth must learn the consequences of various sexual behaviors and where to get more information.

Schools, with the help of various community individuals, can develop programs targeted at different developmental levels: elementary school, junior high, and senior high. Those planning such courses should remember that there are different developmental levels in adolescents: early, middle, and late (see Chapter 1). As noted by Uslander et al., even children in the first, second, and third grades can benefit from introductory family life education; they easily accept it, learn increased respect for each other, and learn appropriate words for human sexuality. As reviewed by Brick, the questions asked by children become more complex as they get older. In first grade, children wonder why people get married or how a baby comes out. Such students can benefit from reading books geared to their level, such as *Did the Sun Shine Before You Were Born?* by Gordon and Gordon. By third grade, students wonder why men can't have babies and how babies grow. In the fourth grade, they ask why their parents argue with them and why boys don't know about girls' feelings. By the fifth and sixth grades, they wonder when it is too young to have sex, why some adults are gay, why some babies are born premature, and what the white material is that comes from one's penis. The students, as they mature, reveal increased self-consciousness, reasoning ability, and concern for others.

Table 10-2. Five Essential Sexual Freedoms (Gordon, 1973).

1. No one has the right to exploit another person's body commercially or sexually.
2. No one has the right to bring an unwanted child into the world.
3. No one has the right to spread VD.
4. No one has the right to exploit children sexually or take advantage of a mentally or physically handicapped individual.
5. No one has the right to impose his sexuality preferences, including when and with whom to have sex. Sexual choice must be voluntary.

Table 10-3. Family Life Education in Elementary Schools (Paramus, NJ Public Schools, 1984).

Kindergarten:	Terminology of external genitalia
	Instruction that some body parts are "private"
Second Grade:	Variation of normal bodies
	Basic facts of sexual development
Fourth Grade:	Events of puberty
	Discussion of different growth rates
	Reproduction
Sixth Grade:	Coitus
	Masturbation
	Pregnancy control

Table 10-3 outlines an approach to family life education in elementary schools. A sensitive, well-trained teacher is, of course, important to the success of this program. Teachers can present many negative or positive messages about human sexuality by providing answers to certain questions and selecting certain books. As noted by Kirby, the best sex education program is *holistic* (covering kindergarten through grade 12), teaches a *preventive*-type attitude, espouses a *developmental* approach (validating human sexuality through the lifespan), encourages an *anthropologic* approach (emphasizing the varieties of human sexuality in different individuals), and incorporates a *sociologic* approach (stimulating the students to evaluate their own enrichment).

Clinicians who care for youth can do much in their own communities to encourage an extensive family life education program to help patients learn important aspects of human sexuality. Clinicians can also encourage parents to provide needed sexuality education to their children. Parents can be shown that teaching their children will not harm their children's peers who may not be so educated. As noted by Lief, "sex education begins on the day that the child is born." If we agree that human sexuality is a critical component of life, then surely our children deserve as thorough an education in this important topic as we can provide.

BIBLIOGRAPHY

American Association of Sex Educators, Counselors and Therapists. The Professional Training and Preparation of Sex Educators. Washington, D.C., 1972.

American School Health Association. Growth Patterns and Sex Education: A Suggested Program Kindergarten through Grade 12. Kent, OH, 1978.

An Analysis of the U.S. Sex Education Programs and Evaluation Methods. Springfield, VA, National Technical Information Service, US Dept. of Commerce, 1979.

Borneman E: Progress in empirical research on children's sexuality. SIECUS Rep 1983;12(2):1-6.

Brick P: Sexuality education in the elementary school. SIECUS Rep 1985;13(3):1-4.

Brick P: Adolescence in perspective: a life span approach to sexuality education. Semin Adolesc Med 1985;1(2):139-144.

Bowlby J: Attachment and Loss. New York: Basic Books, 1969.

Brookman RR: Adolescent sexuality and related health problems. In: Hofmann AD, Greydanus DE: Adolescent Medicine. Menlo Park, CA: Addison-Wesley, 1983:243-245.

Brown J: Sexuality Education: A Curriculum for Parent/Child Programs. Santa Cruz, CA: Network, 1984.

Brown L, ed: Sex Education in the Eighties: The Challenge of Healthy Sexual Evaluation. New York: Plenum, 1981.

Burt JI, Meeks LB: Education for Sexuality: Concepts and Programs for Teaching. Philadelphia: W.B. Saunders, 1975.

Byler R, Lewis G, Totman R: Teach Us What We Want to Know. New York: Mental Health Materials Center, 1969.

Calderone MS, Johnson EW: The Family Book about Sexuality. New York: Harper and Row, 1981.

Calderone MS: Sexuality: a continuum from early childhood through adolescence. In: Blum R, ed: Adolescent Health Care, Clinical Issues. New York: Academic, 1982:157-158.

Calderone MS, Ramsey J: Talking with Your Child About Sex. New York: Random House, 1982.

Calderwood DD, Calderwood M: Human sexuality college textbooks: an experiment in evaluation. SIECUS Rep 1982;10(4):1-12.

Campbell PJ: Sex Education Books for Young Adults, 1892-1979. New York: R.R. Bowker, 1979.

Caplow T, Bahr H, Chadwick B: Middletown Families. Minneapolis: University of Minnesota Press,1982.

Carton J, Carton J: Evaluation of a sex education program for children and their parents. Fam Coordinator 1971;20:4.

Clauat SS: Resistance to sex education. J Sex Educ and Therapy 1977;3(1):28-32.

Cook A, Kirby D, Wilson P, et al: Sexuality Education: A Guide to Developing and Implementing Programs. Santa Cruz, CA: Network, 1984.

Crosbie JF: The effect of family life education on the values and attitudes of adolescents. Fam Coordinator 1971;20:2.

Daniel RS: Human Sexuality: Methods and Materials for the Education, Family Life and Health Professionals. Vol I: An Annotated Guide to the Audiovisuals. Brea, CA: Heuristicus Pub. Co., 1979.

Davis JA, Smith AW: General Social Surveys, 1972-1984: Cumulative Code Book. Chicago: National Opinion Research Center, 1984.

Dawson DA: The effects of sex education on adolescent behavior. Fam Plann Perspect 1986;18(4):162-170.

Deisher RW, Remafedi G: Adolescent sexuality. In: Hofmann AD, Greydanus DE, eds: Adolescent Medicine. Norwalk, CT: Appleton & Lange, 1989:337-346.

Dickman IR: Winning the Battle for Sex Education. New York: SIECUS, 1982.

Edwards LE: Adolescent pregnancy prevention programs in high school clinics. In: Furstenberg FF, Lincoln R, Menken J, eds: Teenage Sexuality, Pregnancy and Childbearing. Philadelphia: University of Pennsylvania Press, 1981.

Erikson EH: Childhood and Society. New York: W.W. Norton, 1950.

Faust B: Women, Sex and Pornography: A Controversial Study. New York: MacMillan, 1986.

Fine M: Sexuality, schooling and adolescent females: the missing discourse of desire. Harvard Educational Review 1988;58(1):29-53.

Film: Seasons of Sexuality and Human Growth III. Highland Park, IL: Human Relations Media, 1983.

Filmstrip: Human Sexuality: The Lifelong Experience. Pleasantville, NY: Human Relations Media, 1984.

Filmstrip: Human Sexuality and the Life Cycle. Perennial Education, Inc., 1983.

Finkelhor D: Child Sexual Abuse: New Theory and Research. New York: Free Press, 1984.

Forrest JD, Silverman J: What public school teachers teach about preventing pregnancy, AIDS and sexually transmitted diseases. Fam Plann Perspect 1989;21:65-72.

Gallup G: Gallup Youth Survey. New York: Associated Press, 1980.

Gebhard PH, Johnson AB: The Kinsey Data: Marginal Tabulation of the 1938-1963 Interviews Conducted by the Institute for Sex Research. Philadelphia: W.B. Saunders, 1979.

Goldman R, Goldman J: Children's Sexual Thinking. Boston: Routledge and Kegan Paul, 1982.

Gordon S: The Sexual Adolescent. North Scituate, MA: Durbury Press, 1972.

Gordon S, Gordon J: Did the Sun Shine Before You Were Born? Fayetteville, NY: ED-U Press,1977.

Greydanus DE: Adolescent sexuality: an overview and perspective for the 1980s. Pediatr Ann 1982;11(9):714-726.

Haffner DW: The AIDS epidemic: implications for the sexuality education of our youth. Siecus Rep 1988;16(6):1-5.

Haffner DW: AIDS and adolescents: school health education must begin now. J. Sch. Health; 1988:58(4):154-155.

Hatcher RA, et al: Contraceptive Technology 1988-1989. New York: Inrvington Publishing, Inc., 1988.

Herold ES, Benson RM: Problem of teaching sex education. Fam Coordinator 1979;28(2):199-204.

Homel SR, ed: Symposium on the physician and sex education. Pediatr Clin North Am 1969;16(2):237-528.

Jones EF, et al: Teenage Pregnancy in Industrialized Countries. New Haven, CT: Yale University Press, 1986.

Kappelman MM: The pediatrician as physician, human sexuality educator and counselor of young people and parents. SIECUS Rep 17(3):1-8, 1989.

Kaufman-Dressler B, Hallingby L: Sexuality education pamphlets: a selected annotated bibliography of resources for sale. SIECUS 1986;15(2):13-20.

Kelander HF: Sex Education in the Schools. New York: MacMillan, 1970.

Kenney AM, Guardado S, Brown J: Sex education and AIDS education in the schools: what states and large school districts are doing. Fam Plann Perspect 1989;21:56-64.

Kinsey AC, Gebbard PH: Sexual Behavior in the Human Female. Philadelphia: W.B. Saunders, 1953.

Kirby D, Alter J, Scales P: An Analysis of U.S. Sex Education Programs and Evaluation Methods. Atlanta: Public Health Service, 1979, vol 2.

Kirby D: Sexuality Education: A Handbook for Evaluating Programs. Santa Cruz, CA: Network, 1984.

Levitan J: Evaluation of family living sex education programs. SIECUS Rep 1986;15(2):7-9.

Lief HI: Preparing the physician to become a sex counselor and educator. Pediatr Clin North Am 1969;16(2):447-458.

Madaras, L. Lynda Maradas talks to teens about AIDS: an essential guide for parents, teachers, and young people. New York: Newmarket Press; 1988; ISBN: 1-55704-010-9.

Marsiglio W, Mott FL: The impact of sex education on sexual activity, contraceptive use and premarital pregnancy among American teenagers. Fam Plann Perspect 1986;18(4):151-162.

Manley J: Teacher selection for sex education. SIECUS Rep 1986;15(2):10-11.

Masters WH, Johnson VE, Kolodney RC: Human Sexuality. Boston, MA: Little, Brown, 1982.

McCaffree K: Sex education curricula: selection for elementary and secondary school students. SIECUS Rep 1986;15(2):4-6.

McCary JL, McCary SP: Human Sexuality, ed 4. Florence, KY: Wadsworth, 1982.

Miller L, Downer A. AIDS: what you and your friends need to know—a lesson plan for adolescents. J. Sch. Health; 1988;58(4):137-141.

Money J, Musaph H, eds: Handbook of Sexology. New York: Excerpta Media/Elsevier North Holland, 1977.

Montagu A: Touching: The Human Significance of the Skin. New York: Columbia University Press, 1971.

Muraskin LD: Sex education mandates: are they the answer? Fam Plann Perspect 1986;18(4):171-174.

National Association of Student Councils: Proceedings from Annual Conference. Reno, NV, 1982.

National Council of Churches, Synagogue Council of America, U.S. Catholic Conference: Interfaith Statement on Sex Education. New York, National Council of Churches, 1968.

New Jersey Department of Education: Family Life Education: Curricula Guidelines. Trenton: New Jersey Department of Education, 1981.

Paramus Public Schools: Human Reproduction and Sexuality Curriculum: Scope and Sequence Chart, Grades K-8. Paramus, NJ: Paramus Public Schools, 1984.

Parcel G, Gordon S, eds: Sex education in the public schools: A symposium. J. School Health March 1981.

Peterson L: The issue and controversy surrounding adolescent sexuality and abstinence. SIECUS Rep 1988;17(1):1-8.

Purdy C, Kendziorski S: Understanding Your Sexuality. Glenview, IL: Scott, Foreman, 1980.

Remafedi GJ, ed: Symposium on adolescent homosexuality. J Adol Health Care 1988;9(2):93-143.

Roberts ET, ed: Childhood Sexual Learning: The Unwritten Curriculum. Cambridge, MA: Ballinger, 1980.

Roberts J, Holt A: Parent-child communication about sexuality. SIECUS Rep 1980;8:1-10.

Rush F: The Best Kept Secret: Sexual Abuse of Children. Englewood Cliffs, NJ: Prentice-Hall, 1980.

Ryan IJ, Dunn PC: Sex education from perspective teachers' view pose a dilemma. J Sch Health 1979;49(1):573-575.

Scales P: How we guarantee the ineffectiveness of sex education. SIECUS Rep 1978;6:4.

Schlafly P: School-based clinics v. sex respect. The Phyllis Schlafly Report 1986;19(11):1-3.

Selverstone R: Sex education and the adolescent: perspectives from a sex educator. Semin Adolesc Med 1985;1(2):145-151.

Semmens JP, Semmens JH: Sex education of the adolescent female. Pediatr Clin North Am 1972;19(3):765-778.

Sex Education for Adolescents: A Bibliography of Low-Cost Materials (1980). American Library Association, Order Department, 50 East Huron Street, Chicago, IL, 60611.

Sgroi SM: Handbook of Clinical Intervention in Child Sexual Abuse. Lexington, MA: Lexington Book, 1984.

Silcox JA: Sex education—the social impact. In: Barwin BN, Belisle S, eds: Adolescent Gynecology and Sexuality. New York: Masson, 1982.

Stout JW, Rivara FP: Schools and sex education: does it work? Pediatrics 1989;83:375-379.

The fear of AIDS: guidelines to the counseling and HTLV-III Antibody screening of adolescents. J Adol Health Care 1988;9(1):84-86.

Uslander A, Weiss C: Dealing with questions about sex. Belmont, CA: Pitman Learning, 1975.

Uslander A, et al: Their Universe; The story of a Unique Education Program. New York: Delacorte, 1973.

Vincent CE, ed: Human Sexuality in Medical Education and Practice. Springfield, IL: Charles C. Thomas, 1969.

Wagman E, Cooper L: Family Life Education-Teacher Training Manual. Santa Cruz, CA: Network, 1981.

Westheimer R, Lieberman L: Sex and Morality: Who Is Teaching Our Sex Standards? New York: Harcourt Brace Jovanovich, 1988.

Wilson SN, Sanderson CA: The sex respect curriculum: is "just say no" effective? SIECUS Rep 1988;17(1):10-11.

Winship B: Masculinity and Femininity. Boston, MA: Houghton Mifflin, 1987.

Winship E, Caparulo F, Harlan VK: Human Sexuality. Boston, Mass: Houghton Mifflin Co., 1988. (Student's edition, 158 pages; teacher's edition.)

Wolbert BA, Clark ML, eds: Child Pornography and Sex Rings. Lexington, MA: Lexington Books, 1984.

Yates W: The church and its holistic paradigm of sexuality. SIECUS Rep 1988;16:1-5.

Zabin LS, Hirsch MB, Smith EA, et al: Evaluation of a pregnancy prevention program for urban teenagers. Fam Plann Perspect 1986;18:19.

11

*Adolescent Nutrition and Substance Abuse Disorders**

Although the primary focus of this book is adolescent sexuality and gynecology, youth often present with nutritional and substance abuse disorders that primary care physicians must address. This chapter includes practical, up-to-date descriptions of appropriate nutritional requirements for adolescents, including the requirements of teenage athletes, weight loss, obesity, hyperlipidemia, anorexia nervosa and bulimia, and other disorders. Furthermore, in this era of drug use and abuse among adolescents, health care providers must understand substance epidemiology, etiology, symptomatology, types, and general treatment protocols, which are also presented. This chapter, of course, cannot cover all aspects of nutrition and substance abuse confronting adolescents; consequently, the chapter concludes with a detailed list of references to augment the material presented.

NUTRITION

The nutritional needs of each adolescent can vary, depending on his or her growth phase and specific activity level. In general, puberty adds the final 50% of a person's weight and 15% of the final height. Males tend to develop increased muscle mass but decreased body fat. Females tend to develop increased muscle mass but increased body fat as well. Females gain twice as much adipose tissue but two thirds the lean muscle mass as males. Energy is needed by these youth to allow such growth and to maintain body function.

The health care professional can be of considerable help to the adolescent by providing professional advice about sound nutrition, whether in regard to maintaining a specific weight or in changing weight (losing or gaining). It is important to stress that a well-balanced diet administered over regular eating periods provides nearly all the essential nutrients for active, growing youth. A basic plan, as recommended by professional nutritionists, provides youth with 12 basic servings from the 4 main food groups: fruit and vegetables, grain or cereal, protein, and dairy. A basic diet of 1500 kilocalories (K.Cal) can be devised to include 2 servings from the protein and dairy groups with 4 servings from the others. Various supplemental foods can be added to this basic plan for the additional

---

* Adapted from Greydanus DE: Adolescence: A Continuum: From Childhood to Adulthood. 2nd ed. Des Moines, IA: Iowa Department of Public Health, 1988.

calories needed by the active, growing teenager. In general, 2800 to 3000 K.Cal are needed by male youth and 2100 to 2400 K.Cal are needed by female youth each day. Specific and often expensive supplementation with proteins, vitamins, or minerals is unnecessary. Pregnant youth need 2400 K.Cal during the first trimester and about 2700 K.Cal per day for the rest of the pregnancy.

Table 11-1 reviews the recommended daily dietary allowances (RDA) for youth, as developed by the Food and Nutritional Board from the National Academy of Sciences. These RDAs do not measure individual nutritional status, but serve as general, chronologically oriented indicators which, if followed, can preclude severe nutritional deficiencies with some probability.

As noted, nearly all of these nutrients can be found in a well-balanced diet. Protein can be found in meat (beef, lamb, pork, veal), poultry, fish, dairy products, and eggs. Those on a vegetarian diet get their protein from beans, cereal and grains, nuts, and various seeds. Iron can be found in lean meats, eggs, dried beans, peas, green leafy vegetables, dried fruits, nuts, fortified wheat products and whole grain products. Calcium is found in dairy products, milk, and dark green leafy vegetables, as well as in some nuts and legumes. Zinc is found in various meats, nuts, cheese, wheat germ, and beans. Table 11-2 identifies some vitamin sources.

A sound diet seeks to limit the fat intake to 30% of calories, with less than one third coming from saturated fats, one third from monosaturated fats, and one third from polyunsaturated fats. The protein content should be limited to 15% of calories; carbohydrates should constitute 55% of the caloric intake. Cholesterol should be limited to under 100 mg per 1000 K.Cal. The use of added salt should be limited, as should the use of highly salted, processed foods. Lean meats and fish are recommended over high-fat lunch meats and hamburgers. Foods should be baked or broiled, and vegetables should be fresh and steamed without salt or butter added. Two-percent-fat milk can be substituted for whole milk. Fiber can be increased by using bran cereal. Vegetable oils can be added to the food intake as well.

Unfortunately, many teenagers will not eat a sound diet and do develop nutritional deficiencies, including those of calcium, iron, vitamin A, vitamin B, vitamin C, folacin, zinc, and others. Over half of teenagers eat no breakfast, and few eat three "traditional" meals each day. Many teenagers are snackers, choosing the most available foods. Those with fewer than three daily meals generally have poorer diets than the frequent snackers. The value of foods from the fast-food chains (a favorite of many if not most teenagers) remains controversial. Although the protein content is adequate, much of the food is too high in calories, too high in sodium content, and too low in fiber. Also, this food is often too high in fat because of the usual process of frying and the high cooking temperatures, which increases the saturation of frying oils or fats.

Some female adolescents are at particular risk for deficiencies of iron, vitamin B_1 (thiamine), and vitamin B_2 (riboflavin). Females using an intra-

Table 11-1. Food and Nutrition Board, National Academy of Sciences—National Research Council, Recommended Daily Dietary Allowances (Revised 1980).

	Age (years)	Energy (K. Cal)	Protein (g)	Water-Soluble Vitamins				
				Ascorbic acid (mg)	Thiamine (mg)	Ribo-flavin (mg)	Niacin (mg)	Vitamin (mg)
Males	11–14	2800	45	50	1.4	1.6	18	1.8
	15–18	3000	56	60	1.4	1.7	18	2.0
Females	11–14	2400	46	50	1.1	1.3	15	1.8
	15–18	2100	46	60	1.1	1.3	14	2.0
Pregnant		+300	+30	+20	+0.4	+0.3	+2	+0.6
Lactating		+500	+20	+40	+0.5	+0.5	+5	+0.6

	Age (years)	Fat-Soluble Vitamins			Minerals				
		Vitamin A activity (U)	Vitamin D activity (IU)	Vitamin E activity (IU)	Calcium (mg)	Phosphorus (mg)	Iodine (mg)	Iron (mg)	Magnesium (mg)
Males	11–14	1000	10	8	1200	1200	150	18	350
	15–18	1000	10	10	1200	1200	150	18	400
Females	11–14	800	10	8	1200	1200	150	18	300
	15–18	800	10	8	1200	1200	150	18	300
Pregnant		+200	+5	+2	+400	+400	+25	A*	+150
Lactating		+400	+5	+5	+3	+400	+400	+50	A*

* Not determined.

Table 11-2. Food Sources of Vitamins.

Vitamin A:	Whole milk, fruits, yellow vegetables, fortified margarine, butter, liver, some green leafy vegetables
Vitamin C:	Citrus fruits, lettuce, green leafy vegetables, broccoli, uncooked potatoes, tomatoes, strawberries, and currants
Vitamin D:	Milk, canned fish, egg yolk, and sunlight
Vitamin B12:	Fish, eggs, milk, fortified soy milk meals
Thiamine:	Beans, nuts, peas, pork, wheat products (enriched and whole grain)
Folacin:	Fresh oranges, nuts, liver, navy beans, dark leafy vegetables and whole wheat products

uterine device are at great risk for deficiency of iron, whereas birth control pill users may develop deficiencies in pyridoxine (vitamin B_6), vitamin B_{12}, and vitamin C. A well-balanced diet is important for those individuals already at risk for vitamin and mineral deficiencies. Some individuals with iron deficiency may need iron supplementation; others who are unable to eat a well-balanced diet may need vitamin supplementation. This chapter's bibliography includes articles outlining specific dietary needs of youth.

Teenage athletes may have special needs because of their vigorous exercise schedule and their desire to optimize their athletic progress. A health care professional who is knowledgeable about nutrition and sports can be helpful for the serious teenage athlete. A balanced diet with intermittent high carbohydrate intake with adequate hydration is important for the youth competing in the short duration events; this allows him or her to develop maximum outbursts of anaerobic energy, as supplied by adenosine triphosphate and phosphocreatinine. On the other hand, athletes involved in endurance sports need advice on improvement of both aerobic and anaerobic energy metabolism. Such advice centers on increasing the glycogen content of muscles, or glycogen-loading programs. Also, proper water replacement must be assured with athletes exercising in hot, humid weather.

Losing Body Weight

A well-balanced diet is necessary for youth, whether maintaining or changing body weights. Some teenagers wish to lose weight because they feel they are obese or because they are athletes and seek to develop a more optimal ratio of body fat to body weight. The next section presents a brief discussion on adolescent obesity. Although many male teenagers have a body fat to body weight ratio of 14 to 16%, champion high school athletes often have much lower ratios, even 5 to 7%. Likewise, although many female adolescents have a ratio of 20 to 22%, champion women athletes often have a ratio of 14 to 16% or lower.

Thus, many adolescent athletes seek to reduce their weight to gain better fat-to-weight ratios and improve their athletic performance. This can be done if proper guidelines are established to ensure gradual weight loss (not over 1½ to 2 lbs. per week) and adequate hydration. An individual program with close supervision by a health care professional is important to ensure a basic diet of 1800 to 2000 K.cal per day for the male or 1600 to 1800 K.cal for the female, combined with a daily increase of energy expenditure of 600 K.cal or more. The weight loss program should not compromise water intake, slow growth, reduce lean body weight, or interfere with fluid and electrolyte status. Weight loss in wrestlers has been linked to reduced testosterone levels in some. The use of drugs (such as diuretics or cathartics) or measures to increase diaphoresis (such as plastic suits) are to be avoided. Also, individuals with a desire to lose weight for athletic purposes should not be confused with the teenager developing anorexia nervosa.

Gaining Body Weight

The teenage athlete wishing to gain weight must avoid drugs (such as cyproheptadine and anabolic steroids). He or she should also avoid diet plans based on an increase of fatty foods. An individualized program can be developed to combine increased balanced calories with a muscle training program so that lean body mass (not fat stores) are gradually increased. Protein and vitamin supplementation is expensive and not necessary or helpful. As with all these plans, consultation with a knowledgeable nutritionist is helpful.

Obesity

Obesity remains one of the most frequent nutritional dysfunctions noted in teenagers. Perhaps 5% of youth are obese (defined as excess fat deposition resulting in a weight 20% or more over the ideal body weight). Current estimates are that 5 to 10% are also "overweight"—that is, 10 to 20% over their ideal body weight. Obesity induces low self-esteem and can limit the psychologic development of the teenager, which can continue on into adult life. The obese youth may have difficulty dealing with peers, and this can seriously affect normal adolescent development. Potential complications noted in later life include hypertension, coronary disease, diabetes, cholecystitis, premature joint destruction, and others.

"Simple" obesity is usually caused by a variety of complex factors, such as genetics, excessive dietary intake, and a reduced-exercise lifestyle. According to some research, risk factors for obesity also include a low socioeconomic status and being black. Depression can play a primary or secondary role in many cases. The individual may have an early puberty, and the height is often normal or above normal. Most causes of adolescent obesity are "idiopathic" and related to childhood obesity. In a few instances, other causes are found such as Cushing's syndrome, prolonged use of corticosteroids, hypothalamic lesions, Prader-Willi syndrome, and others. A careful medical evaluation will distinguish common "idiopathic" or "simple" obesity from secondary (such as primary endocrinologic or other organic disorders).

Treatment of exogenous obesity is difficult. Sensible reduction in caloric intake with an increase in physical activity will result in slow, steady weight reduction. This requires considerable motivation, which is often not found in many individuals. The measure discussed previously can be used, and the weight reduction program should be undertaken with the supervision of a knowledgeable health care professional. The youth should be *motivated* to lose weight. It is not enough for the parent and health care professional to be the only ones interested in the youth's weight loss. A poorly designed program can result in the worsening of an individual's depression through the development of a sense of failure. If the individual does not want to lose weight, the health care professional should be patient and wait until motivation develops.

A variety of "diets" have been developed over the past years to encourage weight loss (Table 11-3). In general, these are ill advised, and some (such as the Zen macrobiotic diet or liquid protein diet) are dangerous, leading to major nutritional deficiencies and increased morbidity as well as mortality. The individual needs to develop a *life-long pattern* of sensible caloric intake balanced by appropriate energy expenditure. "Crash diets," which are not helpful in causing weight loss, cannot be used for extended periods of time, and may have negative side effects; they are not to be encouraged. We must help our patients avoid negative consequences of "diets" that greedy "diet creators" develop for their own but not the patient's overall welfare. Obesity remains a complex nutritional disturbance that causes frustration for patients and health care professionals as well.

Hyperlipidemia

Primary hyperlipidemia is a genetically determined disorder that is a major risk factor for early development of coronary heart disease. Detection and treatment of this condition during adolescence is important to prevent premature death in adulthood. Although controversy exists, it is generally agreed that fasting cholesterol levels over 200 to 230 mg and serum triglyceride levels over 110 to 140 mg per ml are abnormal. Secondary hyperlipidemia can occur with various disorders, such as those listed in Table 11-4. The diagnosis of hyperlipidemia should be considered in any adolescent or young adult with a first-degree relative under age 50

Table 11-3. List of Miscellaneous "Diets."

High Carbohydrate Diet
Low Carbohydrate Diet
High Protein Diet
High Fat Diet
Beverly Hills Diet
Carbohydrate Craver's Diet
Drinking Man's Diet
Last Best Diet
Zen Macrobiotic Diet
Liquid Protein Diet
Protein-sparing, Modified Fast
Many others (Optifast, Medifast, HMR)

Table 11-4. Causes of Secondary Hyperlipidemia.

Diabetes mellitus
Hypothyroidism
Nephrotic syndrome
Chronic renal disease
Obstructive liver disease
Alcohol abuse
Other drugs (glucocorticosteroids, oral contraceptives)
Others

to 55 with coronary artery disease or when hyperlipidemia is a known family risk factor. If fasting serum cholesterol or triglyceride or both are elevated, further assessment is necessary, including evaluation for underlying organic disorders and diagnosis of the specific type.

There are six classic types of primary hyperlipidemia: I, IIA, IIB, III, IV, and V. Types IIA, IIB, and IV account for 95% of adult types. In type IIA, there is an increased cholesterol level and an even greater increase in low-density (beta) lipoprotein. In type IIB, there is an increase in beta lipoprotein, very low-density (prebeta) lipoprotein, triglyceride, and cholesterol. In type IV, there is an increase in triglyceride and a marked increase in prebeta lipoprotein.

The symptomatology of the forms of hyperlipidemia varies with the type and duration of the specific disease complex. Most affected youth have no clinical evidence and appear normal. Those with long-standing lipid elevations may develop xanthomas. Individuals can develop a variety of symptoms in adulthood, including coronary artery disease, pancreatitis, xanthomas, aortic stenosis, retinal damage, and many others. General treatment measures include controlling blood pressure, maintaining ideal body weight, avoiding cigarette smoking, and regular exercise. Individuals with elevated lipid levels should be referred to health care professionals knowledgeable in the care of these disorders. A number of lipid-lowering drugs are available, such as cholestyramine, clofibrate, nicotinic acid, and others. Dietary measures may be sufficient for a time in some cases (Greydanus DE, Hofmann AD, 1989).

The health care professional should remember that it can be difficult for the hyperlipidemic youth to follow a special diet or stay on specific medications. It is difficult for some youth to feel "different," and lack of compliance with recommended treatment regimens is common in adolescence. Patience and tolerance should be displayed by the health care professional, and it may be a number of years before sustained compliance is noted. Careful and continued assessments of the lipid levels from adolescence through adulthood are necessary.

Anorexia Nervosa

This uncommon eating disorder is characterized by a bizarre attitude toward eating in which the youth seeks to lose weight by a marked reduction in caloric intake. The weight loss can become severe, including

20 to 40% or more of the original body weight. There is no primary organic or psychiatric disorder causing the weight loss. Clinical evaluation reveals an individual with a distorted body image in which she perceives herself as "fat" despite obvious emaciation. Over 95% of cases occur in females, and the diagnosis, by definition, should be made in patients under age 25, often during adolescence. To achieve the low body weight, periods of excess physical activity may develop in addition to the reduction in caloric intake. Self-induced vomiting may develop as well. The need to lose weight can continue despite the attempts of others to reverse this trend.

A variety of physical and metabolic abnormalities are well described in anorexics and are reflective of the characteristic state of severe malnutrition: amenorrhea, lanugo hair, hypothermia, bradycardia, hypotension, electrolyte abnormalities, iron deficiency anemia, and many others. Other causes of weight loss must be considered in the differential diagnosis, including inflammatory bowel disease, malignancy, chronic infection, severe depression, and others. The cause(s) of anorexia nervosa is complex and not really understood. The treatment of this disorder is varied and controversial as well. Attention toward dehydration and electrolyte dysfunction as well as other medical abnormalities is important. The psychiatric or psychologic treatment of this disorder involves a variety of outpatient and inpatient therapy methods: individual psychotherapy, group psychotherapy, family therapy, nutritional counseling, antidepressant medication, and others. A variety of therapeutic approaches have been developed. Early diagnosis and treatment of this potentially fatal disorder is recommended. Mortality rates of 5 to 20% are reported in adults (Comerci, 1989).

Bulimia (Bulimia Nervosa)

Another well-known eating disorder is bulimia, in which the individual engages in binging-purging cycles that become uncontrollable. The incidence of bulimia is currently controversial. Previous studies noted a 5 to 15% range in the older adolescent, whereas more recent research has reduced this to as low as 1 to 2% of college-age females. Bulimia may become a part of anorexia nervosa or remain a separate disorder. Large amounts of food (usually easily consumed carbohydrates) are consumed in private and within a short time. The binging stops only if the individual is discovered, develops severe abdominal pain, or falls asleep. The individual becomes concerned about the binging and seeks to remove the food by purging or self-induced vomiting. The cycles can vary in frequency, even occurring daily or several times per day. There is often much denial of this activity and its need for treatment. An underlying depression is frequently reported in many if not most cases. Medical side effects are described, including enamel erosion, pharyngitis, gastritis, hiatal hernia, hypokalemia, and others. Further complications can be seen with the use of diuretics and cathartics. Severe constipation and renal and liver abnormalities have been reported in such cases. Treatment, as with anorexia nervosa, involves attention to medical and psychiatric difficulties, and a variety of treatment approaches are reported (Comerci, 1989).

Others

Youth are at risk for other nutritional difficulties, including *dental caries* and *iron deficiency anemia*. Poor eating habits involving excess sugar intake and poor dental hygiene result in a high rate of dental disorders in youth, including dental caries and periodontal disease. Only 4% of youth are caries-free, and the average 12- to 17-year-old has 6.2 diseased teeth (decayed, missing, or filled). Improved dental hygiene (including proper flossing and brushing techniques) and better habits may reduce the incidence of this widespread adolescent disorder.

Finally, *iron deficiency anemia* can occur in virtually any youth, male or female. Estimates vary, but perhaps 20% are at considerable risk, and 3% of males and 8 to 10% of females have overt iron-deficiency anemia. Iron deficiency is the most common cause of anemia in youth and is precipitated by the rapid growth spurt of adolescents, along with other factors such as menstruation and an iron-poor diet. Iron-deficiency anemia can be defined by a hemoglobin level under 11.5 g/dl or a hematocrit under 35% in 12-year-old males or females, a hemoglobin level under 12.0 (hematocrit under 36%) in 12- to 18-year-old females, and a hemoglobin level under 12. 5 to 13.0 (hematocrit under 38%) in 12- to 18-year-old males. Studies have correlated the hemoglobin/hematocrit levels with the Tanner stage and have noted that blacks average a hematocrit 1 to 3% lower than whites. Improvement in the iron content of the diet or iron supplementation or both will adequately treat this condition.

ADOLESCENT SUBSTANCE ABUSE DISORDERS

The sociomedical phenomenon of drug use and abuse among our adolescent population is among the most critical issues facing our society today. Our environment is permeated with drugs of all kinds; currently, it is not a question of whether most teenagers will use drugs, but which ones they will try and how many will become drug abusers. In 1971 a Gallup poll revealed that Americans felt that drug use was one of the most serious health problems facing our country. Unfortunately it still is. Recent epidemiologic surveys confirm that most youth experiment with such drugs as alcohol and marijuana, and that many try other drugs, such as tobacco, amphetamines, hallucinogens, barbiturates, narcotics, and others. The distinction between drug use and abuse is not always clear, and controversy exists over labeling a youth using drugs as dependent or not. Some individuals accept limited experimentation as normal, whereas others equate any use as abnormal. This review suggests that abnormalities exist when the drug use begins to interfere with childhood and adolescent development, subsequently threatening adulthood. The medical and psychologic effects of drug use and abuse are many and vary with the individual, the extent of the drug use, and the drugs involved.

A major difficulty that exists in dealing with this issue is the acceptance our society has for drugs. Chemicals are frequently prescribed to improve various medical conditions, reduce pain, improve sleep disorders, improve scholastic or sports performances, improve appearance, treat behavioral disorders (psychologic or psychiatric), allow individuals to feel better, and others. An effective solution to the drug abuse problem must start with making the automatic use of chemicals or drugs less acceptable to society than now is the case. This section will review certain aspects of the substance phenomenon: epidemiology, etiology, symptomatology (including stages of drug use and abuse), types, and general treatment issues.

Epidemiology of Drug Abuse

America has had a long historic struggle with drugs. Narcotic addiction was rampant in the last third of the nineteenth century. Marijuana was little used before 1930; prior to 1960, drug use was mainly a problem of adults, not children or teenagers. Unfortunately, a considerable increase in drug use was noted in youth between 1960 and 1980. In the late 1960s, there was widespread use of hallucinogens, opiates, amphetamines, barbiturates, and inhalants. Marijuana and alcohol use increased dramatically in the 1970s, and cocaine abuse had become a serious additional problem in the 1980s. The sharpest increase in drug use among junior high students and senior high students occurred between 1975 and 1978. Although some decrease has been noted since then, the problem remains severe. Many studies demonstrate this trend, and only a few are cited here. The University of Michigan Annual Drug Survey surveyed 16,000 high school students in 1984 and noted that 30% admitted some type of drug use over the previous 30 days (Johnson, 1984). Recent studies regarding four commonly abused drugs—alcohol, marijuana, cigarettes, and cocaine—will be reviewed.

Alcohol. Johnston et al. (1982) reviewed 17,000 high school seniors and noted that 75% had experimented with alcohol and that 5% used it daily. Another study under the guidance of the National Institute of Drug Abuse (NIDA) reported that 93% of the surveyed youth tried alcohol; 87% had done so during the past year, 70% in the past month; 5% were daily users (Johnson, 1984; Clayton, 1985). Such data underestimates the real numbers, since the group with a higher incidence of drug abuse—the school drop-outs and expelled students (15–25% of youth)—are not included. A study published in 1983 revealed that by age 13, 30% of males and 20% of females were experimenting with alcohol; this climbs to 93% of the males and 73% of females at age 18 (Clayton and Ritter, 1983). Forster (1984) studied upper-middle-class adolescents and reported that 73% of fifth to sixth graders had tried wine and 23% had tried other types of alcohol. In this same study, 27% had experimented with cigarettes and 4% with marijuana.

Such early use of alcohol, cigarettes, and marijuana is important to note, as these substances are called "gateway drugs"—drugs which can lead to polydrug abuse in later adolescence and adulthood. A well-recognized pattern is cigarette and alcohol experimentation in early adolescence, followed by marijuana use and polydrug abuse of these and other drugs, including cocaine. Kandel et al., as well as Mills and Noyes, have documented this malignant gateway progression. Current estimates are that 15% of high school seniors drive while intoxicated. Annually, there are 18,000 alcohol-related fatalities noted in youth under age 18 as well as 18,000 in those 18 to 25 years of age. The National Council on Alcoholism estimates that there are over 3 million teenage problem drinkers in this country; many more become problem drinkers as adults. The NIDA estimates that 15 million children (one of every five in the physician's office) live with an alcoholic parent. Much recent literature has accumulated on the extensive psychologic damage that a child of an alcoholic (COA) sustains. The acceptance by general society of alcohol makes it especially difficult to prevent alcohol abuse by adolescents.

   Cigarettes. Although not fully appreciated by health care professionals, the use of tobacco by adolescents remains a major health problem that serves as a time bomb for these individuals later in their adulthood. Forster's study revealed that 27% of fifth to sixth graders tried cigarettes; this rose to 55% for seventh to eighth graders. The NIDA study of high school seniors revealed that 70% have tried cigarettes (30% during the previous month) and 21% used cigarettes on a daily basis in 1982. Johnson et al.'s 1982 study noted that 12% of American high school seniors used tobacco on a daily basis. In 1982, Holleb summarized the literature by noting that 11% of boys and 13% of girls 12 to 18 years of age smoked 10 or more cigarettes per day. Statistics currently note that cigarettes remain the most popular drug used on a daily basis (20% of females and 16% of males); 12% smoke over a half a pack per day. The consequences of such action are enormous. An increase in the use of chewing tobacco is also noted, leading to more difficulties in adulthood. Cigarettes remain one of the few drugs abused by adolescent females more than adolescent males, possibly because of the anorexic effect of tobacco. Unfortunately, with 55 million cigarette smokers in the United States, the problem of tobacco is enormous.

   Marijuana. As previously noted, marijuana was unusual in adolescent populations before 1960. Prior to 1962, 1% of 12- to 17-year-olds experimented with marijuana, versus 4% of 18- to 25-year-olds (DuPont, 1985). In 1979, 31% of 12- to 17-year-olds tried marijuana, versus 68% of 18- to 25-year-olds. In 1978, 60% of American high school seniors tried marijuana; 5% used it daily. It remains the most popular illicit drug, and current statistics note that over half of high school seniors have tried it. As noted, marijuana is a gateway drug, and its use in early to mid-adolescence is suggestive of future polydrug use or abuse. Forster noted that 4% of fifth to sixth graders tried marijuana, versus 19% of seventh to eighth graders and 58% of high school seniors. Schwartz observed that 4% of 1300 eighth graders in Maryland used marijuana on a daily basis. In 1982, NIDA noted that 6.3% of high school seniors used marijuana on a daily basis, and that 59% had tried it. Overall drug use among eighth graders rose from 8% in 1971 to 20% in 1978. Marijuana use is still unusual under age 10, but its use increases significantly in adolescence and adulthood. The acceptance by much of current society for marijuana constitutes a major problem for those seeking to reduce marijuana abuse. In 1982, it was estimated that 64 million Americans had tried marijuana and that 20% were active users (at least once in 30 days prior to the survey).

As noted, the gateway significance of marijuana is serious. Marijuana use can become a chronic pattern. A study of high school seniors who used marijuana daily noted that 50% were still daily users 5 years later (Johnston et al., 1982). Kandel studied 1325 young adults aged 24 to 25, of whom 15% used marijuana 4 or more times per week and 23% used it once or more per month. Such individuals revealed more psychiatric dysfunction than non-marijuana-user controls. If marijuana (or alcohol or cigarettes) use does not start by age 20 to 21, it rarely starts at all.

Cocaine. American youth are in the middle of a serious cocaine epidemic in which all strata of youth are abusing this drug. In 1975, 9% of youth tried cocaine; in 1983, this had risen to 17%. The NIDA estimates that 1% of youth are daily cocaine users (versus 12% daily using tobacco, 5% marijuana, and 5% alcohol). In 1975, 1.9 high school seniors used cocaine during the month prior to the survey, versus 5% in 1982. According to Gold et al. (1982), a survey of high school seniors noted that 88% reported that it was very easy to obtain marijuana, and that 47% said the same of cocaine. These and other studies confirm the growing use and abuse of cocaine by youth. Cocaine is also a classic gateway drug that leads to further (polydrug) abuse.

Etiology of Drug Abuse

The reasons for use and abuse of drugs by adolescents are complex and numerous. Table 11-6 reviews a few of these factors, which operate in diverse ways for different youth. The rite of pubertal passage may be seen in some early to mid-adolescents who use chemicals as proof of maturation, demonstrating how they have left childhood and entered adolescence or even "pseudo-adulthood." From an anthropologic view, a number of societies have celebrated or marked the arrival of adolescence or adulthood with various social and religious ceremonies, with or without the use of drugs. Further drug use may be precipitated by other factors.

Both youth and adults can turn to drugs to escape environmental chaos and tension. It may prove difficult to face current problems, as high unemployment rates, limited financial stability, uncomfortable crime rates, high divorce rates with considerable family dysfunction, widespread poor

Table 11-5. Gateway Drugs.

Alcohol
Tobacco
Marijuana
Cocaine

parental skills, and other factors of youth may make it difficult if not impossible to deal with life involving rape, incest, other crimes, ineffective or unloving parents, inadequate schools, physical limitations, intellectual dysfunction, psychiatric illnesses, and others. The youth who live in the latter part of the twentieth century must contend with an increasingly complex world. Modern technology is changing as the jet age gives way to the computer and superconductor age. Many cannot deal with these pressures and turn to drugs as a way of escaping the pain and anxiety modern life may produce.

Adolescent developmental issues can be difficult enough to accept without exposure to parental and environmental chaos. Drugs can be used as part of attempts to rebel against authority (such as parents or school officials) or to acquiesce to peer pressure for drug experimentation. The use of drugs may provide some youth with "courage" to face social pressures, including sexual experimentation. Unfortunately, many teenage athletes are convinced that the use of certain drugs (such as amphetamines, anabolic steroids, excess vitamins, and others) will improve sports performance. Drugs may also be used to improve mood swings and depression noted with youth.

A vicious cycle can occur when the individual starts experimenting with drugs. The choice of certain chemicals (such as heroin or cocaine) can lead to further failure of life events, compounding the youth's circumstances. The gateway drugs (Table 11-5) can lead to polydrug abuse by middle to late adolescence. Physiologic and psychologic dependency can develop long before the individual is aware of it. Such individuals may be taking what they consider to be a safe drug, only to find out too late how dangerous it is. Most of them do not really know the contents of the street drugs they buy. As the youth observe adult society and its problem with chemical dependency, their decision to try drugs is confirmed. Not only do adults consume large amounts of alcohol and many cigarettes, many parents grew up on marijuana and continue with marijuana use into the middle years and beyond. It is not a rare parent of the 1990s who will reward his or her child with a marijuana joint!

Drugs are widespread in our society and easy to find. Various media are influential in promoting drug use, which quickly turns into drug abuse. Both legal and illicit drugs are encouraged by various individuals. We are all greatly encouraged on a daily basis to try various chemicals and drugs.

Table 11-6. Causes of Drug Abuse.

Rite of passage into puberty
Sequence of middle adolescent issues (Chapter 1)
Environmental chaos
Adult lifestyle mirroring
Polydrug accessibility
Media influence
Result of malignant adolescent processes
Others

Youth are directly encouraged by diverse newspaper, magazine, and television ads to consume alcohol and cigarettes. Women are encouraged by clever, expensive commercials to celebrate and announce "modern femininity" by choosing a certain brand of cigarettes. Alcohol commercials are almost impossible to escape in which movie stars and well-known athletes exhort us to drink. Why should youth not use drugs? Successful athletes openly encourage certain drugs to improve sports performances. The voices offering resistance to such brainwashing are not clearly heard by our youth.

Drug use and abuse can be intimately tied to diverse malignant adolescent processes. Youth who are undergoing extreme rebellion often turn to drugs. Thus, drug use commonly occurs alongside juvenile delinquency, school failure, school dropout behavior, runaway behavior, conduct disorder, and others. Drug use and antisocial behavior can be intimately interwoven into a web, causing considerable problems for our youth. Adolescents can turn to crime, such as mugging or prostitution, to support their habits. Those involved in such lifestyles often find drugs to be an accepted part of the lifestyle. A vicious, self-perpetuating cycle ensues and can consume patients and their families.

Symptoms and Stages of Drug Use and Abuse

A number of risk factors have been identified for drug abuse, which are listed in Table 11-7. A number of warning signs should alert the parent or health care professional to possible drug use in the youth (Table 11-8). Remember that drug experimentation with gateway drugs (Table 11-5) during the "gateway years" (early and middle adolescence) may lead to polydrug abuse in late adolescence and adulthood. A variety of symptoms of drug use and abuse have been described, as reviewed in Table 11-9. Drug abuse may mimic most psychiatric disorders, including major affective disorders (bipolar disorder or major unipolar depression), anxiety disorders, personality disorders, schizophrenia, severe adjustment disorders, and others. General laboratory screenings are often unhelpful. Youth with a history of alcohol abuse may have anemia, macrocytosis, and elevated

Table 11-7. Risk Factors for Drug Abuse.

Positive history for drug use (parents, grandparents, other relatives)
Family dysfunction
Divorce
Separation
Inadequate parenting skills
Others
Family history of total drug abstinence
Adolescent depression, low self-esteem and shyness, possibly due to the following:
Learning disorders
Attention-deficit disorders
Other neurologic-behavioral disorders
General drug accessibility
Association with drug-abusing peers
Peers

Table 11-8. Potential Indicators of Drug Abuse.

Depression
Reduced school performance
Dropping two or more grade levels below known abilities
Frank scholastic failure
Truancy
Worsening parent-child conflicts
Unexplained negative behaviors
Worsening communication skills with family or peers
Preference for drug-abusing peers
Conduct-disorder behavior
Runaway behavior
Conflicts with public officials
Overt evidence of drug intoxication

liver enzymes (especially gamma-glutamyl transpeptidase). A serum or urine drug screen may be positive, but such results must be correlated with other factors about the patient and family. The ability of such tests to detect drugs varies with the test being used, whether thin-layer chromatography, enzyme immunoassay, radioimmunoassay, gas chromatography, or mass spectroscopy.

A number of scales outlining stages of use and abuse have been proposed. A widely used clinical scale has been developed by MacDonald (Table 11-10). In stage 0, there is no overt drug use, but there is curiosity about drugs, low self-esteem, a need for peer acceptance, and other factors that may predispose the individual to later drug use. Stage I refers to an experimentation stage in which the individual experiences the euphoria drugs can bring (usually at weekend parties) but without development of overt consequences to the experimentation. Experience with the gateway drugs (Table 11-5) is gained. When stage II develops, the individual seeks the drug-induced euphoria, widens his or her drug experience, often uses personal drug paraphernalia, regularly buys or steals

Table 11-9. Symptoms of Drug Abuse.

Reduced attention span
Poor/short memory skills
Limited fine motor controls
Poor oral/general hygiene
Injected conjunctiva
Nasal irritation and/or discharge
Episodes of abdominal pain (including the epigastrium)
Weight loss
Emesis
Melena
Hepatomegaly
Chronic cough with recurrent bronchitis
Tachycardia
Poor muscle tone
Multiple skin bruises
Skin tracks (uncommon in adolescence)
Various sexually transmitted diseases
Many others

Table 11-10. MacDonald's Scales of Drug Abuse

Stage 0—Non-use
Stage 1—Experimental use
Stage 2—Recreational use (social involvement)
Stage 3—Interference with school performance and developmental tasks
Stage 4—Compulsive abuse or addiction

drugs, develops identifiable changes in his or her life (with school performance, choice of friends, change in clothes, or behavior), and becomes more adept at denying the developing drug dependence. In stage III the youth becomes preoccupied with achieving the euphoria and his or her life becomes more out of control with a wide list of drug use, more depression, more mood swings, acting out behavior, lethargy, and malaise. Many of the consequences of drug abuse are seen here. Stage IV is the burnout or end stage in which the abuser seeks drugs to maintain the euphoria and feel "normal." A wide variety of psychiatric reactions can occur, including suicide, violence, unpredictable behavior, and others. The progression from stage 0 to IV can take from months to years.

Types of Drugs

Alcohol. Many abused drugs are available to youth (Table 11-11). *Alcohol* is one of the most used and abused drugs in society. It is classified as a central nervous system depressant that causes a euphoric feeling most find pleasant. Tolerance and psychologic dependence develop in many individuals, and physiologic dependence is well recognized in alcoholics. The actual reaction to alcohol depends on the type and amount consumed. The alcohol content varies widely, whether in beer (3 to 6% alcohol), wine (12%), or various liquors (50%). Mild intoxication can occur at blood alcohol levels of 0.05 to 0.15 mg/dl. Legal intoxication is sometimes defined by 0.15 mg/dl or greater. Judgment can be impaired at a blood alcohol level as low as 0.1 mg/dl. Increasing amounts of alcohol lead to respiratory depression, coma, and even death. The mixture of drinking and driving has proven to be a dangerous one for both the drinkers and

Table 11-11. Abused Drugs.

1. Alcohol
2. Marijuana
3. Tobacco
4. Cocaine
5. Hallucinogens
a. Lysergic acid diethylamide (LSD)
b. Phencyclidine HCL (PCP)
c. Others
6. Amphetamines
7. Barbiturates
8. Narcotics
9. Hydrocarbons and other solvents
10. Miscellaneous

numerous innocent victims. Youth at parties should be urged to have a nondrinking peer or other sober individual (such as parents) drive them home.

Alcoholism is a major disease in adults that has roots in adolescence. The importance of genetic factors in the development of alcoholism, including biochemical depression, is being discussed in current research. Many youth are unable to stop at the social drinking or experimentation stage. Rapid progression through the MacDonald stages can then ensue. Problem teenage drinkers tend to come from homes in which parents are excessive drinkers or from homes in which no alcohol is consumed. Medical complications of excess alcohol consumption are well known, including overt intoxication, gastritis, pancreatitis, toxic psychosis, worsening of diabetes, epilepsy, and others. Problem teenage drinkers may develop elevated serum gamma glutamyl transpeptidase, glutamic-oxaloacetic or pyruvic transaminases, alkaline phosphatase, bilirubin, and uric acid levels. The *alcohol withdrawal syndrome* is characterized by tremor, hallucinations, seizures, and overt delirium tremens. The *fetal alcohol syndrome* is a well-recognized consequence of alcohol consumption during pregnancy.

Marijuana. *Marijuana* can be categorized as a sedative or hallucinogen and is a popular illicit drug for millions of individuals. It comes from the *Cannabis sativa* plant, and its active ingredient is delta-9-tetrahydrocannabinol (THC). Street marijuana can vary widely in its THC content, from 1 to 4% and more. The plant also contains over 400 other chemicals, including benzopyrine, a recognized carcinogen also seen in tobacco. Although usually smoked, marijuana can also be taken orally. It produces an intense feeling of relaxation within minutes of initial use, and this euphoria can last several hours. Classic physical addiction is not proven, but tolerance and psychologic dependency is a well-accepted consequence of heavy marijuana use. Frequent marijuana use by youth may lead to confused thinking, shortened memory span, and dulled reflexes, which can be detrimental to a youth's ability to successfully carry out daily tasks in school, at home, and in other environments.

Marijuana is a dangerous drug for youth. Chronic use may become part of the classic *amotivational syndrome,* with extreme lethargy, lack of interest in work or school, and various difficulties in society. Psychologic reactions are well described in some marijuana users; these reactions include depression, anxiety, fear, violent behavior, delusions, and in a few, overt hallucinations. Chronic cough and bronchitis are noted in marijuana users. Marijuana smoke is more potent than cigarette smoke; since it is held in the lungs longer than cigarette smoke in many cases, more destructive pulmonary effects can be experienced.

More research is clearly needed to further understand all of marijuana's complications. Some studies suggest that marijuana reduces male sperm count, induces amenorrhea, interferes with DNA functioning at a cellular level, and may induce immunologic dysfunction. Further research is necessary to understand the full effects of various levels of marijuana use on specific individuals. The fact that marijuana remains in the body for several days after a single episode is worrisome. Marijuana and alcohol can lead to thousands of car-deaths each year. The effect on the offspring of pregnant individuals who use marijuana can be negative. It is a dangerous drug, and youth must be thoroughly educated to abstain from it. Unfortunately, it enjoys widespread acceptance among the adult as well as adolescent population of the 1990s.

Tobacco. Tobacco is another widely abused drug in modern society. Profound physical addiction or chemical dependency is characteristic of tobacco use. Today's teenage smokers eventually become adults with significant risks for emphysema, lung cancer, laryngeal carcinoma, other forms of cancer, heart disease, and other medical disorders. Lung cancer is now a more common cause of cancer deaths in adult females than breast cancer because of the increase in the number of women who smoke within the past few decades. Smoking cigarettes leads to chronic exposure to many detrimental chemicals, such as tar, nicotine, benzopyrine, carbon monoxide, arsenous oxide, radioactive polonium compounds, and others. Recent research has noted negative effects that smoking during pregnancy has on the offspring, who are smaller than the offspring of nonsmokers. The negative effects of passive smoking are becoming even clearer. Although legal and well accepted, tobacco is a drug whose use must be discouraged. The recent increase in chewing tobacco among youth will lead to a dramatic rise in oral cancer within a generation.

Cocaine. Cocaine is a central nervous system stimulant that can be taken intranasally, intravenously, by inhalation, and orally. In the past, cocaine was often given in the form of a powder of the hydrochloride salt made from an alkaloid present in coca leaves. Alkaloidal cocaine, or free base, is now widely available in a form used for smoking called "crack" or "rock." Crack is mainly pure cocaine and can be smoked ("freebasing") in a "base pipe." It can also be crushed, mixed with tobacco, and smoked in a cigarette. It induces an intense euphoria which is short-lived and followed by fatigue and irritability. Tolerance and severe psychologic addiction occur. Various side effects include nasal septum infection and perforation, tachycardia, hypertension, hyperpyrexia, seizures, ventricular arrhythmia, angina pectoris, myocardial infarction, and sudden death. Cocaine is recognized as a gateway drug. Previously, cocaine powder, or "snow," was quite expensive and not available to all. Crack is now widely available and relatively inexpensive, and is posing a serious problem for youth. Pregnant youth on cocaine risk abortion, damage to their offspring, or both. Cocaine is sometimes used to induce abortion.

Hallucinogens. The hallucinogens, PCP and LSD (Table 11-11), are still seen, although not as commonly as they were in the 1970s. They are taken orally and produce an intense distortion of reality. Tolerance to these chemicals is well described. Psychoses have developed in a few users, as has the classic flashback phenomenon, which can also be precipitated by marijuana and antihistamines. Overdosing with these agents produces a variety of symptoms, including respiratory depression, coma, and death. Bad reactions, or "trips," may respond to diazepam or haloperidol.

Amphetamines. Amphetamine is a classic central nervous system stimulant that leads to anxiety, hyperactivity, hypertension, tachycardia, insomnia, anorexia with weight loss, mydriasis, and hyperhidrosis. It can be used to reduce fatigue, induce euphoria, attempt improvement of work or sports performances, and lose weight. It can be taken orally, subcutaneously, and intravenously. Tolerance and an abstinence or withdrawal syndrome (apathy, sleep dysfunction, and depression) are classic. Possible complications include infection (such as hepatitis, endocarditis, AIDS, and others) when using an infected needle, personality changes, psychiatric disturbances, and others. Overdose can lead to hypertension, mydriasis, hyperthermia, seizures, cardiac arrhythmias, and death.

Barbiturates. Barbiturates are classic central nervous system depressants called hypnotic-sedative drugs. Physical addiction, tolerance, and abstinence syndromes are noted; the latter are characterized by emesis, anxiety, postural hypotension, delirium, seizures, and even death. Acute effects from oral or intravenous use include slurred speech, euphoria, lethargy, ataxia, and myosis. Overdose can occur with hypotension, respiratory depression, bullous skin lesions, coma, and death. Barbiturates should not be prescribed to youth, except with extreme caution.

Opiates. Opiate narcotics were common in the 1960s and are still noted in today's society. Heroin can be taken in a snuff form, subcutaneously, or intravenously. Intense euphoria, tolerance, narcotic abstinence syndrome, physical addiction, and psychologic dependency are associated with heroin. Other abused narcotics include meperidine, codeine, methadone, morphine, propoxyphene, pentazocine, and others. Medical complications are numerous, including HIV infection, multiple skin infections, hepatitis, endocarditis, lung disease (such as pulmonary edema and pneumonia), tetanus, amenorrhea, peptic ulcer, osteomyelitis, and others. Heroin overdose can result in respiratory depression and death. A withdrawal syndrome is observed in newborns of pregnant women who abuse narcotics. A resurgence of narcotic abuse has been noted in the 1980s and 1990s.

Solvents. Solvents are central nervous system depressants that produce transient euphoria in the abusers. Solvents have been commonly abused drugs of young adolescents. There are many types (Table 11-12).

Table 11-12. Types of Solvents.

1. Glue (Toluene)
2. Cleaning fluids (trichloroethylene)
3. Aerosol sprays (Freon)
4. Gasoline
5. Lighter fluids (with Naphtha)
6. Nail product removers (acetone)
7. Nitrous oxide
8. Nitrites (amyl and butyl)
9. Others

The chemicals can be placed in a rag or in a plastic bag and then inhaled. A variety of complications can be noted, including respiratory tract irritation, cardiac arrhythmias, and even death. Renal or hepatic toxicity can occur with trichloroethylene use and plumbism with gasoline sniffing. Finally, there are many other chemicals that can be abused, including phenylpropanolamine, caffeine, ephedrine, pseudoephedrine, pyrilamine, tranquilizers, muscle relaxers, analgesics, anticholinergics, and others.

Drug Use and Abuse in Adolescent Athletes

For centuries, athletes have used various drug mixtures in an attempt to improve athletic performance. Agents that have been used include oxygen, amphetamines, vitamins, anabolic steroids, testosterone, ephedrine, iron, blood, and many others (Table 11-13). The teenage athlete should be carefully counseled that there is no substance that consistently and safely improves the performance of a well-trained individual. Also, the use of these agents has considerable potential to cause physical and psychologic damage. Misuse of drugs, or the *doping phenomenon,* as it is called, should be discouraged.

Anabolic steroids are a class of chemicals that are synthetic derivatives of testosterone and represent the drug class most abused by adolescent athletes. Such drugs include methandrostenolone (Dianabol), nandrolone decanoate (Decaduraboline), stanozolol (Winstrol), oxymetholone (Anadrol-50), and others. Dianabol has been discontinued because of the high level of abuse noted by athletes. If athletes take high doses of anabolic steroids (and some of the androgenic steroids) while undergoing heavy resistance training, there may be an increase in body weight and muscle mass; such use produces an increase in water retention and lean

Table 11-13. Drugs Misused by Adolescent Athletes.

Anabolic steroids
Amphetamines
Caffeine
Vitamins
Sodium bicarbonate
Nonsteroidal anti-inflammatory drugs (ibuprofen, mefenamic acid, naproxen, others)
Ephedrine
Iron
Blood
Oxygen
Dimethyl sulfoxide (DSMO)
Pangamic acid ("Vitamin B15")
Diuretics
Other illicit drugs
  Alcohol
  Marijuana
  Tobacco
  Hallucinogens (lysergic acid diethylamide and phencyclidine hydrochloride)
  Barbiturates
  Opiate narcotics
  Glue solvent
Others

body mass. The exact effects of anabolic steroids are complex and not fully defined. The effect of training is important, since healthy volunteers who take these drugs without training show no increase in muscle strength or size. Some experiments have noted that inexperienced weight lifters taking anabolic steroids may experience an increase in body weight but not in strength. Whether or not athletes experience a significant increase in athletic performance remains controversial. What *is* clear is that many unwanted side effects accompany such drugs. Many athletes, however, are convinced that these drugs are valuable and worth the risk, even in very high doses. The therapeutic doses of such drugs, as used for treatment of various medical disorders, is 8 to 30 mg, depending upon the particular drug. While taking several drugs together in a method called "stacking," some athletes use up to 200 mg per day. Female athletes try to get a high enough dose to get the expected or desired results on muscle mass, but low enough to prevent unwanted side effects such as masculinization. Athletes at particular risk for the use of anabolic steroids include those engaged in such sports as weight lifting, shot putting, discus throwing, body building, sprinting, football, and wrestling.

Side effects include demasculinization, fluid retention, personality changes, gastric ulcers, hepatic neoplasms, hyperglycemia, and others. The maturation process can be accelerated in growing athletes with closure of epiphyses and shortened ultimate adult height. An increase in tendon injuries has also been reported in teenagers on anabolic steroids. Masculinization of females may occur with such changes as hirsutism and clitoromegaly. A recent hepatocellular-carcinoma-induced death in an athlete taking anabolic steroids reminds one of this tragic side effect. There can also be an increase in liver function tests, increased peliosis hepatitis, prostatic enlargement, and acne development. There is also a decrease in glycoproteins (FSH/LH) with decreased sperm, decreased testosterone levels, and reduction in testicular size. This reduction in testicular size is reversible, but abnormalities of germinal elements can persist for several weeks after discontinuation of these drugs. To avoid the reduction in testicular size, some athletes take intramuscular human chorionic gonadotropin (hCG). There is also a reduction in high density lipoprotein (HDL) with a resultant possible increase in cardiovascular risks. One case of a renal tumor (Wilms's tumor) has been reported. Psychologic changes have also been noted, including an increase in aggressiveness, irritability, and depression.

Caffeine is a xanthine derivative that may improve performance in steady-state endurance activities that rely on fat for fuel, since this chemical increases lipid metabolism. It increases the release of free fatty acids from adipocytes and also stimulates catecholamine activity. Studies have noted that ingestion of 2½ to 3 cups of coffee increases the endurance of individuals cycling to exhaustion on bicycle ergometers. It seems to reduce the perception of fatigue and allow further performance. However, excessive amounts increase sympathomimetic stimulation, which can interfere with overall athletic performance. Coffee's diuretic effect can also interfere with such performance. Excessive amounts are banned for Olympic competition. Such amounts are defined as over 15 μg/ml in the urine.

A variety of other agents (Table 11-13) can be abused by athletes in an often fruitless attempt to improve their athletic performance. Despite the claims made for the massive intake of *multiple vitamins,* there is no evidence that such an addition will be of real benefit to the athlete. A well-balanced diet with appropriate training is the key to maximizing athletic performance. Some try to develop a new vitamin as part of this craze over "vitamin therapy." The food additive *pangamic acid* (erroneously called "vitamin B_{15}" by some) is a good example of this unfortunate trend. *Sodium bicarbonate* has been used to delay fatigue during bouts of exercise that are limited by acidosis; this may be helpful in cases in which the blood flow can increase to accommodate the increase in the byproducts of the increased muscle at work.

Nonsteroidal anti-inflammatory agents have been used to relieve pain and allow athletes to increase their performance despite painful injuries; this can lead to greater, longer-lasting injuries. Such medications have erroneously been used to "quicken" muscle-soreness healing after exercise. Side effects of such medications include gastrointestinal bleeding, reduced platelet aggregation, reduced renal perfusion, increased salt and water retention, and thermal regulation dysfunction with resultant heat illness. Another agent falsely used as an anti-inflammatory agent by athletes is *dimethyl sulfoxide (DMSO)*. This chemical is available in over-the-counter preparations and is rubbed onto sore or injured areas. Its effectiveness as an anti-inflammatory agent has never been demonstrated by research, and its production does not occur under standards acceptable for human use. Its use should be discouraged until these problems are resolved.

Ephedrine is an example of a medication that can have beneficial effects in disease states such as asthma, but which is not acceptable to certain committees on sports medicine. In the case of ephedrine, many feel its sympathomimetic action gives the user an unfair advantage, and it is thus banned. However, such beta-2 agonists as terbutaline and salbuterol are accepted in the Olympics if an athlete has documented asthma and informs the Olympic Committee of use of such drugs. The purpose is to allow the athlete proper treatment of a verified disorder, but not to allow him or her an unfair advantage over fellow competitors. Athletes should win by superior performance secondary to better skill and training, not by the use of drugs or so-called ergogenic aids.

As noted in Table 11-13, other drugs are abused by athletes. The use of various *diuretics* to lose weight quickly is not an unusual plan of wrestlers. The use of such medications can result in increased weakness such that a wrestler can be injured by competing against a stronger opponent. Electrolyte dysfunction and other medical side effects of diuretics may complicate the picture. A report has been issued on pulmonary embolism in a high school wrestler using such a regimen.

Blood doping ("blood boosting" or "blood packing") is an attempt to use one's own blood to increase aerobic performance. Blood doping is impossible to detect by laboratory tests. The frequency of use among athletes is unknown, but is probably low in adolescent athletes.

General Treatment Issues

Unfortunately, there are no clear-cut, easy-to-apply rules for the prevention and treatment of substance abuse. Overall treatment goals are to prevent abuse and, if it is occurring, interrupt it, maintain sobriety, and allow the individual to develop a chemical-free lifestyle. The key to all of this is to provide our youth with good reasons to avoid drugs in the first place or for those already into drugs, good reasons to stop. The first step is to prevent drug use. Children as young as those in the first grade can develop long-term attitudes toward drugs and their use. Education should occur in the home and continue in school and with religious training. We must overcome the powerful positive drug messages our children receive from peers, media, and society in general. Those at increased risk for drug abuse must be identified and given special attention. The major problem we face is the general apathy found in society when attempting to deal with this problem of substance abuse. Remember that use of gateway drugs leads to polydrug abuse in many youth. Depressed youth often turn to drugs; addiction can then develop. Drug dependency and some form of depression are currently viewed as biologic disorders that require behavioral controls. Alternatives to drug dependency must be sought out and emphasized, such as sports, recreational activities, religion, job training, volunteer assignments, and others. Those who have not experimented with tobacco, alcohol, or illicit drugs by 18 to 21 years of age are unlikely to do so.

Once the drug-dependent youth is identified through careful assessments, a variety of programs can be tried, including inpatient short-term treatment, residential care, outpatient treatment with partial hospitalization, and others. Some programs are basically psychiatric in nature, whereas others emphasize the "12-Step" anonymous program (Alcoholics Anonymous, Narcotics Anonymous, Al-Anon, and Families Anonymous).

A careful assessment of each patient is recommended to identify underlying causes of substance abuse and to then identify the treatment programs that are necessary. A multidisciplinary approach that emphasizes family therapy—seeking to get the youth back into the family, if there is one—is good for many patients. The current family dysfunction seen in general society complicates this task. Children of alcoholics are a special group often requiring extensive individual and family therapy. Keeping the recovering drug abuser away from past and potentially new drug-using peers is important to prevent relapse. Remember that current theories of drug dependency consider such dependency to be biologically based, with some environmental influence. Controlling the youth's environment is important. Current adolescent treatment programs are often based on adult models. More study is necessary to determine the best program for different subgroups of adolescent drug abusers.

Decreasing society's acceptance of drugs would go a long way in preventing and reducing drug addiction. Some limited success has been noted with programs seeking to reduce society's tolerance of cigarette smoking; these efforts should be expanded. Such programs as "Say No to Drugs" and Mothers Against Drunk Drivers, raising the legal age of drinking alcohol to 21, keeping drugs out of the workplace—these are all good starts. Self-help groups for youth and parents have also been positive steps in the difficult task of treating societal drug dependency.

BIBLIOGRAPHY

Nutrition

American Academy of Pediatrics, Committee on Nutrition: Prudent lifestyle for children: dietary fat and cholesterol. Pediatrics 1986;78:521-525.

Barnes HV, Berger R: An approach to the obese adolescent. Med Clin North Am 1975;59:1507-1516.

Bruch H: The Golden Cage: The Enigma of Anorexia Nervosa. Cambridge, MA: Harvard University, 1978.

Comerci GD, ed: Symposium on eating disorders: anorexia nervosa and bulimia. Sem Adol Med 1986;2:1-220.

Comerci GD: Adolescent nutrition and eating disorders. In: Hofmann AD, Greydanus DE, eds: Adolescent Medicine. 2nd ed. Norwalk, CT: Appleton-Lange, 1989:441-462.

Dwyer J: Diets for children and adolescents that meet the dietary goals. Amer J Dis Child 1980;134:1073-1080.

Fahagy P, Boltri JM, Monk JS: Key issues in nutrition during childhood and adolescence. Postgrad Med 1987;81(4):301-305.

Formula diets for obesity. Med Lett Dr Ther 1989;31:22-23.

Friedman RB: Fad diets: evaluation of five common types. Postgrad Med 1986;79(1):249-258.

Grandgan AC: Vitamins, diet and the athlete. Clin Sports Med 1983;2(1):105-114.

Greydanus DE, Hofmann AD: Hyperlipidemia. In: Hofmann AD, Greydanus DE, eds: Adolescent Medicine. 2nd ed. Norwalk, CT: Appleton-Lange, 1989:111-114.

Heald FP: Teenage obesity. Pediatr Clin North Am 1973;20:807.

Hecker AL: Nutritional conditioning and athletic performance. Prim Care 1982;9(3):545-556.

Kirschenbaum DS, Johnson WG, Stalonas PM: Treating Childhood and Adolescent Obesity. New York: Pergamon Press, 1987.

Marks A, Fisher M: Health assessment and screening during adolescence. Pediatrics 1987;80(1:Suppl):135-155.

Marino DD, King JC: Nutritional concerns during adolescence. Pediatr Clin North Am 1980;27:125.

Mellendick GJ: Nutritional issues in adolescence. In: Hofmann AD, Greydanus DE, eds. Menlo Park, CA: Addison-Wesley, 1983:309-327.

Moses N, Banilivy MM, Lifshitz F: Fear of obesity among adolescent girls. Pediatrics 1989;83:393-398.

Palazzoli MS: Self-Starvation: From Individual to Family Therapy in the Treatment of Anorexia Nervosa. New York: Jason Aronson, 1987.

Schotte DE, Stunkard AJ: Bulimia v. bulimic behaviors on the college campus. JAMA 1987;258:1213-1215.

Smith NJ: Gaining and losing weight in athletes. JAMA 1976;236:149-151.

Smith NJ: Nutrition and the young athlete. Pediatr Ann 1978;7(10):49-63.

Spear BA: Adolescent nutrition. Sem Adol Med 1985;1(1):55-65.

Wolff LH: Obesity. In: Ziai M, ed. Pediatrics. 3rd ed. Boston: Little, Brown, 1984:735-737.

Young EA, Sims OL, Bingham C: Fast food update: nutrient analyses. Feelings. Ross Lab 1987;29:15-26.

Substance Abuse Disorders

Adams GR, Montemayor R, Gullotta TP, eds: Biology of Adolescent Behavior and Development. Newbury Park, CA: Sage Publications, 1989:1-308.

American Academy of Pediatrics Task Force on Substance Abuse: Substance Abuse: A Guide for Health Professionals. Elk Grove Village, IL: 1988:1-193.

Bennett DL: Young people and their health needs: a global perspective. Semin Adol Med 1985;1:1-14.

Blum R: Contemporary threats to adolescent health in the United States. JAMA 1987; 257:3390-3395.

Clayton RR, Ritter C: The epidemiology of alcohol and drug use among adolescents. Adv Alcohol and Substance Abuse 1985;4(3-4):69-97.

Cohen AV: Alternatives to drug abuse: Steps toward prevention. Institute for Drug Abuse Education and Research. The John F. Kennedy University National Clearing House for Drug Abuse Information reprinted by Wisconsin Clearing House, Madison, WI, 1984:1-34.

Comerci GD: Spotting young substance abusers in your practice. Diagnosis 1985;7(3):78-97.

Crack. Med Lett Dr Ther 1986;28:69-70.

DuPont RL: Marijuana, alcohol and adolescence: a malignant synergism. Semin Adol Med 1985;1(4):311-315.

DuPont RL: Substance abuse. JAMA 1985;254:2335-2337.

DuPont RL: Prevention of adolescent chemical dependency. Pediatr Clin No Amer 1987;34:495-505.

Dyment PG: Drug misuse by adolescent athletes. Ped Clin No Amer 1982;29:1363-1368.

Forster B: Upper middle class adolescent drug abuse: patterns and factors. Adv Alcohol and Substance Abuse 1984;4(2):27-36.

Galanter L, Gleaton T, Marcus CE, et al: Self-help groups for parents of young drug and alcohol abusers. Am J Psychiatr 1984;141(7):889-891.

Gold MS, Verebey K, Dackis CA: Diagnosis of drug abuse, drug intoxication and withdrawal states. Psychiatr Lett (Fair Oaks Hospital) 1985;3(5):23-34.

Gold MS, Semlitz L, Dackis CA, et al: The adolescent cocaine epidemic. Semin Adol Med 1985;1(4):303-309.

Greydanus DE: Adolescent drug abuse. Crit Probl Pediatr (Eds: J.F. Mellinger and G.B. Stickler). Philadelphia: JB Lippincott, 1985:191-205.

Greydanus DE: Risk-taking behaviors in adolescence. JAMA 1987;258:112-114.

Greydanus DE: Routing a modern pied piper of Hamelin. JAMA 1989;261:99-100.

Hofmann AD: Drug and alcohol use and abuse: medical and psychologic aspects. In: Hofmann AD, Greydanus DE, eds. Adolescent Medicine. Menlo Park, CA: Addison-Wesley, 1983:328-349.

Holleb AI: Smoking, the ticking time bomb for teenage girls. Cancer 1981;31(1):44.

Irwin CE Jr, Millstein SG: Biopsychosocial correlates of risk-taking behaviors in adolescence: can the physician intervene? J Adol Health Care 1986;7(6 Suppl):82S-96S.

Johnson GM, Shontz FC, Locke TP: Relationships between adolescent drug use and parental drug behaviors. Adolescence 1984;19(74):295-299.

Johnston L, Bachman J, O'Malley P: Highlights from students drug use in America 1975-1980, NIDA, U.S. Government Printing Office, 1982.

Johnston LD, O'Malley PP, Bachman JG: Use of licit and illicit drugs by America's high school students: 1975-1984. National Institute on Drug Abuse, DHHS Publ No (ADM) 85-1393, Washington DC, U.S. Government Printing Office, 1985.

Jones R: The toxic adolescent: substance and alcohol abuse. Semin Adol Med 1985;1(4):231-324.

Kandel DB: Marijuana users in young adulthood. Arch Gen Psychiatr 1984;41(2):200-209.

Kandel DB, Logan JA: Patterns of drug use from adolescence to young adulthood: I: Periods of risk for initiation, continued use and discontinuation. AJPH 1984;74(7):660-666.

Kashani JH, Keller MB, Solomon N, et al: Double depression in adolescent substance users. J Affect Dis 1985;8:153-147.

MacDonald DI: Drugs, Drinking and Adolescence. Chicago: Yearbook, 1984.

MacDonald DI: Drugs, drinking and adolescence. AJDC 1984;138(2):117-125.

MacDonald DI: Drug abuse in adolescents. When to intervene, how to help. Postgrad Med 1985;78(4):109-113.

MacDonald DI: Patterns of alcohol and drug use among adolescents. Pediatr Clin No Amer 1987;34:275-288.

MacKenzie RG, Jacobs EA: Recognizing the adolescent drug abuser. Prim Care 1987; 14:225-236.

Mills CG, Noyes HL: Patterns and correlates of initial and subsequent drug use among adolescents. J Consult Clin Psychol 1984;52(2):231-243.

National Academy of Sciences, Institutes of Medicine, Marijuana and Health, 1982.

Parcel GS: The pediatrician's role in drug education. Pediatrics-in-Rev 1982;4(5):144-149.

Robinson TN, Killen JD, Taylor CB, et al: Perspectives on adolescent substance use: a defined population study. JAMA 1987;257:98-101.

Rogers PD: Symposium on chemical dependency. Pediatr Clin No Amer 1987;34(2):275-539.

Schwartz RH: Frequent marijuana use in adolescence. Am Fam Phys 1985;31(1):201-205.

Schwartz RH: Are you ready to deal with the pot-smoking patient? Contemp Pediatr 1987;April:84-106.

Shearin RB, Jones R: Drug and alcohol abuse. In: Hofmann AD, Greydanus DE, eds. Adolescent Medicine. 2nd Ed. Norwalk, CT: Appleton & Lange, 1989:561-613.

Sommer B: The troubled teen: suicide, drug use and running away. Women and Health 1984;9(2-3):117-141.

Stephenson JN, Moberg PJ, Daniels RF, et al: Treating the intoxicated adolescent. JAMA 1984;252(15):1884-1888.

Yamaguchi K, Kandel DB: Patterns of drug use from adolescence to young adulthood: II: Sequences of progression. AJPH 1984;74(8):668-672.

Yamaguchi K, Kandel DB: Patterns of drug use from adolescence to young adulthood: III: Predictors of progression. AJPH 1984;74(7):673-681.

Zucker RA, Harford TC: National study of the demography of adolescent drinking practices in 1980. J Stud Alcohol 1983;44(6):974-985.

Appendix

MISCELLANEOUS SEXUALITY EDUCATION MATERIALS

A. School Curricula
   1. American School Health Association: Growth Patterns and Sex Education: Suggested Program Kindergarten through Grade 12. Kent, Ohio, 1978.
   2. Brick P: Sexuality education in the elementary school. SIECUS 1985; Rep 13(3):1-4.
   3. Brown J: Sexuality Education: A Curriculum for Parent/Child Programs. Santa Cruz, CA: Network Publications, 1984.
   4. Brown L, ed: Sex Education in the Eighties: The Challenge of Healthy Sexual Evaluation. New York: Plenum Press, 1981.
   5. Burt JI, Meeks LB: Education For Sexuality: Concepts and Programs For Teaching. Philadelphia: W.B. Saunders, 1975.
   6. Cook A, Kirby D, Wilson P, Alter J: Sexuality Education: A Guide to Developing and Implementing Programs. Santa Cruz, CA: Network Publications, 1984.
   7. Dickman IR: Winning the Battle for Sex Education. New York: SIECUS, 1982.
   8. Kirby D, Alter J, Scales P: An Analysis of the U.S. Sex Education Programs and Evaluation Methods, Vol. II. Atlanta: Public Health service, U.S. Dept. of Health, Education and Welfare, 1979.
   9. Kirby D: Sexuality Education: A Handbook for Evaluating Programs. Santa Cruz, CA: Network Publications, 1984.
   10. Levitan J: Evaluation of Family Living Sex Education Programs. SIECUS 1986; Rep 15(2):7-9.
   11. Manley J: Teacher Selection for sex education. SIECUS 1986; Rep 15(2):10-11.
   12. McCaffree K: Sex education curricula: selection for elementary and secondary school students. SIECUS 1986; Rep 15(2):4-6.
   13. NJ Dept of Education: Family Life Education: Curricula Guidelines. Trenton, NJ, 1981.
   14. Paramus Public Schools: Human Reproduction and Sexuality Curriculum: Scope and Sequence Chart, Grades K-8. Paramus, NJ, 1984.
   15. Roberts ET, ed: Childhood Sexual Learning: The Unwritten Curriculum. Cambridge, MA: Ballinger Publications, 1980.
   16. Wagman E, Cooper L: Family Life Education-Teacher Training Manual. Santa Cruz, CA: Network Publications, 1981.
B. Sexuality Education Materials For Adolescents
   1. Campbell PJ: Sex Education Books for Young Adults, 1892-1979. New York: RR Bowker, 1979.
   2. Films: Seasons of Sexuality and Human Growth III. Highland Park, IL: Perennial Education, Inc, 1983.

    3. Filmstrip: Human Sexuality: The Lifelong Experience. Pleas-
antville, NY: Human Relations Media, 1984. Also: Human Sexuality and the Life Cycle. Human Relations Media, 1983.

    4. Kelly GF: Learning About Sex: A Contemporary Guide for Young
Adults. Woodbury, NY: Barron's Education Series, 1977.

    5. Purdy C, Kendziorski S: Understanding your Sexuality. Glenview,
IL: Scott, Foreman and Co, 1980. (Textbook for adolescents)

    6. Winship B: Masculinity and Femininity. Boston, MA: Houghton
Mifflin, 1987. (Textbook for adolescents)

C. Sexuality Education Textbooks for Professionals

    1. Calderwood DD, Calderwood M: Human sexuality college text-
books: an experiment in evaluation. SIECUS 1982; Rep 10(4):1, 2,
11-12. (Reviews 25 college textbooks on human sexuality)

    2. Daniel RS: Human Sexuality: Methods and Materials for the Ed-
ucation, Family Life and Health Professionals. Vol I: An annotated
Guide to the Audiovisuals. Brea, CA: Heuristicus Publishing Co,
1979.

    3. McCary JL, McCary SP: Human Sexuality, 4th ed. Florence, KY:
Wadsworth, 1982. (College textbook; its first edition was in 1967,
and it was the first college textbook summarizing available data on
human sexuality)

    4. Masters WH, Johnson VE, Kolodney RC: Human Sexuality. Bos-
ton, MA: Little, Brown and Company, 1982.

    5. Money J, Musaph H, eds: Handbook of Sexology. New York:
Excerpta Media/Elsevier North Holland, 1977.

D. Sexuality Education Material for Parents

    1. Calderone MS, Johnson EW: The Family Book about Sexuality.
New York: Harper and Row, 1981.

    2. Calderone MS, Ramsey J: Talking with your Child about Sex. New
York: Random House, 1982.

E. Miscellaneous Sexuality Education Material

    1. Kaufman-Dressler B, Hallingby L: Sexuality Education Pamphlets:
a selected annotated bibliography of resources for sale. SIECUS
1986; 15(2):13-20. (Lists over 130 resources)

    2. Sex Education for Adolescents: A Bibliography for low-cost mate-
rials. Amer Libr Assoc., (1980)., Order Dept, 50 East Huron St.,
Chicago, IL, 60611.

    3. SIECUS (Sex Information and Education Council of the United
States), 32 Washington Place, New York, NY, 10003. (Provides
lists of materials related to sexuality education for various individuals: parents, students, professionals.)

F. Kinsey Scale of Sexual Orientation

    Rating   Description

      0   Exclusive heterosexual (in sexual behavior and fantasy)

      1   Essentially heterosexual with incidental or limited homo-
                sexual history

      2   Largely heterosexual with distinct homosexual history

3   Equal heterosexual and homosexual orientation ("ambisexuality")
4   Largely homosexual with distinct heterosexual history
5   Essential homosexual with limited heterosexual history
6   Exclusive homosexual (in sexual behavior and fantasy)

REFERENCES

1. Gebhard PH, Johnson AB: The Kinsey Data: Marginal Tabulation of the 1938-1963 Interviews Conducted by the Institute for Sex Research. Philadelphia: W.B. Saunders, 1979.
2. Greydanus DE: Homosexuality in adolescence. Sem Adol Med 1985;1:117-129.
3. Greydanus DE: Adolescence: A Continuum From Childhood to Adulthood. Des Moines, Iowa: Iowa Department of Public Health, 1988.
4. Kinsey AC, Gebhard PH: Sexual Behavior in the Human Female. Philadelphia: W.B. Saunders, 1953.
5. Kinsey A, Pomeroy W, Martin C: Sexual Behavior in the Human Male. Philadelphia: W.B. Saunders, 1948.
6. Masters WH, Johnson VE, Kolodney RC: Human Sexuality. Boston, MA: Little, Brown, 1982.
7. Money J, Musaph H, eds: Handbook of Sexology. New York: Excerpta Media/Elsevier North Holland, 1977.

G. Troiden's Four-Stage Model: Development of Gay Identity*

Stage One: Sensitization

Gains homosexual experiences in childhood and adolescence while learning of general society's view on homosexuality.

Stage Two: Dissociation and Signification

Struggles to reject the concept that society's negative views on homosexuality applies to one's self.

Stage Three: Coming Out

Identifies one's self as "gay" and reaches out to become involved in some aspect of the gay society subculture. Begins to consider homosexuality as a viable lifestyle option.

Stage Four: ACCEPTANCE

Fuses one's concepts of sexuality and emotionality as an adult. Some are "arrested" at Stage Three while others will arrive at Stage Four.

* Troiden R: Becoming homosexual: a model of gay identity acquisition. Psychiatry 1979;42:363-373.

Index